The Rising Glory of America

The American Culture

NEIL HARRIS—General Editor

THE
RISING
GLORY
OF AMERICA
1760-1820

Edited,
with Introduction and Notes by

Gordon S. Wood

George Braziller   New York

Standard Book Number: 0-8076-0611-1, cloth
                         0-8076-0610-3, paper

Library of Congress Catalog Card Number: 75-151798
FIRST PRINTING
Printed in the United States of America.

Preface

"Do not tell me only of the magnitude of your industry and commerce,"
wrote Mathew Arnold during his visit to the United States in the 1890's;
"of the beneficence of your insitutions, your freedom, your equality: of
the great and growing number of your churches and schools, libraries and
newspapers; tell me also if your civilization—which is the grand name you
give to all this development—tell me if your civilization is *interesting*."

The various volumes that comprise THE AMERICAN CULTURE series
attempt to answer Mathew Arnold's demand. The term "culture," of
course, is a critical modern concept. For many historians, as for many
laymen, the word has held a limited meaning: the high arts of painting,
sculpture, literature, music, architecture; their expression, patronage, and
consumption. But in America, where physical mobility and ethnic diversity have been so crucial, this conception of culture is restricting. The
"interesting" in our civilization is omitted if we confine ourselves to the
formal arts.

The editors of THE AMERICAN CULTURE, therefore, have cast a wider
net. They have searched for fresh materials to reconstruct the color and
variety of our cultural heritage, spanning a period of more than three
hundred years. Forgotten institutions, buried artifacts, and outgrown
experiences are included in these books, along with some of the sights
and sounds that reflected the changing character of American life.

The raw data alone, however fascinating, are not sufficient for the task
of cultural reconstruction. Each editor has organized his material around
definitions and assumptions which he explores in the volume introductions. These introductions are essays in their own right; they can be read
along with the documents, or they can stand as independent explorations
into social history. No one editor presents the same kind of approach;
commitments and emphases vary from volume to volume. Together,
however, these volumes represent a unified effort to restore to historical
study the texture of life as it was lived, without sacrificing theoretical rigor
or informed scholarship.

NEIL HARRIS

Contents

Illustrations

PEALE'S MUSEUM / 203

1. Charles Willson Peale, *Exhuming the First American Mastodon* (1806-1808). The Peale Museum, Baltimore, Maryland.
2. Titian Ramsay Peale, *The Peale Museum* (1822). Detroit Institute of Arts.

PAINTING AND ENGRAVING / 272

1. The Advertising of Art, 1790: *Proposals by John Trumbull* (1790). John Carter Brown Library.
2. John Trumbull, *Battle of Bunker's Hill* (1775). Yale University Art Gallery.
3. John Trumbull, *The Declaration of Independence* (1786-1797). Yale University Art Gallery.
4. Gilbert Stuart, *George Washington* (The Lansdowne Portrait) (1796). Pennsylvania Academy of the Fine Arts.
5. Edward Savage, *The Washington Family* (1798). New York Public Library.
6. Anonymous, *Polly Botsford and Her Children* (c. 1813). Abby Aldrich Rockefeller Folk Art Collection.
7. Amos Doolittle, *A New Display of the United States* (1799). Library of Congress.
8. Catherine T. Warner, *Mourning Picture: George Washington* (c. 1800). Abby Aldrich Rockefeller Folk Art Collection.

ARCHITECTURE / 306

1. Model of the Virginia State Capitol (1785-1790) by Thomas Jefferson and Charles Louis Clerisseau. Virginia State Library.
2. Design for President's House (1792) by "A.Z." [Thomas Jefferson]. Maryland Historical Society.
3. Monticello (originally built in 1770's, remodeled in 1796-1809) by Thomas Jefferson. Thomas Jefferson Memorial Foundation.
4. The University of Virginia (1819-1826) by Thomas Jefferson. Old Print Shop, New York.
5. Design of the East Elevation of the U.S. Capitol (1794) by William Thornton. Library of Congress.
6. "Cornstalk" and "Tobacco Leaf" Capitals (1809 and 1816) by Benjamin Latrobe. Library of Congress.

Introduction

GORDON S. WOOD

I

The period between 1760 and 1820 in America spans two eras and two worlds. At the beginning of the imperial controversy with Britain, America was only a collection of disparate colonies with about two million settlers huddled along a narrow strip of the Atlantic coast—European outposts whose cultural focus was still London, the metropolitan center. Yet scarcely fifty years later, following the second war with Britain, these insignificant provinces had become a single continental republic with nearly ten million citizens, "a large and unexpected portion" of whom, as *Nile's Weekly Register* of 1815 put it, had already spilled into the lands beyond the Appalachian mountains—a huge expansive nation whose cultural focus was no longer abroad, but inward at its own boundlessness.

By 1820 Americans had moved into another century, not only in time but in thought, in the way they perceived themselves and the world. They had experienced a social and cultural transformation as great as any in American history, a transformation marked by the search for an American identity and by the climax and fall of the Enlightenment in America. The American Revolution seemed to present Americans with the opportunity to realize an ideal world, to put the Enlightenment into practice, to create the kind of ordered society and illustrious culture that men since the Greeks had yearned for. But the Revolution and the ideas of the Enlightenment that accompanied it contained within themselves the sources of their own disillusionment and destruction. By 1820 the Enlightenment in America was over, the ideals of the Revolution changed and perverted. Yet the transformation was so complicated, so indeliberate, so much a medley of responses to fast-moving events, that Americans scarcely knew how they got from one point to the other.

They began their Revolution seeking a classic destiny in a world they felt very much a part of; they ended by perceiving their destiny in America itself, by becoming a peculiar and unprecedented kind of republic. It was an unintended revolution, for the character they saw revealed in Andrew Jackson and the Hunters of Kentucky—the romantic, undisciplined, and untutored heroes of the battle of New Orleans—was scarcely the character they had sought in 1776. The bumptious nationalism and the defiant abandonment of Europe expressed at the end of the War of 1812 represented both a repudiation of the classic ideals of the Revolution and an attempt to come to terms with the largely unanticipated society that had emerged from the Revolution. A new culture had been created both because and in spite of the Revolution. With the Peace of Ghent and the end of the Napoleonic wars, the new American republic seemed at last secure and ready to comprehend itself. Yet by that time some Americans were no longer sure that this was the kind of republic they wanted after all.

II

The most obvious characteristic of mid-eighteenth-century colonial American culture was its intense provinciality. Educated men throughout the colonies were keenly aware that most of their art and literature, their standards and values, and their canons of taste came not from among themselves, but from the metropolitan center of the empire across the Atlantic. During the first half of the eighteenth century the growth and consolidation of a colonial elite, together with the steady imposition of a network of British officialdom on the colonies, had led to an increasing imitation of English manners and customs. By 1760 the American colonies were more English in their culture than at any time since the first settlements; in fact, to some observers the Americans seemed more English than the English themselves.

The inevitable corollary of such Anglophilism by the colonists was a pervasive sense of cultural inferiority, of feelings of awe and mortification when confronted with the contrast between the achievements of English and colonial society. American travelers in England in the eighteenth century were continually struck with the size and grandeur of English social and cultural life, with London and its social complexity, with the parks, the buildings, the art, the extravagance and sumptuousness of it all. Most Americans reacted to this discrepancy and to the condescension emanating from London and from the would-be English sophisticates in their midst with increasing defensiveness, and they felt repeatedly pressed to apologize for the crudity of their society, the insignificance of their art and literature, and the triviality of their affairs.

It is too easy to interpret the American Revolution as simply an attempt to escape from these provincial feelings of inferiority by rejecting English culture. The Revolutionaries never meant to repudiate English culture but rather to embrace and fulfill it. Indeed, what is important about the Americans' relation to eighteenth-century English culture is their deep involvement in it, at least in its literary expression, and the seriousness with which they took it. Ultimately it was the very internalization of values set forth by English writers themselves that contributed to American estrangement and eventual revolution from the mother country.

The English literature of the Augustan age—both belles lettres and political polemics—the literature the colonists read, imitated, and drew most of their conceptions of English life from, was above all a literature of social criticism. Most of the English writers of the first half of the eighteenth century—whether notables or coffeehouse hacks, whether on the right or the left of the political spectrum, whether Augustan satirists or radical Whigs, whether Bolingbroke, Pope, Swift or Moyle, Trenchard, and Gordon—all wrote out of a deep and bitter hostility to the great social, economic, and political changes taking place in England during the decades following the Glorious Revolution of 1688—changes fostered by a great financial and commercial revolution that was as unsettling and as important as the subsequent industrial revolution for which it prepared the way. The rise of huge banks, trading companies, and stock markets, plus the growing capitalization of land, the emergence of new moneyed men, the increasing debt, the corruption of politics, and the general commercialization of life threatened all traditional values and led most English intellectuals to conclude that England was dangerously diseased—indeed on the verge of ruin, eaten away by vice, luxury, and money. Such a pessimistic conclusion was not the consequence of mere nostalgia, but was in fact a response to the most rational conception of social development of the day—a conception originating in the classic Latin literature, revived by Machiavelli, and carried into the eighteenth century by everyone who laid claim to being enlightened.

The eighteenth century still thought of the social development of states in cyclical terms. States were like human beings: they were born, they matured, and they died; hence change and the process of time were necessarily identified with decay. The Enlightenment, whether expressed in American commencement speeches or in the writings of Edward Gibbon, was fascinated with this problem of political disease and decay—"political pathology," as one American called it. Thus for the eighteenth century, history, particularly that of antiquity, became a kind of laboratory in which autopsies of the deceased classical states would lead to a science of social sickness and health. Rome's fate especially interested eighteenth-century Englishmen, for it seemed to foretell what was happening to England itself. Rome, it was evident from all the literature, was destroyed not by forces from without, but by decay from within. Once the Roman people had become too luxurious, too obsessed with refinements and magnificent living, and too preoccupied with money, their politics had become corrupted, selfishness had dominated, and dissolution had to follow. The lesson for the Augustans was obvious, and they continually drew parallels with the development of the British empire, sinking under the weight of its own prosperity. In their polemics and in their satires they offered classical republican values and idealized images of the ancient republics as counterforces to eighteenth-century English materialism and corruption.

Obsessed with this neoclassical and radical Whig criticism as the principal source of their knowledge of the mother country and defensive about their own provincial simplicity, the colonists inevitably came to take this literature more seriously than the English themselves. Gradually it came to lend a new significance to the discrepancy between English and American life. The very crudities of American society—the absence of an aristocracy, the prevailing rusticity, the relative lack of luxury and polish, the equality —now seemed to be advantages, not deficiencies. The colonists began to see themselves as more capable than the English in realizing the values and norms articulated by British intellectuals. They were still, as they told themselves and Londoners over and over, "a young and forming people" whose greatness lay ahead of them. Throughout the eighteenth century they had eagerly received and extolled Bishop Berkeley's "Verses on the Prospect of Planting Arts and Learning in America," which set forth the conventional notion of a western cycle of empire passing from the Near East to Greece, from Greece to Rome, from Rome to Western Europe, and from Western Europe eventually across the Atlantic to the New World. By 1760, noted the unsympathetic English traveler Andrew Burnaby, the colonists were "looking forward with eager and impatient expectation to that destined moment when America is to give the law to the rest of the world." They believed, as Philip Freneau's and Hugh Henry Brackenridge's 1771 commencement poem, "The Rising Glory of America," declared, that they would in time have their own Homers and Miltons and their own states, "not less in fame than Greece and Rome of old." .The future seemed to belong to this newer, fresher, less developed, and more ideal English society in the New World.

By the middle of the eighteenth century, and especially after the British attempt to reorganize the empire in the 1760's, American Whigs came to conclude that England was truly corrupt and bent on the subjugation and corruption of America as well. There were alarming signs appearing in the colonies of increasing individualism, widening social cleavages, and enhanced luxury, characteristics brought on by the colonists' emergence into more complicated and dynamic market societies, but interpreted by them as symptoms of regression and decay, a falling away of traditional moral and social values. All these changes bore a resemblance to what was happening in England and seemed to be connected in some way to English corruption. By the 1770's some of the Calvinist clergy began to shift the blame for these vices from Americans onto England, and on the eve of the Revolution the English Crown had become a scapegoat for a multitude of American sins. Even the "insignificance, insipidity, and ignorance" of America's provincial culture, one Virginian argued in 1776, were products not of the wilderness, but of the colonists' "connexion and dependence on Britain." England stood as "an insuperable barrier between us and the polished world, who, dazzled with the view of the primary planet, either knew not, or disregarded, the humble satellites which served to increase her splendor."

The Revolution thus became not only a rejection of the corrupted British empire, but as well an attempt to reform American society and to realize once and for all the moral values intellectuals had espoused for centuries—values that the Americans found summed up in the tradition of civic humanism or classical republicanism. For Americans in 1776, this republicanism represented an eighteenth-century secularized version of Puritanism, an updated, reactionary effort to bring under control the selfish and individualistic impulses of an emergent capitalistic society that could not be justified. It stressed a morality of social cohesion and promised the kind of organic state where men, as citizens, were indissolubly linked to one another in harmony and benevolence. It was a very beautiful but fragile ideal, for republics by definition and by their utter dependence on the people were the states most intimately related to the character of their people, both in their capacity for reformation and in their sensitivity to changes in that character. More than any other kind of polity, republics required an absence of selfishness and luxury; their existence in fact demanded an extraordinary moral quality in their people, a moral quality that the eighteenth century, like previous ages, designated as virtue—that is, the willingness of the people to sacrifice their private desires for the good of the whole. "A Citizen," declared Samuel Adams in a common exhortation of the Revolutionary years, "owes everything to the Commonwealth." He was, in fact, as Benjamin Rush said, "public property. His time and talents—his youth—his manhood—his old age—nay more, life, all belong to his country."

This virtue, or the unselfish devotion to the collective good, represented all that men of the eighteenth century, from Benjamin Franklin to Jonathan Edwards, sought in social behavior. It was generally assumed that those most willing to forego their selfish interest for the public good were those who privately practiced a mixture of classical and Puritan virtues—temperance, industry, frugality, simplicity, and charity. Hence, the sturdy independent yeomen, Jefferson's "chosen people of God," who were commonly regarded as the most free of private temptations and the most incorruptible, were considered to be the best citizens and the firmest foundation of a republic. The celebration of the farmer in the years following the Revolution was thus not a literary conceit, but a scientifically based imperative of republican government. It followed too that only a society marked by equality, where distinctions would be naturally rather than artificially based, could encourage men's willingness to obey authority and to subordinate their private desires to the general will. Hence, as American actions demonstrated in 1776, laws abolishing all legal distinctions and privileges were a necessary concomitant of republican government. The goal, however, was not to create a leveled society, but an organic hierarchy led by natural aristocrats who would resemble not the luxury-loving, money-mongering lackeys of British officialdom but the stoical and disinterested heroes of antiquity—men like Washington, who seemed to Americans to embody perfectly the classical ideal of a republican leader.

The republican obsession with virtue colored the entire Revolutionary movement and in time helped to shape America's cultural history in a way no part of the environment, the frontier included, ever could have. Indeed, much of what Americans came to believe and value grew out of their Revolutionary republicanism. It was a radical doctrine because, like Puritanism, it flew in the face of man's natural selfishness. Yet, in this new enlightened age, the most hopeful of the Revolutionaries believed that man was a malleable creature and that America especially was "in a plastic state" where "the benefactor of mankind may realize all his schemes for promoting human happiness." In fact, "it was possible," said Benjamin Rush, who personified the American Enlightenment, "to convert men into republican machines." As Samuel Stanhope Smith, soon to be president of Princeton, told James Madison shortly after Independence, new habitual principles, "the constant authoritive guardians of virtue," could be created and nurtured by republican laws, and these principles, together with the power of the mind, could give man's "ideas and motives a new direction." By the repeated exertion of reason—by "recalling the lost images of virtue: contemplating them, and using them as motives of action, till they overcome those of vice again and again . . . until after repeated struggles, and many foils, they at length acquire the habitual superiority"—by such exertions it seemed possible for the Americans to create a society of "habitual virtue." From these premises flowed the Revolutionaries' efforts at moral and social reformation; much of their republican iconography—the "Pomp and Parade," as John Adams called it, the speeches and orations, the bells and bonfires, the didactic history, even the "Painting, Sculpture, Statuary, Medalling, and Poetry"; and the republicans' devotion, in Smith's words, to "the great importance of an early virtuous education"—education that was designed not to release the talents of the individual, but to turn him into "public property." When the Americans of 1776 talked of their intention to "form a new-era and give a new turn to human affairs" by becoming the "eminent examples of every divine and social virtue," they meant that they would become the special kind of simple, austere, egalitarian, and virtuous people that history and enlightened social science said was essential for the sustenance of a republic. The moral quality of their society thus became a measure of the success of their Revolution.

Despite all the seeds of later American exceptionalism embedded in this emphasis on virtue, the American Revolution was not meant to be a national revolution in any modern sense. The Revolutionary generation was the most cosmopolitan of any in American history. The Revolutionaries were patriots, to be sure, but they were not obsessed, as were later generations, with the unique character of America or with separating America from the broad course of western civilization. Their republicanism was no indigenous ideology, but in fact represented a tradition of civic humanism covering twenty centuries of western civilization, which was grounded in the eighteenth-century's image of classical antiquity, especially as it had been refracted through the writings of Europeans since the Renaissance. The Americans of 1776 were seeking not to cut themselves off from this classical heritage but to embody it. "I us'd to regret," said the Revolutionary general Charles Lee shortly after Independence, "not being thrown into the World in the glorious third or fourth century of the Romans." But now it seemed to Lee and other American Whigs that their classical republican dreams "at length bid fair for being realiz'd." Americans were treading, as Edmund Randolph said, not upon new ground but "upon the Republican ground of Greece and Rome." Every American leader, following Swift and other Augustan writers, hoped to become another Cato; Addison's play about that

Roman patriot was presented over and over throughout the Revolutionary era, was printed in at least nine American editions before 1800, and was even performed at Washington's insistence during the trying days at Valley Forge.

It was a neoclassical age, and it was a neoclassical revolution the Americans undertook. Believing, as all educated men in that era of reason did, in standards of behavior and thought that transcended temporal and national boundaries, the Revolutionaries aimed not at becoming more American but at becoming more enlightened. It was not native originality, but universal and eternal truth they sought—in their constitutions, their literature, and their art—a truth that was as easily taken from Plutarch and Tacitus as it was from Milton and Burlamaqui. They hoped to realize what England, according to its classical republican critics, had been unable to realize—the age-old values of the good society, free of contention, selfishness, and materialism; and yet, at the same time, they hoped to create a worthy place—a Columbia, the poets called it—where, in the words of Ezra Stiles, the enlightened president of Yale, "all the arts may be transported from Europe and Asia and flourish . . . with an augmented lustre."

III

The cultural relics of these classical dreams are with America still: in the names of towns and streets, like Syracuse and Troy; in the designation of political institutions, like the senates and capitols; in the political symbols, like the goddess Liberty, the numerous Latin mottoes, and the Great Seal of the United States with its *novo ordo seclorum* and its Roman numerals, MDCCLXXVI, for greater dignity; in the poetry and the songs, like "Hail Columbia"; and of course in the endless proliferation of Greek and Roman temples. But the spirit that once inspired these things, the meaning they had for the Revolutionaries, has been lost; and it was being lost even as they were being created. Americans began their Revolution seeking to republicanize their culture, to form a classic homogeneous community of calculated austerity infused with reason and civic virtue. By 1820 the culture had become thoroughly republicanized, but scarcely in the way most Revolutionaries had intended.

Instead of becoming a new and grand incarnation of the spirit of the ancient republics, a fit repository for the cultural heritage being passed from Europe, America had become a sprawling, materialistic, and licentious popular democracy unlike anything that had ever existed before. Prosperity replaced austerity, and the meaning of virtue was transformed. Far from sacrificing their private desires for the good of the whole, nineteenth-century Americans came to see that the individual's pursuit of wealth was not only inevitable but justifiable as the only proper basis for a free state. Their cultural provinciality was conquered not by emulating and surpassing Europe but by ignoring it, and fifty years after the Revolution Americans were more isolated from the sources of western culture than they had been as colonists. This vast transformation, this move from classical republicanism to romantic democracy in a matter of decades, was the real American revolution, creating for many Americans a cultural crisis as severe as any in American history.

Beneath all the changes lay a basic social revolution. In the three or four decades following the Revolution, the whole eighteenth-century hierarchy seemed to come crashing down under the impact of pent-up forces released by the Revolution. Economic and demographic changes that seemed to have been momentarily slowed in the middle years of the eighteenth century were now accelerated at unprecedented rates, and more territory was occupied in the first post-Revolutionary generation than was occupied in the entire colonial period. Instead of braking these developments, the Revolution and republicanism lubricated them. Republican equality became a rallying cry for new men seeking to challenge all sorts of authority and superiority, whether naturally derived or not, and distinctions of every kind were put on the defensive, as the creators of the Order of the Cincinnati in 1783 and the supporters of the Boston Tea Club in 1785 discovered. The broadening opportunities for wealth turned mobility into a scramble, as men previously satisfied with humble stations in life became infected with the expectation of material gain. Instead of inculcating a new respect for order, simplicity, and selflessness, republicanism was breeding disorder, extravagance, and individualism.

The Federal Constitution of 1787 was in large part a response to these social developments, an attempt to mitigate their effects by institutional arrangements. Yet this effort to create governmental institutions that would stand apart from the society and at the same time control it nearly brought America to the point of rebellion in the 1790's. The political antagonists of these years, the Federalists and the Republicans, were not, like later political parties, divided simply over issues of financial or foreign policy. They represented conglomerations of social groups split over the very nature of the emerging republic: the Federalists seeking a strengthening of the social hierarchy and cultural fabric through artificial means if necessary, and the Republicans remaining generally confident of and backed by the democratic forces unleashed by the Revolution. Because the future of the republic seemed so unformed and problematical to both sides, every issue, including the proper title to address the President (which involved a month of debate in the first Congress), seemed crucial and loaded with significance.

In such a climate political passions ran as high as they ever have in American history, and every aspect of American life—business groups, banks, militias, dance assemblies, even funerals—become politicized. As personal and social ties fell apart, differences and strains easily broke into violence, even to the point of spitting and fist fighting in the state and federal legislatures. Mobs, which had been common in colonial times, now assumed a more sinister character; with the disintegration of deferential social relationships, butchers, tavern keepers, and other ordinary people took to the streets to close presses, destroy property, and beat men without waiting for the tacit consent of elites. Dueling became more common than at any other time in American history, spreading to all ranks of the society. With the rumblings of Negro slave rebellion fed by the language of the Revolution, the South began developing a self-conscious sense of difference from the rest of America that it had never had to the same degree earlier. Everything seemed to be coming apart, and murder, suicide, and drunkenness became prevalent responses to the terrific burdens individualism and the expectation of gain were placing on men.

IV

The response to all of these social developments was diverse and confused, ranging from deep despair to anxious hope. But among all the groups in American society, it was the Protestant clergy who, having always at hand a means of interpreting chaotic events, remained beneath their talk of depravity and sin the most optimistic about America's future. The ministers had been deeply involved in every social crisis since the seventeenth century. With the exception of the Anglicans, they had in fact been in the vanguard of the Revolutionary movement, perceiving no threat whatsoever to religion in the ideas of republicanism. Unlike the church in Europe, the American churches were neither the enemies nor the victims of the Enlightenment. While secular-minded elites were absorbed in their rational classicism, the American clergy saw in the break with England and in the morally regenerative effects of republicanism a heaven-sent opportunity to cleanse America of sin once and for all. Some even came to see in the Revolution the advent of the millennium itself.

Apocalyptic impulses run through a great deal of the Revolutionary literature, being revealed, for example, even in such a Whiggish piece as

John Adams' "Dissertation on the Canon and the Federal Law," published in 1765. Beneath his outward celebration of knowledge and enlightenment, Adams posited a titanic struggle against the combined forces of darkness that had begun with the Reformation and hopefully would end with the providential fullfillment of America. From such scattered hints and from the significance given to America by the evangelicals of the Great Awakening, millennial thinking was carried to a crescendo at the end of the eighteenth century and firmly linked with the fate of the new republic. In 1794, in a collected edition of millennial pieces, the evangelical enthusiast, David Austin, pictured the Biblical "eagle of liberty" fleeing from the Old World to the New and taking "her station upon the broad seal of the United States" as "an emblem of this protection of Providence towards our present government, and towards this, our happy land." With Stephen Hopkins, the greatest of the post-Revolutionary millennialists, the coming New Jerusalem achieved a degree of concreteness and worldly detail that made his *Treatise on the Millennium* something of an Enlightenment tract. By giving the millennium such a temporal and secular character and by identifying the Kingdom of God with the prospects of the American republic, the Protestant clergy created the most important element feeding into the Americans' gradually evolving idea of progress.

Despite the clergy's enthusiasm for the new republican experiment, however, the alliance between the Enlightenment and American Protestantism forged at the Revolution was never an easy one. Although Presbyterians and Baptists had backed Jefferson's successful effort to disestablish the Anglican church in Virginia, they could never share his rationalistic belief, expressed in the Act for Establishing Religious Freedom, that religion was only a matter of opinion, having no more relation to government than "our opinions in physics or geometry." Since religion was the principal promoter of morality and virtue, without which no republic could long exist, many of the clergy, like Henry Cumings of Massachusetts in 1783, soon began to question carrying the "idea of religious liberty so far, as . . . to rob civil government of one of its main supports." Even someone like the Baptist leader, Isaac Backus, despite his passion for the separation of church and state, supported religious tests for governmental office and laws compelling church attendance and recognition of the Sabbath.

As long as the enlightened deism of Jefferson, Madison, and other Revolutionary leaders was confined to the uppermost social levels and was not publicized, it posed little threat to Protestant orthodoxy. But when in the 1790's, at the time of the French Revolution, rationalistic, natural religion seemed to be spreading to the lower classes, especially through the writings of Thomas Paine and Ethan Allen and the organization of deistic societies, the Calvinistic clergy became alarmed and began a counter movement on behalf of orthodox Christianity that eventually became part of the Second Great Awakening and the emerging nineteenth-century revivalism.

This revivalism led to a further disintegration of orthodox authority and a continuing proliferation of religious groups, all intensely interested in their denominational purity and all competing with one another in a religious marketplace. Yet this organizational fragmentation was offset by a blurring of theological distinctions and by the espousing of a common creed of identity with the destiny of the nation that worked to unify the culture more than any legal establishment ever could have. In this coalescence of piety and patriotism, the classical republicanism of the Revolution became Christianized.

Both ministers and politicians in the early nineteenth century emphasized over and over that America, although without an established church, was nevertheless a nation of God—not a Newtonian God, but an evangelical one. Throughout the period religious groups resisted the disintegrating effects of the secular Enlightenment and urged the republic to recognize its basis in Christianity by instituting chaplains in Congress, proclaiming days of fasting and prayer, and by ending mail delivery on the Sabbath. In 1811, in a notable blasphemy decision of Chancellor James Kent, *The People of New York v. Ruggles*, the Christianizing of republicanism was acknowledged in law. Although the state had no established church and its constitution guaranteed freedom of religious opinion, Kent declared that to revile with contempt the Christian religion professed by almost the whole community, as Ruggles had done, was "to strike at the root of moral obligation and weaken the security of the social ties." Christianity in fact seemed to have become the only cohesive force holding the nation together—"the central attraction," said Lyman Beecher in 1820, "which must supply the deficiency of political affinity and interest." It had become patriotism itself.

The bond holding the fragmented denominations and the nation together was a common obsession with morality. At the outset of America's republican experiment, the clergy had been repeatedly told that, whatever their doctrinal differences, "you are all united in inculcating the necessity of morals," and that "from the success or failure of your exertions in the cause of virtue, we anticipate the freedom or slavery of our country." Faced with such awesome responsibility, religious groups and others responded to the cause of virtue with a stridency and zeal that went beyond what any classicist in 1776 could have imagined possible. Missionary, education, tract, and Bible societies—some even composed of combinations of the various denominations—spilled out to moralize and tame the barbarians, both in the American west and throughout the world.

It was no longer enough to expose the community's guilt through jeremiads and to reform merely the "better part" of the society. Even government, ministers complained, was incapable of creating the right "moral effect." The growing weakness of elites and government meant that the great emerging force of American democratic society, public opinion— "that invisible guardian of honour—that eagle-eyed spy on human actions— that inexorable judge of men and manners—that arbiter, whom tears cannot appease, nor ingenuity soften—and from whose terrible decisions there is no appeal"—had to be mobilized in the cause of virtue, largely through the creation of local voluntary associations. The proliferation in the early nineteenth century of these local moral societies—"disciplined moral militia," Beecher called them—eventually transformed and often eclipsed the previously founded humanitarian and benevolent societies that had popped up in the cities in the immediate post-Revolutionary years as products of the Enlightenment. By 1800 or shortly after, the social complexion of these humane associations had become less elitist and more middle class, less rational and more moral, and less concerned with relieving the suffering of the unfortunate and more with the shaping of everyone's conduct. Reformers responding to the democratic impulses of the new century were now more interested in working on the character of the American people from the bottom up rather than from the top down.

Under these kinds of pressures the morality of civic humanism became evangelized, and the middle-class genteel tradition of nineteenth-century America was born. Virtue to most Revolutionary leaders had possessed a rational, austere, and detached quality befitting the classical heroes they emulated. It consisted, as one essayist in the *New York Magazine* wrote in 1790, "in a conformity of temper to the requirements of reason and revelation, a practice influenced by prudence, honour and honesty, a control over the passions, and a check to inordinate desires," resulting in a "serenity of mind" amidst all adversity. Such a conception was thoroughly classical and elitist; it set the stoical and benevolent leader, "like the towering cedar," above the mass of mankind to whom the influence of his virtue would be carried through a process of deferential imitation. With the growing democratization of American society in the early years of the nineteenth century, however, the classical virtues became less a means by which enlightened men could improve mankind and more a means by which moralizing men could control the masses. Temperance, for example, that self-control of the passions so valued by the ancients, became largely identified with the elimination of drunkenness. By 1820 republican virtue and morality were no longer a matter of the inward serenity of the rational few; they had become a matter of the outward behavior of the unruly many. The republican citizen had become a Christian democrat.

V

This democratization and vulgarization of American life was not what most men had expected from the Revolution; hence, the social and cultural developments of the post-Revolutionary years had a bewildering effect on American attitudes. While some continued to talk of the dangers to the new republic of luxury, overrefinement, and decay, others soon perceived threats from another direction on the spectrum of civilization. Americans, or at least some of them, seemed to have reversed the process of time. Unlike any other people in history, wrote one analyst in the *Panoplist* in 1818, Americans were going backwards, moving in an unnatural direction in the cycle of history. Usually the first settlers of any country were barbarians who, through time, gradually became civilized and cultivated. "The progress has been from ignorance to knowledge, from the rudeness of savage life to the refinements of polished society. But in the settlement of North America the case is reversed. The tendency is from civilization to barbarism." Under the impact of the New World environment, "the tendency of the American character is then to degenerate, and to degenerate rapidly." Such thoughts were doubly frightening because they only confirmed what some European theorists had been saying for centuries about the harmful effects of the environment of the New World.

By the middle of the eighteenth century, America had become an issue in the debate by European intellectuals over the destiny of the Old World. For some, America with its simplicity and egalitarianism was "a mirage in the west," a symbol of all that a decadent Europe lacked. But for others, America with its primitiveness posed a threat to the carefully cultivated refinements of centuries of Old World maturity and therefore needed to be disparaged. With the writings of the great French naturalist, the Comte de Buffon, the problem of American degeneracy was pitched onto a new scientific level. In his long, rambling *Natural History of Man*, written during the third quarter of the eighteenth century, Buffon concluded pessimistically that there was in the New World "some combination of elements and other physical causes, something that opposes the amplification of animated Nature." The American environment—the great irregularity of its topography, the violent variability of its climate, the excessive moisture in its air, the extent of its forests and miasmatic swamps—appeared to have a deleterious effect on all life, including human beings. Not only, said Buffon, were the animals smaller and less vigorous, but the original inhabitants of the American environment, the Indians, were incapable of progress. Taken up by others, including Corneille de Pauw, the Abbé Raynal, and William Robertson, these notions entered the popular literature about America and were on the mind of every European traveler who visited the New World.

Nothing angered Americans more than these European charges that their country was not a suitable human habitat, and they reacted in every conceivable fashion, with indignant dismissal, scientific comparison, or anxious boasting. They continually found themselves torn between the need to defend the honor and virtue of the native Indian and the desire to distinguish themselves from the state of savagery. Still, there was always the thoroughgoing environmentalism of their Enlightenment thought, an environmentalism so intense that some even concluded that skin color was a product of the environment, a position that Benjamin Rush pushed to ludicrous extremes when he hypothesized in a paper delivered to the American Philosophical Society in 1799 that the Negro's blackness was a consequence of a disease, leprosy, and thus could, in good enlightened manner, be cured. If the environment, including the climate, was powerful enough to inhibit the Indians' development and to affect skin color, then obviously the Americans had to learn about the environment of the New World.

Calls thus went out to all levels of the intellectual community for information about the American habitat. Ministers in such insignificant places as Mason, New Hampshire, faithfully compiled meteorological and demographic records, and otherwise exclusively literary journals like the *North American Review* published periodic weather charts sent from distant outposts in Brunswick, Maine, and Albany, New York. Temperature-taking became everyone's way of participating in the Enlightenment. During the years from 1763 to 1795, Ezra Stiles filled six volumes with his daily temperature and weather readings. Volume IV of the *Transactions of the American Philosophical Society* contained no less than six papers dealing with America's climate. Men grasped at the possibility that they might by their own efforts order their natural environment, and the journals and newspapers of the period were filled with accounts of how Americans, by clearing their forests and draining their marshes, had moderated their weather over the previous decades. Jefferson put his friends to work weighing and measuring American animals, "from the mouse to the mammoth." While minister to France in the 1780's, he wrote home for a variety of bones and horns to convince Buffon of his errors, apologizing for the small size of the specimens, when in fact he had requested the largest specimens available. The most exciting scientific event of the period was Charles Willson Peale's exhumation of the bones of the mastodon or mammoth in 1801, which he proudly displayed in his museum as "the LARGEST of *terrestrial* beings" and "the nineth wonder of the world!!!" In an effort to bring all this information gathering together, the Philosophical Society in 1800 formally petitioned Congress to transform the decennial census into a detailed mortality and occupational survey "to determine the effect of the soil and the climate of the U.S. on the inhabitants thereof," promising even before the data were in that "truths will result very satisfactory to our citizens that under the joint influence of soil, climate and occupation the duration of human life in this position of the earth will be found at least equal to what it is in any other; and that its population increases with a rapidity unequaled in all others."

Through all of these efforts to justify the American environment ran a pervasive sense of anxiety. Whether it was the Hartford Wits in their poetry, Jefferson in his *Notes on Virginia*, Jedidiah Morse in his *Geography*, or William Bartram in his *Travels*—all felt a need to examine and to extol the nature of America not only to European critics but to themselves. Despite the growing celebration of the American landscape in this period, however, the eighteenth-century American philosopher always knew that it was never going to be enough for America to have more magnificent rivers, more stupendous mountains, more expansive forests, or more sublime cataracts than other nations. What ultimately counted to the generation of the Enlightenment was whether or not, as De Witt Clinton said in an 1814 address to the Literary and Philosophical Society of New York, "our country will be the chosen seat, and favourite abode of learning and science." One writer in the *Port Folio* of 1810 joked that the only thing separating civilized men from the savage was the invention of the razor strop. Beneath such Federalist sarcasm lay the hope of the eighteenth-century Enlightenment: that differences among men were more matters of human invention and cultural creation than of the natural environment. Americans told themselves repeatedly, and the *American Museum* put it in 1787, that "the time is come to explode the European creed, that we are infantine in our acquisitions, and savage in our manners, because we are inhabitants of a new world, lately occupied by a race of savages." Although it may have been true that "the age of ultimate refinement in America is yet to arrive," American philosophes were convinced that it would eventually arrive and demonstrate, as the American Philosophical Society said in 1785, "the favourable influence that Freedom has upon the growth of useful Sciences and Arts."

Yet by demanding that "the learned of our country . . . no longer shine in borrowed beams, but in their own native lustre," free from "servile imitation" of Europe, Americans so entangled the claims of patriotism with their efforts in the arts and sciences that in the end they undid their enlightened classical hopes. Although nature had been important to Revolutionary Americans, it was not the American wilderness or landscape they had sought to celebrate, but the natural order of a Newtonian universe that transcended all national boundaries. All of the learned and scientific societies formed in the period, from the American Philosophical Society in 1769 to the Literary and Philosophical Society of New York in 1814, rested on the eighteenth-century assumption that science was what distinguished cultivated men from savages and made them citizens of the world. To the eighteenth-century Enlightenment, science was cosmopolitan, taxonomic, and contemplative. The study of nature raised man "above vulgar prejudices" and enabled him "to form just conceptions of things." It expanded "his benevolence," extinguished "everything mean, base, and selfish in his nature," gave "a dignity to all his sentiments," and taught "him to aspire to the moral perfections of the great author of all things." While no philosophe doubted the usefulness of science in bettering mankind, its real value lay in the aesthetic contemplation of an ordered universe. "The cultivation of knowledge, like the cultivation of virtue, is its own reward," said De Witt Clinton in one of the last echoes of the Enlightenment's impulse. By 1814, not only had classical virtue become a behavioristic morality for the American masses, but enlightened knowledge was no longer its own reward: it had become an instrument for the promotion of American prosperity.

By the early nineteenth century, scientists, under pressure to explain their serene detachment, were strenuously subverting the Enlightenment for the sake of "the dignity of independence and the glory of usefulness" and urging each other to turn their backs on the generalities of European science in the name of American particularities. The contemplative and cosmopolitan sciences of the eighteenth century, physics and astronomy, now gave way to the more vital and patriotic sciences of biology and chemistry. In its search for some sort of foundation in the popular mass, science kept sinking into curiosity-hunting and gimmickry. Peale, despite his rhetorical devotion to the taxonomic majesty of the natural world, loved novelties himself and used all sorts of amusements to attract customers to his museum; in 1820 he resorted to a popular musical performer who played five different instruments simultaneously, using all parts of his body. Doctor Benjamin Rush sought to republicanize medicine by purging it of its mysteries and making it possible to be "taught with less trouble than is taken to teach boys to draw, upon paper or slate, the figures in Euclid." He succeeded in reducing all diseases to one—fever caused by capillary tension, with the cure being purging and bleeding; but the simplification was so extreme that the inevitable revulsion left medicine drowning in a sea of empiricism and increasing complaints against quackery. As the chemist Thomas Cooper declared in 1817, "The days of metaphysical philosophy when the learned argued from generals to particulars . . . are gone by." Knowledge could no longer be the business of the learned, elevated few; it belonged to everyone and had to enter "into our everyday comforts and conveniences," chemistry even being justified by Cooper for its usefulness in the preparing and marinating of food!

The eighteenth-century conception of the benefaction of science to mankind became increasingly identified with hardheaded materialistic utilitarianism. The rush of technological inventions in the post-Revolutionary years—steamboats, clocks, lamps, and numerous machines for doing everything from carding wool to cutting nails—were not unanticipated by Enlightenment philosophers like Jefferson, but the new business significance given to them was. While many of the devices of these years were the results of the detached ingenuity of enlightened gentlemen-scientists like Jefferson or Peale, most were the products of bourgeois-minded men of humble background, like John Fitch, Peter Cooper, or Oliver Evans, seeking not fame but more efficient and more profitable ways of doing things. Education became explained more and more as a means of releasing individual talents for the individual's benefit, and science was being identified solely with those who had an interest in it, which was increasingly a pecuniary one. In Europe, said the *North American Review* in 1818, wealth was a prerequisite to new discoveries in science. In America, "we do all these as a means of acquiring wealth." Lacking the "large establishments and expansive endowments" of Europeans, the Americans, said Jacob Bigelow in a notable address in 1816, had fundamentally altered the nature and sociology of scientific investigation and had become "a nation of inventors."

By the early nineteenth century, technology and prosperity began assuming for Americans the same sublime and moral significance that the Enlightenment had reserved for the classical state and the Newtonian universe. Roads, bridges, and canals were justified by their fostering of "national grandeur and individual convenience," the two now being inextricably linked. It was not virtue that held this restless and quarrelsome people together, wrote Samuel Blodgett in 1806; it was commerce, "the most sublime gift of heaven, wherewith to harmonize and enlarge society." If America were ever to "eclipse the grandeur of European nations," said Charles G. Haines in 1818 in an enthusiastic promotion of the Erie Canal, it had to be in America's own terms: in its capacity to further the material welfare of its citizens. The "American Athens" was bound to have a commercial flavor, and the nature of all the arts, fine as well as useful, had to change.

VI

With this rising emphasis on materialism and utility, the role of the fine arts in American culture became increasingly defensive. Indeed, from the very beginning of the Revolution, the position of the fine arts in the republican ideology was ambiguous. On the one hand, the Revolutionaries hoped to emulate and eventually to surpass Europe in the cultivation of all those arts that gave western civilization its distinctiveness. Yet, on the other hand, they knew very well that the fine arts, like painting or sculpture, in Benjamin Rush's words, "flourish chiefly in wealthy and luxurious countries" and therefore were symptoms of social decadence. To the end of his life John Adams, despite his sensuous attraction to the world of art, remained convinced, as he told his wife in 1778 in a letter from France, "that the more elegance, the less virtue, in all times and countries." Buildings, paintings, sculpture, music, gardens, and furniture—however rich, magnificent, and splendid—were simply "bagatelles introduced by time and luxury in change for the great qualities and hardy, manly virtues of the human heart." If Americans were to exceed Europe in dignity, grandeur, and taste, they would somehow have to create a republican art that avoided the vices of over-refinement and luxury.

The solution lay in the taut rationality of republican classicism, which allowed artistic expression without fostering corruption and social decay. Classicism to the American Revolutionaries, and to the eighteenth century generally, was a means of freezing time and defying change, a set of values emphasizing, as the commissioners who were charged with supervising the construction of public buildings in Washington put it in 1793, "a grandeur of conception, a Republican simplicity, and that true elegance of proportion, which correspond to a tempered freedom excluding Frivolity, the food of little minds." Such a neoclassical art was not an original art in any modern sense, but it never intended to be. The Americans' aim, in their literature, painting, and architecture of the 1780's and 1790's, was to give a new and fresh republican spirit to old forms, to isolate and exhibit in their art the external and universal principles of reason and nature. Poets in the wilds of the New York frontier thus saw nothing incongruous in invoking comparisons with Virgil or Horace. Milton, Dryden, and Pope were all adopted without embarrassment as models for imitation. Even Noah Webster, despite his talk of the cultural independence of America, never intended that the elegant style of Addison should be abandoned.

For the neoclassicist the criterion of art lay not in the genius of the artist or in the novelty of the work, but in the effect of the art on the audience or spectator. Hence, Joel Barlow could believe that his epic of America, the *Columbiad,* precisely because of its high moral and republican message, could excel in grandeur even Homer's *Iliad.* And John Trumbull could conclude that the profession of painting was not trivial and socially useless as long as the artist depicted great events and elevated the spirit of the viewer. Washington, as much as he loved the theater, justified it on the grounds that it would "advance the interest of private and public virtue" and "polish the manners and habits of society." There was nothing startling about Thomas Jefferson's choice of the Maison Carrée, a Roman temple at Nîmes from the first century A.D., as a model for the new republican state capitol to be built along the mud-lined streets of a backwoods town in Virginia. Since architecture to Jefferson was "an art which shows so much," it was particularly important for the new nation, as his rebuilding of Monticello and his plans for the University of Virginia demonstrated, that appropriate inspirational forms be used, even at the expense of functional considerations. In much of the art of the period—from the epic visions of the poetry to the planning for the city of Washington—Americans aimed to create a moral and symbolic effect consonant with the hope, expressed by Benjamin Latrobe in 1811, that "the days of Greece may be revived in the woods of America."

Yet the rapid democratization of American society following the Revolution ultimately left most of these artistic achievements as simply awkward reminders of the brevity of America's neoclassical age. The didactic function of art was not lost but transformed and vulgarized: the elevated morality of classical art, designed for an elite, became more and more identified, especially under the influence of Scottish common-sense philosophy, with a popular kind of prudery. In Susannah Rowson's sentimental novel, *Charlotte Temple,* first published in America in 1794, every character, every detail, and even the tone itself were used for moral instruction in domestic behavior, making the book the best-selling novel in America until *Uncle Tom's Cabin,* with forty-two editions in the years up to 1820. In this kind of moral atmosphere, the theater with its reputation for licentiousness was especially vulnerable to criticism, and it sought continually through various ways to justify its propriety in a moral republic. During the debate over the establishment of a theater in Boston in 1792, William Haliburton was reduced to defending the stage as simply an "engine" of government designed "to *impel, direct,* or *restrain* the spirits of a nation" and to suppress vulgar vices like gambling and drinking. Under pressure from critics to perform nothing that "savours of indelicacy" or "tends to loosen the ties of morality," the theater in the early nineteenth century gradually degenerated into popular melodrama whose blatant moralism and strident patriotism were in accord with the new democratic age.

These developments, however, did more than change the nature of art from neoclassical to romantic; by threatening to destroy the learned community—the "republic of letters"—that made eighteenth-century artistic standards meaningful, they created a serious cultural crisis out of which the modern distinction between high and popular culture was born.

To eighteenth-century literati, culture or cultivation was unitary and homogeneous, and was identified almost exclusively with the sharing of a common body of letters that transcended national boundaries. In the predemocratic age cultivation or learning was a personal qualification for participation in polite society. Men of learning had no doubt of the existence of vulgar habits and customs among the common people, but they did not yet see these as a popular culture set in opposition to the republic of letters. Only when the social hierarchy and homogeneity that made such a conception possible began to break down, only when the audience for the artist became disparate and democratized, did an adversary tension between high and popular culture begin to rise. The forces that led to this growing cultural division were inherent in America's republican ideology.

Cultivation, Americans in 1776 believed, could no longer be merely a means of entry into aristocratic society. In the new republic cultivation necessarily had to be socialized and become something in which the whole citizenry was involved. The problem of refining and elevating the moral and aesthetic sensibilities of the American people inevitably came to focus on education. The attacks during this period on the use of the "dead" languages of Latin and Greek in the schools did not represent a philistine assault on classical western culture but, on the contrary, represented a revolutionary desire to make that culture more available and communicable to ordinary people. The artists themselves, with a rising sense of urgency, were encouraged to join in this educational process—in the words of William Tudor, to "feel something of a *missionary* spirit" in improving "the taste of the publick." Learned academies and critical journals were formed not simply, as in Europe, for professional recognition and communication, but for the instruction and guidance of the people's artistic judgment.

Yet it soon became evident that, instead of refining the taste of the American people, art itself was becoming vulgarized. Painters had difficulty in gaining support for anything but portraiture, and the commemoration of great historical events on canvas soon degenerated into "panoramics," over-sized spectacles designed for carnival-like exhibition. Literary journals such as the *Port Folio* and the *Monthly Anthology* were filled with hand wringing analyses of the forces retarding the development of American literature. America was simply too money-grubbing, too factious, too barbaric for the proper appreciation of the fine arts. "To imagine that a refined and classical style of writing will be encouraged here," wrote Joseph Dennie, the high-toned editor of the *Port Folio*, "is as absurd as for a thief to break into a Log House in the expectation of stealing Silver Tankards."

Suddenly these mostly Federalist literati, who clung to the standards of the eighteenth century, found themselves in hostile isolation from the main currents of American life, standing outside a growing popular culture that was corrupting classic art and tastes. The eighteenth-century republic of letters was rapidly being engulfed by nineteenth-century democracy. By 1810, even the Revolutionary enthusiast Benjamin Rush had become alarmed at the vulgarization of art taking place in America. It was all right, he said, for practical knowledge to be "as common and as cheap as air," but "a *learned* education" should once again "become a luxury in our country," for "should it become *universal*," as recent tendencies had shown, "it would be as destructive to civilization as universal barbarism." But it was already too late: the arts in America would thereafter be involved in a continual resistance to popular absorption.

Amidst the lamentations of America's cultural deficiencies, however, were other voices beginning to celebrate the unforeseen consequences of the Revolution. Instead of becoming an austere and ordered community, Americans had become a nation of materialistically-minded individualists. Instead of creating a cosmopolitan culture resting on permanent standards, they had turned inward to their own pecularities and had defied Europe and its cultural heritage. A new generation was no longer interested in the Revolutionary dream of building a classical republic of elitist virtue out of the inherited materials of the Old World. As early as 1807, a young Philadelphia lawyer, Charles Ingersoll, caught the emerging national mood, soon to be violently expressed in a final war against Britain and the cultural tradition she represented. America, concluded Ingersoll, would find its greatness not by emulating the states of classical antiquity celebrated by the poets, but by creating a prosperous, free society, rooted in the nature of America and belonging to ordinary obscure men. With the rise of these kinds of sentiments, the Enlightenment in America was at an end.

PART ONE

THE PROMISE
OF AMERICA

1. New World Enlightenment

Perhaps no single document captures the character of the American Enlightenment more than does John Adams' "Dissertation on the Feudal and the Canon Law." It was the immediate product of the incipient crisis between Great Britain and her colonies, prompted by the conjunction of the English move to establish an episcopacy in America with the passage of the Stamp Act. The piece was first published in 1765 as a series of four untitled articles in the *Boston Gazette* and later reprinted in England under its remembered title, furnished by Thomas Hollis. But the "Dissertation" was far more than a response to the events of the early 1760's. It was, as Adams later suggested, "an Essay upon Forefathers Rock," an impassioned attempt to explain the significance in history of the settlement of America.

On the Feudal and the Canon Law
JOHN ADAMS

"IGNORANCE and inconsideration are the two great causes of the ruin of mankind." This is an observation of Dr. Tillotson, with relation to the interest of his fellow men in a future and immortal state. But it is of equal truth and importance if applied to the happiness of men in society, on this

EDITOR'S NOTE: In this document, as in all others throughout the volume, I have retained the original spelling and punctuation. G.S.W.

John Adams, "Dissertation on the Feudal and the Canon Law" (1765), in Charles F. Adams, ed., *The Works of John Adams* . . . (Boston, 1851), Vol. III, pp. 447–64.

side the grave. In the earliest ages of the world, absolute monarchy seems to have been the universal form of government. Kings, and a few of their great counsellors and captains, exercised a cruel tyranny over the people, who held a rank in the scale of intelligence, in those days, but little higher than the camels and elephants that carried them and their engines to war.

By what causes it was brought to pass, that the people in the middle ages become more intelligent in general, would not, perhaps, be possible in these days to discover. But the fact is certain; and wherever a general knowledge and sensibility have prevailed among the people, arbitrary government and every kind of oppression have lessened and disappeared in proportion. Man has certainly an exalted soul; and the same principle in human nature,—that aspiring, noble principle founded in benevolence, and cherished by knowledge; I mean the love of power, which has been so often the cause of slavery, —has, whenever freedom has existed, been the cause of freedom. If it is this principle that has always prompted the princes and nobles of the earth, by every species of fraud and violence to shake off all the limitations of their power, it is the same that has always stimulated the common people to aspire at independency, and to endeavor at confining the power of the great within the limits of equity and reason.

The poor people, it is true, have been much less successful than the great. They have seldom found either leisure or opportunity to form a union and exert their strength; ignorant as they were of arts and letters, they have seldom been able to frame and support a regular opposition. This, however, has been known by the great to be the temper of mankind; and they have accordingly labored, in all ages, to wrest from the populace, as they are contemptuously called, the knowledge of their rights and wrongs, and the power to assert the former or redress the latter. I say RIGHTS, for such they have, undoubtedly, antecedent to all earthly government,—*Rights*, that cannot be repealed or restrained by human laws—*Rights*, derived from the great Legislator of the universe.

Since the promulgation of Christianity, the two greatest systems of tyranny that have sprung from this original, are the canon and the feudal law. The desire of dominion, that great principle by which we have attempted to account for so much good and so much evil, is, when properly restrained, a very useful and noble movement in the human mind. But when such restraints are taken off, it becomes an encroaching, grasping, restless, and ungovernable power. Numberless have been the systems of iniquity contrived by the great for the gratification of this passion in themselves; but in none of them were they ever more successful than in the invention and establishment of the canon and the feudal law.

By the former of these, the most refined, sublime, extensive, and astonishing constitution of policy that ever was conceived by the mind of man was framed by the Romish clergy for the aggrandisement of their own order. All the epithets I have here given to the Romish policy are just, and will be allowed to be so when it is considered, that they even persuaded mankind to believe, faithfully and undoubtingly, that God Almighty had entrusted them with the keys of heaven, whose gates they might open and close at pleasure; with a power of dispensation over all the rules and obligations of morality; with authority to license all sorts of sins and crimes; with a power of deposing princes and absolving subjects from allegiance; with a power of procuring or withholding the rain of heaven and the beams of the sun; with the management of earthquakes, pestilence, and famine; nay, with the mysterious, awful, incomprehensible power of creating out of bread and wine the flesh and blood of God himself. All these opinions they were enabled to spread and rivet among the people by reducing their minds to a state of sordid ignorance and staring timidity, and by infusing into them a religious horror of letters and knowledge. Thus was human nature chained fast for ages in a cruel, shameful, and deplorable servitude to him, and his subordinate tyrants, who, it was foretold, would exalt himself above all that was called God, and that was worshipped.

In the latter we find another system, similar in many respects to the former; which, although it was originally formed, perhaps, for the necessary defence of a barbarous people against the inroads and invasions of her neighboring nations, yet for the same purposes of tyranny, cruelty, and lust, which had dictated the canon law, it was soon adopted by almost all the princes of Europe, and wrought into the constitutions of their government. It was originally a code of laws for a vast army in a perpetual encampment. The general was invested with the sovereign propriety of all the lands within the territory. Of him, as his servants and vassals, the first rank of his great officers held the lands; and in the same manner the other subordinate officers held of them; and all ranks and degrees held their lands by a variety of duties and services, all tending to bind the chains the faster on every order of mankind. In this manner the common people were held together in herds and clans in a state of servile dependence on their lords, bound, even by the tenure of their lands, to follow them, whenever they commanded, to their wars, and in a state of total ignorance of every thing divine and human, excepting the use of arms and the culture of their lands.

But another event still more calamitous to human liberty, was a wicked confederacy between the two systems of tyranny above described. It seems to have been even stipulated between them, that the temporal grandees should contribute every thing in their power to maintain the ascendency of the priesthood, and that the spiritual grandees in their turn, should employ their ascendency over the consciences of the people, in impressing on their minds a blind, implicit obedience to civil magistracy.

Thus, as long as this confederacy lasted, and the people were held in ignorance, liberty, and with her, knowledge and virtue too, seem to have deserted the earth, and one age of darkness succeeded another, till God in his benign providence raised up the champions who began and conducted the Reformation. From the time of the Reformation to the first settlement of America, knowledge gradually spread in Europe, but especially in England; and in proportion as that increased and spread among the people, ecclesiastical and civil tyranny, which I use as synonymous expressions for the canon and feudal laws, seem to have lost their strength and weight. The people grew more and more sensible of the wrong that was done them by these systems, more and more impatient under it, and determined at all hazards to rid themselves of it; till at last, under the execrable race of the Stuarts, the struggle between the people and the confederacy aforesaid of temporal and spiritual tyranny, became formidable, violent, and bloody.

It was this great struggle that peopled America. It was not religion alone, as is commonly supposed; but it was a love of universal liberty, and a hatred, a dread, a horror, of the infernal confederacy before described, that projected, conducted, and accomplished the settlement of America.

It was a resolution formed by a sensible people,—I mean the Puritans,— almost in despair. They had become intelligent in general, and many of them learned. For this fact, I have the testimony of Archbishop King himself, who observed of that people, that they were more intelligent and better read than even the members of the church, whom he censures warmly for that reason. This people had been so vexed and tortured by the powers of those days, for no other crime than their knowledge and their freedom of inquiry and examination, and they had so much reason to despair of deliverance from those miseries on that side the ocean, that they at last resolved to fly to the wilderness for refuge from the temporal and spiritual principalities and powers, and plagues and scourges of their native country.

After their arrival here, they began their settlement, and formed their plan, both of ecclesiastical and civil government, in direct opposition to the canon and the feudal systems. The leading men among them, both of the clergy and the laity, were men of sense and learning. To many of them the historians, orators, poets, and philosophers of Greece and Rome were quite familiar; and some of them have left libraries that are still in being, consisting chiefly of volumes in which the wisdom of the most enlightened ages and nations is deposited,—written, however, in languages which their great-grandsons, though educated in European universities, can scarcely read.[1]

Thus accomplished were many of the first planters in these colonies. It may be thought polite and fashionable by many modern fine gentlemen, perhaps, to deride the characters of these persons, as enthusiastical, superstitious, and republican. But such ridicule is founded in nothing but foppery and affectation, and is grossly injurious and false. Religious to some degree of enthusiasm it may be admitted they were; but this can be no peculiar derogation from their character; because it was at that time almost the universal character not only of England, but of Christendom. Had this, however, been otherwise, their enthusiasm, considering the principles on which it was founded and the ends to which it was directed, far from being a reproach to them, was greatly to their honor; for I believe it will be found universally true, that no great enterprise for the honor or happiness of mankind was ever achieved without a large mixture of that noble infirmity. Whatever imperfections may be justly ascribed to them, which, however, are as few as any mortals have discovered, their judgement in framing their policy was founded in wise, humane, and benevolent principles. It was founded in revelation and in reason too. It was consistent with the principles of the best and greatest and wisest legislators of antiquity. Tyranny in every form, shape, and appearance was their disdain and abhorrence; no fear of punishment, nor even of death itself in exquisite tortures, had been sufficient to conquer that steady, manly, pertinacious spirit with which they had opposed the tyrants of those days in church and state. They were very far from being enemies to monarchy; and they knew as well as any men, the just regard and honor that is due to the character of a dispenser of the mysteries of the gospel of grace. But they saw clearly, that popular powers must be placed as a guard, a control, a balance, to the powers of the monarch and the priest, in every government, or else it would soon become the man of sin, the whore of Babylon, the mystery of iniquity, a great and detestable system of fraud, violence, and usurpation. Their greatest concern seems to have been to establish a government of the church more consistent with the Scriptures, and a government of the state more agreeable to the dignity of human nature, than any they had seen in Europe, and to transmit such a government down to their posterity, with the means of securing and preserving it forever. To render the popular power in their

---

[1]"I always consider the settlement of America with reverence and wonder, as the opening of a grand scene and design in Providence for the illumination of the ignorant, and the emancipation of the slavish part of mankind all over the earth."

new government as great and wise as their principles of theory, that is, as human nature and the Christian religion require it should be, they endeavored to remove from it as many of the feudal inequalities and dependencies as could be spared, consistently with the preservation of a mild, limited monarchy. And in this they discovered the depth of their wisdom and the warmth of their friendship to human nature. But the first place is due to religion. They saw clearly, that of all the nonsense and delusion which had ever passed through the mind of man, none had ever been more extravagant than the notions of absolutions, indelible characters, uninterrupted successions, and the rest of those fantastical ideas, derived from the canon law, which had thrown such a glare of mystery, sanctity, reverence, and right reverend eminence and holiness, around the idea of a priest, as no mortal could deserve, and as always must, from the constitution of human nature, be dangerous in society. For this reason, they demolished the whole system of diocesan episcopacy; and, deriding, as all reasonable and impartial men must do, the ridiculous fancies of sanctified effluvia from episcopal fingers, they established sacerdotal ordination of the foundation of the Bible and common sense. This conduct at once imposed an obligation on the whole body of the clergy to industry, virtue, piety, and learning, and rendered that whole body infinitely more independent of the civil powers, in all respects, than they could be where they were formed into a scale of subordination, from a pope down to priests and friars and confessors,—necessarily and essentially a sordid, stupid, and wretched herd,—or than they could be in any other country, where an archbishop held the place of a universal bishop, and the vicars and curates that of the ignorant, dependent, miserable rabble aforesaid,—and infinitely more sensible and learned than they could be in either. This subject has been seen in the same light by many illustrious patriots, who have lived in America since the days of our forefathers, and who have adored their memory for the same reason. And methinks there has not appeared in New England a stronger veneration for their memory, a more penetrating insight into the grounds and principles and spirit of their policy, nor a more earnest desire of perpetuating the blessings of it to posterity, than that fine institution of the late Chief Justice Dudley, of a lecture against popery, and on the validity of presbyterian ordination. This was certainly intended by that wise and excellent man, as an eternal memento of the wisdom and goodness of the very principles that settled America. But I must again return to the feudal law. The adventurers so often mentioned, had an utter contempt of all that dark ribaldry of hereditary, indefeasible right,— the Lord's anointed,—and the divine, miraculous original of government, with which the priesthood had enveloped the feudal monarch in clouds and mysteries, and from whence they had deduced the most mischievous of all doctrines, that of passive obedience and non-resistance. They knew that government was a plain, simple, intelligible thing, founded in nature and reason, and quite comprehensible by common sense. They detested all the base services and servile dependencies of the feudal system. They knew that no such unworthy dependencies took place in the ancient seats of liberty, the republics of Greece and Rome; and they thought all such slavish sub-ordinations were equally inconsistent with the constitution of human nature and that religious liberty with which Jesus had made them free. This was certainly the opinion they had formed; and they were far from being singular or extravagant in thinking so. Many celebrated modern writers in Europe have espoused the same sentiments. Lord Kames, a Scottish writer of great reputation, whose authority in this case ought to have the more weight as his countrymen have not the most worthy ideas of liberty, speaking of the feudal law, says,—"A constitution so contradictory to all the principles which govern mankind can never be brought about, one should imagine, but by foreign conquest or native usurpations." Rousseau, speaking of the same system, calls it,—"That most iniquitous and absurd form of government by which human nature was so shamefully degraded." It would be easy to mul-tiply authorities, but it must be needless; because, as the original of this form of government was among savages, as the spirit of it is military and despotic, every writer who would allow the people to have any right to life or property or freedom more than the beasts of the field, and who was not hired or en-listed under arbitrary, lawless power, has been always willing to admit the feudal system to be inconsistent with liberty and the rights of mankind.

To have holden their lands allodially, or for every man to have been the sovereign lord and proprietor of the ground he occupied, would have consti-tuted a government too nearly like a commonwealth. They were contented, therefore, to hold their lands of their king, as their sovereign lord; and to him they were willing to render homage, but to no mesne or subordinate lords; nor were they willing to submit to any of the baser services. In all this they were so strenuous that they have even transmitted to their posterity a very general contempt and detestation of holdings by quitrents, as they have also a hereditary ardor for liberty and thirst for knowledge.

They were convinced, by their knowledge of human nature, derived from history and their own experience, that nothing could preserve their posterity from the encroachments of the two systems of tyranny, in opposition to which, as has been observed already, they erected their government in church and state, but knowledge diffused generally through the whole body of the people. Their civil and religious principles, therefore, conspired to prompt them to use every measure and take every precaution in their power to propagate and perpetuate knowledge. For this purpose they laid very early the foundations of colleges, and invested them with ample privileges and emoluments; and it is remarkable that they have left among their posterity so universal an affection and veneration for those seminaries, and for liberal education, that the meanest of the people contribute cheerfully to the support and maintenance of them every year, and that nothing is more generally popular than projections for the honor, reputation, and advantage of those seats of learning. But the wisdom and benevolence of our fathers rested not here. They made an early provision by law, that every town consisting of so many families, should be always furnished with a grammar school. They made it a crime for such a town to be destitute of a grammar schoolmaster for a few months, and subjected it to a heavy penalty. So that the education of all ranks of people was made the care and expense of the public, in a manner that I believe has been unknown to any other people ancient or modern.

The consequences of these establishments we see and feel every day. A native of America who cannot read and write is as rare an appearance as a Jacobite or a Roman Catholic, that is, as rare as a comet or an earthquake. It has been observed, that we are all of us lawyers, divines, politicians, and philosophers. And I have good authorities to say, that all candid foreigners who have passed through this country, and conversed freely with all sorts of people here, will allow, that they have never seen so much knowledge and civility among the common people in any part of the world. It is true, there has been among us a party for some years, consisting chiefly not of the descendants of the first settlers of this country, but of high churchmen and high statesmen imported since, who affect to censure this provision for the education of our youth as a needless expense, and an imposition upon the rich in favor of the poor, and as an institution productive of idleness and vain speculation among the people, whose time and attention, it is said, ought to be devoted to labor, and not to public affairs, or to examination into the conduct of their superiors. And certain officers of the crown, and certain other missionaries of ignorance, foppery, servility, and slavery, have been most inclined to countenance and increase the same party. Be it remembered, however, that liberty must at all hazards be supported. We have a right to it, derived from our Maker. But if we had not, our fathers have earned and bought it for us, at the expense of their ease, their estates, their pleasure, and their blood. And liberty cannot be preserved without a general knowledge among the people, who have a right, from the frame of their nature, to knowledge, as their great Creator, who does nothing in vain, has given them understandings, and a desire to know; but besides this, they have a right, an indisputable, unalienable, indefeasible, divine right to that most dreaded and envied kind of knowledge, I mean, of the characters and conduct of their rulers. Rulers are no more than attorneys, agents, and trustees, for the people; and if the cause, the interest and trust, is insidiously betrayed, or wantonly trifled away, the people have a right to revoke the authority that they themselves have deputed, and to constitute abler and better agents, attorneys, and trustees. And the preservation of the means of knowledge among the lowest ranks, is of more importance to the public than all the property of all the rich men in the country. It is even of more consequence to the rich themselves, and to their posterity. The only question is, whether it is a public emolument; and if it is, the rich ought undoubtedly to contribute, in the same proportion as to all other public burdens,—that is, in proportion to their wealth, which is secured by public expenses. But none of the means of information are more sacred, or have been cherished with more tenderness and care by the settlers of America, than the press. Care has been taken that the art of printing should be encouraged, and that it should be easy and cheap and safe for any person to communicate his thoughts to the public. And you, Messieurs printers, whatever the tyrants of the earth may say of your paper, have done important service to your country by your readiness and freedom in publishing the speculations of the curious. The stale, impudent insinuations of slander and sedition, with which the gormandizers of power have endeavored to discredit your paper, are so much the more to your honor; for the jaws of power are always opened to devour, and her arm is always stretched out, if possible, to destroy the freedom of thinking, speaking, and writing. And if the public interest, liberty, and happiness have been in danger from the ambition or avarice of any great man, whatever may be his politeness, address, learning, ingenuity, and, in other respects, integrity and humanity, you have done yourselves honor and your country service by publishing and pointing out that avarice and ambition. These vices are so much the more dangerous and pernicious for the virtues with which they may be accompanied in the same character, and with so much the more watchful jealousy to be guarded against.

"Curse on such virtues, they've undone their country."

Be not intimidated, therefore, by any terrors, from publishing with the utmost freedom, whatever can be warranted by the laws of your country; nor suffer yourselves to be wheedled out of your liberty by any pretences of politeness, delicacy, or decency. These, as they are often used, are but three different names for hypocrisy, chicanery, and cowardice. Much less, I presume, will you be discouraged by any pretences that malignants on this side the water will represent your paper as factious and seditious, or that the great

on the other side the water will take offence at them. This dread of representation has had for a long time, in this province, effects very similar to what
the physicians call a hydropho, or dread of water. It has made us delirious;
and we have rushed headlong into the water, till we are almost drowned, out
of simple or phrensical fear of it. Believe me, the character of this country has
suffered more in Britain by the pusillanimity with which we have borne
many insults and indignities from the creatures of power at home and the
creatures of those creatures here, than it ever did or ever will by the freedom
and spirit that has been or will be discovered in writing or action. Believe me,
my countrymen, they have imbibed an opinion on the other side the water,
that we are an ignorant, a timid, and a stupid people; nay, their tools on this
side have often the impudence to dispute your bravery. But I hope in God
the time is near at hand when they will be fully convinced of your understanding, integrity, and courage. But can any thing be more ridiculous, were
it not too provoking to be laughed at, than to pretend that offence should be
taken at home for writings here? Pray, let them look at home. Is not the human understanding exhausted there? Are not reason, imagination, wit, passion, senses, and all, tortured to find out satire and invective against the
characters of the vile and futile fellows who sometimes get into place and
power? The most exceptionable paper that ever I saw here is perfect prudence and modesty in comparison of multitudes of their applauded writings.
Yet the high regard they have for the freedom of the press, indulges all. I
must and will repeat it, your paper deserves the patronage of every friend to
his country. And whether the defamers of it are arrayed in robes of scarlet
or sable, whether they lurk and skulk in an insurance office, whether they
assume the venerable character of a priest, the sly one of a scrivener, or the
dirty, infamous, abandoned one of an informer, they are all the creatures
and tools of the lust of domination.

The true source of our sufferings has been our timidity.

We have been afraid to think. We have feld a reluctance to examining into
the grounds of our privileges, and the extent in which we have an indisputable right to demand them, against all the power and authority on earth.
And many who have not scrupled to examine for themselves, have yet for
certain prudent reasons been cautious and diffident of declaring the result of
their inquiries.

The cause of this timidity is perhaps hereditary, and to be traced back in
history as far as the cruel treatment the first settlers of this country received,
before their embarkation for America, from the government at home. Everybody knows how dangerous it was to speak or write in favor of any thing, in
those days, but the triumphant system of religion and politics. And our

fathers were particularly the objects of the persecutions and proscriptions of the times. It is not unlikely, therefore, that although they were inflexibly steady in refusing their positive assent to any thing against their principles, they might have contracted habits of reserve, and a cautious diffidence of asserting their opinions publicly. These habits they probably brought with them to America, and have transmitted down to us. Or we may possibly account for this appearance by the great affection and veneration Americans have always entertained for the country from whence they sprang; or by the quiet temper for which they have been remarkable, no country having been less disposed to discontent than this; or by a sense they have that it is their duty to acquiesce under the administration of government, even when in many smaller matters grievous to them, and until the essentials of the great compact are destroyed or invaded. These peculiar causes might operate upon them; but without these, we all know that human nature itself, from indolence, modesty, humanity, or fear, has always too much reluctance to a manly assertion of its rights. Hence, perhaps, it has happened, that nine tenths of the species are groaning and gasping in misery and servitude.

But whatever the cause has been, the fact is certain, we have been excessively cautious of giving offence by complaining of grievances. And it is as certain, that American governors, and their friends, and all the crown officers, have availed themselves of this disposition in the people. They have prevailed on us to consent to many things which were grossly injurious to us, and to surrender many others, with voluntary tameness, to which we had the clearest right. Have we not been treated, formerly, with abominable insolence, by officers of the navy? I mean no insinuation against any gentleman now on this station, having heard no complaint of any one of them to his dishonor. Have not some generals from England treated us like servants, nay, more like slaves than like Britons? Have we not been under the most ignominious contribution, the most abject submission, the most supercilious insults, of some custom-house officers? Have we not been trifled with, browbeaten, and trampled on, by former governors, in a manner which no king of England since James the Second has dared to indulge towards his subjects? Have we not raised up one family, in them placed an unlimited confidence, and been soothed and flattered and intimidated by their influence, into a great part of this infamous tameness and submission? "These are serious and alarming questions, and deserve a dispassionate consideration."

This disposition has been the great wheel and the mainspring in the American machine of court politics. We have been told that "the word *rights* is an offensive expression;" "that the king, his ministry, and parliament, will not endure to hear Americans talk of their *rights*;" "that Britain is the mother

and we the children, that a filial duty and submission is due from us to her,''
and that ''we ought to doubt our own judgment, and presume that she is
right, even when she seems to us to shake the foundations of government;''
that ''Britain is immensely rich and great and powerful, has fleets and armies
at her command which have been the dread and terror of the universe, and
that she will force her own judgment into execution, right or wrong.'' But let
me entreat you, sir, to pause. Do you consider yourself as a missionary of
loyalty or of rebellion? Are you not representing your king, his ministry, and
parliament, as tyrants,—imperious, unrelenting tyrants,—by such reasoning
as this? Is not this representing your most gracious sovereign as endeavoring
to destroy the foundations of his own throne? Are you not representing every
member of parliament as renouncing the transactions at Runing Mede, (the
meadow, near Windsor, where Magna Charta was signed;) and as repealing
in effect the bill of rights, when the Lords and Commons asserted and vin-
dicated the rights of the people and their own rights, and insisted on the
king's assent to that assertion and vindication? Do you not represent them as
forgetting that the prince of Orange was created King William, by the people, on purpose that their rights might be eternal and inviolable? Is there not
something extremely fallacious in the common-place images of mother
country and children colonies? Are we the children of Great Britain any more
then the cities of London, Exeter, and Bath? Are we not brethren and fellow
subjects with those in Britain, only under a somewhat different method of
legislation, and a totally different method of taxation? But admitting we are
children, have not children a right to complain when their parents are attempting to break their limbs, to administer poison, or to sell them to enemies for slaves? Let me entreat you to consider, will the mother be pleased
when you represent her as deaf to the cries of her children,—when you compare her to the infamous miscreant who lately stood on the gallows for starv-
ing her child,—when you resemble her to Lady Macbeth in Shakspeare, (I
cannot think of it without horror,) who

> ''Had given suck, and knew
> How tender 't was to love the babe that milked her,''

but yet, who could

> ''Even while 't was smiling in her face,
> Have plucked her nipple from the boneless gums,
> And dashed the brains out.''

Let us banish for ever from our minds, my countrymen, all such unworthy
ideas of the king, his ministry, and parliament. Let us not suppose that all are
become luxurious, effeminate, and unreasonable, on the other side the water,

as many designing persons would insinuate. Let us presume, what is in fact true, that the spirit of liberty is as ardent as ever among the body of the nation, though a few individuals may be corrupted. Let us take it for granted, that the same great spirit which once gave Caesar so warm a reception, which denounced hostilities against John till Magna Charta was signed, which severed the head of Charles the First from his body, and drove James the First from his kingdom, the same great spirit (may heaven preserve it till the earth shall be no more) which first seated the great grandfather of his present most gracious majesty on the throne of Britain,—is still alive and active and warm in England; and that the same spirit in America, instead of provoking the inhabitants of that country, will endear us to them for ever, and secure their good-will.

This spirit, however, without knowledge, would be little better than a brutal rage. Let us tenderly and kindly cherish, therefore, the means of knowledge. Let us dare to read, think, speak, and write. Let every order and decree among the people rouse their attention and animate their resolution. Let them all become attentive to the grounds and principles of government, ecclesiastical and civil. Let us study the law of nature; search into the spirit of the British constitution; read the histories of ancient ages; contemplate the great examples of Greece and Rome; set before us the conduct of our own British ancestors, who have defended for us the inherent rights of mankind against foreign and domestic tyrants and usurpers, against arbitrary kings and cruel priests, in short, against the gates of earth and hell. Let us read and recollect and impress upon our souls the views and ends of our own more immediate forefathers, in exchanging their native country for a dreary, inhospitable wilderness. Let us examine into the nature of that power, and the cruelty of that oppression, which drove them from their homes. Recollect their amazing fortitude, their bitter sufferings,—the hunger, the nakedness, the cold, which they patiently endured,—the severe labors of clearing their grounds, building their houses, raising their provisions, amidst dangers from wild beasts and savage men, before they had time or money or materials for commerce. Recollect the civil and religious principles and hopes and expectations which constantly supported and carried them through all hardships with patience and resignation. Let us recollect it was liberty, the hope of liberty for themselves and us and ours, which conquered all discouragements, dangers, and trials. In such researches as these, let us all in our several departments cheerfully engage,—but especially the proper patrons and supporters of law, learning, and religion!

Let the pulpit resound with the doctrines and sentiments of religious liberty. Let us hear the danger of thraldom to our consciences from ignorance,

extreme poverty, and dependence, in short, from civil and political slavery.
Let us see delineated before us the true map of man. Let us hear the dignity
of his nature, and the noble rank he holds among the works of God,—that
consenting to slavery is a sacrilegious breach of trust, as offensive in the sight
of God as it is derogatory from our own honor or interest or happiness,—and
that God Almighty has promulgated from heaven, liberty, peace, and good-
will to man!

Let the bar proclaim, "the laws, the rights, the generous plan of power"
delivered down from remote antiquity,—inform the world of the mighty
struggles and numberless sacrifices made by our ancestors in defence of freedom. Let it be known, that British liberties are not the grants of princes or
parliaments, but original rights, conditions of original contracts, coequal
with prerogative, and coeval with government; that many of our rights are
inherent and essential, agreed on as maxims, and established as prelimin-
aries, even before a parliament existed. Let them search for the foundations
of British laws and government in the frame of human nature, in the constitution of the intellectual and moral world. There let us see that truth, liberty, justice, and benevolence, are its everlasting basis; and if these could be
removed, the superstructure is overthrown of course.

Let the colleges join their harmony in the same delightful concert. Let
every declamation turn upon the beauty of liberty and virtue, and the deformity, turpitude, and malignity, of slavery and vice. Let the public disputa-
tions become researches into the grounds and nature and ends of government, and the means of preserving the good and demolishing the evil. Let
the dialogues, and all the exercises, become the instruments of impressing on
the tender mind, and of spreading and distributing far and wide, the ideas of
right and the sensations of freedom.

In a word, let every sluice of knowledge be opened and set a-flowing. The
encroachments upon liberty in the reigns of the first James and the first
Charles, by turning the general attention of learned men to government,
are said to have produced the greatest number of consummate statesmen
which has ever been seen in any age or nation. The Brookes, Hampdens,
Vanes, Seldens, Miltons, Nedhams, Harringtons, Nevilles, Sidneys, Lockes,
are all said to have owed their enimence in political knowledge to the ty-
rannies of those reigns. The prospect now before us in America, ought in the
same manner to engage the attention of every man of learning, to matters of
power and of right, that we may be neither led nor driven blindfolded to
irretrievable destruction. Nothing less than this seems to have been meditated for us, by somebody or other in Great Britain. There seems to be a
direct and formal design on foot, to enslave all America. This, however, must

be done by degrees. The first step that is intended, seems to be an entire subversion of the whole system of our fathers, by the introduction of the canon and feudal law into America. The canon and feudal systems, though greatly mutilated in England, are not yet destroyed. Like the temples and palaces in which the great contrivers of them once worshipped and inhabited, they exist in ruins; and much of the domineering spirit of them still remains. The designs and labors of a certain society, to introduce the former of them into America, have been well exposed to the public by a writer of great abilities; and the further attempts to the same purpose, that may be made by that society, or by the ministry or parliament, I leave to the conjectures of the thoughtful. But it seems very manifest from the Stamp Act itself, that a design is formed to strip us in a great measure of the means of knowledge, by loading the press, the colleges, and even an almanack and a newspaper, with restraints and duties; and to introduce the inequalities and dependencies of the feudal system, by taking from the poorer sort of people all their little subsistence, and conferring it on a set of stamp officers, distributors, and their deputies. But I must proceed no further at present. The sequel, whenever I shall find health and leisure to pursue it, will be a "disquisition of the policy of the stamp act." In the mean time, however, let me add,—These are not the vapors of a melancholy mind, nor the effusions of envy, disappointed ambition, nor of a spirit of opposition to government, but the emanations of a heart that burns for its country's welfare. No one of any feeling, born and educated in this once happy country, can consider the numerous distresses, the gross indignities, the barbarous ignorance, the haughty usurpations, that we have reason to fear are meditating for ourselves, our children, our neighbors, in short, for all our countrymen and all their posterity, without the utmost agonies of heart and many tears.

2. The Kingdom of God in America

Millennialism to most twentieth-century readers denotes a kind of fanatic, even freakish, enthusiasm that is usually associated in American history with the most marginal and eccentric religious sects. Only recently have we become aware of how central to our religious, indeed, to our entire cultural, history is the belief in redemption. Literally, millennialism referred to the doctrine held by some Christians on the authority of *Revelation* xx, 4-6, that after his cataclysmic Second Coming, Christ would establish a messianic kingdom on earth and would reign over it for a thousand years before the Last Judgment. Flowing out of the heart of seventeenth-century Puritanism, this eschatological tradition was significantly altered in America by the great eighteenth-century theologian Jonathan Edwards. He conceived of the millennium occurring within history; that is, the Coming of Christ would follow, not precede, the happy and glorious final age of man on earth.

In the Revolutionary generation Edwards' millennial views were evangelized by a number of American ministers, including Timothy Dwight, Joseph Bellamy, and perhaps most important, Samuel Hopkins (1721-1803). Hopkins' brand of post-millennialism was particularly relevant to the needs of the new republic, and his *Treatise on the Millennium* became a handbook to a generation of American theologians. Hopkins set out to give Americans a detailed description of the coming golden age of benevolence, prosperity, and righteousness, and thus helped to prepare them for their peculiar progressive conception of the process of redemption within the temporal confines of a regenerated republic.

A Treatise on the Millennium
SAMUEL HOPKINS

There have been, and still are, very different opinions, respecting the Millennium, and the events which will take place in that day; which are grounded chiefly on the six first verses in the twentieth chapter of the Revelation. . . .

Some have supposed, that this passage is to be taken literally, as importing that at that time, Jesus Christ will come in his human nature, from heaven to earth; and set his kingdom up here, and reign visibly, and personally, and with distinguished glory on earth. And that the bodies of the martyrs, and other eminent christians, will then be raised from the dead, in which they shall live and reign with Christ here on earth, a thousand years. And some suppose, that all the saints, the true friends to God and Christ, who have lived before that time, will then be raised from the dead, and live on earth perfectly holy, during this thousand years. And this they suppose, is meant by the first resurrection. Those who agree in general in this notion of the Millennium, differ with respect to many circumstances, which it is needless to mention here.

Others have understood this paragraph of scripture, in a figurative sense. That by this reign of Christ on earth, is not meant his coming from heaven to earth, in his human, visible nature; but his taking to himself his power, and utterly overthrowing the kingdom of satan, and setting up his own kingdom in all the world, which before this had been confined to very narrow bounds; and subduing all hearts to a willing subjection, and thus reigning over all men, who shall then be in the world, and live in that thousand years. And by "The souls of them which were beheaded for the witness of Jesus, and for the word of God, and which had not worshipped the beast, neither his image, neither had received his mark upon their foreheads, or in their hands," living again and reigning with Christ a thousand years; they suppose, is not meant a literal resurrection, or the resurrection of their bodies, which is not asserted here, as there is nothing said of their bodies, or of their being raised to life: But that they shall live again and reign with Christ, in the revival, prosperity, reign and triumph of that cause and in-

Samuel Hopkins, *A Treatise on the Millennium* . . . (Boston, 1793), pp. 42–44, 52, 55–67, 69–73.

terest in which they lived, and for the promotion of which they died; and in whose death, the cause seemed in a measure, and for a time, to die and be lost. And they shall live again in their successors, who shall arise and stand up with the same spirit, and in the same cause, in which they lived and died, and fill the world and reign with Christ a thousand years, agreeable to ancient prophecies. "The meek shall inherit the earth. And the kingdom and dominion, and the greatness of the kingdom under the whole heaven, shall be given to the people of the saints of the Most High; whose kingdom is an everlasting kingdom, and all dominions shall serve him." And they suppose, that this revival of the truths and cause of Christ, by the numerous inhabitants of the earth, rising up to a new and holy life, and filling the world with holiness and happiness, is that which is here called the *first resurrection*, in distinction from the second, which will consist in the resurrection of the truths and cause of Christ, which had been in a great degree, dead and lost; and a resurrection of the souls of men, by the renovation of the Holy Ghost.

That this important passage of scripture, is to be understood in the figurative sense, last mentioned, is very probable, if not certain. . . .

In the Millennium, there will be a spiritual resurrection, a resurrection of the souls of the whole church on earth, and in heaven. All nations will be converted, and the world will be filled with spiritual life, as it never was before; and this will be a general resurrection of the souls of men. This was represented in the returning prodigal. The father says, "This my son was dead, and is alive." And the Apostle Paul speaks of christians as raised from the dead to life. "But God, who is rich in mercy, for the great love wherewith he loved us, even when we were dead in sins, hath quickened us together with Christ." "If ye then be *risen* with Christ." And this will be a most remarkable resurrection of the church on earth from a low, dark, afflicted state, to a state of great life and joy. It will be multiplied to an exceeding great army, which will cover the face of the earth. And heaven will in a sense and degree, come down to earth; the spirit of the martyrs, and of all the just made perfect, will now revive and appear on earth, in their numerous successors, and the joy of those in heaven will be greatly increased.

The way is now prepared, to consider and show more particularly, in what the happiness and glory of the Millennium will consist; and what particular circumstances will attend the church at that day: What is revealed concerning this by express prophecies and what is implied in them, or may be deduced as consequences from what is expressly declared. It will be no wonder if some mistakes should be made on this point; but it is hoped if there should be any, there will not be very hurtful: And it is apprehended that the greatest error will be in falling short, and not coming up to the reality, in the description of the happiness and glory of that day; for doubtless, our ideas of these, when raised to the highest of which we are at present capable, fall vastly short of the truth. There is good reason to conclude, however, that the church, and christians, will not be perfectly holy in that day; but that every one will be attended with a degree of sinful imperfection, while in the body, however great may be his attainments and advantages in knowledge and holiness. Doubtless the inspired declarations, that "There is no man which sinneth not—There is not a just man upon earth, that doeth good and sinneth not—That if any who professes to be a christian, say he hath no sin, he deceiveth himself, and the truth is not in him," will remain true to the end of the world, even in the Millennium; and there will be no perfection on this side heaven. The apostacy which will take place at the end of the Millennium, can be better accounted for, on the supposition that the saints will not be perfect in that time, and seems to suppose it. Though they may, and doubtless will, have vastly higher degrees of light and holiness, than any shall have before that time; yet they will be far from being wholly without sin.

It is most probable that every individual person who shall then live will be a real christian; and all will doubtless be members of the church, in that day. That is the time when "all shall know the Lord, from the least to the greatest." God says to his church, speaking of that day, "Thy people also shall be all righteous." "Awake, awake, put on thy strength, O Zion, put on thy beautiful garments, O Jerusalem, the holy city: For henceforth there shall no more come unto thee the uncircumcised and the unclean."

The following things will take place in the Millennium in an eminent degree, as they never did before; which may be mentioned as generals, including many particulars, some of which will be afterwards suggested.

I.   That will be a time of eminent holiness, when it shall be acted out by all, in a high degree, in all the branches of it, so as to appear in its true beauty, and the happy effects of it. This will be the peculiar glory, and the source of the happiness of the Millennium. The Prophet Zechariah, speaking of that day, says, "In that day, shall there be upon the bells of the horses, HOLINESS UNTO THE LORD; and the pots of the Lord's house shall be like the bowls before the altar. Yea, every pot in Jerusalem and in Judah, shall be holiness unto the Lord of hosts."—In these metaphorical expressions, is declared the eminent degree of holiness of that day, which will consecrate every thing, even all the utensils and the common business and enjoyments of life, unto the Lord.

Holiness consists in love to God, and to man, with every affection and exercise implied in this, which being expressed and acted out, appears in the exercise of piety towards God, in every branch of it; and of righteousness and goodness, or disinterested benevolence towards man, including ourselves. This, so far as it shall take place, will banish all the evils which have existed and prevailed in the world; and becoming universal, and rising to a high and eminent degree, will introduce a state of enjoyment and happiness, which never was known before on earth; and render it a resemblance of heaven in a high degree. . . .

II.   There will be a great increase of light and knowledge to a degree vastly beyond what has been before. This is indeed implied in the great degree of holiness, which has been mentioned. For knowledge, mental light, and holiness, are inseparably connected; and are, in some respects, the same. Holiness is true light and discerning, so far as it depends upon a right taste, and consists in it; and it is a thirst after every kind and degree of useful knowledge; and this desire and thirst for knowledge, will be great and strong, in proportion to the degree of holiness exercised: And forms the mind to constant attention, and to make swift advances in understanding and knowledge; and becomes a strong guard against mistakes, error and delusion. Therefore, a time of eminent holiness, must be a time of proportionably great light and knowledge. . . .

The holy scriptures will then be attended to by all, and studied with care, meekness, humility and uprightness of heart, earnestly desiring to understand them, and know the truth; and the truths they contain will be received with a high relish and delight: And the Bible will be much better understood, than ever before. Many things expressed or implied in the scripture, which are now overlooked and disregarded, will then be discovered, and appear important and excellent; and those things which now appear intricate and unintelligible, will then appear plain and easy. Then public teachers will be eminently burning and shining lights; apt to teach; scribes well instructed into the things of the kingdom of heaven, who will bring out of their treasures, things new and old: And the hearers will be all attention, and receive the truth in the love of it, into honest and good hearts; and light and knowledge will constantly increase. The conversation of friends and neighbours, when they meet, will be full of instruction, and they will assist each other in their inquiries after the truth, and in pursuit of knowledge. Parents will be able and disposed to instruct their children, as soon as they are capable of learning; and they will early understand what are the great and leading truths which are revealed in the Bible, and the duties and institutions there prescribed. And from their childhood they will know and understand the holy scriptures, by which they will grow in understanding and wisdom; and will soon know more than the greatest and best divines have known in ages before. And a happy foundation will be laid for great advances in knowledge and usefulness to the end of life. Agreeable to this, the scripture, speaking of that day, says, "There shall be no more thence (i. e., in the church) an infant of days, nor an old man that hath not filled his days; for the child shall die an hundred years old." "An infant of days," is an *old infant*. That is, an old man who is an infant in knowledge, understanding and discretion. Many such aged infants have been, and still are to be found. In that day all shall make advances in true knowledge, discretion and wisdom, in some proportion to their years. "Nor an old man that hath not filled his days." That is, an old man who has not improved in knowledge and usefulness and every good attainment, according to his age. "For a child shall die an hundred years old." That is, children in years shall then make such early progress in knowledge, and in religion, and in all excellent and useful attainments, that they shall equal, if not surpass, the highest attainments in these things, of the oldest men who have lived in former ages.

They will then have every desirable advantage and opportunity to get knowledge. They will all be engaged in the same pursuit, and give all the aid and assistance to each other, in their power. —They will all have sufficient leisure to pursue and acquire learning of every kind, that will be beneficial to themselves and to society; especially knowledge of divinity. And great advances will be made in all arts and sciences, and in every useful branch of knowledge, which tends to promote the spiritual and eternal good of men, or their convenience and comfort in this life.

III. It will be a time of universal peace, love and general and cordial friendship. War and all strife and contention shall then cease, and be succeeded by mutual love, friendship and benificence. Those lusts of men, which originate in self love, or selfishness, which produce all the wars and strifes among men, shall be subdued and mortified, and yield to that disinterested benevolence, that heavenly wisdom, which is peaceable, gentle and easy to be intreated. This will effectually put an end to war, as the scripture teaches. "And he shall judge among the nations, and shall rebuke many people: And they shall beat their swords into plowshares, and their spears into pruning hooks: Nation shall not lift up sword against nation, neither shall they learn war any more. And my people shall dwell in a peaceable habitation, and in sure dwellings, and in quiet resting places." The whole world of mankind will be united as one family, wisely seeking the good of each other, in the exercise of the most sweet love and friendship, founded upon the best and everlasting principles. "The meek shall inherit the earth, and shall delight themselves in the abundance of peace.". . .

IV.   In that day, men will not only be united in peace and love, as brethren; but will agree in sentiments, respecting the doctrines and truth contained in the Bible, and the religious institutions and practice, which are
there prescribed.

Professing christians have been from the beginning of christianity to this
day, greatly divided, and have opposed each other in their religious sentiments and practices; and are now divided into various parties, sects and
denominations, while all appeal to divine revelation, and profess to take their
sentiments and practices from that.

It has been often said by some professing christians, and is a sentiment
which appears to be spreading at this day, That difference in religious sentiments, and in attendance on the institutions of the gospel, and modes of
worship, is attended with no inconvenience, but is rather desirable, and
advantageous; and by this variety, christianity is rendered more agreeable
and beautiful. That it is impossible that all men, whose capacities and genius
are so different and various, and their minds, and way of thinking and conception are naturally so far from being alike, should ever be brought to think
alike, and embrace the same religious sentiments. That this difference in
man's belief and sentiment cannot be criminal; for men are no more obliged
to think alike, than they are to look alike, and have the same bodily features
and stature. All the union that is required, or that can take place, is that of
kind affection, love and charity.

But such sentiments as these are not agreeable to reason or scripture.
Error in judgment and sentiment, especially in things of a moral nature, is
always wrong; and does not consist or originate merely in any defect of the
moral faculties of the mind; but is of a moral nature, in which the taste, affection, or inclination of the heart is concerned; and therefore is always, in
every degree of it, morally wrong, and more or less criminal. Were the moral
faculties of the mind, were the heart, perfectly right, man would not be
capable of error, or of judging wrong, or making any mistake, especially in
things of religion. The natural faculties of the mind, of perception and
understanding or reason, considered as separate from the inclination or will,
do not lead, and have no tendency in themselves, to judge wrong, or contrary to the truth of things. To do so, is to judge without evidence, and
contrary to it, which the mind never would or could do, were not the inclination or heart concerned in it, so as to have influence, which must be a wrong
inclination, and contrary to the truth, and to evidence; and therefore is
morally wrong, or criminal.

Therefore, all the mistakes and wrong opinions which men entertain,
respecting the doctrines, institutions and duties revealed in the Bible, are

criminal, and of a bad tendency. They must be so, as they are contrary to man's obligation and duty to believe all revealed truth; and are wholly owing to a wrong bias of inclination, or the depravity and corruption of the heart. What God has revealed in his word, he has declared to man, to be received by him, and believed to be the truth; of which he has given sufficient evidence. And the man who does not believe what God has clearly revealed, and of which he has given sufficient evidence, even all that can be reasonably desired, does abuse and pervert his own under-standing, and shuts his eyes against the truth, and refuses to receive the testimony which God has given. And who will say there is no crime in this!

Since therefore, all mistakes and errors, contrary to the truths made known in the Bible, are criminal, and owing to the corruption of the heart of man, then perfect holiness will exclude all error, and there neither is, nor can be, any wrong judgment in heaven; and in the Millennium, which will be a greater image of heaven than ever was before on earth, holiness, light and knowledge, will rise so high, that the former errors in principle and practice will subside, and there will be a great and general union in the belief and practice of the truth, contained in divine revelation. . . .

And they will have one common Lord, will understand, and obey all the commands of Christ; and they will know what are the institutions and or-dinances which Christ has appointed, which are all implied in baptism: They will understand what is the import of this, and implied in it, and be united in sentiments and practice, so as to form a beautiful, happy union and harmony; which will put an end to the variety and opposition of opin-ions, and practices, which now divide professing christians into so many sects, parties and denominations. . . .

Those of every denomination will doubtless expect, that the doctrines they hold, and their mode of worship and discipline, and practice, with respect to the institutions and the ordinances of Christ, will be then estab-lished as agreeable to the truth; and all others will be given up; and all men will freely conform to them. But the most, and perhaps all, will be much disappointed in this expectation; especially with regard to the different modes of worship, and practises relating to discipline, and the ordinances of the gospel. When the church comes to be built up in that day, and put on her beautiful garments, it will doubtless be different from any thing which now takes place; and what church and particular denomination is now nearest the truth, and the church which will exist at that time, must be left to be decided by the event. It is certain, that all doctrines and practices which are not agreeable to the truth, at that day, as wood, hay, and stubble, be burnt up. Therefore, it now highly concerns all, honestly to seek and find, love and practice, truth and peace. . . .

V. The Millennium will be a time of great enjoyment, happiness and universal joy. . . .

And this great increase of happiness and joy on earth will be the natural and even necessary consequence, of the great degree and universality of knowledge and holiness, which all will then profess. The knowledge of God, and the Redeemer, and love to him, will be the source of unspeakable pleasure and joy in his character, government and kingdom. And the more the great truths of divine revelation are opened and come into view, and the wisdom and grace of God in the work of redemption, are seen; the more they are contemplated and relished, the greater will be their enjoyment and happiness; and great will be their evidence and assurance of the love and favour of God, and that they shall enjoy him, and all the blessings and glory of his kingdom forever. —Then, as it is predicted of that time, "The work of righteousness shall be peace, and the effect of righteousness, quietness and assurance forever." Then the eminent degree of righteousness or holiness, to which all shall arrive, will be attended with great enjoyment and happiness, which is often meant by *peace* in scripture. And the effect and consequence of this high degree of holiness, and happiness, in seeing and loving God and divine truth, shall be, that they shall have a steady, quiet assurance of the love of God, and of his favour forever, which will greatly add to their happiness. . .

Then religious enjoyment, whether in company or alone, will appear to be a reality, and of the highest and most noble kind; and every one will be a witness and instance of it. There will then be no briar and thorns to molest enjoyment, or render company disagreeable; but all will be amiable, happy and full of love, and render themselves agreeable to every one. Every one will behave with decency and propriety towards all, agreeable to his station and connections. The law of kindness will be on the tongues of all; and true friendship, of which there is so little among men now, will then be common and universal, even christian love and friendship, which is the most excellent kind of friendship, and is indeed the only real, happy, lasting friendship. And this will lay a foundation for a peculiar, happy intimacy and friendship, in the nearest relations and connections: By which conjugal and domestic duties will be faithfully performed; and the happiness of those relations will be very great; and the end of the institutions of marriage, and families, be answered in a much greater degree, than ever before, and they will have their proper effect, in promoting the enjoyment of individuals, and the good of society. . . .

There are many other things and circumstances which will take place in that day, which are implied in what has now been observed, or may be inferred from it, and from the scripture, by which the advantages, happiness and glory of the Millennium will be promoted; some of which will be mentioned in the following particulars:

All outward worldly circumstances will then be agreeable and prosperous, and there will be for all, a sufficiency and fulness of every thing needed for the body, and for the comfort and convenience of every one. . . .

There will then be no war to impoverish, lay waste and destroy. This has been a vast expense and scourge to mankind in all ages, by which poverty and distress have been spread among all nations; and the fruits of the earth, produced and stored by the hard labour of man, have been devoured, and worse than lost. Then there will be no unrighteous persons, who shall be disposed to invade the rights and property of others, or deprive them of what justly belongs to them; but every one shall securely sit under his own vine, and fig tree; and there shall be none to make him afraid. Then there will be no law suits, which now, in civilized nations, are so vexatious and very expensive of time and money. Then, by the temperance in all things, which will be practised, and the prudent and wise care of the body, and by the smiles of heaven, there will be no expensive, distressing, desolating pestilence and sickness; but general health will be enjoyed; by which much expense of time and money will be prevented.

The intemperance, excess, extravagance and waste, in food and raiment, and the use of the things of life, which were before practised, will be discarded and cease in that day. By these, a great part of the productions of the earth, which are for the comfort and convenience of man, are now wasted and worse than lost, as they are, in innumerable instances, the cause of debility of body, sickness and death. But every thing of this kind will be used with great prudence and economy; and in that way, measure and degree, which will best answer the ends of food, drink, and clothing, and all other furniture, so as to be most comfortable, decent and convenient, and in the best manner furnish persons for their proper business and duty. Nothing will be sought or used to gratify pride inordinate, sensual appetite or lust: So that there will be no waste of the things of life: Nothing will be lost.

And at that time, the art of husbandry will be greatly advanced, and men will have skill to cultivate and manure the earth, in a much better and more easy way, than ever before; so that the same land will then produce much more than it does now, twenty, thirty, sixty, and perhaps an hundred fold more. And that which is now esteemed barren, and not capable of producing any thing, by cultivation, will then yield much more, for the sustenance of man and beast, than that which is most productive now: So that a very little spot will then produce more of the necessaries and comforts of life, than large tracts of land do now. And in this way, the curse which has hitherto been upon the ground, for the rebellion of man, will be in a great measure removed.

There will also doubtless, be great improvement and advances made in all those mechanic arts, by which the earth will be subdued and cultivated, and all the necessary and convenient articles of life, such as all utensils, clothing, buildings, &c. will be formed and made, in a better manner, and with much less labour, than they now are. There may be inventions and arts of this kind, which are beyond our present conception. And if they could be now known by any one, and he could tell what they will be, they would be thought by most, to be utterly incredible and impossible; as those inventions and arts, which are now known and familiar to us, would have appeared to those who lived before they were found out and took place.

It is not impossible, but very probable, that ways will yet be found out by men, to cut rocks and stones into any shape they please; and to remove them from place to place, with as little labour, as that with which they now cut and remove the softest and lightest wood, in order to build houses, fences, bridges, paving roads, &c. And those huge rocks and stones, which now appear to be useless, and even a nuisance, may then be found to be made, and reserved by him who is infinitely wise and good, for great usefulness, and important purposes. Perhaps there is good reason not to doubt of this. And can he doubt of it, who considers what inventions and arts have taken place in latter ages, which are as much an advance beyond what was known or thought of in ages before, as such an art would be, beyond what is now known and practiced? The art by which they removed great stones, and raised them to vast heights, by which they built the pyramids in Egypt; and that by which huge stones were cut and put into the temple of Jerusalem, is now lost, and it cannot be conceived how this was done. This art may be revived in the Millennium; and there may be other inventions and arts, to us, inconceivably greater and more useful than that. Then, in a literal sense, The vallies shall be filled, and the mountains and hills shall be made low, and the crooked shall be made straight, and the rough ways shall be made smooth, to render travelling more convenient and easy, and the earth more productive and fertile.

When all these things are considered, which have now been suggested, and others which will naturally occur to them who attend to this subject, it will appear evident, that in the days of the Millennium, there will be a fulness and plenty of all the necessaries and conveniences of life, to render all much more easy and comfortable, in their worldly circumstances and enjoyments, than ever before, and with much less labour and toil; And that it will not be then necessary for any men or women to spend all, or the greatest part of their time in labour, in order to procure a living, and enjoy all the comforts and desirable conveniences of life. It will not be necessary for each one, to labour more than two or three hours in a day, and not more than will conduce to the health and vigour of the body. And the rest of their time they will be disposed to spend in reading and conversation, and in all those exercises which are necessary and proper, in order to improve their minds, and make progress in knowledge; especially in the knowledge of divinity: And in studying the scriptures, and in private and social and public worship, and attending on public instruction, &c. When the earth shall be all subdued, and prepared in the best manner for cultivation, and houses and inclosures and other necessary and convenient buildings shall be erected, and completely finished, consisting of the most durable materials, the labour will not be hard, and will require but a small portion of their time, in order to supply every one with all the necessaries and conveniences of life: And the rest of their time will not be spent in dissipation or idleness, but in business, more entertaining and important, which has been now mentioned.

And there will be then such benevolence and fervent charity in every heart, that if any one shall be reduced to a state of want by some casuality, or by inability to provide for himself, he will have all the relief and assistance that he could desire; and there will be such a mutual care and assistance of each other, that all worldly things will be in a great degree, and in the best manner common; so as not to be withheld from any who may want them; and they will take great delight in ministering to others and serving them, whenever, and in whatever ways, there shall be opportunity to do it.

PART TWO

THE MORAL REPUBLIC

3. The Need for Virtue

In his Fourth of July oration in 1783, for the first of Boston's commemorations of America's Independence, John Warren (1753-1815) dwelt on a persistent theme of post-Revolutionary America—the special fragility of republican states. Revolutionary Americans had little sense of the linear inevitability of the promise of the United States. Right from the beginning they expressed doubts and apprehensions about the republican experiment they were entering upon. States, they knew, were like human beings: they existed in cycles of birth, maturation, and death. For Warren, the leading doctor and surgeon in post-Revolutionary Boston and member of a distinguished medically-minded Massachusetts family, the biological analogy in discussing politics was especially appropriate; but it was not peculiar to him. All American intellectuals were aware that republics were the states most susceptible to disease, requiring an extraordinary moral quality in their citizens if they were to survive.

An Oration, Delivered July 4th, 1783

JOHN WARREN

Fathers, Brethren, and Fellow-Citizens !

To mark with accuracy and precision, the principles from which the great and important transactions on the theatre of the political world originate, is indispensable duty, not only of legislators, but of every subject of a free State; fraught with the most instructive lessons on the passions that actuate the human breast, the inquiry is amply adapted to the purpose of regulating the social concerns of life.

John Warren, *An Oration, Delivered July 4th, 1783 . . . in Celebration of The Anniversary of American Independence* (Boston, 1783).

The laws and penalties by which subjects are compelled to promote the general interests of a community, should ever be instituted with a special reference to these principles, and the greatest perfection of human government consists in the judiciousness of this application.

The constitution or frame of government in a republican State, is circumscribed by Barriers, which the ambitious or designing cannot easily remove, without giving the alarm to those whose priviledges might be infringed by the innovation; but that the principle of administration may be grossly corrupted, that the people may be abused, and enslaved under the best of constitutions, is a truth to which the annals of the world may be adduced to bear a melancholy attestation.

So silently have the advances of arbitrary power been made, that a community has often been upon the verge of misery and servitude, whilst all was calm and tranquil in the State.

To revert to first principles is so essentially requisite to public happiness and safety, that Polybius has laid it down as an incontrovertible axiom, that every State must decline more or less rapidly, in proportion as she recedes from the principles on which she was founded.

That virtue is the true principle of republican governments° has been sufficiently proved by the ablest writers on the subject, and, that whereas other forms of government may be supported without her, yet that in this she is absolutely necessary to their existence.

A general prevalence of that love for our country which teaches us to esteem it glorious to die in her defence, is the only means of perpetuating the enjoyment of that liberty and security, for the support of which all government was originally intended.

Laws and punishments are but the ensigns of human depravity, to render them as few as the public safety will admit, is the study of every wise, humane legislature.† The happy influences of this noble passion, by precluding the necessity of a multiplicity of Laws will free a People from those spectacles of misery and horror, which the penalties annexed to the breach of them must inevitable create.

The contempt of dangers, and of death, when liberty was the purchase, has been the means of elevating to the highest pitch of glory, those famed Republics of antiquity, which later ages have considered as the models of

---

°Aristotle thinks there is not any one virtue belonging to the subjects of a despotic government.

†A multiplicity of rigorous penal laws is not only incompatible with the liberty of a free state, but even repugnant to human nature. Montesquieu.

political perfection; instructed from early infancy to deem themselves the property of the State, they were ever ready to sacrifice their concerns to her interests; "dear to us (says the eloquent Cicero) dear to us are our Parents, dear are our Children, our Neighbours and Associates, but above all things, dear is our Country;" the Injuries that are done to an individual are limited, those to a community may involve millions in destruction.

"It is impossible not to love a patriot, it is only loving him who loves us,"° —it is impossible not to be charmed with the influences of those divine sentiments, which induced the brave Decii to devote themselves to certain Death, that they might ensure the Roman armies victory and glory.

The celebrated story of the two Carthaginian brethren, who consented to be buried alive, to increase the boundaries of their Country, shews us to what an enthusiastic height this virtue may be carried.

Amongst the Spartans, to return from the field of battle *with* or *upon* their shields, was equally glorious, and subject of joy and acclamation; to escape without them, an indelible mark of infamy and disgrace.

From *public* spirit proceeds almost every other virtue. The man who willingly would die to save his Country, would surely sacrifice his fortune and possessions, to secure her peace and happiness. The noble examples of frugality which were exhibited in the conduct of the Spartan governors, who began the reformation of the state, by delivering up their own private property, to convince the citizens that their intentions were sincere, is a proof how much it may be made to triumph over avarice and selfishness.

The Thebans, under the matchless Epaminondas, when they were deserted by their allies, and reduced to the greatest extremities, were by the wise example of their general, and frequent skirmishes with the enemy, inspired with a spirit of enterprize and bravery, which at length enabled them to vanquish thrice their number of Lacedemonian troops, and having slain their general, to march in hostile array to the very gates of Sparta.

These are the principles which have more or less animated the subjects of every state, that has arrived to any considerable degree of opulence and grandeur, and it is of the greatest use to observe how others have gradually crept into governments, and suppressed, or eradicated the public virtue of a people.

Alas! to what amounts the summit of all human greatness! Sparta, the nurse of heroes and legislators, Athens, the seat of arts and sciences, Carthage the mart of all the trading nations, and even Rome, the haughty mistress of the world, have all long since been level'd with the dust! Of all

°Gordon, *Sallust,* p. 41.

the states and cities of the globe that have experienced the like catastrophe, scarce can we mention one that has not met her ruin, in a forgetfulness of those *fundamental principles* on which her happiness depended.

So nearly is the most prosperous condition of a people, allied to decay and ruin, that even this flattering appearance conceals the seeds, that finally must produce her destruction.°

The object of public virtue, is to secure the liberties of the community, a security of liberty admits of every man's pursuing, without molestation, the measures most likely to increase his ease, and to place him in a state of independent affluence, nothing is more conducive to these ends than a free and unlimited commerce, the encouragement of which is undoubtedly the duty of the Commonwealth, and the feelings of humanity are, in a general sense, highly interested in the prosecution of it.

Commercial intercourse and connection have perhaps contributed more towards checking the effusion of blood, than all the obligations of morality and religion, in their usual state of debility, could ever have effected.† The ideas of conquest and destruction amongst the ancients, were commonly comprehended under the same term, and torrents of human blood have been shed to gratify a spirit of revenge; in latter times the views of almost every powerful nation with whom civilization has been the effect of trade, have been directed to the support of that political balance, upon which this intercourse depends.

In the quarrel between the Swedes and Danes, a short time previous to the restoration of Charles the second of England, and again in the reign of William the third, the Dutch and the English sent their fleets into the Baltic, to prevent those inconveniences that would have resulted to the commerce of the maritime powers, had either of those kingdoms been destroyed, and the same thing has taken place in the general wars against France.

Considered then as an instrument for lessening the calamities of war, humanity must ever exult in the countenance given to trade; the immediate effect of it, when extensive, is usually an augmentation of wealth, but as it is generally impossible for every subject to acquire a great degree of opulence, the riches of the state become accumulated in the coffers of a few;‡

°It was the victory over the Persians, obtained in the straits of Thalamis, that corrupted the Republic of Athens, and the defeat of the Athenians, ruined the Republic of Syracuse. Montesquieu, *Spirit of Laws*, vol. I, p. 163.

†Peace is the natural effect of Trade. Montesquieu, vol. II, p. 2.

‡Luxury is always proportional to the inequality of fortune. Montesquieu, vol. I, p. 137.

the passions of the great almost invariably extend to the body of the people, who to gratify an unbounded thirst for gain, are ready to sacrifice every other blessing to that, which in any degree, furnishes them with the means of imitating their superiors; bribery and venality, the grand engines of slavery, have been called in to the assistance of the aspiring nobles, who, in this case, never fail to make the deluded people pay them the full price of their prostitution.

This accession of power, acquired by the consent of the people themselves, enables their governors to assume the reins of absolute controul, to burst all the bonds of social obligation, and finally to extort by violence, what formerly they were obliged to purchase; accustomed to a habit of sloth and idleness, the subjects are rendered too effeminate to apply themselves to labor and fatigue, or if they do it, are soon discouraged by the rapaciousness of their rulers, a spirit of faction and uneasiness becomes generally prevalent; impressed with that awful respect with which the trappings of wealth universally inspire a people that have been accustomed to view it as the measure of human felicity, they are too pusillanimous to relieve themselves from their burden by an united effort of the whole,° and the only object of intestine commotion, is the plunder of the rich, that they may sell the acquisition to the highest bidder; insurrections of this kind are most commonly easily suppressed, and farther impositions are forever the consequence.

The extortion exercised on the earnings of the labourer is an effectual check upon the pursuit of agriculture;† Population, universally in a great measure proportionable thereto, being by this means limited, and discouraged, the number of subjects, the real source of strength and support, daily diminishes, 'till at length they fall an easy prey to the first Despot, whether foreign or domestic, who offers them the yoke;—Such is the fatal operation of luxury, almost invariably the consequence of unbounded wealth.‡

The Carthaginians, says Montague, stand single upon the records of history, the only people in the universe upon whom immense wealth has never been able to work its usual effects; but even in this instance it may perhaps reasonably be questioned, whether the factions that prevented the illustrious

°China, the *richest* and most populous commercial empire of the universe, was subdued by a handful of *poor* Tartars.

†Countries are not cultivated in proportion to their fertility but to their liberty. Montesquieu, *Spirit of Laws,* vol. I, p. 388.

‡The Spaniards, since the discovery of the American mines, have been incessantly declining. Montesquieu, *Spirit of Laws,* vol. I, p. 64.

Hannibal from entering the gates of Rome, whilst he had filled that city with terror and dismay, were not the effect of opulence, and loss of public virtue. The introduction of wealth in the Roman republic, is dated at the conquest of Antiochus the great, and the era of corruption from the same memorable period; what sluices of depravity and misery did they not open in the state! That senate which once resembled an assembly of Kings, whose rigid faith had rendered them the objects of universal veneration whilst frugality and patriotism were held in estimation, can *now* meanly stoop to avail themselves of a quibble in terms of a treaty, to destroy a City they had pledged their honour to preserve; that senate from which a single deputy had once caused a mighty monarch to tremble and obey, and barely by the motion of his cane, obliged him, at the head of a victorious army, to resign his conquest, can now condescend to flatter the vilest passions, and bear to be insulted with the most humiliating usage without daring to murmur or complain.

The unparalleled usurpations of Sylla, Marius, and Caesar are but variegated forms, in which are exhibited, the baneful effects of that adulatory submission, with which a base, degenerate, and corrupted people have become the instruments of tyranny and murder; the bloody proscriptions and licensed executions of those pests of the human race, which have disgraced the Roman name, were generally accompanied with the thanks of the Senate. Jugurtha, that infamous Numidian Prince, who ungratefully murdered the children of his benefactor, in this corrupted age of the Republic, secures himself from the punishment due to his crimes by bribing his judges, and by the same means enables himself to enter the Roman camp, and make that army whose force he once had dreaded, submit to *pass the yoke*, the most ignominious punishment that could have been inflicted.

The Roman Provinces would never so generally have submitted to the impositions of their rapacious governors, had not the minds of the people been prepared for them by their participation in the manners of the citizens.

When once a State has arrived to this extreme degree of corruption, nothing short of a miracle can wrest it from destruction; luxury and venality become a branch of education, and as nothing can operate so strongly on the minds of youth, as examples set by parental authority,° the evil becomes ingrafted into the opinions of the people; whilst the Spartan Republic retained her virtue, she was free and invincible, she made the mighty army of the Persian monarch flee before her, and with three hundred soldiers

---

°The surest way of instilling into children a love for their country is, for parents to set the example. Montesquieu, *Spirit of Laws,* vol. I, p. 49.

stopped the march of more than three millions of men; with the exception only of a single man they died in the contest, with their arms in their hands, and a magnificent monument was erected to their memory, with an inscription that comprehends the finest eulogium, "Go traveller and tell at Lacedemon, that we died here in defence of her sacred laws." —Philopaeman, the general of the Achaeans, was so fully persuaded that the only means of reducing this brave people to subjection and dependence, was to eradicate the principle of public virtue, that he attempted it, by endeavouring to change the manner of their education.° A change was afterwards effected, a taste for luxury inculcated, Athens subjected to her arms, her spoils and riches seized with greediness, corruption ensued, and ruin closed the drama.

We are charmed with the noble exertions of the United Provinces in their opposition to despotic government, yet how soon are we astonished to see that brave people in the greatest danger of a total subjection from that passion for commerce, which by attracting their whole attention, and confining their views to the objects of gain, induced them, that they might not be interrupted in their favorite pursuits, to confide in foreign mercenaries for their defence and protection; such was the general depravity of morals at one unhappy period of the Republic, that their excellent Stadholder, the Prince of Orange and Nassau, exhibited the most brilliant virtues, to little other purpose than to convince himself and the world, that loss of public virtue is an infallible mark of real, or approaching declension.

The Republic of Venice which for twelve centuries has maintained her freedom and independence, and which has been independently a match for the whole Ottoman Power, has preserved herself solely by her wise maxims of Legislation, founded on the first principles of her government.

The thirteen independent cantons of Switzerland, preserved from slavery by resistance to tyranny, retain the same unchangeable character for simplicity, honesty, frugality, and modesty, with which they first set out.[†] It would be endless to enumerate all the instances that might be offered, of the miseries and wretchedness that have been heaped upon mankind, by a

---

°The people will never fail to pursue right measures for the security of their liberties, if they are but rightly informed; and it is a pleasing consideration, that the means of education, and the promotion of the sciences, are so generally the objects of public attention in these *rising confederated states.*

†They have no corrupt or corrupting court, no blood sucking placemen, no standing army, the ready instruments of tyranny, no ambition for conquest, no luxury, no citadels against invasion, and against liberty, their mountains are their fortifications, and every householder is a Soldier ready to fight for his country. *Political Disquisitions,* vol. III, p. 410. Quot. Voltaire.

general adoption of the contrary qualities, we need but advert to the history of that nation, whose extreme degeneracy, has induced them to acquiesce in these enormous impositions, which a braver people have resisted, at the hazard of their lives and fortunes, and even to become the willing tools for enforcing a servile subjection, upon those, whom they were bound by ties of blood, to love and succour.

That we may learn wisdom by the misfortunes of others, that by tracing the operation of those causes which have proved ruinous to so many states and kingdoms, we may escape the rocks and quicksands on which they have been shipwreck'd, it may be useful to take a cursory retrospect of the motives and opinions, which have effected the dismemberment of a very large and valuable part of the British dominions, and thereby deprived them of a principal source of strength and greatness; under a constitution which has ever been the boast of Englishmen, we have seen a most shameful prostitution of wealth to the purposes of bribery and corruption, with a view still farther to augment that opulence of individuals, which when exorbitant, must always be injurious to the common interest.°

We have seen the members of a House of Commons, which was once the bulwark of the nation, and the palladium of Liberty, availing themselves of the meanest artifices for securing a seat, because it enabled them to gratify their favorite passions; and shame to human nature! We have seen a people, once famed for honesty and temperance,intoxicated at the gambols of an election, and stupidly selling their suffrages for representatives in Parliament!

The whole business of government had become an affair of trade and calculation, the representative who expended his property for the purchase of a vote, was sure to make his profits, by the sale of his influence for the support of ministerial prodigality, or absolute domination; and to extend the security with which the members might plunder the people and trample on their rights, the prolongation of their parliaments to a term of time sufficient to inveterate their power, was at length adopted, for the purpose of riveting those chains which an undue influence in elections had previously forged.

°The great increase of our commerce after the peace of Utrecht, brought in a vast accession of wealth; and that wealth revived, and gradually diffused that luxury through the whole nation, which had laid dormant during the warlike reigns of William and Ann; to this universal luxury, and to this only, we must impute the amazing progress of corruption which seized the very vitals of our constitution. Montague, on *Republics*, p. 376.

Religious tyranny had forced from the unnatural bosom of a parent, a race of hardy sons, who chose rather to dwell in the deserts of America with the savage natives, than in the splendid habitations of *more* savage men.

Scarcely had these persecuted fugitives breathed from the fatigues of a dangerous voyage, when behold the cruel hand of power stretched over the Atlantic to distress them in their new possessions! Having found a rude uncultivated soil, inadequate to the supply of the conveniences of life, they attempted those arts of which they stood immediately in need; a prohibition of the manufactures necessary to cloath them in these then inhospitable wilds was early threatened, and though they were afterwards permitted, yet it was under the most humiliating restrictions.

From a principle of avarice and the most unjustifiable partiality in prejudice of these infant settlements, all commercial communication between them was forbidden, the importation of mercantile articles was laid under the heaviest restraints, none were to be freighted, not even the produce of foreign countries, from any other than British ports, and all exportations were finally to terminate in Britain.

The manifest object of these measures, was to enrich some crouching favorites at home, 'till at length, plunged into debt, even in the midst of success and conquest, by the rapaciousness of an insatiable ministry, and a general corruption of manners, every sinew was strained amongst their domestic subjects for the acquisition of a large revenue, but this resource having been found insufficient for the purpose, the expences of the war, out of which they had just emerged, were made the pretext for levying taxes on the unrepresented subjects of America; the first requisition for the supply of an army was too readily submitted to, and the subsequent acts, which have led to that war, in which these states have been called upon to contend for every thing dear in life, are too recent to be yet forgotten by you my fellow citizens, on whom the vengeance they were designed to execute has so largely fallen.

The mild voice of supplication and petition had in vain assailed the royal ear, the blood of your fellow-countrymen was wantonly shed on the memorable plains of *Lexington*, you flew to arms and made *your last appeal to Heaven*.

Never did an enthusiastic ardor in the cause of an injured country blaze forth with such resistless fury, never did patriotic virtue shine out with such transcendent lustre, as on that solemn day! scarcely was there to be seen a peasant through the land "whose bosom beat not in his country's cause." Angels must have delighted in the fight! A wide extended country, roused into action at the first flash of arms, and pouring forth her thousands of virtuous yeomen to avenge the blood of their slaughtered bretheren on the unprincipled aggressors! Quickly they fled from merited destruction, and fleeing, shed their blood, an immolation to the beloved names of those who fell the early martyrs to this glorious cause; you then convinced *deluded* Britons, that bravery was not the growth of any one *peculiar* spot or soil.

The enterprize 'tis true was bold and daring! The nations of the world stood still, astonished at the desperate blow! The brave alone are capable of noble actions. Defenseless, and unfurnished with the means of war, you placed your confidence in that God of armies who approves the struggles of the oppressed, and relying on the honest feelings of the heart for your success, you ventured to contend with veteran armies, and to defy the formidable power of a nation accustomed to success and conquest.

Your Guardian Genius patronized your cause, presided in your counsels, inspired you with intrepidity and wisdom, and mysteriously infatuated the British chiefs; protected in the days of weakness and of danger, by the concealment of your real wants, the boasted wisdom of your crafty foe was baffled and confounded.

Through all the various fortunes of the field, you persevered with an undaunted front, and whilst your coasts were swarming with fleets, full freighted with the choicest legions of the enemy, a force that would have stiffened with dispair a less determined people, you dared to pass the irrevocable decree, that forever cut asunder the ties that bound you to a cruel parent, assumed your rank amongst the nations of the world, and instituted a new Epoch in the annals of your country; with solemn oaths, you pledged your sacred honor, to die united in defence of your much injured rights, or live in virtuous possession of *peace*, of *liberty* and *safety*.—The generations yet unborn shall read with rapture that distinguished page, whereon in capitals shall stand recorded, the important transaction of that day, and celebrate to the latest ages of this republic, the anniversary of that resolution of the American Congress, which gave the rights of sovereignty and independence to these United States.

Long may they retain that spirit of union which has enabled them to withstand the mighty force of Britain, and never be persuaded, through the artifice of their enemies, to violate the articles of that confederation to which they owe their liberty; should ever the constitutional authority of the legal representative body of the nation be annihilated, the bond of union will be dissolved, and we shall be reduced to the greatest hazard of misery and subjection.

By means of their union, the states, alone and unassisted, have vanquished a numerous army of brave and veteran troops, and led their chief a captive to your capital.—As long as time shall last the noble example you have set the world shall be produced, to shew what wonders may be done by men united, and determined to be free.

Your virtue has supplied the place of wealth in the prosecution of the war; the taxes that have been levied, have generally been submitted to with chearfulness, and in a free state, where the people themselves are the assessors, so far were they from being considered as a grievance, that you wisely *esteemed them* as the symptoms of virtue, because they evince that the safety of the public is the supreme object of attention.°

Nor shall the powerful aids of a magnanimous Ally be suffered here to pass unnoticed; the generous terms on which assistance and support were granted, shall leave impressions of esteem and friendship which time and age shall not be able to efface. Under the conduct of *One*† illustrious General, the brave allied armies have together contended for the rights of human nature, have mingled blood, conquered a formidable host of *chosen* troops, *and laid the British Standard at your feet.*

At length, ye favoured Sons of freedom, THE GLORIOUS WORK IS DONE! Heralds of Peace proclaim the joyful tidings! Let the remotest corners of the globe resound with acclamations of applause, 'till even the inanimate creation shall join the concert, and dance to more sublime than *Orphean* strains! Genius of liberty rejoice, for Heaven has opened a new asylum to your long persecuted sons! Rejoice ye inhabitants of this chosen land! Let songs of joy dwell long upon your thankful tongues, and notes of gratitude to Heaven be raised on ten thousand strings, 'till angels catch the sound, and echo back, *Peace and good will to men*! Had I a thousand tongues, and all the eloquence of Cicero or Demosthenes, too feeble were my accents, too small my energy for this *transporting* theme!

°It is a general rule that taxes may be heavier in proportion to the liberty of the subject, and that there is a necessity for diminishing them in proportion to the increase of slavery. Montesquieu, vol. I, p. 305.

How much these States enjoy advantages superior to Great Britain, with respect to the payment of their public debt, is sufficiently obvious.

†It greatly redounds to the honour of these states, as well as that of their great General, that whilst the British have four or five times changed their commander in chief, the same has continued at the head of the American forces through the whole war; has this been the case, because amongst our enemies it was more difficult to find a virtuous man, or because the government under which they held their places was more factious and corrupt? The long continuance of the hannibalic war, in which the Carthaginians maintained their ground above 16 years against the whole force of the Romans, is imputed to the annual change of Generals amongst the *latter,* whilst the *former* were constantly commanded by the *same* extraordinary man.

What miseries and tortures have we not escaped! Go search the records of tyranny and usurpation, and learn the insolence forever consequent on the suppression of insurrections in the behalf of violated rights! Agis, the brave reformer of the Spartan manners, was condemned by the tyrant who owed his life to *him*, to die an ignominious death for an unsuccessful opposition to the torrent of vice which had overwhelmed that republic; a fond and anxious mother presented at the door of his prison, a petition, that her son might be indulged with a hearing before the people; the unfeeling minister of cruelty had already perpetrated the execrable deed, and sneeringly replied, no farther injury should be done him; he then introduced her to the apartment where laid the body of her murdered son, with that of her aged mother who had attended him; sensible that his misfortunes were the consequence of lenity carried to a degree that rendered it impolicy, she could not forbear kissing the bloody corpse, and uttering aloud the sentiments of her soul; in the midst of this affecting scene, that would have extorted pity from a savage breast, the ruffian, exasperated at these effusions of grief, as expressing her justification of his conduct, rushed on the distracted *mother*, and plunged his dagger in her breast!

The history of that brave and honest nation, whose spirited exertions have lately extricated them from that subjection and dependance, to which the arms and artifice of a neighbouring kingdom had reduced them, sufficiently evinces, that resistance to arbitrary power, needs but the name of *rebellion*, to furnish out a pretext for every form of violence and cruelty; often have the scaffolds smoked with gore pour'd from the veins of patriots and of heroes, and the destroying sword of despotism been drunk with the richest blood of a community!

Had conquest crowned the efforts of our enemies, numbers of our *worthy patriots*, had *now* been bleeding under the vindictive hand of a successful foe, and *we* perhaps in mines or dungeons, been dragging out a life of wretchedness, and weeping in silence, over the memory of *those*, to whom were justly due, the applause and gratitude of every friend to liberty and virtue.

What a contrast to this frightful picture does the joyfulness of the occasion which has this day assembled us together, exhibit to our view! Many of these illustrious freemen now meet us here, and mingle tears of joy and gratitude with ours!

Thousands of brave, deserving members of society, have fallen an untimely prey to the poisonous exhalations of a *prison*, and *filthy guardships*, have been the charnel houses of our brethren; confined within those dreadful regions of horror and dispair, where no refreshing breezes ever entered, the tainted element itself was charged with pestilence and death! You who have seen the helpless victim of a merciless disease, groaning under the agonies of a relentless fever, can tell what epithets to use in the description of the tortures they endured; their tongues were parched with raging heat! Their boiling blood scalded the very veins in which it circulated—and did ye then, ye ministers of wrath, supply a single cup of water to refresh their thirsty souls? Verily, ye unworthy offspring of a *christian* land, *inasmuch as ye did it not to one of these*, ye did it not to *him* who shortly will avenge the cause of *innocence*.

But smiling peace returns, and death and carnage shall prevail no more to swell the number of the slain; we wish not Britons, too severely to upbraid you, we only mean to hold you up as an example to the world, from which the best of lessons may be learnt.

—Let us however contemplate those unfictitious scenes of misery and distress, which an arduous struggle for our liberties have cost us; let us remember the principles that produced the opposition, as well as those that gave occasion for it, and then if we can tamely bear to see our liberties destroyed, let us flee, *quickly* flee, from these yet hallowed shores, nor dare pollute the land which holds *our fathers' tombs.*

A time of *tranquility* and *peace* is often a season of the greatest danger,° because it is too apt to involve a general opinion of perfect security. The Roman state, whilst Carthage stood her rival, retained her virtue, Carthage was destroyed, and Rome became corrupt†; unless *we* are properly apprized of, and duly armed against this evil, the *United States* will *one day* experience a similar fate.

Transported from a distant clime, less friendly to its nurture, you have planted here the *stately Tree of Liberty*, and lived to see it flourish! But whilst you pluck the fruit from the bending branches, remember that *its roots were watered with your blood!*—Remember the price at which you purchased it, "Nor barter liberty for gold."

Go search the vaults, where lay enshrined the relicks of your martyred fellow-citizens, and from their dust receive a lesson on the value of your

---

°When once a state has struggled through many and great difficulties, and emerged at last to freedom and wealth, men begin to sink gradually into luxury, and to grow more dissolute in their morals. Montague, on *Republics*, p. 362.

†Baron de Montesquieu speaking of Carthage and Rome says, they were alarmed and strengthened by each other, strange that the greater security those states enjoyed, the more like stagnated waters they were subject to corruption! vol. I, p. 164.

freedom! When virtue fails, when luxury and corruption shall undermine the pillars of the state, and threaten a total loss of liberty and patriotism, then solemnly repair to those *sacred repositories* of the dead, and if you *can*, return and sport away your rights.

When you forget the value of your freedom, read over the history that counts the wounds from which your country bled; peruse the picture which brings back to your imaginations, in the lively colours of undisguised truth, the wild, distracted feelings of your hearts!—But if your happy lot has been not to have felt the pangs of a convulsive separation from *friend* or *kindred*, learn them of *those that have.*—

Behold the *hoary head of age*, descending to the grave with sorrow and despair; pleased with enchanting prospects, in a *son* with whom his very soul was bound together, a *son* who promised to have been the stay and staff of his defenceless years, the *good old man* insensibly declined along the path of life, and scarcely felt the weight of *three score years and ten*—the deadly shaft pierced through the bosom of his hopes, and doomed him to breathe out the residue of life in solitude and wretchedness.—

Observe the *Youth* whose *parent, guardian,* and *protector,* just at the time when the faculties of reason were beginning to put forth their buds, and court the fostering hand of culture, snatched from their dutiful embraces, and all the *endearing ties* of life.—

But, if suspicious of a counterfeited grief, you seek an instance where sorrow *cannot* be feigned, go follow *her* whose streaming eyes, distracted mein, and bursting heart, announce the pangs that nature feels, in the sudden and violent dissolution of the *nearest* and *most dear connection.*—

I might proceed—but permit me *here* to draw the sable veil, and leave to your imaginations to suggest the rest—but stay—forbear, nor longer mourn for those who have no cause for tears.—

> "Glory with all her lamps shall burn
> "To watch the warrior's sleeping clay,
> " 'Till the last trump shall raise his urn,
> "To share the triumphs of the day."

If to latest ages we retain the *spirit* which gave our INDEPENDENCE birth; if taught by the fatal evils that have subverted so many *mighty states,* we learn to sacrifice our dearest interests in our country's cause, enjoin upon our children a *solemn veneration* for her laws, as next to adoration of their God, the *great* concern of man, and seal the precept with our last expiring breath, these STARS, that even now enlighten half the world, shall shine a glorious constellation in this *western hemisphere*, 'till *stars* and suns shall shine no more, and all the kingdoms of *this* globe shall vanish like a scroll.

4. Church and State

Isaac Backus (1724-1806) was one of America's great contributors to the tradition of separation of church and state. Indeed, as his biographer William G. McLoughlin has stated, Backus is a much more representative exponent of the peculiar American relationship between government and religion—at least until recent times—than even Thomas Jefferson. For Americans, despite their abhorrence of religious orthodoxy and legal establishments, have been an intensely religious people. Thomas Jefferson and James Madison, with their latitudinarian, secular-minded deism, could never really speak for the evangelical Christianity of nineteenth-century America. Backus, however, could. Liberty of conscience for Backus, a New Light Separate Baptist, was not a consequence of the rationalistic and pagan Enlightenment. Backus and the Baptists came to their belief in the separation of church and state out of the exigencies of being a minority sect within tax-supported established church systems and out of the pietistic desire to create gathered, voluntaristic churches of individual believers. Disestablishment for Backus did not signify the end of what he called the "sweet harmony" between church and state; it meant only that Christ's kingdom should be free to evangelize the society aided by sympathetic but nonsectarian governments.

The tract reprinted here describes a decision of the Bristol County Court of Massachusetts in 1782 invalidating the famous and controversial Article Three of the Massachusetts Constitution of 1780. This Article, by granting each town or parish the power to provide for the public support of religion, seemed to violate the Constitution's Declaration of Rights, which stated that no one could be hurt or restrained for worshiping God in his own way. When Elijah Balkom, a member of the Baptist church in Attleboro, was jailed for refusing to pay religious taxes, he sought through a suit against the tax assessors to test the constitutionality of Article Three. The decision, in his favor, in effect disestablished the Massachusetts churches; together with the success of the action of Baptist Richard Lee against rioters in Hingham, it convinced Backus that the prospects for equal Christian liberty and evangelical reformation in America had been so opened that they could never be stifled again. Although Backus' optimism about disestablishment in Massachusetts was short-lived (the Balkom decision being reversed two years later), his vision anticipated America's nineteenth-century experience.

A Door Opened for Equal Christian Liberty

ISAAC BACKUS

The return of peace to the nations, and to this land in particular, with its circumstances and privileges, is a very great event indeed; which calls loudly to all for gratitude and thankfulness, to be manifested by a wise improvement of the favours granted us, and a faithful discharge of duty in our several stations. And as contentions about religious liberty have caused much difficulty among ourselves, whereby our enemies hoped to have got advantage against us, it may be of public benefit to lay open the prospect we now have of their being happily terminated.

The east parish in Attleborough, supposing that our laws about worship were the same as formerly, taxed and made distress upon several persons, for the support of their worship, who did not attend thereon. One of them thought proper to try how our laws now are in that respect; and for that end sued their assessors before a justice of peace in Norton, February 22, 1782; when and where he fully proved, that he had usually attended public worship with the first baptist church in Attleborough, ever since May 1780, and had communicated to its support to their satisfaction. Yet judgment was given against him; from which he appealed to the country court at Taunton. And it being a matter of great importance, to have points of law well defined, and settled under our new constitution of government, both parties agreed to have the case tried by the honorable justices of the court; namely, Walter Spooner, Thomas Durfee, Benjamin Williams, and William Baylies, Esquires. The council for the appellant were the honorable William Bradford, and James-Mitchel Varnum, Esquires. For the appellees was the honorable Robert Treat Paine, Esq; attorney general for this Commonwealth.

The latter, when pleading for said parish, owned that religion must at all times be a matter between God and the individuals, and declared that he disclaimed all subordination of any one sect to another; but pleaded, that the certificates, formerly required by law, were not tokens of subordination of

Isaac Backus, *A Door Opened for Equal Christian Liberty, And No Man Can Shut It* . . . (Boston [1783]).

one sect to another, but of subordination to the government; and accused the baptists of refusing to be subordinate to government. He also pleaded, that the appellant was born in the second parish in Attleborough, was baptized there, and therefore was to all intents a member of that society; so that if he thought he had cause to leave them, the law, reason, and even common civility, required that he should give them notice of it, which he had not done.

The chief pleas for the appellant were, that RELIGION was prior to all states and kingdoms in the world, and therefore could not in its nature be subject to human laws; that the certificates heretofore required, were given to parish officers, officers of one particular sect, and not to officers of government; and as our constitution says, "No subordination of any one sect or denomination to another, shall ever be established by law," those laws are repealed thereby. And as the constitution was established by the people, it is stronger than any law the assembly can make, it being the foundation whereon they stand. Also the society to which the appellant joined, is as regular a society as the other that taxed him.

These points were learnedly discussed, on March 16, 1782; after which the justices retired a little by themselves, and then returned, and declared, "that they were unanimously agreed in giving the appellant damages and costs." Which judgment not only settled the controversy in Attleborough, but has been extensively beneficial elsewhere.

As far as my memory and judgment serve me, this is a fair representation of those transactions; and if any can set them in a more just light, they are welcome to do it. And since some in Attleborough accused the baptists of great inconsistency, in protesting against the third article in our bill of rights, and yet now making use of it against them, I shall take leave to make a few remarks upon this subject.

1. It is well known that on December 2, 1779, three months before the constitution was finished, as agent for our churches, I published that article in the independent chronicle, with exceptions against the power claimed therein; when I declared, that I "fully concurred" with that part of it which we have now made use of; and none could tell how it would operate but by experience.

2. If natural birth, and the doings of others, could make a person a member of a religious society, without his own consent, we should have no objection against the way of withdrawing from such a society, that our opponents plead for. But since religion is ever a matter between God and individuals, how can any man become a member of a religious society without his own consent? And how can a man who believes it to be impossible, practically

say, that it is possible, without contracting guilt to his conscience? This is the exact state of our controversy about religious liberty. We have been very far from perfection in our behaviour therein; but we have not been accused of disobedience to government, and of disturbing the public peace, because of our ever invading the rights of others; but only because we will not give up our own. It is because we have chosen sufferings, rather than to sin against God. We believe that attendance upon public worship, and keeping the first day of the week holy to God, are duties to be inculcated and enforced by his laws, instead of the laws of men; but we have had no controversy with our rulers about that matter. The town of Boston must now look at home, for a want of subordination to government in that respect.°

3.   The first, and most essential article in the order of Christ's kingdom, is that no man *can see it*, not have any right to *power* therein, until he is *born again*. John I. 12, 13. III. 3. And the fathers of the Massachusetts government paid such a regard to this truth, that, during their first charter, none were admitted to full communion in their churches, not to govern in the choice and support of ministers, without a credible profession of that great change. And their excluding of all others from a vote in civil government, and yet compelling of them to attend and support their worship, gave the most plausible handle that the British court ever had, to rob us of the stipulated privilege of choosing our own governors, while they demanded our property to support governors arbitrarily set over us. And contentions upon this point was the root of the late bloody war, which has cost a multitude of lives, and involved both countries amazingly in debt. Yet many are still attached to the errors of our fathers, while they are resolutely set against their virtues.

After a glorious reformation, the first church in Middleborough, were bereaved of their beloved pastor, in April 1744. The church then consisted of above an hundred male communicants; but after they had voted to hear Mr. Silvanus Conant four sabbaths upon probation, the parish committee went and got another minister to supply the pulpit the same days. And a council of six ministers, approved of their so doing, and advised them to persist in that way. By this means the society was divided; and a pastor chosen by three quarters of the church, and who proved to be one of the best ministers in the county, had no better place than a barn to preach in, till they built a new meeting house for him. The ministers who *caused that division*, belonged to Scituate, Hingham, Hanover, Pembroke, and Bridge-

---

°A law about these things was made here last fall, which, after repeated meetings, is not obeyed by this town.

water. And the setting up of the world to govern the church about soul guides, was the evident cause of the following prophane, cruel, and scandelous actions.

Mr. Richard Lee, a gifted member of one of our churches having laboured with success in Scituate, was earnestly requested by a man in Hingham, to come and hold a meeting at his house, which he consented to. The meeting was appointed to be in the evening of May 28, 1782; but as the people were assembling for worship, a large mob came up, armed with clubs and staves, and warned Lee and his friends to depart out of Hingham immediately, or it would be much worse for them. He inquired whether they came with any authority? and finding that they did not, he, with the bible in his hand, began to exhort the people to fear God rather than man. Upon which one of them violently seized him by his arm and collar, and others also laying hold of him, halled him away out of the house, and out of the town. When he attempted to speak, and to recite passages of scripture, they repeatedly smote him on his mouth, with the palms of their hands, and also made loud noises to prevent his being heard. As one who had hold of him blundered down, and another shook a club over his head, and swore that if he flung another down, he would sink Lee to hell in a moment. He then said, "I look upon this holy bible to be the "very best law that ever I heard of." Upon which it was spitefully struck out of his hand, and stamped under foot, with curses and execrations too horrid to be here repeated! When the mob had got him over the town line, their captain shook a club over Lee's head, and swore, that if he ever came into that town again, he would tie him up, and whip him thirty stripes. Said our suffering brother, "that's not so much as they whipt Paul." *What! d—n you,* said one, *do you compare yourself with Paul!* A Hingham man said, Mr. Lee may go and hold a meeting at my house.— But others declared that if he did, they would burn his house down, and carry him out of town. One of the mob cast soft cow-dung in Lee's face, and then they insulted him because of that defilement, with a great deal more of abuse to men, and blasphemy against God. Two other baptist brethren were then hauled by violence out of Hingham, and they went and held a religious meeting in Scituate the same night.

In the above actions they tore Mr. Lee's cloaths considerably, and also bruised and injured his body so much that he was ill for some days, and then he returned home to Glocester in the county of Providence. In July I met him at Scituate, where we were credibly informed, that his safety, and even his life, were still threatened by those rioters. We then went to Boston to ask advice; and many there as well as in the country, advised him to present a complaint to the grand jury of Suffolk county, against those rioters, as a necessary means of securing the public peace, and the liberties of mankind. This was accordingly done, when the county court sat at Boston in October. Thirteen men were named in the complaint, which was supported by the testimony of eight witnesses; and a warrant was granted against five of the rioters, four of whom were taken, and pleaded not guilty before the court; upon which their trial was appointed to be on January 14, 1783.

Snow, ice, and a very sharp air, caused the traveling to be exceeding difficult; yet Mr. Lee travelled seventy miles from his house to Scituate, and, with other witnesses, twenty-three more from thence to Boston, at the appointed time. But after an expensive attendance of two days, the case was put off till April. And the ill treatment he then met with made him determine not to appear there again, without somebody from a distance to speak for him; and the event justified this determination. For no sooner did a lawyer from Providence appear for him in Boston, on April 23d, than a proposal was made to leave the whole affair to chosen men to settle it. This was agreed to; and the gentlemen appointed met upon it in Bridgwater the 6th instant. But then the defendants could not bear to have their case publicly opened; and Mr. Lee was prevailed with to settle the matter with them, upon their promising to pay a sum far short of what many thought they ought to have done. So that none can justly charge him with prosecuting them out of a revengeful spirit, nor with taking all the advantages of them that the law would have given him. And their names are not omitted in this publication, out of any fear of not being able fully to prove every article; but because we could expose, and give proper warnings against such actions for the future, without mentioning their names; and we hope and pray for their repentance and salvation.

The fathers of this town and government mistook the work of civil rulers so much, as to imagine that they were to inflict corporal punishments upon men, as sinners against God, and not only for crimes against the community. They therefore banished several persons upon pain of death for adultery, before they did any for heresy; and some were hanged here for adultery near twenty years before they hanged the quakers. But the Apostle has plainly taught the churches, to put away wicked persons out of their communion; and says upon it, *Them that are without God judgeth.* 1 Cor. v. 13. And in the parable of the tares of the field, our Lord has commanded his servants, to let the children of his kingdom, and the children of the wicked one, grow together in the world, till the end of it. Which divine laws have ever been violated by all those who have confounded the government of the church and state together. On the one hand they have been deficient about, if they have not wholly neglected, gospel discipline in the church;

while they have ever invaded their neighbours' rights in the state, under religious pretences. And for twelve or thirteen centuries, all colleges and places for superior learning, were under the government of men, who assumed the power to lay religious bands upon children before they could choose for themselves, and to enforce the same by the sword of the magistrate all their days. But I congratulate my countrymen upon the arrival of more agreeable times, and upon the prospect of a much greater reformation before us. For the following reasons convince me, that God has now set before us an open door for equal christian liberty, which no man can shut.

1. Not only America, but all the kingdoms and states of Europe, who have acknowledged the authority of our Congress, have set their seal to this truth, that the highest civil rulers derive their power from the consent of the people, and cannot stand without their support. And common people know, that nothing is more contrary to the rules of honesty, than for some to attempt to convey to others things which they have no right to themselves; and no one has any right to judge for others in religious affairs.

2. All former taxes to support worship, were imposed in each government by a particular sect, who held all others in subordination thereto; which partiality is now expressly excluded from among us.

3. No man can take a seat in our legislature, till he solemnly declare, "I believe the christian religion, and have a firm persuasion of its truth." And as surely as it is true, Christ is the only HEAD of his church, and she is COMPLETE in him, and is required to do all her acts IN HIS NAME; and all worship of a contrary nature, is *will worship*, and is only to *satisfy the flesh*. Col. II. 10, 19-23. III. 17. And all ministers who were supported by tax and compulsion among us before the late war, received that power in the name of the king of Great Britain, and not King Jesus; and they are the only officers in this land, that have retained the power over the people, which they have received in that name. Whatever gifts and graces any of them have received from Jesus Christ, let them faithfully improve the same according to his direction; but, as they would appear loyal to him, or friends to their country, let them renounce the holding of any earthly head to the church.

4. If this be not done, none can tell who they will have for their head. For the name protestant is no longer to be a test of our legislators; and to pursuade the people to yield thereto, the compilers of the constitution said to them, "your delegates did not conceive themselves to be vested with power to set up one denomination of christians above another; for religion must at all times be a matter between God and individuals." This is a great truth; and it proves, that no man can become a member of a truly religious society without his own consent; and also that no corporation that is not a

religious society can have a right to govern in religious matters. Christ said, *who made me a judge, or a divider over you?* And Paul said, *what have I to do to judge them also that are without?* Luke xii. 14. i Cor. v. 12. Thus our divine Lord, and the great apostle of the Gentiles, explicitly renounced any judicial power over the world by virtue of their religion. And to imagine that *money* can give any *power* in religious matters, is the doctrine of Simon the *sorcerer;* and by such *sorceries* the whore of Babylon hath *deceived all nations.* Acts viii. 18, 19. Rev. xviii. 23. It was from thence that the Pope, on May 4, 1493, the year after America was first discovered, presumed to give away the lands of the heathen therein. And the same power was claimed by the crown of England, in granting several charters of this country; from whence some of the states were lately contending in Congress with others, about the western lands of this continent.

5. All the power that the constitution gives our legislature in this respect, is to make "suitable provision" for christian teachers; and, according to their declaration, divine revelation must determine what is suitable; and that determines that they *shall live of the gospel.* i Cor. ix. 14. Those who under the law collected support for religious teachers *by force*, brought compleat destruction upon themselves therefore. i Sam. ii. 16, 25. Micah iii. 5-12. Christianity is a voluntary obedience to God's revealed will; and every thing of a contrary nature is antichristianism. And all teachers who do not watch for souls as those who must give an account to God; and all people who do not receive and support his faithful ministers, as they have opportunity and ability, are daily exposed to punishments infinitely worse than men could inflict. Luke x. 3-12. Gal. vi. 6-9. Heb. xiii. 7, 17, 18.

6. Reason and revelation agree, in determining that the end of civil government is the *good* of the governed, by defending them against all such as would *work ill to their neighbours;* and in limiting the power of *rulers* there. And those who invade the religious rights of others, are *self-condemned*, which of all things is the most opposite to *happiness*, the great end of government. Rom xiii. 3-10. xiv. 10-23.

7. If men will refuse to be happy themselves, yet their power to enslave others is now greatly weakened. And a faithful improvement of our privileges will weaken it more and more, till there shall be no more use for *swords*, because there shall be *none to hurt or destroy in all God's holy mountain.* Isaiah xi. 9. Micah iv. 1-4. And who would not be in earnest for that glorious day?

5. Republican Religion

Revivals were not a new phenomenon in the early republic. Ever since the late seventeenth century, ministers had been sporadically gathering harvests of believers, culminating with the Great Awakening of the mid-eighteenth century. The disruption and demoralization of religion caused by the Revolution—the destruction of churches, the scattering of congregations—were only temporary setbacks in the development of American revivalism. By the 1790's Americans were ready to continue their evangelical efforts. But the Second Great Awakening, at the turn of the century, did not represent as much a new intensification of religion as it did the mobilization of unprecedented numbers of hitherto unchurched people into religious communion. The great revival was thus the working out of the Revolution in religion. By popularizing religion as never before and by extending organized Christianity into the remotest areas of America, the revival marked the beginning of the republicanizing and nationalizing of American religion. By meeting the countless social and psychic needs unleashed by the Revolution, it transformed American religion, Calvinism included, into a participatory affair in which all who wished could order their own salvation.

Richard McNemar (1770-1839) was one of the leaders of the western phase of the revival. In 1797, four years after Kentucky had been admitted to the union, McNemar was licensed by the Presbyterian church to preach at Cane Ridge, Kentucky, the site of the most remarkable of the early camp meetings. Under pressure from the Kentucky synod for preaching erroneous Calvinistic doctrine—that is, the belief in God's love for the whole world and the possibility of salvation for all sinners—McNemar and four other Kentucky ministers formed a new presbytery; they later broke with Presbyterianism altogether and created an independent church of a universal Christianity in which all denominations could unite. While several of his fellow seceders drifted back into Presbyterianism, McNemar eventually joined and became spokesman for the Western Shakers, one of the earliest of communalistic sects soon to become a familiar part of the nineteenth-century American religious scene.

The Kentucky Revival

RICHARD McNEMAR

To The Reader

You have been probably waiting for something to be published from this quarter, and may be a little surprised to find the *Kentucky Revival* our theme; as it is generally known that we profess to have advanced forward into a much greater work.

Admitting this to be the case (which we do not deny) it would nevertheless be improper to forget, or set light by any operation or work of the true spirit, however small it might seem. But far from esteeming the Kentucky Revival a day of small things, we believe it was nothing less than an *introduction* to that work of *final redemption*, which God had promised in the latter days. And to preserve the memory of it among those who have wisely improved it as such, the following particulars have been collected for the press, by one, whose spirit was in it from the beginning, and who is a living witness of the most important particulars which occurred in every stage of it, until the present day.

For the better understanding of the following history, it will be proper to make a few preliminary observations.

I.   It will be granted, that God has a particular order and manner of working, in which one thing goes before another. Thus: *the law and the prophets were until John*, after that *the kingdom of heaven is preached*. It then follows that *all men press into it*. The first thing is the *law*, which convinces of sin. 2. The *Prophets*, who minister the promise and hope of salvation. 3. The *kingdom of heaven is preached*; the way and method of salvation made manifest in word and doctrine: and last of all we must *press into it*. This is the order of God, and there is no other. Nothing short of pressing into the kingdom can save the soul. Conviction may die away; hope and comfort desert the breast; and the most lively views of the kingdom be forgotten. Hence the necessity of so often reviving these things among professors. But whatever can die away, is short of the kingdom of God; those who are in the kingdom have everlasting life. Therefore it is plain that the constituent parts

Richard McNemar, *The Kentucky Revival, Or A Short History of the Late Extraordinary Out-Pouring of the Spirit of God, in the Western States of America* . . . (Cincinnati, 1808), pp. *v-viii*, 19–20, 22–24, 27, 29–31.

of a revival (which are conviction of sin, a hope of deliverance from it, and a manifestation of the *heavenly state*) can only be preparative to entering into it. How many revivals have taken place in these latter days, which for a season would raise the people, as it were, to heaven's gate; and after all, leave them to fall back into their former lifeless state. And why so? Because they did not take the last step, and press into that state which in word and doctrine was opened.

II.   It will be granted, that whoever preaches the kingdom of heaven, must preach deliverance from all sin: For where sin is, there can be no heaven. Now when the kingdom has been preached, and honest souls have fixed their eye of faith upon it—longed with intense desire to be in it, and solicitously enquired for the footsteps of those who have already entered: then has been the time for the grand deceiver to come in with his doctrine of procrastination, and preach up sin for term of life;—appeal to the doleful experience of past generations, and confirm the fatal error by the doctrines and decrees of a corrupt church. Thus the most promising revivals have been blasted, and all that near sense of heaven's pure enjoyments (common under the preaching of the kingdom) extinguished by men of corrupt minds.

But the *Kentucky Revival*, from the beginning, spoke better things. Those who were the genuine subjects of it, ever expressed the fullest confidence that it would not terminate as revivals had generally done. It was not a common portion of law conviction; nor that faith in the promise which puts heaven at a distance; nor merely preaching about the kingdom, that drew out the multitudes to encamp for days and nights in the wilderness, &c. It was a near prospect of the true kingdom of God, into which many were determined to press at the expense of all that they held dear upon earth. The late revival was not sent to RE-FORM the churches. It did not come with a piece of new cloth to patch the old garment, to mend up the old hope with some new experience; but to prepare the way for that kingdom of God, in which all things are new: and whether it be in many or few, the purposes whereunto it was sent, shall undoubtedly be answered.

III.   That this extraordinary work sprung from some supernatural cause has been universally granted; but whether the cause was good or evil, has been a matter of much debate, even among those who profess to take the scripture for their only guide. Christians so called, of all others have been the most divided in their judgment concerning it; and while some without hesitation have pronounced it a glorious work of God; others who professed to be children of the same father, followers of the same Saviour, and instructed by the same word of God, have with equal confidence pronounced it *witchcraft, enthusiasm, fanaticism*, and *the very energy of delusion*. Hence the various predictions concerning it: Some affirming that it would shortly terminate and leave the unhappy subjects of it, in a worse condition than ever; others that it should *cover the earth, as the waters cover the sea,* and gather the nations into one united body.

IV. As the continuance of the revival was so strongly predicted and asserted by its subjects, it will be proper to consider how far and upon what footing, those predictions and assertions are tenable. That it should always continue in the same measure and appearance without any increase, was never intended; therefore if that same power continues to work, though it should be in a greater degree and more extraordinary manner, and tho' it should be among a different people, this will not prove the above predictions false, provided it be the same power working to the same end.

While the extraordinary power of the revival was exterraneous; while irresistible beams of light presented objects to the view which persons could not avoid seeing, and they were rushed into exercises of body by a force of operation which they could not withstand, the continuance of the work in this fashion, was precarious, knowing that God will not always work upon man like a machine. Therefore in order to [allow?] the continuance of the work, a number of its subjects have found it necessary to receive this extraordinary power as an in-dwelling treasure, to unite with this supernatural agent, to dwell in him and he in them, and become workers together with him, and without force or violence, believe and practise whatever he teaches. And on this pivot the revival turns with each individual. The power or light of God, continues with those who continue in it, his spirit abides only with those who abide in him, and do continually the things that please him; of course such as are willing that Christ and Belial should have day about, light and darkness alternately prevail, must fall off and wither; for no man can serve two masters.

V. Since the spirit and power of the revival has been established upon the above principles, and the divine agent has found a habitation with men, less attention has been paid to former appearances. This new and strange doctrine of receiving Christ, and walking in him, has engrossed the general concern: and while the singular manner of worship, strange bodily exercises, &c. of those the world around, their distinguishing faith has been a matter of serious enquiry with many; especially those who have begun to open their eyes on the hidden glories of the kingdom of Christ, and are beginning to move Zion-ward. But before the *temple of God* can be opened in heaven and the ark of his testament be seen, it will be proper to recognise the various operations by which the materials of the tabernacle were prepared: According as it is written—"*Behold I send my messenger, and he shall prepare the way before me: and the Lord whom ye seek, shall suddenly come to his temple."*

Turtle-Creek, June 20, 1807.   R.M.

Of the first appearances of the extraordinary work, in different parts of Kentucky, in 1800 and 1801.

The first extraordinary appearances of the power of God in the late revival, began about the close of the last century, in Logan and Christian counties; on the waters of Gasper and Red Rivers. And in the spring of 1801, the same extraordinary work broke out in Mason county, upper part of Kentucky; of which I was an eye witness, and can therefore, with greater confidence, testify what I have heard, seen and felt.

It first began in individuals who had been under deep convictions of sin, and great trouble about their souls, and had fasted and prayed, and diligently searched the scriptures, and had undergone distresses of mind inexpressibly sore, until they had obtained a comfortable hope of salvation. And from seeing and feeling the love of Christ, and his willingness to save all that would forsake their sins and turn to God through him; and feeling how freely his love and goodness flowed to them, it kindled their love to other souls, that were lost in their sins; and an ardent desire that they might come and partake of that spiritual light, life, and comfort, which appeared infinite in its nature, and free to all. And under such an overpowering weight of the divine goodness, as tongue could not express, they were constrained to cry out, with tears and trembling, and testify a full and free salvation in Christ, for all that would come; and to warn their fellow-creatures of the danger of continuing in sin; and entreating them in the most tender and affectionate manner, to turn from it; and seek the Lord, in sure and certain hope that he would be found.

Under such exhortations, the people began to be affected in a very strange manner. At first they were taken with an inward throbbing of heart; then with weeping and trembling: from that to crying out, in apparent agony of soul; falling down and swooning away till every appearance of animal life was suspended, and the person appeared to be in a trance. From this state they would recover under different sensations. . . .

And here a new scene was opened, while some trembled like one in a fit of the ague; wept or cried out, lamenting their distance from God, and exposedness to his wrath; others were employed in praying with them, encouraging them to believe on the Son of God—to venture upon his promise—give up their wicked rebellious heart, just as it was; for God to take it away, and give them a heart of flesh;—singing hymns, and giving thanks to God, for the display of his power, without any regard to former rules of order. At this, some were offended and withdrew from the assembly, determined to oppose it, as a work of the wicked one. But all their objections, only tended to open the way for the true nature and spirit of the work to shine out; and encourage the subjects of it, to set out with warmer zeal to promote it. Accordingly a meeting was appointed a few evenings after; to which a crowd of awakened souls flocked, and spent the whole night in singing hymns, praying, and exhorting one another, &c. At this meeting, one man was struck down and lay for about an hour, in the situation above mentioned. This put the matter beyond dispute, that the work was supernatural; and the outcry which it raised against sin, confirmed a number in the belief that it was from above.

From small beginnings, it gradually spread. The news of these strange operations flew about, and attracted many to come and see; who were convinced, not only from seeing and hearing, but feeling; and carried home the testimony, that it was the living work of God. This stirred up others, and brought out still greater multitudes. And these strange exercises still increasing, and having no respect to any stated hours of worship, it was found expedient to encamp on the ground, and continue the meeting day and night. To these encampments the people flocked in hundreds and thousands, on foot, on horseback, and in waggons and other carriages.

At first appearance, those meetings exhibited nothing to the spectator, but a scene of confusion that could scarce be put into human language. They were generally opened with a sermon; near the close of which, there would be an unusual out-cry; some bursting forth into loud ejaculations of prayer, or thanksgiving for the truth. Others breaking out in emphatical sentences of exhortation. Others flying to their careless friends, with tears of compassion, beseeching them to turn to the Lord. Some struck with terror, and hastening through the croud to make their escape, or pulling away their relations.—Others, trembling, weeping and crying out for the Lord Jesus to have mercy upon them: fainting and swooning away, till every appearance of life was gone, and the extremities of the body assumed the coldness of a dead corpse.—Others surrounding them with melodious songs, or fervent prayers for their happy resurrection, in the love of Christ.—Others collecting into circles around this variegated scene, contending with arguments for and against. And under such appearances, the work would continue for several days and nights together. . . .

The next general camp-meeting was held at Concord, in the county of Bourbon, about the last of May, or beginning of June. The number of people was supposed to be about 4,000, who attended on this occasion. There were present seven Presbyterian ministers, four of whom were opposed to the work and spoke against it until the fourth day about noon, the evidence then became so powerful, that they all professed to be convinced that it was the work of God; and one of them addressed the assembly with tears, acknowledging that notwithstanding they had long been praying to the Lord to pour out his spirit, yet when it came they did not know it, but wickedly opposed the answer of their own prayers. On this occasion, no sex nor color, class nor description, were exempted from the pervading influence of the spirit; even from the age of eight months to sixty years, there were evident subjects of this marvellous operation.

The meeting continued five days and four nights; and after the people generally scattered from the ground, numbers convened in different places and continued the exercise much longer. And even where they were not collected together, these wonderful operations continued among every class of people and in every situation; in their houses and fields, and in their daily employments, falling down and crying out under conviction, or singing and shouting with unspeakable joy, were so common, that the whole country round about, seemed to be leavened with the spirit of the work. . . .

The people among whom the revival began, were generally Calvinists, and altho' they had been long praying in words for the out-pouring of the spirit, and believed that God had "*foreordained whatsoever comes in to pass;*" yet, when it *came to pass* and their prayer was answered, and the spirit began to flow like many waters, from a cloud of witnesses, and souls were convicted of sin and cried for mercy, and found hope and comfort in the news of a Saviour; they rose up and quarreled with the work, because it did not *come to pass* that the subjects of it were willing to adopt their soul stupifying creed. Those who had laboured and travailed to gain some solid hope of salvation, and had ventured their souls upon the covenant of promise, and felt the living zeal of eternal love; could not, dare not preach that salvation was restricted to a certain *definite number*; nor insinuate that any being which God had made, was, by the Creator, laid under the dire necessity of being damned forever. The love of a Saviour constrained them to testify, that one had died for all. This truth, so essential to the first ray of hope in the human breast, was like a dead fly in the ointment of the apothecary, to the Calvinist; hence all this trembling, weeping and groaning under sin, rejoicing in the hope of deliverance and turning from the former practice of it, sent forth a disagreeable savor. Yet these exercises would no doubt, have passed for a good work of God, had they appeared as seals to their doctrine of election, imperfection, and final perseverance. But every thing appeared new, and to claim no relation to the old bed of sand upon which they had been building; and rather than quit the old foundation, they chose to reject, oppose and persecute the truth, accompanied with all that evidence which many of them were obliged to acknowledge was divine. . . .

Of the distinguishing doctrines and manner of worship, among the first subjects of the revival.

The first point of doctrine which distinguished the subjects of the revival, was that which respected divine revelation.

The established opinion in the churches had been, that the *Scriptures*, explained according to sound reason and philosophy, was light sufficient; and simply to believe, what we were thus taught, was the highest evidence we could have of the truth of spiritual things. But *these* adopted a very different faith, and taught, as an important truth, that the will of God was made manifest to each individual who honestly sought after it, by an inward light, which shone into the heart. —Hence they received the name of *New-Lights*. Those who were the subjects of this inward light, did not call it *new light*, but a renewed manifestation of *that*, which at sundry times and in divers manners, had been opened to those who were willing and desirous to know the truth for themselves.

This inward light, they denominated *the Lord*, because by it they were instructed, influenced and governed. Hence they spake of seeing *the Lord*, finding *the Lord*, loving *the Lord*, following *the Lord*, offending *the Lord*, &c. by all which expressions was meant, that *inward light* and revelation of truth, by which they could see things in their true colors, and find a measure of peace and consolation, and a comfortable hope of eternal life.

This *new light* first broke out in the Presbyterian church, among those who held the doctrines of Calvin, and therefore it is considered as more immediately contrasted with that system. Those who first embraced it, had also been reputed Calvinists, and belonged to the Presbyterian church, among whom were several persons of distinction in the ministry; of course, the existence of sentiments so very different in the same church, rendered a division unavoidable. This division was gradual, and had its foundation in the above principle of a direct manifestation of spiritual light from God to the soul, which was superior to all the comments that natural men had ever made upon the scriptures. This division in sentiment, with its concomitant effects, drew together a vast multitude out of different churches, who formed a general communion, and for a time, acceded to the doctrines, manner of worship, &c. first opened and practised among the *New-Lights*; a brief sketch of which is as follows, viz: that all creeds, confessions, forms of worship, and rules of government invented by men, ought to be laid aside; especially the distinguishing doctrines of Calvin. —That all who received the true light of the spirit in the inner man, and faithfully followed it, would naturally see eye to eye, and understand the things of the spirit alike, without any written tenet or learned expositor. That all who received this true light, would plainly see the purity of God—the depravity of man—the necessity of a new birth, and of a sinless life and conversation to evidence it. —That God was no respecter of persons—willeth the salvation of all souls—has opened a door of salvation, through Christ, for all—will have all invited to enter, and such as refuse to come in, must blame themselves for their own perdition.

As to worship, they allowed each one to worship God agreeably to their own feelings, whatever impression or consciousness of duty they were under; believing the true wisdom, which "lives through all life," to be a safer guide than human forms, which can only affect the outer man: and hence, so wide a door was opened, and such a variety of exercises were exhibited at their public meetings. All distinction of names was laid aside, and it was no matter what any one had been called before, if now he stood in the present light, and felt his heart glow with love to the souls of men; he was welcome to sing, pray, or call sinners to repentance. Neither was there any distinction as to age, sex, color, or any thing of a temporary nature: old and young, male and female, black and white, had equal privilege to minister the light which they received, in whatever way the spirit directed. And it was moreover generally considered, that such as professed to stand in the light and were not actively engaged some way or other, in time of public meeting, were only dead weights upon the cause.

No one, who has not been an eye witness, can possibly paint in their imagination the striking solemnity of those occasions, on which the thousands of Kentuckians were convened in one vast assembly, under the auspicious influence of the above faith. How striking to see hundreds who never saw each other in the face before, moving uniformly into action, without any preconcerted plan, and each, without intruding upon another, taking that part assigned him by a conscious feeling, and in this manner, dividing into bands over a large extent of ground, interspersed with tents and waggons: some uniting their voices in the most melodious songs; others in solemn and affecting accents of prayer: some lamenting with streaming eyes their lost situation, or that of a wicked world; others lying apparently in the cold embraces of death: some instructing the ignorant, directing the doubtful, and urging them in the day of God's visitation, to make sure work for eternity: others, from some eminence, sounding the general trump of a free salvation, and warning sinners to fly from the wrath to come:—the surrounding forest at the same time, vocal with the cries of the distressed, sometimes to the distance of half a mile or a mile in circumference.

How persons, so different in their education, manners and natural dispositions, without any visible commander, could enter upon such a scene, and continue in it for days and nights in perfect harmony, has been one of the greatest wonders that ever the world beheld.

6. Organizing for Morality

The post-Revolutionary era saw a fantastic proliferation of voluntary associations and organizations. Indeed, more such societies were formed in the dozen years following the Declaration of Independence than in the entire colonial period. By the early nineteenth century, America had already become famous as a nation of joiners. Some of the organizations, like the Democratic-Republican Societies of the 1790's, were openly political; others, like the American Academy of Arts and Sciences, were educational; others, like the New York Society for the Relief of Distressed Debtors, were humanitarian; and still others, like the Masonic lodges, were ostensibly private and fraternal. But nearly all of the voluntary associations formed in the early years of the republic were avowedly moral, designed in their various ways to influence the character of the new society.

Probably the single most important fraternal and benevolent society of the early republic was the Masonic Order. Freemasonry was in fact something of a surrogate religion for many Americans. Little is known about the secret fraternity in early America, except that many of the Revolutionary leaders—Washington, Jefferson, James Otis, Richard Henry Lee—were members. Yet it is obvious from simply the nature of the membership roll and from the prevalence of Masonic imagery everywhere during the period that the influence of Freemasonry on the culture of the early republic was profound. As the eulogy by Thaddeus Mason Harris (1768-1842), a Boston Unitarian clergyman who disliked all denominational distinctions, suggests, Freemasonry was very much a rational Enlightenment organization, based on a hierarchical conception of society and a classical sense of order. With the growing democratization of American society, its secrecy and elitism came under increasing attack, reaching a crescendo in the 1820's with the formation of the Anti-Masonic Party.

Whereas Freemasonry saw reformation flowing downward, from the society's emulation of the virtuous behavior of its natural leaders, the multitudes of moral societies organized in the early years of the nineteenth century, like the Columbia Moral Society of New York, sought to attack the vices infecting the society directly at the base—by persuasion if possible, by compulsion if necessary. With this declining confidence in the natural workings of the social and intellectual hierarchy, the Enlightenment in America had come to an end.

A Masonic Eulogy

THADDEUS MASON HARRIS

RESPECTED HEARERS,

You see before you A BAND OF BROTHERS connected with each other by the firmest engagements and most affectionate ties. Warmed with the most general philanthropy, they profess to unite their endeavours in the benevolent design of assisting the perfection of the human character, and the harmony and happiness of society. Their institution boasts its origin in the earliest ages of the world; and it retains its ancient *laws* uncorrupted, its venerable *rites* and expressive *symbols* unchanged, and its primeval *ceremonies* intire. The stupendous pyramids which were raised, the lofty obelisks inscribed, and the magnificent temples built *by masonic hands*, have yielded to the ravages of time; but the institution itself has survived their overthrow, and outlived their glory. It will continue still, and flourish, till

> "The great globe itself,
> And all which it inherit, be destroyed,
> And, like the baseless fabric of a vision,
> Leave not a wreck behind."

HAD we leisure, it would be an interesting and entertaining research to trace its progress through the various stages of society it has successively improved and adorned: To see its early honours in Egypt; its CONSECRATION at Jerusalem; its subsequent glory; and its preservation, and extension "in ages long gone by." It is true that in recurring to some periods of its remote history, we should have occasion to lament that the unfounded and illiberal prejudices of too many which it could not soften, and their corrupt passions which it could not subdue, at times denied the craft its merited honours, opposed its cause, and impeded its progress. Like the SUN, its emblem, it has at times been obscured. Clouds and darkness have overshadowed its lustre: The clouds of error and the darkness of ignorance. But from the temporary penumbra it always emerged with increased splendour. And though from low minds mists of prejudice may still arise, and dim the clearness of its horizon, before the meridian light of *reason, truth* and *wisdom*, they will quickly disappear.

Thaddeus Mason Harris, "A Masonic Eulogy, Delivered at Worcester, June 24, A.L. 1794 . . ." in *Discourses Delivered on Public Occasions, Illustrating the Principles, Displaying the Tendency, and Vindicating the Design of Free Masonry* (Philadelphia, 1819), pp. 231–242.

IN the DARK AGES Masonry yielded only a faint and glimmering radiance: "A light that shined in a dark place." But, when the gloom of ignorance and barbarism was dispelled, it revived in its pristine consequence and glory.

THOSE who enter minutely into the history of this society, will find it eventful and interesting. Various have been the efforts wantonly used, even in later times, to disturb its tranquility and diminish its importance. Dissatisfaction has, however, been obliged to yield to conviction; and the groundless imputations of enmity, have been silenced by a display of the virtues the institution recommends and excites, and the laudable effects it produces. Among all nations, at last, its salutary influence is felt, and its beneficial tendency acknowledged. And, (though, like the common blessing of light, unheeded in its silent operation,) men are ignorantly indebted to it, as a principle, for some of the most disinterested exertions of generosity, and some of the sweetest intimacies of endearing friendship and social life.

FREE MASONS have always considered liberality as a virtue of the most general obligation and diffusive nature. To administer relief to the needy, and consolation to the distressed, is their most constant wish, and their highest pride; establishing friendship and forming connections not by receiving but conferring benefits; and diffusing the conveniences and comforts of life with that cheerful readiness and benevolent impartiality which heightens their value and sweetens their possession. Their bounty is not dissipated among those who can return the obligation; but is frequently conveyed to distant lands and foreign cities, to the naked and the hungry who see not the hand that reaches out the kind supply, and can make no acknowledgment to their unknown benefactors but the ardent benediction of gratitude.

To communicate the blessings of which we are partakers; to contribute to the successful propagation of knowledge, virtue and peace, of the sciences and the arts, and of whatever cultivates and adorns social life; and to assist the advancement of human happiness; have ever been the great objects of this venerable association. Impressed with a due sense of their obligation to the discharge of their duties, the members of it have steadily pursued such means as were apparently most conducive to the accomplishment of so desirable an end: And they hope to surmount the obstacles and discouragements which retard its more general propagation.

To reflect on the rapid progress and present general diffusion of the ROYAL ART through almost every part of the habitable world, must be particularly agreeable to all its friends, to every one sincerely interested in the cause of humanity; the happiness of his species.

AT the present, as in every former age over which it hath spread its principles, Masonry constitutes the affectionate and indissoluble alliance which unites man in warm cordiality with man. It forms the most liberal and extensive connections. No private prepossession nor national predilection, no civil policy nor ecclesiastical tyranny, no party spirit, nor dissocial passion, is suffered to prevent the engagement, nor interfere with the free exercise of that *brotherly love, relief, and fidelity*, it fails not to produce. It has for ages been lamented, that petty distinctions and partial considerations, irrational prejudices and contracted sentiments, should so much obstruct the friendly intercourse of mankind. Masonry breaks down these formidable barriers. In its solemn assembly, around its social altar, meet the inhabitants of different countries with benignant looks of esteem, and sentiments of unfeigned friendship. Around distant lands it casts Philanthropy's connecting zone, and binds together in the same sympathies the whole family on earth.

BY the use of the *universal language of Masons,* members of the fraternity of all nations communicate easily and freely with each other. On every quarter of the globe they can make known their wishes, and be sure of finding an attentive friend, a hospitable asylum, and liberal assistance.

WITH RELIGION, whose sublime *doctrines* it cannot increase, whose noble *precepts* it cannot improve, and whose *sanctions* it dare not adjudge, Masonry does not interfere. The duties of *piety* must be the voluntary and spiritual intercourse of man with heaven. Over them it usurps no controul and claims no jurisdiction. It is satisfied with teaching all the brethren to remember that "THE EYE WHICH SEETH IN SECRET" observes all their conduct; that they must therefore "live as seeing him who is invisible," and have their souls raised superior to the gross indulgences of vice, and their affections refined by the sublime energies of virtue; that they must be alive to all the engaging duties of benevolence, and be attached to their fellow men by all those tender ties of friendship and good will which hold the heart in the most permanent captivity.

SUCH, my hearers, is the genius, the design, and tendency, of this institution.

BUT faint and imperfect is the representation I have given. Yet I cannot but hope that, though it be but as the sun painted in the dew drop, it will be found to have the merit of reflecting something of the splendour of its original.

AT the door of Masonry I stand with my taper. Would you view the glories of the temple, enter in, and dwell there.

THE ingeniousness of nature, my brethren, kindles a blush at the praise which comes so near to ourselves. Yet, who, but one of its own members, can speak the eulogy of an establishment, all of whose regulations, and most of whose effects, are not open to general inspection, but designedly concealed from all but the initiated? Determined by his conviction, and in the cause of TRUTH, REASON and PHILANTHROPY, indifferent alike to ridicule and censure, the speaker asserts the high utility and value of this society, for the encouragement and cultivation of those attainments and qualities which are of vital consequence to *moral* and *social* man. He honours from his soul its laws: Those laws which softening nature by humanity melt nations into brotherhood. Happy would it be for the peace of the world were they more universally acknowledged. They would give quiet to the nations. They would annihilate the spirit of martial glory, and utterly debase the pomp of war. They would be instrumental in meliorating the dispositions of men; in awakening and exercising their virtues; in exalting their condition and their happiness.

SEEK ye a pure source of joys to enliven your prosperity? Ask ye for consolation in adversity? Want ye relief from poverty? Enter our temple and share our blessings. FRIENDSHIP will conduct your faultering step, VIRTUE will *strengthen* your resolutions, and WISDOM enlighten your mind. There, also, PITY and CHARITY will direct your benevolence, and give value to the exercise of your kindness. There HOPE will brighten your prospects, and GLORY crown your deeds.

To this commendation of our society, my beloved brethren, your knowledge and your hearts will bear willing testimony. Let the actions of your lives afford corroborative evidence. Answer the raised expectations of the world. While ambitious of extending the influence, neglect not to support the credit of this ancient and venerable society. May the amiable simplicity and goodness of your manners produce sentiments of esteem in others for the principles from which they arise! Disgrace not your profession by any unworthy action. Masonry may indeed suffer awhile from the suspicions of the ignorant and the censure of its enemies, but it can be lastingly injured only by the imprudences and ill conduct of its members and friends. Let me therefore enjoin it upon you, while you treat with just indifference the insinuations and surmises of the disingenuous and the perverse, to silence the tongue of reproach by the rectitude of your conduct, and the brillance of your virtues. Let it be seen in you that our institution produces the good effects we have so openly boasted, and the virtues we have so frequently recommended and warmly approved. Fix your eyes steadily on *the important object* of your association. Let it open the affectionate embrace of large philanthropy, and lift up the hands of rational devotion! Let it exalt the capacity of the mind, refine the social sympathies, and form you for the noblest purposes of reasonable life!

The Columbia Moral Society

On Tuesday the 10th of January last [1815], a great number of the friends of good morals, of various religious and political denominations, from different parts of the county of Columbia, met at the court-house in this city, for the purpose of forming a Moral Society for the suppression of vice. Previous notice was given in this Magazine, and in each of the papers published in this city, and also by circular letters sent to gentlemen residing at a distance. The meeting was one of the largest and one of the most respectable that we have ever witnessed. It was gratifying beyond expression, to behold men of various religious and political feelings and sentiments, unite cordially for the suppression of vice, and laying aside every feeling but the benevolent desire to promote the happiness of community. There were very many who would have attended this meeting, but found it impossible to get into the court-room, which was full to overflowing. A spirit of unanimity, of cordial good will, and of ardent zeal to attain the object in view, marked all the proceedings, and gave the best pledge of the good motives and final success of the Society. Here were seen Episcopalians, Dutch Reformed, Baptists, Congregationalists, Methodists and Presbyterians. The Rev. Mr. Sickles, of Kinderhook, was called to preside, and the Rev. Mr. Clark, of Canaan, and J. Kittle, Esq., of Kinderhook, were appointed Secretaries. The President opened the meeting with prayer.

The Rev. Mr. Chester, of Hudson, from a committee appointed for that purpose, reported a Constitution, which was read, discussed, and unanimously adopted.

CONSTITUTION

Article I. The name of this association shall be, "The Columbia Society for the promotion of Good Morals."

II. The members of this Society shall, by their conversation and example, encourage all virtuous conduct, and in aid of the laws of the State will oppose and discountenance vice generally, and particularly the vices of Sabbath-breaking, intemperance, profane swearing and horse-racing. They shall use their influence for the execution of the laws of the State against vice and immorality—especially the vices above named, and for enforcing the laws made for regulating licensed houses and shops.

"Formation and Constitution of the Columbia Moral Society," *Columbia Magazine,* vol. I (1814–15), pp. 179–185.

III.   And in order more fully to carry into effect the objects of this society, it shall be the duty of its members to exert their influence in promoting the formation of auxiliary societies in the towns and districts to which they respectively belong, to be connected with this Society, and to make report of their proceedings to this association at its annual meetings; and the members of this Society shall unite with such auxiliary Societies.

IV.   Any person of fair moral character may become a member of this Society. And all persons upon their admission shall subscribe the Constitution.

V.   The officers of this Society shall be a President, six Vice-Presidents, eight Counsellors, a Corresponding Secretary, Recording Secretary, and Treasurer, who together shall form an Executive Committee, and shall be chosen annually by ballot.

VI.   It shall be the duty of the President, and in his absence of one of the Vice-Presidents, to preside at all meetings of the Society, and at the meetings of the Executive Committee; and the President shall have power to convene the Executive Committee whenever he thinks proper; and it shall be his duty to call a meeting of the Executive Committee, whenever he shall be thereto requested by two members of that body. And the President shall call a special meeting of the Society whenever requested by a majority of the said Committee.

VII.   The Corresponding Secretary shall open and maintain correspondences with other similar institutions, for the purpose of collecting facts relative to the objects of this Society, and of obtaining the results of the experience of other similar associations, and shall make report in writing to this Society at the annual meeting.

VIII.   The Treasurer shall take the charge of the monies and other property of the Society, and shall exhibit an account of his receipts and expenditures to the Society, at the annual meeting thereof.

IX.   The Recording Secretary shall keep a fair record of the proceedings of the Society.

X.   The Executive Committee shall meet upon their own adjournment, and shall manage the concerns of the Society during the intervals of its meetings—shall arrange and exhibit to the Society any plans which they shall deem proper for the furtherance of its objects—shall have power to appropriate its monies and property, and shall make report of their doings to the Society at its annual meetings.—Seven members shall constitute a quorum.

XI.   Twenty-one members of this Society shall constitute a quorum.

XII.   If any member shall, by his conduct, exhibit a spirit hostile to the expressed views of this Society, he may be dismissed at any regular meeting thereof, by the votes of two thirds of the members present.

XIII. There shall be an annual meeting of the Society on the second Tuesday of January, at such place as shall be appointed by the Society at the previous meeting. The annual and special meetings of the Society shall be publicly notified in each of the newspapers printed in the county, during two weeks immediately preceding the meeting. At each annual meeting a sermon shall be delivered before the society by some person elected for that purpose, and a contribution shall then be made for the benefit of the Society.

XIV. This Constitution may be amended by a vote of two thirds of the members present at any annual meeting. . . .

The Society then passed the following resolutions:—

1. *Resolved*, That an extra meeting of this Society be held at Hudson, in the Presbyterian meeting-house, on the last Monday in May next, at two o'clock, P.M.—that the Rev. Jacob Sickles, of Kinderhood, preach a sermon on that day before the Society and that the Rev. Mr. Clark, of Canaan, be his second.

2. That the Rev. John Chester and Hezekiah Dayton, Esq. be a committee to cause these proceedings to be published in both the papers printed in this county, and also in the Columbia Magazine.

The meeting closed by prayer, by the Rev. Mr. Clark, of Canaan.

We cannot fail to congratulate our readers upon the result of this meeting. We consider it as one of the most interesting events that have occurred in the history of religion in this county. It proves that its inhabitants are awake to their most important interest, and that multitudes consider "Jerusalem their chief joy." The friends of good order, good morals, and of pure and undefiled religion, have now united under favourable and most flattering prospects. It is ascertained that *public sentiment* is decidedly in favour of the execution of the wise and wholesome laws of this state, for the suppression of vice and immorality. It is a delightful reflection, that amid the confusion and acrimony of party, the good sense and virtuous feelings of the community may be called into vigorous exercise, unimpeded by the line of a *sect*, and unrestrained by the magic of a name,—to unite upon a subject where the animosity of contention is lost in the ardour of benevolence, and the virulence of party is sacrificed at the shrine of public happiness. If this was the only result of this institution, it would have a blessed effect upon society. But this is not all. This union will produce a vigour in the execution of the laws, which has long been lost,—it will give tone and effect to public opinion,—it will present a formidable front to vice, and give new dignity and importance to the officers of justice.

Experience has already taught, that similar institutions in other places have had an extensive and beneficial influence. Those who have doubted the expediency of their formation, have in many instances been fully convinced of their utility when they have marked their progress and witnessed their operation. There is one class in community who may be expected to revile and oppose them. It is composed of those who hate the restraints of law, and of public opinion; and who wish to trample upon the commands of God and man with impunity.

To enable this Society to carry its designs into effect, the third article in the constitution must be promptly attended to. Auxiliary Societies must be formed in the various towns and districts. The rules by which they will be governed, must be suggested, in a considerable degree, by the peculiar situation of the places in which they are formed. Without Auxiliary Societies are formed, who shall report to the county Society, its influence will be very much circumscribed, if not wholly destroyed.

We had intended in this article to have attempted a full explanation of the objects which this Society contemplates. One of our kind correspondents has very obligingly sent us the able piece below, which while it relieves our labours, treats the subject in a very satisfactory manner.

THE MORAL SOCIETY OF COLUMBIA COUNTY!

What is its object? How is this to be effected? And what probable good will result from it? These questions, interesting to the public mind, have grown out of the late proceedings of a county meeting, held at Hudson on Tuesday the 10th day of January, 1815. A public transaction of this nature, cannot fail to awaken a degree of curiosity. This may be partly satisfied by a very concise answer to the questions stated above.

1. As to the object of this society:—It is to turn the attention of the public to some of those vices which are prostrating all laws, and endangering the dearest interests of men; and at the same time, if possible, to effect a reformation. A deep concern for the welfare of the rising generation is spreading through the country. All men of correct sentiments, and the lovers of virtue of every name, have imbibed these feelings—have groaned in anxious silence, and longed to see some standard lifted against these evils. Until lately, however desirable, the thing has seemed impossible. But, as men in general act more from habit than reflection, it has been presumed that if they can be led to reflect, habits of vice may be in some good degree controlled. Not only all law, human and divine, but the conscience of every man is armed against vice. And such are the charms of virtue, that she stands recommended to all, even to the most vicious. At no time is the state of society so bad, but that far the greatest weight of worth and influence will be found on

her side. And when this influence is concentrated and properly directed, she is sure to find support. To collect and give scope to this influence, we conceive to be the sole object of the Moral Society.

2. The next question is, How is this to be effected? In one word, it is to be effected by *union*. Experience testifies that insolated individuals, be their motives never so pure and their weight of character never so great, cannot act with success against the encroachments of vice. Owing to this circumstance, all former attempts to bring about a reformation have proved ineffectual. The great object of the county Society is, to form a bond of union —to concentrate its energies, and to erect a citadel, from which extended observations may be made. By the constitution of this Society, its members are bound to use their influence to discountenance vice generally, in particular certain kinds of vice therein specified, and to make all persuasive exertions to have auxiliary societies established in the several towns and districts in the county. These societies, by collecting the lovers of virtue of every name, will present a bold front to the growing licentiousness of the day. If a man has virtue enough to unite with such a society, it is taken for granted that such a man will be virtuous enough not to violate its rules. This being admitted, it is calculated that reformation may be effected in its own members. Members of such a society will, at least, be more watchful over their own deportment. Every man also has some degree of influence over the moral conduct of others. The proof of this may be found in inticements to vice. Turn this about, and bring it to bear on the object now contemplated, and certainly some good may be done by a proper direction of this influence. Man is a reasonable being, has an instinctive sense of right and wrong, and is capable of feeling and yielding to the power of arguments. Few are so shockingly depraved, and inflexibly bent upon open wickedness, as to resist every consideration of friendship and interest. And when a friend interferes, with the strongest testimonials and assurances of love, he must, in nineteen cases out of twenty, be successful. Such are the weapons in general to be used by the Moral Society, which like those of the Gospel, are "addressed to every man's conscience in the sight of God." But if men cannot be reasoned with—if such mild and friendly efforts cannot restrain them—the members of these societies are pledged to expose them to the penalties of law. No process of this kind, however, is to be commenced, until every milder measure has been patiently tried, and completely exhausted. Nor will any be taken unawares, or without an opportunity to know their duty. It is contemplated to spread the laws before the public in such a way, that every one may know them; and when this is once done, it is presumed that they will command respect.

The third and last question here to be answered, is this—What probable benefit will result from such a Society? By giving efficacy to the restraints of law, it will strengthen the hands of magistrates, and save them from the necessity of perjury in their oath of office. Through fear of giving offence, they now let the laws sleep, satisfied that in a faithful execution of their solemn trust they cannot be supported. This embarrassment will be done away, by the unfailing and united support of the Moral Society. And if its members are faithful in setting good examples, and in using those friendly, conciliating and persuasive measures which its constitution contemplates, the legal alternative will seldom need to be resorted to. Parents and heads of families will have a vast advantage in restraining those who are intrusted to their care. Character, that dearest earthly interest of man, will thus be protected, and thousands who are now settling down into incurable habits of licentiousness, will by these means be reclaimed. Many are now gone beyond all hope of recovery. These no arm aside from omnipotence can save. But such desperate cases can be tested only by experiments: means must yet be used, and the event left to God. But if any are reclaimed by means of these Societies, an infinite benefit will grow out of them; and every individual thus rescued from destruction, will be a monument raised up by Providence to testify to their utility. As many as are diverted from courses of vice, will, by the same means, be guided into those of virtue. While many are rescued from the devouring vortex of licentiousness, a salutary barrier will be erected around the rising generation. Children will be better educated, and less exposed by bad examples before them. Communities will assume a new and more respectable character; the means of grace will be better attended to; the churches will be built up, and thousands yet unborn will bless God for the disinterested, self-denying efforts of these Societies. But notwithstanding all these vast advantages, which, in the use of proper means, we may confidently hope for, still these associations will have to contend with the most formidable opposition. Prejudice, ignorance and vice, will all unite to counteract their efforts. The two last of these will be by far the most easily overcome. Ignorance will dissipate at the approach of correct information; and vice itself will yield to arguments, or submit to the restraints of law. But prejudice cannot be reasoned with, nor can any thing control its stubborn dominion. In listing licentiousness, slander, and detraction on its side, it will seek to prostrate all before it. May both the writer and the reader of these remarks be kept from its influence! The object contemplated by this institution, is one in which all good men may with cordiality unite; and certain it is, that this object cannot be in any good degree answered without such a union. Every one who reforms himself, and joins in this attempt to effect a reformation in others, will have not only the comfort of doing good in the world, but a rich dividend in "The blessings of many souls now ready to perish."

7. Messages of Morality

Broadsides

The LIFE, and dying SPEECH of *ARTHUR*, a Negro Man;
Who was Executed at *Worcester*, October 20th 1768.
For a Rape committed on the Body of one *Deborah Metcalfe*.
I Was born at *Taunton*, January 15. 1747, in the House of *Richard Godfrey*,
Esq; my Mother being his Slave, where I lived fourteen Years; was learned
to read and write, and was treated very kindly by my Master; but was so
unhappy as often to incur the Displeasure of my Mistress, which caused
me then to run away: And this was the beginning of the many notorious
Crimes, of which I have been guilty. I went first to *Sandwich*, where I fell
in Company with some Indians, with whom I lived two Months in a very
dissolute Manner, frequently being guilty of Drunkenness and Fornication;
for which Crimes I have been since famous, and by which I am now brought
to this untimely Death.

At *Sandwich*, I stole a Shirt, was detected, and settled the Affair, by paying
twenty Shillings. My Character being now known, I thought proper to leave
the Place; and accordingly shipped my self on board a Whaling Sloop, with
Capt. *Coffin*, of *Nantucket:* We were out eight Months, and then returned to
Nantucket, from whence we sailed, where I tarried six Weeks. In which
Time I broke a Store of Mr. *Roach*'s, from which I stole a Quantity of Rum,
a pair of Trowsers, a Jacket, and some Calicoe.—The next Day I got drunk,
and by wearing the Jacket, was detected, for which Offence I was whip'd
fifteen Stripes, and committed to Gaol, for the Payment of Cost &c from
whence I escaped in half an Hour by breaking the Lock. Being now hardened in my Wickedness, I the next Night broke another Store in the same
Place, from which I took several Articles, and then shipped myself on
board a Vessel bound to *Swanzey*, where I was discovered, taken on Shoar,
and whip'd sixteen Stripes; being then set at Liberty, I returned to *Taunton*,
after one Year's Absence, where my Master received me kindly, whom I
served three Years: In which Time I followed the Seas, sailing from
Nantucket, and *Newport*, to divers parts of the *West-Indies*, where I whored
and drank, to great Excess. Being now weary of the Seas, on the 27th of
October 1764, I came again to live with my Master at *Taunton*, where I
behaved well for six Weeks; at the Expiration of which Time, going to Town
with some Negroes, I got intoxicated; on returning home went into an House
where were several Women only, to whom I offered Indecencies, but was
prevented from executing my black Designs, by the coming in of *James
Williams*, Esq; upon which I left the House, but was overtaken by him, who
with the Assistance of Mr. *Job Smith*, committed me to *Taunton* Gaol: On
the next Day I was tried before the same Mr. *Williams*, and was whip'd
thirty-nine Stripes for abusing him, uttering three profane Oaths, and

threatning to fire Mr. *Smith*'s House. My Master being now determined, by the Advice of his friends, to send me out of the Country. I was sold to———— *Hill*, of *Brookfield*, with whom I lived only one Week; was then sold to my last Master, Capt. *Clarke*, of *Rutland* District, where I behaved well for two Months, and was very kindly treated by my Master and Mistress. I then unhappily commenced an Acquaintance with a young Squaw, with whom (having stole Six Shillings from one of my Master's Sons) I was advised by other Negroes, to run away, to avoid being taken up. By Advice of my Companion (who like the rest of her Sex, was of a very fruitful Invention) I had recourse to the following Expedient: I dressed in the Habit of a Squaw, and made of my own Cloaths a Pappoose; in this manner we proceeded to *Hadley* undiscover'd, where I was introduced by my Companion, to an Indian Family, where I tarried only one Night, being discover'd in the Morning by one Mr. *Shurtless*, a Person who had been sent after me; with him I went to *Springfield*, where I met my Master, who took me down to *Middletown* with a Drove of Horses where he sold me to a Dutch Gentleman, whose Name I have since forgot. The very Night after I stole from the Widow *Sherley*, (a Person who kept a public House in that Place) five Pounds; and the next Night, by getting drunk and loosing some of my Money, I was detected and put under the Custody of two Men, for Trial the next Day: From whom I escaped, and went to *Farmington*, where being advertised, I was immediately taken up by Mr. *John Petterill*, who carried me to my old Master *Clarke*'s in *Rutland* District, with whom I spent the Summer, frequently stealing and getting drunk. My Master being now wearied by my repeated Crimes, was determined to part with me: And accordingly we set off for *Boston*, at which Time I took two Dollars from my Master's Desk. On our Way thither, tarrying some Time at Mr. *Fisk*'s in *Waltham*; I went with some Negroes to a Husking, at Mr. *Thomas Parkes*'s, in *Little Cambridge*, where they on the same Night introduced me to a white Woman of that Place: And as our Behaviour was such, as we have both Reason to be ashamed of, I shall for her sake pass over in Silence. On the next Day I went to *Boston*, was pursued by her Husband, who found me at the Sign of the white Horse, where I left him in Conversation with my Master, who sent me to *Little Cambridge* with his Team; he again came up with me on *Boston* Neck, where we came to Blows, and coming off Conqueror, put on for *Cambridge*. The next Night I went to another Husking at Mr. *John Denney*'s, of that Place; after husking, I went to a Tavern opposite Mr. *Denney*'s, and took from a Team there, a Horse, Saddle and Bridle, and rode to *Natick*, where I met with the Squaw, with whom I formerly made my Tour to *Hadley*, and with her spent the Day; and returning to *Cambridge*,

I met my Master, with another Man, in pursuit of me. At our Arrival there, I was sentenced by five Men (to whom the Matter was left) to receive fifteen Stripes, or pay four Dollars; and my Master was so good natur'd, or rather silly, as to pay the Money and let me go with Impunity.

From there we went to *Waltham*, where my Master heard that the injured Husband before mentioned, was after me with a Warrant, which determined him to ship me off; accordingly he went to *Boston* to get a Berth for me, and order'd me to come in the Night: In Pursuance of which Order, I set off, but having a natural Aversion to walking, for my own Ease, and that I might make the greater Dispatch, I took a Horse from the Stable of one Mr. *Cutting*, rode to *Roxbury*, and let him go: I walked over the Neck, and took Lodging in a Barn belonging to one Mr. *Pierpoint*, where I was met by my Master, who told me to tarry 'till the next Day, when I should be taken on board a Vessel bound for *Maryland*. But they not coming at the Time appointed, and I not having had any Victuals since I left *Waltham*, tho't proper to leave the Barn for better Quarters; and accordingly made the best of my way to *Dorchester*, where I stole a Horse, Saddle and Bridle, and proceeded to *Easton*, to pay a Visit to my Parents: who suspecting my Situation, insisted on my returning to my Master, which I promised without either Thoughts or Inclination of performing: For instead of returning to *Boston*, I steered my Course for *Sandwich*. On my way there, *at Rochester*, stole a Bason. When I got to *Sandwich*, I went to an Indian House, where I had been formerly acquainted, and with the Squaws there, spent my Time in a manner which may be easily guessed; but was taken up on Suspicion, by one Mr. *Fish*, and by him carried before Col. *Otis*, who on my confessing that I stole the Horse at *Dorchester*, committed me to *Barnstable* Gaol for Trial, from whence I escaped in two Days. I then went to *Southsea*, an Indian Village in *Sandwich*, where I tarried six Weeks, spending my Time in drinking and whoreing with the Squaws. By this Time I had got almost naked; and on going to *Falmouth* with some Indians, went into a Shoemaker's Shop, and from thence stole a pair of Shoes: And from a House in the same Place, I stole a Shirt, and a pair of Trowsers. At Night my Companions getting drunk, I left them; and at a Tavern there, stole a Horse, Saddle and Bridle, on which I returned to the Indian Village, and then let him loose. After tarrying one Week more, I was again taken up and committed to *Barnstable* Gaol, where after laying three Weeks, I was tried and sentenced to receive twenty Stripes; but being unwell, the Man from whom I stole the Horse at *Dorchester*, coming to *Barnstable*, and by paying the Cost, took me out of Gaol, so that I again got off unpunished: With him I lived about three Weeks, and behaved well.

In the mean Time, my Master being sent for, once more took me home, where I had not been three Weeks, before another Negro of my Master's told me that the young Squaw, so often mentioned, was very desirous of seeing me. I one Night, after having stole some Rum from my Master, got pretty handsomely drunk, took one of his Horses, and made the best of my way to her usual Place of Abode; but she not being at home, the Devil put it into my Head to pay a Visit to the Widow *Deborah Metcalfe*, whom I, in a most inhumane manner, ravished: The Particulars of which are so notorious, that it is needless for me here to relate them. The next Morning the unhappy Woman came and acquainted my Master of it, who immediately tyed me, to prevent my running away, and told her (if she was desirous of prosecuting me) to get a Warrant as soon as possible; but she being unwilling to have me hanged, proposed making the Matter up for a proper Consideration, provided my Master would send me out of the Country; to which he agreed, and accordingly set off with me for *Albany:* But we were overtaken at *Glasgow*, by Mr. *Nathaniel Jennison*, who it seem'd had got a Warrant for me. On our return to *Rutland* District, we stop'd at a Tavern in *Hardwick*, where after I had warmed my self, *Jennison* was Fool enough to bid me put along, and he would overtake me; accordingly I went out of the Door, and seeing his Horse stand handily, what should I do, but mount him, and rode off as fast as I could, leaving *Jennison* to pursue me on Foot. I got home before Bed-time, and took up my Lodging in my Master's Barn for the Night, where I had a Bottle of Cherry-Rum (which I found in Mr. *Jennison's* Baggs) to refresh my self with.

On the next Day, being the 30th of March 1767, was discovered and committed to *Worcester* Gaol, where I continued 'till the 20th of April following; at which Time I broke out with the late celebrated *FRASIER*, and a young Lad, who was confined for stealing. After which, at *Worcester* we broke into a Barber's Shop, from whence we stole a Quantity of Flour, a Comb, and a Razor: We then set off for *Boston*. At *Shrewsbury*, we stole a Goose from Mr. *Samuel Jennison;* and from the Widow *Kingsley*, in the same Place, we stole a Kettle, in which we boiled the Goose, in *Westborough* Woods. At *Marlborough*, we broke into a Distill-House, from whence we stole some Cyder Brandy: In the same Town we broke into a Shoe-maker's Shop, and took each of us a pair of Shoes. We like wise broke into Mr. *Ciperon Howe*'s House, in the same Place, from whence we stole some Bread, Meat and Rum. At *Sudbury*, we stole each of us a Shirt, and one pair of Stockings. At *Weston* we stole some Butter from off a Horse. At *Waltham* we broke into a House belonging to one Mr. *Fisk*, from whom we took a small Sum of Money, some Chocolate and Rum. At *Watertown* we stole a

Brass Kettle from one Mrs. *White* of that Place. My Companions now left me; upon which I went to Mr. *Fish's* in *Waltham*, who knew me. And having heard of my Escape from *Worcester* Gaol, immediately secured me, and with the Assistance of another Man, brought me back again, where on the 17th of September following, I was tryed and found guilty. Upon which, by the Advice of my Counsel, I prayed for the Benefit of the Clergy; which after a Year's Consideration, the Court denied me: And accordingly I was, on the 24th of Sept. last, sentenced to be hanged, which I must confess is but too just a Reward for my many notorious Crimes.

I cannot conclude this my Narrative, without gratefully acknowledging the unwearied Pains that was taken by the Rev. Mr. *Mccarty*, to awaken me to a proper Sense of my miserable and wretched Condition, whose frequent Exhortations, and most fervent Prayers, together with those of the rest of God's People, and my own sincere Endeavours after true Repentance, will I hope prove the Means of my eternal Well-being; which I hope is still the Prayers of every Christian, to whom my unhappy Situation is known.—I earnestly desire that this Recital of my Crimes, and the ignominious Death to which my notorious Wickedness has bro't me, may prove a Warning to all Persons who shall become acquainted therewith. But in a particular Manner, I would solemnly warn those of my own Colour, as they regard their own Souls, to avoid Desertion from their Masters, Drunkenness and Lewdness; which three Crimes was the Source from which have flowed the many Evils and Miseries of my short Life: Short indeed! For I am now at the Age of 21 Years only, just going to launch into a never-ending eternity; not by a natural Death, but to the Dissolution of Soul and Body, so dreadful in itself, are added the Ignominy and Terror of that particular kind of Death, which I am now going to suffer.—I freely acknowledge I have been better treated by Mankind in general, than I deserved: Yet some Injuries I have received, which I now freely forgive. I also humbly ask Forgiveness of all whom I have injured, and desire that they would pray that I may receive the Forgiveness of God, whom I have most of all offended; and on whose Pardon and Grace depends my eternal Happiness or Misery.—

Worcester Gaol,
Oct. 18, 1768.   *Arthur.*

Boston: Printed and Sold in Milk-Street. 1768.

1.   Paul Revere, engraver, *Boston Massacre* (1770).

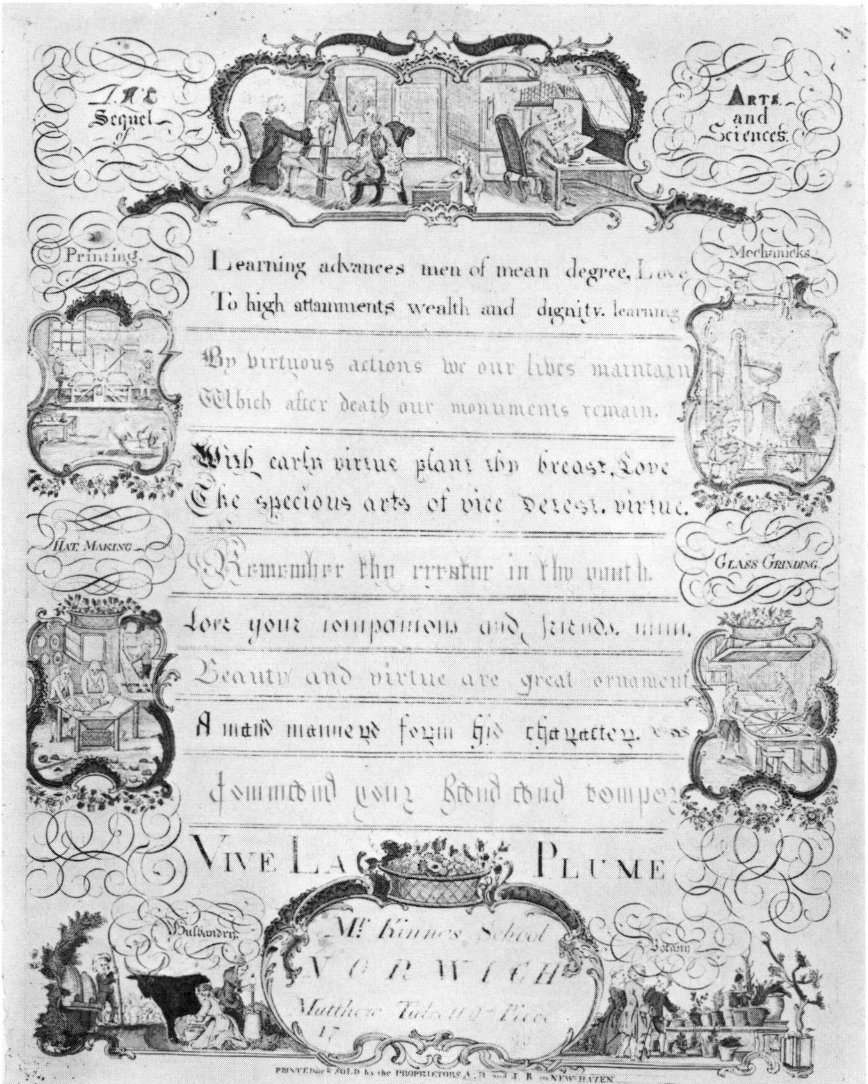

2. Abel Buell, *The Sequel of Arts and Sciences* (c. 1774).

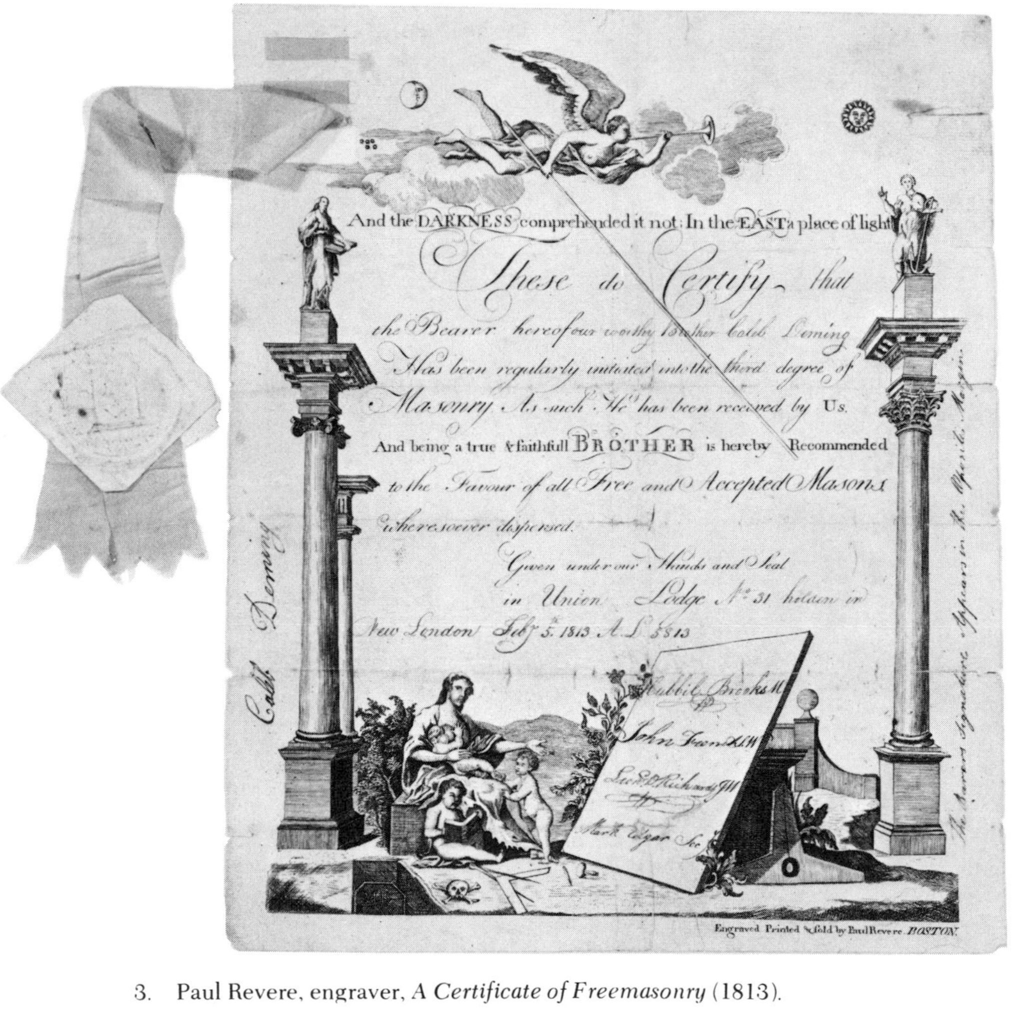

3. Paul Revere, engraver, *A Certificate of Freemasonry* (1813).

4. Anon., *The Tree of Life* (1791).

THE
CLOSET COMPANION:
OR,

An HELP to serious Persons, in the important Duty of SELF-EXAMINA-
TION.

Intended to be fixed up in the Christian's usual Place of Retirement, in
order to *remind* him of, as well as to *assist* him in, the Work.

> *Commune with your own Heart.* Psalm iv. 4.
> *Beloved, if our Heart condemn us not, then have we Confidence toward
> God.* 1 John iii, 21.
> *For the Spirit itself beareth Witness with our Spirit, that we are the
> Children of God.* Rom vii, 16.

DIRECTIONS.

I.   MAKE *Conscience of performing this Duty.* The Necessity of it will
appear, if you consider (1.) God has repeatedly commanded it. (2.) The
People of God have always practised it. (3.) There is great Danger of being
deceived; for every Grace in the Christian has its Counterfeit in the Hypo-
crite. (4.) Many Professors have been deceived, by neglecting it, and are
ruined forever. (5.) Your Comfort and Holiness depend, in a great Measure,
upon knowing your real State.

II.   *Be very serious in the Performance of it.* Set your Heart to the solemn Work, as in the Presence of the Searcher of Hearts, who will judge the
Secrets of all Men, in the great Day. Heaven and Hell are no trifles. The
question before you is no less than this: Am I a Child of Wrath, or a Child of
God? If I should die, when I have done reading this, where would this precious Soul of mine be, forever, forever, forever?

III.   *Be impartial,* or you lose your Labour; nay, you confirm your mistakes. On the one Hand, resolve to know the *worst* of yourself, the very
worst. Some are afraid to know the worst, lest they should fall into Despair,
and this fear makes them partial. Suppose the worst, and that, after serious
Examination, it should appear, that you have neither Faith nor Holiness, yet
remember, your Case is not desperate. The Door of Mercy is ever open to the
returning Sinner. It remains a blessed Truth, that *whoever cometh to Christ,
shall in no wise be kept out.* John vi. 37.

On the other Hand, be willing to know the *best* of yourself, as well as the
worst. Do not suppose, that Humility requires you to overlook your Graces,
and notice only your Corruptions.

IV.   Judge of your Graces by their *Nature,* rather than their *Degree.* You
are to try inherent Graces by the *Touchstone,* not by the *Measure.* The
greatest Degree is to be desired and aimed at, but the smallest Degree is

Matter of Praise and Rejoicing. Don't conclude there is no Grace, because there is some Corruption; or, that the Spirit does not strive against the Flesh, because the Flesh strives against the Spirit.

V.   Let not the Issue of this Trial depend at all upon your Knowledge of the exact Time of your Conversion, or the particular Minister or Sermon first instrumental in it. Some, yea, many, are wrought upon by flow and insensible Degrees. Grace increases like the Day-light. No Man doubts whether the Sun shines at Noon, because he did not see the Day-break.

VI.   Take this Caution, lest you stumble at the Threshold. Think not that you must begin this Work with doubting whether God will extend Mercy to you, and save you; and that you must leave this a Question wholly under Debate, till you have found out how to resolve it, by Self-Examination. This is a common and pernicious Error, laying the very Foundation of this Work in the great Sin of Unbelief. The Question before you is not, Will God accept and save me, though a vile Sinner, if I believe on Christ? But you are to inquire, *Am I now, at this Time, in an accepted State?* The former Question is already resolved by God himself, who cannot lie. His Word positively declares, that every coming Sinner shall be accepted and saved. This being determined, is not to be questioned. But you are to try, Whether you are now in a State of Grace?

VII.   Take Care, that you do not *trust* on your Self Examination, rather than on Christ. There is a Proneness in our Natures to put Duties in the Place of Christ.

VIII.   Be not content merely to read over the following Questions, but stop and dwell on each: nor suffer yourselves to proceed to another, till you have put the first home to your Conscience, and have got an honest Answer to it.

IX.   Examine yourself *frequently*; at least, once a Week. The Lord's Day Evening is a most suitable Season. The oftener you perform this Work, the easier it will become. If you do not obtain Satisfaction at first, you may by repeated Endeavours; and a scriptural, solid Hope will amply repay your utmost Labour.

N.B. The above Directions are taken, in Part, from that excellent Book, *Marshall on Sanctification.*

QUESTIONS,

With Respect to *Faith*, and the *Fruits of Faith.*

I.   Do I Believe on the Son of God? Surely this is an important Question. My Bible assures me, that *He that believeth shall be saved.* Do I then believe? And here, let me carefully distinguish between Faith, and its Fruits. *What is Faith?* The simple Meaning of Faith is, believing; and believing always refers to something spoken or written. Divine Faith is the Belief of a divine Testimony, as John speaks, *He that hath received his Testimony, hath set to his Seal that* GOD *is* TRUE. John iii. 33. And on the contrary, the Apostle *John* says, *He that believeth not God, hath made him a Liar, because he believeth not the Record that God gave of his Son. And this is the Record, that* GOD HATH GIVEN TO US ETERNAL LIFE, *and this Life is in his Son.* I John v. 10, 11. I must first believe the Truth of God, as revealed in his Word; I must credit his Report, and believe his Testimony concerning Christ; and then, *receive* and *trust upon Christ*, so revealed, for my own personal Salvation. But to be more particular:

1. Do I really believe that I am a fallen Creature—that I derived from Adam a Nature wholly corrupt, depraved, and sinful—and that I am a Child of Wrath, by Nature, even as others?—Have I ever considered the unspotted and infinite Purity and Holiness of God's Nature, and that he abhors, detests, and hates Sin, wherever he sees it?—Have I considered that his Law, contained in the Ten Commandments, is a Copy and Transcript of that holy Nature; and by comparing myself with that eternal Rule of Right and Wrong, have I been led to see my horrible Wickedness and Vileness?—O what Multitudes of Sins have I committed, in Thought, Word and Deed!—Am I really sick of Sin, sorry for Sin, and do I abhor myself as a vile Sinner?

2. Have I duly considered what my Sins have deserved?—Do I sincerely think that if God were to send *me* to Hell, because I am *a Sinner*, he would do justly?

3. Do I see my utter, *Helplessness*, as well as my Sin and Misery?—Am I perfectly assured, that I cannot by any Works, Duties, or Sufferings of my own, in the least help myself; but that if ever I am saved, it must be the Effect of free Mercy?

4. Are the Eyes of my Understanding enlightened, to know Christ?—What do I think of Christ? Who is he?—Do I believe that he is *God manifest in the flesh*, uniting in his *one* Person the human and divine Natures; *Man*, that he might suffer; and *God*, that he might redeem?—Do I know *why* he suffered; that it was to make Satisfaction to divine Justice, for the Injury done to God's Law and Government by Man's Sin?—Do I believe, that *the Father is well pleased for his Righteousness Sake; and that he has magnified the Law*, both by his Obedience and Sufferings, *and made it honourable*?—Do I therefore look upon Christ, as the only WAY to the Father; as the only FOUNDATION to build on, the only FOUNTAIN to wash in?—Am I persuaded of his ability to save, to the utmost, all who come to God by him?

5. Am I satisfied from God's own Word and Promise, that whoever, let them be ever so vile and wicked, coming to Christ, by Faith, shall be saved?

the Promise being, without Exception, *Whosoever believeth on him shall not be ashamed.*

6. Am I led and assisted by the Spirit of God, to believe this general Promise, in *my own* particular Case? As God has made no Exceptions, why should I except myself? True, no Tongue can tell how vile I have been, only God Knows the Greatness of my Sins, and the Wickedness of my Heart! But shall I then *despair*, and so add, to my other Sins, the *worst* and *greatest* Sin of all, UNBELIEF? God forbid! *It is a faithful saying, and worthy of* MY *Acceptation that Christ came to save the chief of Sinners.* Do I then, sensible of my Sin, Misery and Helplessness, look upon Christ as an all-sufficient Saviour, and commit my precious, immortal Soul to him, relying upon him *only*, and endeavouring to rely upon him *confidently*, for eternal Salvation? —If so, surely I am a Believer, and shall receive the End of my faith, the Salvation of my Soul.

HAVING thus examined my Faith, let me proceed impartially to examine THE FRUITS AND EFFECTS OF MY FAITH. Many pretend to Faith, whose Works give the Lie to their Pretentions; let me therefore *show my Faith by my Works.* James ii. 18.

Quest. II. WHAT ARE THE FRUITS OF MY FAITH? Does it produce those Effects which the Word of God points out, as the Proof and Evidence of its Sincerity, with Respect to my *Conscience*, my *Heart*, and my *Life*?

1. *What are the Effects of my Faith, as to my Conscience?* The Scripture says, *We which have believed do enter into Rest.* Heb. iv. 3. Do I rest from my former legal *Attempts* to justify myself, going about to establish my own Righteousness? Am I satisfied with Christ's Righteousness, as a complete Title to Glory? I read of *Peace in believing.* Have I Peace in my Conscience? Being justified by Faith, have I *Peace with God?*—When my Soul is alarmed with the Remembrance of former Sins, or those lately committed, how do I obtain Peace? Is it by forgetting them as soon as I can, and then fancying that God has forgotten them too?—Is it by resolving to do so no more, and so making future Obedience atone for past Offences?—Is it by performing religious Duties, and so making Amends?—Or, is it by a fresh Application to the pardoning, peace-speaking Blood of Christ?—When my Sins stare me in the Face and my Duties themselves appear Sins, whence, O my Soul, proceeds thy Comfort?—*Is it the Blood of Christ,* my Sacrifice, *that purges my Conscience from dead Works?*—Does Faith in the Atonement of his Death, free me from the dreadful Apprehension of Condemnation and Wrath, due to sin?—Do I, or do I not, believe that *God is reconciled,* through the Death of his Son, and therefore look up to him with Freedom and Delight?—If I have not this Peace, why is it? What hinders? Either I do not clearly under-

stand the Nature of the Gospel, or I do not fully believe it: for it provides for every possible Case. If I have this, blessed be God for it! Lord, help me to keep it, that it may keep me! Lord, I believe; help thou mine Unbelief!

2. *I would try, what are the Effects of my Faith, as to my* HEART, *and its Affections.*

(1.) Do I love GOD, God the *Father?* Do I think of him, and go to him as a loving Father, in Christ? Have I the Spirit of Adoption, so that I cry, *Abba Father?*—Do I love him as the Father of Mercies, the God of Hope, the God of Peace, the God of Love?

(2.) *Do I love Christ?*—To those who believe, he is precious; is he precious to me?—Do I see infinite Beauty in his Person? Is he the Chief among ten Thousands to me, and altogether lovely?—Do I admire the Length, and Breadth, and Depth, and Height of his Love?—Is it the Language of my very Soul, *None but Christ, None but Christ?*—Is it my Grief and Shame, that I love him no more?

(3.) *Do I love the Holy Spirit?* (Rom. xv. 30.) Do I honour him, as the great Author of Light and Life, Grace and Comfort? Do I maintain a deep Sense of my Dependence on his divine Agency, in all my religious Performances? Do I desire my Heart to be his Temple?—Am I cautious lest I quench his holy Motions, or grieve him by my Sins? Am I sensible, that without his Influences I cannot pray, hear, read, communicate, nor examine myself as I ought?

(4.) *Do I love God's Law?*—Do I delight in the Law of the Lord, after the inward Man, not wishing it less strict and holy, but loving it because it is holy?—Am I as willing to take Christ for my *King* to rule over me, as for my *Priest* to atone for me?—Do I hunger and thirst after Righteousness?—Do I pant, and long, and pray to be holy?—Do I wish to be holy, as I wish to be happy? Do I hate all Sin, especially that Sin which most easily besets me, and labour daily to mortify it, and to deny myself? Do I sigh for complete Deliverance from remaining Corruption, and rejoice in the Hope of it, through a holy Jesus?—Do I long for Heaven, that there I may be satisfied with his Likeness?

(5.) *Do I love God's People?*—Can I say to Christ, as *Ruth* to *Naomi, Thy People shall be my People?*—Do I love them, because they love Christ, and bear his Image?—Do I feel an Union of Spirit with them, though they may not be of my Party, or think exactly as I do?—Can I say, *I know that I have passed from Death to Life, because I love the Brethren?*

3. *What are the Effects of my Faith, as to my daily* WALK *and Conversation?*—The Word of God tells me, that he who is in Christ, is *a new Creature;*

old Things are passed away, all Things are become new.—If ye love me, said Christ, *keep my Commandments.* Let me review the Decalogue, and see how my Love to Christ is manifested by my Obedience.

(1.) Do I know and acknowledge God to be the only true God, and *my* God, and do I worship and glorify him accordingly? Is he the supreme Object of *my* Desire and Delight?—Do I trust him, hope in him, love to think of him?—Do I pray to him, do I praise him, am I careful to please him?

(2.) Do I receive, observe, and keep pure and entire all such religious Worship and Ordinances as God hath appointed in his Word? How is it with me in secret Prayer, in Family Prayer, in public Prayer?—With what Views do I go to hear the preached Gospel, and what Good do I get by it?

(3.) Do I make a holy reverend Use of God's Names, Titles, Attributes, Ordinances, Word, and Works, avoiding the Profanation or Abuse of any Thing whereby God makes himself known?

(4.) Do I keep holy to God the Sabbath Day, resting *all* that Day from worldly Employments, Recreations, and Conversation? And do I spend *the whole Time* in public and private Exercises of divine Worship, except so much as is to be taken up in the Works of Necessity and Mercy? Is the Sabbath my Delight, and are the Ordinances of God's House very precious to my Soul?

(5.) Do I endeavour to preserve the Honour, and perform all the Duties, which I owe to my *Superiors, Inferiors,* or *Equals*; remembering, that true Religion makes good Husbands, Wives, Children, Masters and Servants? If I am *really* holy, I am *relatively* holy.

(6.) Do I use all lawful Means to preserve my own Life, and the Life of others?—Do I avoid all Intemperance?—Do I resist passionate Tempers?—Do I labour to promote the Welfare of Men's Souls?—Do I exercise Love, Compassion, and Succour to the Poor and Distressed, according to my Ability? Can I, and do I, freely forgive those who have injured me? Can I, and do I, pray for them; and instead of hating, do I love my very Enemies?

(7.) Do I earnestly strive to preserve my own, and my Neighbour's Chastity, in *Heart, Speech,* and *Behaviour*; avoiding all the Incentives to Lust, such as Intemperance in Food, lascivious Songs, Books, Pictures, Dancings, Plays, and debauched Company; remembering that my Body is the Temple of the Holy Ghost?

(8.) Do I use the lawful Means of moderately procuring and furthering the Wealth and outward Estate of myself, and others?—Do I abhor every Species of Robbery and Injustice?—Am I strictly and conscientiously honest in all my Dealings, not overreaching or defrauding any Person, in any Degree?

(9.) Do I studiously maintain and promote TRUTH, between Man and Man; not only abhorring Perjury, but hating all Falsehood? And do I, as a Professor of Religion, avoid both ludicrous and pernicious Lies, being as tender of my Neighbour's Character as of my own?—Am I very *cautious* in making Promises, and very *careful* to keep them?

(10.) Am I contented with the Condition God has allotted me, believing that he orders all Things for the best?—And do I avoid, as much as possible, envying my Neighbour's Happiness, or inordinately desiring any Thing that is his?

Conclusion

And now, dear Reader, What is the Result of your Inquiry? Have you made a solemn Pause, at the Close of every Question, and obtained an honest Answer? And are you, notwithstanding many unhallowed Imperfections, able to conclude, That your Faith is of God's Operation; and proved so to be, by its holy Fruits of Peace, Love, and Obedience?—Then take the Comfort, and give God the Glory.

But if, on the other Hand, the Evidence of Scripture and Conscience is against you, and you are forced to conclude, that your Heart is not right with God—then, for God's Sake, and for your Soul's Sake, cry instantly and mightily to him to have Mercy upon you, and change your Heart; remembering, that though your Case is awful, it is not desperate; and that still you, even you, coming to Christ, shall in no wise be cast out.

G. B.

Boston:—Printed and sold by MANNING & LORING, No. 2, Cornhill.

BY THE PRESIDENT
Of the United States of America.

A Proclamation.

As no truth is more clearly taught in the volume of inspiration, nor any
more fully demonstrated by the experience of all ages, than that a deep sense
and a due acknowledgment of the governing providence of a Supreme Being
and of the accountableness of men to Him as the searcher of hearts and
righteous distributor of rewards and punishments, are conducive, equally, to
the happiness and rectitude of individuals and to the well being of communities; as it is, also, most reasonable in itself, that men who are made capable
of social acts and relations, who owe their improvements to the social state,
and who derive their enjoyments from it, should, as a society, make their
acknowledgments of dependance and obligation to Him who hath endued
them with these capacities, and elevated them in the scale of existence, by
these distinctions; as it is, likewise, a plain dictate of duty, and a strong
sentiment of nature, that in circumstances of great urgency and seasons of
imminent danger, earnest and particular supplications should be made to
Him who is able to defend or to destroy; as, moreover, the most precious
interests of the people of the United States are still held in jeopardy, by the
hostile designs and insidious arts of a foreign nation, as well as by the dissemination among them of those principles subversive of the foundations of
all religious, moral and social obligations, that have produced incalculable
mischief and misery in other countries; and as, in fine, the observance of
special seasons for public religious solemnities, is happily calculated to avert
the evils which we ought to deprecate, and to excite to the performance of
the duties which we ought to discharge,—by calling and fixing the attention
of the people at large to the momentous truths already recited, by affording
opportunity to teach and inculcate them, by animating devotion and giving
to it the character of a national act:—For these reasons, I have thought
proper to recommend, and I do hereby recommend accordingly, that
Thursday, the 25th day of April next, be observed, throughout the United
States of America, as a day of solemn humiliation, fasting and prayer—That
the citizens, on that day, abstaining as far as may be from their secular
occupations, devote the time to the sacred duties of religion, in public and
in private: That they call to mind our numerous offences against the most
High GOD, confess them before him with the sincerest penitence, implore
his pardoning mercy, through the great Mediator and Redeemer, for our
past transgressions, and that, through the grace of his Holy Spirit, we may be
disposed and enabled to yield a more suitable obedience to his righteous

requisitions in time to come: That he would interpose to arrest the progress of that impiety and licentiousness in principle and practice, so offensive to himself and so ruinous to mankind: That he would make us deeply sensible that "righteousness exalteth a nation, but that sin is the reproach of any people": That he would turn us from our transgressions and turn his displeasure from us: That he would withhold us from unreasonable discontent, —from disunion, faction, sedition and insurrection: That he would preserve our country from the desolating sword: That he would save our cities and towns from a repetition of those awful pestilential visitations under which they have lately suffered so severely, and that the health of our inhabitants, generally, may be precious in his sight: That he would favour us with fruitful seasons, and so bless the labors of the husbandman as that there may be food in abundance for man and beast: That he would prosper our commerce, manufacturers, and fisheries and give success to the people in all their lawful industy and enterprize: That he would smile on our colleges, academics, schools and seminaries of learning, and make them nurseries of sound science, morals and religion: That he would bless all magistrates from the highest to the lowest, give them the true spirit of their station, make them a terror to evil doers and a praise to them that do well: That he would preside over the councils of the nation at this critical period, enlighten them to a just discernment of the public interest, and save them from mistake, division and discord: That he would succeed our preparations for defence, and bless our armaments by land and by sea: That he would put an end to the effusion of human blood, and the accumulation of human misery, among the contending nations of the earth, by disposing them to justice, to equity, to benevolence, and to peace: And that he would extend the blessings of knowledge, of true liberty, and of pure and undefiled religion, throughout the world.

AND I do, also, recommend that with these acts of humiliation, penitence and prayer, fervent thanksgiving to the author of all good be united, for the countless favors which he is still continuing to the people of the United States, and which render their condition as a nation eminently happy, when compared with the lot of others.

GIVEN under my hand and the seal of the United States of America, at the city of Philadelphia, this sixth day of March in the year of our Lord one thousand seven hundred and ninety-nine and of the Independence of the said States the twenty-third.

JOHN ADAMS.

By the President,

TIMOTHY PICKERING,

Secretary of State.

PART THREE

RUDENESS AND REFINEMENT

8. Republican Barbarism

Charles W. Janson was an English immigrant to America who spent more than thirteen years (1793-1806) trying to understand the new country. He came to America, as he put it, "with an intention of passing a considerable part of his life there," but a series of land-speculating and business failures and his "perpetual uneasiness" among Americans eventually drove him back to England. His account of American customs and manners, "in every respect uncongenial to English habits, and to the tone of an Englishman's constitution," was therefore critical and bitter; but it was a criticism and bitterness about the emerging nature of the American character shared by many Americans equally fearful of the brutality and vulgarity the republican society seemed to be breeding. By the early nineteenth century, there were many native Americans who too were beginning to feel that they were strangers in their own land.

Stranger in America
CHARLES WILLIAM JANSON

I shall now shew the reader, without the most distant idea of giving of-fence, what must sometimes be endured from the manners and customs of the people.

Arrived at your inn, let me suppose, like myself, you had fallen in with a landlord, who at the moment would condescend to *take the trouble* to pro-

Charles William Janson, *The Stranger in America: Containing Observations Made During a Long Residence in that Country, on the Genius, Manners and Customs of the People of the United States* . . . (London, 1807), pp. 85–88, 202–207, 297, 300–305, 356–358, 363, 373–377, 416–417, 422–424.

cure you refreshment after the family hour, and that no *pig*, or other trifling circumstance called off his attention, he will sit by your side, and enter in the most familiar manner into conversation; which is prefaced, of course, with a demand of your business, and so forth. He will then start a political question (for here every individual is a politican), force your answer, contradict, deny, and, finally, be ripe for a quarrel, should you not acquiesce in all his opinions. When the homely meal is served up, he will often place himself opposite to you at the table, at the same time declaring, that "though he thought he had eaten a hearty dinner, yet he will pick a bit with you." Thus will he sit, drinking out of your glass, and of the liquor you are to pay for, belching in your face, and committing other excesses still more indelicate and disgusting. Perfectly inattentive to your accommodation, and regardless of your appetite, he will dart his fork into the best of the dish, and leave you to take the next cut. If you arrive at the dinner-hour, you are seated with "mine hostess" and her dirty children, with whom you have often to scramble for a plate, and even the servants of the inn; for liberty and equality level all ranks upon the road, from the host to the hostler. The children, imitative of their free and polite papa, will also seize your drink, slobber in it, and often snatch a dainty bit from your plate. This is esteemed wit, and consequently provokes a laugh, at the expence of those who are paying for the board. No check must be given to these demonstrations of unsophisticated nature; for the smallest rebuke will bring down a severe animadversion from the parent. Many are the instances that could be pointed out, where the writer has undergone these mortifications, and if Mr. Winterbottom has ever travelled in the country parts of the United States, he can, if he pleases, attest the truth of these observations.

"The American farmer, (says this gentleman) has more simplicity and honesty—we more art and chicanery; they have more of nature, and we more of the world. Nature, indeed, formed our features and intellects very much alike; but while we have metamorphosed the one, and contaminated the other, they have retained and preserved the natural symbols of both."

If we credit these assertions, we must admit that the inhabitants of the new world, far excel us, also, in mental acquirements; but I take the very contrary to be the fact. A republican spirit makes them forward and impertinent—a spirit of trade renders them full of chicanery—and under a shew of liberty, they are commonly tyrants to each other. This is observable at their public meetings, when the fumes of whisky or apple-brandy begin to operate—the more opulent will lord it over his poor neighbor; while the robust will attack the weak, till the whole exhibits a scene of riot, blasphemy, and intoxication. . . .

Among the females, a stranger may soon discover the pertness of republican principles. Divested, from that cause, of the blushing modesty of the country girls of Europe, they will answer a familiar question from the other sex with the confidence of a French Mademoiselle. I would not, however, be understood to question their chastity, of which they have as large a portion as Europeans; my object is merely to shew the force of habit, and the result of education.

The arrogance of domestics in this land of republican liberty and equality, is particularly calculated to excite the astonishment of strangers. To call persons of this description *servants*, or to speak of their *master* or *mistress*, is a grievous affront. Having called one day at the house of a gentleman of my acquaintance, on knocking at the door, it was opened by a servant-maid, whom I had never before seen, as she had not been long in his family. The following is the dialogue, word for word, which took place on this occasion: —"Is your master at home?"—"I have no master."—"Don't you live here?" —"I *stay* here."—"And who are you then?"—"Why, I am Mr. _____'s *help*. I'd have you to know, *man*, that I am no *sarvant*; none but *negers* are *sarvants*."

・ ・ ・

To return to the city of Washington—I have remarked, that on my return to London, the first general enquiry of my friends is respecting this far-famed place. The description given of it by interested scribblers, may well serve to raise an Englishman's curiosity, and lead him to fancy the capital of Columbia a terrestrial paradise.

The entrance, or avenues, as they are pompously called, which lead to the American seat of government, are the worst roads I passed in the country; and I appeal to every citizen who has been unlucky enough to travel the stages north and south leading to the city, for the truth of the assertion. I particularly allude to the mail stage road from Bladensburg to Washington, and from thence to Alexandria. In the winter season, during the sitting of Congress, every turn of your waggon wheel (for I must again observe, that there is no such thing in the country as what we call a stage coach, or a post-chaise,) is for many miles attended with danger. The roads are never repaired; deep ruts, rocks, and stumps of trees, every minute impede your progress, and often threaten your limbs with dislocation.

Arrived at the city, you are struck with its grotesque appearance. In one view from the capitol hill, the eye fixes upon a row of uniform houses, ten or twelve in number, while it faintly discovers the adjacent tenements to be miserable wooden structures, consisting, when you approach them, of two or three rooms one above another. Again, you see the hotel, which was vauntingly promised, on laying the foundation, to rival the large inns in England. This, like every other private adventure, failed: the walls and the roof remain, but not a window! and, instead of accommodating the members of Congress, and travellers of distinction, as proposed, a number of the lowest order of Irish have long held the title of *naked possession*, from which, were it ever to become an object, it would be difficult to eject them. Turning the eye, a well finished edifice presents itself, surrounded by lofty trees, which never felt the stroke of the axe. The president's house, the offices of state, and a little theatre, where an itinerant company repeated, during a part of the last year, the lines of Shakespeare, Otway, and Dryden, to empty benches, terminate the view of the Pennsylvania, or Grand Avenue.

Speculation, the life of the American, embraced the design of the new city. Several companies of speculators purchased lots, and began to build handsome streets, with an ardor that soon promised a large and populous city. Before they arrived at the attic story, the failure was manifest; and in that state at this moment are the walls of many scores of houses begun on a plan of elegance. In some parts, purchasers have cleared the wood from their grounds, and erected temporary wooden buildings: others have fenced in their lots, and attempted to cultivate them; but the sterility of the land laid out for the city is such, that this plan has also failed. The country adjoining consists of woods in a state of nature, and in some places of mere swamps, which give the scene a curious patch-work appearance. The view of the noble river Potomack, which the eye can trace till it terminates at Alexandria, is very fine. The navigation of the river is good from the bay of Chesapeak, till the near approach to the city, where bars of sand are formed, which every year encroach considerably on the channel. The frigate which brought the Tunisian embassy, grounded on one of these shoals, and the barbarians were obliged to be landed in boats. This is another great disadvantage to the growth of the city. It never can become a place of commerce, while Baltimore lies on one side, and Alexandria on the other; even admitting the navigation to be equally good—nor can the wild and uneven spot laid out into streets be cleared and levelled for building upon, for many years, even with the most indefatigable exertions.

The Capitol, of which two wings are now finished, is of hewn stone, and will be a superb edifice, worthy of its name. The architect who built the first wing, left the country soon after its completion; the corresponding part was carried on under the direction of Mr. Latrobe, an Englishman; from whose taste and judgment much may be expected in finishing the centre of the building; the design of which, as shewn to me by Doctor Thornton, is truly elegant.

The president's house, of which a correct view is given in the frontispiece to this volume, is situated one mile from the Capitol, at the extremity of Pennsylvania Avenue. The contemplated streets of this embryo city are called avenues, and every state gives name to one. That of Pennsylvania is the largest; in fact I never heard of more than that and the New Jersey Avenue, except some houses uniformly built, in one of which lives Mr. Jefferson's printer, John Harrison Smith, a few more of inferior note, with some public-houses, and here and there a little *grog-shop*, this boasted avenue is as much a wilderness as Kentucky, with this disadvantage, that the soil is good for nothing. Some half-starved cattle browsing among the bushes, present a melancholy spectacle to a stranger, whose expectation has been wound up by the illusive description of speculative writers. So very thinly is the city peopled, and so little is it frequented, that quails and other birds are constantly shot within a hundred yards of the Capitol, and even during the sitting of the houses of congress. . . .

o   o   o

Neither park, nor mall, neither churches, theatres, nor colleges, could I discover so lately as the summer of 1806. A small place has indeed been erected since in the Pennsylvania Avenue, called a theatre, in which Mr. Green and the Virginia company of comedians were nearly starved the only season it was occupied, and were obliged to go off to Richmond during the very height of the sitting of congress. Public offices on each side of the president's house, uniformly built of brick, may also, perhaps, have been built subsequent to that period. That great man who planned the city, and after whom it is named, certainly entertained the hopes that it would at some future period equal ancient Rome in splendor and magnificence. Among the regulations for building were these—that the houses should be of brick or stone—the walls to be at least thirty feet high, and to be built parallel to the line of the street.

The president's house is certainly a neat but plain piece of architecture, built of hewn stone, said to be of a better quality than Portland stone, as it will cut like marble, and resist the change of the seasons in a superior degree. Only part of it is furnished; the whole salary of the president would be in-adequate to the expence of completing it in a style of suitable elegance. Rooms are fitted up for himself, an audience chamber, and apartments for Mr. Thomas Man Randolph, and Mr. Epps, and their respective families, who married two of his daughters, and are members of the house of repre-sentatives.

The ground around it, instead of being laid out in a suitable style, remains in its ancient rude state, so that, in a dark night, instead of finding your way to the house, you may, perchance, fall into a pit, or stumble over a heap of rubbish. The fence round the house is of the meanest sort; a common post and rail enclosure. This parsimony destroys every sentiment of pleasure that arises in the mind, in viewing the residence of the president of a nation, and is a disgrace to the country.

Though the permanent seat of government has been fixed at Washington, its progress has been proved to be less rapid than any other new settlement supported only by trade. The stimulus held out by the presence of congress has proved artificial and unnatural. After enumerating the public buildings, the private dwelling-houses of the officers of government, the accommodations set apart for the members of the legislature, and the temporary tenements of those dependent on them, the remainder of this boasted city is a mere wilderness of wood and stunted shrubs, the occupants of barren land. Strangers after viewing the offices of state, are apt to enquire for the city, while they are in its very centre.

One of the greatest evils of a republican form of government is a loss of that subordination in society which is essentially necessary to render a country agreeable to foreigners. To the well-informed this defect is irksome, and no remedy for it can be applied. The meaning of liberty and equality, in the opinion of the vulgar, consists in impudent freedom, and uncontrolled licentiousness; while boys assume the airs of full-grown coxcombs. This is not to be wondered at, where most parents make it a principle never to check those ungovernable passions which are born with us, or to correct the growing vices of their children. Often have I, with horror, seen boys, whose dress indicated wealthy parents, intoxicated, shouting and swearing in the public streets. In the use of that stupefying weed, tobacco, apeing their fathers, they smoke segars to so immoderate a degree, that sickness, and even death, has been the consequence. . . .

"The delicate and entertaining diversion, with propriety called GOUGING, is thus performed:—When two boxers are wearied out with fighting and bruising each other, they come, as it is called, to close quarters, and each endeavours to twist his fore-fingers in the ear-locks of his antagonist. When these are fast clenched, the thumbs are extended each way to the nose, and the eyes *gently* turned out of the sockets. The victor, for his expertness, receives shouts of applause from the sportive throng, while his poor eyeless antagonist is laughed at for his misfortune." Such are the very words of Morse, in his American Geography, under the head of North Carolina.

That the European reader may give immediate credit to the existence of this most horrible practice called *gouging*, I have quoted the words of a native author. It is in vain for later writers to gloss over the subject; to pretend that this custom was *once* practised in America; or that such was the revenge which *once* prevailed in the breast of civilised man. It is my avowed purpose to paint "the manners living as they rise;" and upon this point, with pain am I compelled to declare, that this more than savage custom is daily practised among the lower classes in the southern states.

Though Mr. Morse gives frequent occasion to differ from him on many points, yet I admit that he did travel through the different states of the Union to collect materials for the work above-mentioned. I farther admit a belief that Mr. Morse did not write to serve any dishonorable purpose—that he meant to instruct, and not to mislead. And, were he divested of that strong prejudice, so prominent a feature in the works of most American authors, when speaking of their country, his Geography might be pronounced an acquisition to the British reader.

It is therefore evident that *gouging* is a barbarity still continued in America; but, as an author, posterior to Mr. Morse, and an Englishman, has attempted to insinuate that it is now no longer practised, I shall relate a few recent instances of its existence, and a painful description of an ocular demonstration of the horrors of its execution.

Passing, in company with other travellers, through the state of Georgia, our attention was arrested by a gouging-match. We found the combatants, as Morse describes, fast clenched by the hair, and their thumbs endeavoring to force a passage into each other's eyes; while several of the bystanders were betting upon the first eye to be turned out of its socket. For some time the combatants avoided the *thumb stroke* with dexterity. At length they fell to the ground, and in an instant the uppermost sprung up with his antagonist's eye in his hand!!! The savage crowd applauded, while, sick with horror, we galloped away from the infernal scene. The name of the sufferer was John Butler, a Carolinian, who, it seems, had been dared to the combat by a Georgian; and the first eye was for the honor of the state to which they respectively belonged.

The eye is not the only feature which suffers on these occasions. Like dogs and bears, they use their teeth and feet, with the most savage ferocity, upon each other.

A brute, in human form, named John Stanley, of Bertie county, North Carolina, sharpens his teeth with a file, and boasts of his dependence upon them in fight. This monster will also exult in relating the account of the noses and ears he has bitten off, and the cheeks he has torn.

A man of the name of Thomas Penrise, then living in Edenton, in the same state, attempting at cards to cheat some half-drunken sailors, was detected. A scuffle ensued; Penrise knocked out the candle, then gouged out three eyes, bit off an ear, tore a few cheeks, and made good his retreat.

Near the same place, a schoolmaster, named Jarvis Lucas, was beset by three men, one Horton, his son, and son-in-law. These ruffians beat the unfortunate man till his life was despaired of, having bitten, gouged, and kicked him unmercifully. On the trial of an indictment for this outrageous assault, a Carolina court of justice amerced them in a small fine only . . . .

Another bestial mode of assault used by men in North Carolina, is properly called butting. This attack is also copied from the brute creation, and is executed nearly in the same manner as practised in battle between bulls, rams, and goats. A traveller has endeavored to confine butting to the negroes; but he must excuse my implicating the white man in this brutal act.

That the reader may become a little familiar with these Columbian accomplishments, I can assure him that disputes terminated in England by fair blows, are *generally* there maintained by the practice of some, and often all of these dreadful stratagems, should opportunities offer during the combat.

An American pugilist is equally dexterous with his feet, which are used, not only against his antagonist's shins, but are applied, with the utmost violence, against those parts which the contending beasts of the field never assail. Hence ruptures, loss of eyes, mutilated noses, and indented cheeks so frequently surprise and shock the traveller. A fellow named *Michie*, in my presence, boasted "that he could kick any man, six feet high, under the chin, and break his jaws." . . .

The lower class in this gouging, biting, kicking country, are the most abject that, perhaps, ever peopled a Christian land. They live in the woods and desarts, and many of them cultivate no more land than will raise them corn and cabbages, which, with fish, and occasionally a piece of pickled pork or bacon, are their constant food. This land, on which, prior to their settlement, no human step had ever marked a path, required clearing of trees, whose tops almost reached the clouds, before a spot could be found large enough to erect a shelter for the women and children. Their habitations are more wretched than can be conceived; the huts of the poor of Ireland, or even the meanest Indian wig-wam, displaying more ingenuity and greater industry. They are constructed of pine trees, cut in lengths of ten or fifteen feet, and piled up in a square, without any other workmanship than a notch at the end of each log, to keep them in contact. When this barbarous pile is raised between six and seven feet, they split the remainder of their logs to the thickness of two or three inches, and by laying them over the whole in a sloping direction, form the roof. The chimney is, if possible, worse than Dr. Johnson describes the hole in the roof of a house in Scotland, through which the smoke found a passage. The summer's scorching sun, and the bleak winds of winter, are equally accessible to this miserable dwelling. The interstices between the logs are often left open to the elements, and are large enough to give admission to vermin and reptiles, which abound in this part of the world.

Amid these accumulated miseries, the inhabitants of log-houses are extremely tenacious of the rights and liberties of republicanism. They consider themselves on an equal footing with the best educated people of the country, and upon the principles of equality they intrude themselves into every company. In the taverns in this part of the United States, there is generally no other accommodation than a large sitting-room, in common, where the governor of the state, and the judge of the district, in travelling, must associate with their fellow-citizens of every degree.

o o o

The state of South Carolina produces abundance of rice, tobacco, cotton, and indigo, for exportation; and contains more slaves, for the number of square miles, than any other part of the United States. It is, indeed, the only one which admits the horrid traffic, and thousands of these miserable people are dispersed over the adjoining states, through the port of Charleston, where there is a greater slave-market than, perhaps, was ever known at one place in the West India islands.

The richest planters in the United States are to be found in South Carolina, some drawing a yearly revenue from the labor of their slaves to the amount of forty or fifty thousand dollars, and many enjoy an income of from twelve to twenty thousand from the same source. A planter in moderate circumstances is in the receipt of from three to six thousand; while others, so capricious is fortune, drag on a miserable existence with large families, on the wretched pittance of eighty or one hundred dollars a year.

The best lands are the tide-swamps, where cotton and rice are grown, and which, in high cultivation, have sold as high as one hundred and seventy dollars per acre;—an enormous price, when it is remembered that land, capable of producing corn, may be had, and in good situations too, from five to fifteen dollars—while uncleared land, that is, land in its original state, inhabited by the beasts of the forest alone, is selling at one third of the last-mentioned price. The value, in short, rises as the land is cleared, while in England we estimate our estates in proportion to the quantity of timber upon them. In general, the tide-swamps command from seventy to one hundred—inland swamps twenty to fifty—while such as bear corn, sweet potatoes, &c. fetch from six to forty dollars, and high uncleared land from one to six dollars per acre, in South Carolina.

The buildings on the plantations are in proportion to the value of the latter—from the cost of thirty thousand dollars, to a miserable log-house. The best houses consist generally, of not more than a ground-floor, with bed-chambers above; and many of them of a ground-floor only; but in this case, they cover a considerable space. At the south-front it is an invariable rule to attach a piazza, which impedes the extreme heat of the sun from penetrating into the sitting and lodging-rooms; and in the evening it affords an agreeable walk. The kitchens and out-offices are always at the distance of several yards from the principal dwelling. This is done as well to guard against the house-negroes through carelessness setting the houses on fire, for they generally sit over it half the night, as to keep out their noise. Negroes are great and loud talkers; and in this warm climate, having wood for the trouble of fetching it, they often sit up, after their work is done, over a large fire, in the summer, when I could scarcely endure the excessive heat of the night in the open air.

The masters here, as in the other southern states, regard their slaves, as English farmers do their live stock. The men are valued, like horses, for their superior properties—the females, for their fecundity. The infant slave is generally valued at a year's service of the mother and as she is compelled to work, three parts of the time she is breeding and nursing, planters are very attentive to this mode of enhancing the value of their estates.

The swamps and low lands are so unhealthy, that they cannot be cultivated by white persons. Here, however, the negro is compelled to work, uncovered, through the sun's meridian heat, and labor till evening, often up to his waist in water, for these lands are generally overflowed with stagnant pools; while his pampered master can barely support himself in the shade in such a relaxing atmosphere. If he be employed in the rice-grounds, he must toil all day long in soft mud, ditching and draining the ground; while to a white person such an occupation would, in a few days, prove certain death. The punishment they often undergo are inflicted with savage ferocity, and frequently at the caprice of a cruel overseer. What else can be expected from the natural brutality of man, in a country where the murder of a slave is only punished by a fine of fifty pounds, and if wilfully perpetrated, or as the law terms it, "with malice aforethought," then the fine is only doubled —but, in fact, the bloody deed, when committed, is seldom looked into . . . .

While such is the condition of slaves in South Carolina, their owners in some cases entertain such high and strict notions of what they call *honor*, and *a good name*, that duels frequently take place among them. In one of these rencounters fell the son of a departed friend of mine, and what rendered the circumstance more afflicting was, that his conduct to his antagonist was of such a nature as to preclude commiseration for his death. The story may prove a lesson worthy of remembrance.

Mr. Rutledge, a gentleman of South Carolina, of considerable property, and a member of congress, left his house, with his wife and children, on the approach of the hot months, to enjoy the salubrious air of Rhode Island. At Newport he became acquainted with the son of my respected friend, the late Doctor Senter. This young man succeeded to his father's business, and had commenced the practice of physic. Mr. Rutledge having staid at Newport as long as he had intended, returned to his home, without any suspicion to the prejudice of his new acquaintance. Soon after their departure, the young doctor likewise made his appearance in South Carolina. Without entering into the cause of this step on the part of the latter, and unwilling to wound the feelings of the survivor, suffice it to say, that the Rhode Islander was so near being detected by his injured friend, in a clandestine visit to his wife, as to owe his safety to immediate flight. Mr. Rutledge pursued, and overtook him at or near Charleston, where they fought. The guilty man fell, being badly wounded in the thigh, and he died under amputation.

o o o

Having shewn the great benefits which slave-owners derive from the labour of this miserable race of their fellow-creatures, we naturally turn our thoughts to the treatment they receive to enable them to undergo the drudgery of the field. When we see men toiling in rice and indigo grounds, which are generally overflowed with stagnant water; enduring the scorching rays of the sun, in raising tobacco, and different kinds of grain, to supply luxuries for their master's tables; we should naturally conclude that their food is of the best quality, and their raiment adapted to their respective employments. I wish any thing could be advanced to palliate the hardship of their lot—but on this subject we only find the horrors of slavery too often aggravated by the neglect of the owner, and the savage ferocity of an overseer.

An opportunity once offered, which gave me full demonstration of the treatment of negroes in North Carolina.—I had hired a small sailing boat to convey me from the island of Mattamuskeet, on Pamlico Sound; the wind proving adverse, with the appearance of an approaching summer squall, the boatman proposed to make a harbour in a small creek which he observed led to a new negro quarter belonging to Mr. Blount,° of Newburn; adding,

°This man is, at this time, a member of the house of representatives in congress for the district of Newburn, in North Carolina.

that as he was acquainted with the overseer, I might there find shelter till the weather proved favorable. This I gladly agreed to, as these summer gusts, which they call "white squalls," are often so sudden as to upset a vessel before the sails can be handed. From the head of the creek a canal had been cut to the quarter, and from thence it was intended to communicate with the Great Alligator river, for the purpose of transporting lumber, with which the country abounds, to a sea-port. For this purpose, Mr. Blount had placed there a gang of about sixty negroes, whose daily work was in water, often up to the middle, and constantly knee-deep. The overseer was a man of some information, and he gave us a hearty welcome to his log-house, which was a few hundred yards from the huts of the slaves. He said, that no human foot had trod upon the spot till his arrival with the negroes; who had penetrated about a mile into the forest with the canal, through haunts of wild beasts. There was an unusual number of children in proportion to the working slaves; and on my noticing this circumstance, the overseer replied, that but few of them belonged to the gang, being sent thither 'to be raised in safety.' From the situation of the place, there was no chance of their escaping; and being fed at a very small expence, and suffered to run wild and entirely naked, he observed, that their encreased value, when the canal was finished, would nearly defray the expence attending it. An infant slave, when born, is computed to be worth thirty or forty dollars, of course, every year increases his value, and a stout 'field fellow,' is worth three or four hundred dollars; a 'field wench' a fourth part less. He had already been two years in this desolate place, and calculated upon remaining three more before the canal would be finished.

The day of our arrival happened to be on Saturday, when the week's allowance if given out. This consisted of salt herrings, of an inferior quality, and a peck of *Indian corn in the cob*, to each, the grinding of which occupied the remainder of the day. Such was the daily food, without variation, of these wretched people, and even of this, the allowance was extremely scanty. No such luxury as salt pork, or beef, had they been indulged with for many months; and Mr. Overseer, with perfect indifference, observed, that he did not expect any fresh supply for some time after what was brought them should be consumed. A few barrels were at first allowed, by way of reconciling them to the place; and so accustomed were they to drag on this miserable existence, that I observed no repining, each receiving his pittance without a murmur. The overseer, however, took special care of himself. His residence was surrounded with turkies and fowls, and his cupboard was supplied with excellent bacon. These provisions were set before us, together with a bottle of brandy. During our repast, we were attended by a stout negro boy, entirely naked, whom the overseer had selected to be about his person. The poor fellow's attention was so riveted on the victuals, that he blundered over his employment in a manner that extorted a threat of punishment from his master, who would not attribute his momentary absence of mind to the cause from which it sprung. As soon as an opportunity offered after dinner, I cut off, unobserved, a piece of bacon, and gave it to the boy, who snatched at it in an extacy, and instantly ran off to the negro huts. On his return, I questioned him what he had done with it; when the grateful and affectionate creature replied, that he had given the morsel to his poor mother, who was sick, and could not eat her herrings. Hear this, ye pampered slave-holders! contemplate the virtues of this boy; and while you teach your own offspring to follow his example, treat his unfortunate race as human beings!

The day proving boisterous, we remained all night with the overseer. He described, with much apparent satisfaction, the means he employed to keep *his gang* under subjection, and the different modes of punishment which from time to time he inflicted on them. Some months ago, it appeared, that he missed some of his fowls; and being convinced they had been stolen by the slaves, he ordered them all into his presence, charged them with the robbery, and ordered them to point out the perpetrator. This not producing the desired effect, he threatened to flog them all, observing, that by so doing he should get hold of the thief without confession; and he actually put this threat into instant execution. The job, he continued, occupied the whole day, as he took his leisure, that it might be complete, and serve as a warning in future. Thus suffered the whole of those innocent miserable people, by way of punishing one, who might have been guilty.

The first week in the year, in this land of slavery, is a kind of fair for the disposal of negroes, some for life, and others for a limited time, by public auction, the sheriff of the county generally acting as auctioneer.

Here is often exhibited a spectacle which would soften the most obdurate heart, that had never participated in the horrid traffic. At these times slave-dealers attend from a distant part of the country, making a trade of their fellow-men. Husbands for ever separated from their wives; mothers torn from their children; brothers and sisters exchanging a last embrace, are subjects of mirth to the surrounding crowd of bidders. Indulgent nature equally formed this sable group; yet, it would seem, that while the exterior of the Ethiopian is tinged with the darkest hue, the heart of the white man is rendered callous to all the finer feelings, which are said to give him rank above the other creatures of the Almighty. Often have I witnessed negroes dragged, without regard to age or sex, to the public whipping-post, or tied up to the limb of a tree, at the will of the owner, and flogged with a cow-skin, without pity or remorse, till the ground beneath is died with the blood of the miserable sufferer. These punishments are often inflicted for an unguarded expression of the slave, while groaning under an oppressive task— for neglectiong to do homage as his master passes by—and too often to indulge private resentment or caprice. Sometimes they are fastened on a barrel, the hands and feet nearly meeting round it, are tied together; thus the breech is presented, and in this position they endure their torments. Shocking cruelties of this nature have been practised, even in the more enlightened state of New York.

º º º

Literature is yet at a low ebb in the United States. During my stay in Philadelphia, where the small portion of genius is chiefly to be found, I heard of very few literary characters, superior to the political scribblers of the day. Joseph Dennie, and Mr. Brown, of that city, with Mr. Fessenden, of Boston, are men of genius. The former is editor of a literary periodical paper, called "The Port-Folio," a publication which would do credit to the most polished nation in Europe. Its cotemporary prints make politics their principal object; the Port-Folio embraces the belles lettres, and cultivates the arts and sciences. The editor, when he touches upon the state of his country, speaks in the cause of federalism; and, from his great abilities, he is consequently obnoxious to the ruling party. The government had long endeavored to control the federal prints, and had already ineffectually prosecuted some of the editors. At length, they denounced Mr. Dennie, who was indicted and tried at Philadelphia, for publishing the following political strictures:—

"A democracy is scarcely tolerable at any period of national history. Its omens are always sinister, and its powers are unpropitious. With all the lights of experience blazing before our eyes, it is impossible not to discern the futility of this form of government. It was weak and wicked in Athens. It was bad in Sparta, and worse in Rome. It has been tried in France, and has terminated in despotism. It was tried in England, and rejected with the utmost loathing and abhorrence. It is on its trial here, and the issue will be civil war, desolation, and anarchy. No wise man but discerns its imperfections; no good man but shudders at its miseries; no honest man but proclaims its fraud; and no brave man but draws his sword against its force. The institution of a scheme of polity, so radically contemptible and vicious, is a memorable example of what the villainy of some men can devise, the folly of others receive, and both establish, in despite of reason, reflection, and sensation."

This paragraph was copied into the federal papers throughout the union, and it became extremely obnoxious to the democratic party. The trial greatly interested all ranks; but, after much time being consumed, and much party spirit evinced by the contending advocates, Mr. Dennie was acquitted. He gives a sketch of the trial in the Port-Folio, and thus concludes:— "The causes of this prosecution, the spirit of the times, and the genius of the commonwealth, must be obvious to every observer. The editor inscribes *vici* on the white shield of his innocence, but is wholly incapable of vaunting at the victory!" . . .

Printing and bookselling have of late years been extended to the most remote parts of the country. Several newspapers are printed in Kentucky; and almost every town of more than a few score houses, in every state, has a printing-office, from which the news is disseminated. There is no tax whatever on the press, and consequently every owner of one can print a newspaper with little risk, among a people who are all politicans. These sheets are the utmost limits of literature in most country towns, and they furnish ample food for disputation. Several hundred different newspapers are daily distributed by the public mail, in all parts, to subscribers, at the small charge of one or two cents, at most, for postage;° but printers exchange their papers with each other, by that mode, free of any charge. I have often seen a printer receive as many newspapers by one mail, as would fill the room of several hundred letters.

○ ○ ○

The English have not yet adopted the enlightened custom of consigning their dead to the parent earth, like some fanatic sects in America, in fields and gardens, without a burial service, or even a prayer. . . .

The truth is, that no people upon earth make a greater parade in the burial of the dead. . . . On such occasions what they call "warnings," is the day before, or early in the morning, given of the funeral. This is a notice or warning of the event in writing, which is regularly carried from house to house, and shewn or read to some of the family. Some hours previous to the procession being put in motion, the neighbors assemble, and the tenement of the deceased is soon filled; to whom wine, punch, toddy, and cakes, are handed round. During this time some dissenting minister is frequently haranguing those within the house, in what is called a funeral sermon, while the great body of those who mean to swell the procession gather together on the outside. In some places they have a vehicle which may be

---

°The post-towns in the United States, and which are rapidly increasing, in the year 1804 amounted to 1,159.

called a hearse, but as rude in comparison to that which diverted the Yankee in London, as their stage-waggons are to the elegant and comfortable public coaches met with on the high roads of Britain. It is in fact, as I have already said, a kind of black box on wheels, and sometimes decorated, not with nodding plumes of feathers, but with miserable daubings, meant to represent human sculls and crossed thigh-bones. This vehicle is, however, seldom to be found; carrying dead bodies upon men's shoulders, the most usual mode, is certainly attended with less expence.

The sermon ended, which generally consumes an hour, and sometimes two, the procession, if the subject of the ceremony has died rich, is conducted in the following order:—First comes the undertaker, in a scarf and hatband of black silk or white linen, according to the state of the deceased, then follow, side by side, the parson and the doctor, personages deemed necessary on those occasions, and who are also complimented with the insignia of mourning; the other clergy of the town; the body, when no hearse or chaise wheels are used, carried by four inferior republicans, without the smallest trappings of woe, while the pall is borne by six of their superiors, in hatbands and scarfs similar to those of the parson and doctor; but which are generally put over a drab or other coloured coat, presenting a motley view; then follow the inhabitants, two and two, beginning with those who arrogate to themselves in this land of liberty a superiority over the others, until the whole is brought up by the slaves of the deceased. These processions, such is the usage, are sometimes the whole length of a large town; and the surviving relatives are gratified in proportion to the number of attendants.

The interment of inferior persons is also generally attended with a procession. Instead, however, of scarfs and hatbands, the mourners content themselves with a piece of black ribbon or crape, tied round the arm above the elbow; and on these occasions, the parading of the priest and the doctor, for reasons which need no explanation, is omitted, and the corpse is committed to the grave without the reading of a prayer, or the singing of a psalm.

9. The Problem of Luxury

Nothing seems more ludicrous than the frenzied outcry against the establishment in 1785 of a Tea Assembly meeting in Boston every other week for dancing and card playing. Yet, to many Americans during the Critical Period, the founding of this "Sans Souci Club," as it was called, was no small laughing matter, for the issue at stake seemed to be nothing less than the kind of society America was creating. Only an appreciation of the classical terms in which eighteenth-century Americans discussed the problems of social character and an understanding of the underlying social resentments against the emergence of a fast and pretentious young set in post-Revolutionary Boston society can make proper sense of the debate. The public uproar continued for nearly two months and involved some of the leading figures of Boston, including Samuel Adams, writing as "The Observer," Benjamin Austin as "Candidus," and twenty-year-old Harrison Gray Otis as "Sans Souci." The issue soon became entangled in the 1785 campaign for the Massachusetts governorship and foreshadowed the eventual split in Massachusetts between federalism and antifederalism.

The Sans Souci Club

THE OBSERVER, NO. VII

Friday, January 14, 1785

If there ever was a period wherein reason was bewildered, and stupified by dissipation and extravagance, it is surely the present. Did ever effeminacy with her languid train, receive a greater welcome in society than at this day. New amusements are invented—new dissipations are introduced,

Boston *Massachusetts Centinel,* January 15, 19, 22, 1785.
Boston *Independent Chronicle,* January 20, 27, 1785.

to lull and enervate those minds already too much softened, poisoned and contaminated, by idle pleasures, and foolish gratifications. We are exchanging prudence, virtue and economy, for those glaring spectres luxury, prodigality and profligacy. We are prostituting all our glory as a people; for new modes of pleasure, ruinous in their expences, injurious to virtue, and totally detrimental to the well being of society.

Did we consult the history of Athens and Rome, we should find that so long as they continued their frugality and simplicity of manners, they shone with superlative glory; but no sooner were effeminate refinements introduced amongst them, than they visibly fell from whatever was elevated and magnanimous, and became feeble and timid, dependent, slavish and false. Will not the corroborating testimony of succeeding nations teach us a similar lesson. Does not reason whisper in our ears that the fate of preceeding ones will certainly be ours? Say my country. Why do you thus suffer all the intemperances of Great-Britain to be fostered in our bosom in all their vile luxuriance? Now is the time to prune the branches 'ere they shoot forth into a strength which cannot be subdued;—'ere the poppy—Pleasure, has too far lulled reason asleep or the poison of dissipation has choaked even the latent spark of virtue.

You who were foremost in defence of your liberties, and whose public virtues have raised the standard of freedom on a once wild uncultivated land! Let not your names which would be otherwise handed as virtuous, brave and good, to ages yet unborn, be thus shaded with infamy. Be not behind your finer states° in extirpating vice, however marked with the epithet of polite.

The stage, which is not permitted among us, might under proper regulations, be a school of morality, but gaming, stript of all the nobleness which attended its first institution, when a parsley garland, or a pine wreath, fully satisfied the desires, is now countenanced by characters, who but a short time since would have blushed at the name of a gamster. But enervated minds by their weaknesses, are subject to every excess, and are guilty of extravagancies directly opposite each other. Suitable recreations, such as do not glaringly tend to levity of behaviour—to the introduction of gaming, and in short to the destruction of everything good or virtuous—the cares, the fatigues of the world require. Rational amusements it would cer-

---

°When the Tea Assembly was introduced at New York, the populace were so enraged they went in a body, burst open the doors, threw water on the floor, and obliged them to break up.

tainly be irrational to deny:—But an Assembly so totally repugnant to virtue, as in its very name (*Sans Souci, or free and easy*) to banish the idea by throwing aside every necessary restraint—those being esteemed the politest, who are the most careless;—and the most genteel and accomplished, who can, like the figures at a masquerade, mix in each scene, however devoid of delicacy, it is therefore to be hoped the citizens of a free republic, will unanimously exert themselves to give a check to so injurious an institution.

TO THE OBSERVER

The *Man who lives under a government whose Constitution is advanced as near perfection as the state of human affairs will permit, and strives, on any occasion, to violate that Constitution is an enemy to his country; and he, whose malignancy of heart fabricates falsehoods to answer his pernicious purposes, is both in the view of Men and Angels a detestable villain.*

Within both these descriptions of character your seventh number published last Saturday, demonstrates you to be concluded. You there manifestly endeavour to attain for your own vicious will the force of legislative authority, and aim at exciting a rabble mob *to carry into effect your fell designs. You are desirous,* because you are pleased to fear that a harmless legal Assembly will hereafter prove baneful to the Community, *to attack and wrest from your fellow subjects, several of this |sic| natural rights never taken away, or even abridged, by the laws of society; and that too by violent measures that reflect supreme disgrace on any government which suffers them.*

You have also published, as truths, the most egregious falsehoods, and with their assistance, basely attempted to brand with infamy the most spotless and respectable characters among us. You have also with the most niggardly meanness, and to your eternal condemnation, compared a collection of your most virtuous and irreproachable country-women, the boast of America, and "chaste as the isicicle that hangs on Diana's Temple," to the most lewd and profligate of females, lately to the honor of New-York, removed from Canvass-Town (not by a mob) *but* by the executive power under due warrants and authority. *The tea party, composed by Gentlemen and Ladies of that city, was dissolved by their own inclinations, without the interposition of any persons.*

You have stigmatized our Tea Assembly (which is not termed a Sans Souci) *as "totally repugnant to virtue, banishing the very idea by throwing aside every necessary restraint. Those being thought most polite who are the most careless—and the most genteel and accomplished, who can, like figures*

*at a masquerade, mix in each scene however devoid of Delicacy." This may
be its complexion to the jaundiced eyes of your envy and malice, but hold
the mirror to the view of truth and candour, and it appears a company
regulated with propriety, governed by decency, and observant of the nicest
and most scrupulous laws of delicacy. A company whose whole deportment
bespeaks purity of mind and manners in the highest degree—evinces such
a portion of republican virtue, as places the inhabitants of this town (here
beheld) on a par with the most celebrated either of Sparta or Lacedaemon.*

*We still boast, contradicting your scandalous insinuation, as great heroick
manliness, and bravery of soul at this moment as could be claimed at any
period while the "standard of liberty was raising on this once wild and uncultivated land;" and that* virtuously energetic spirit, which you aver has
become enervated (should your vile counsels be adopted; by the worthless
and degenerate sons of Boston) will, doubt it not, flash forth in glory to
your and their utter terror and dismay, confounding you with the effulgence
of its brightness. *A Bostonian*

FOR THE CENTINEL

Messrs. Printers,

A Writer in your last number who stiles himself "Observer" has obtruded
sentiments upon the publick which must excite the indignation and
abhorrence of every virtuous citizen. The members of the little Society, so
peculiarly the object of his malevolence, are bound by the justice which they
owe themselves, to repel his invidious suggestions. The members of the
community at large are bound by the more sacred league of patriotism, to
unveil the danger of his principles—to expose their seditious tendency, and
to stamp them with a common and indelible seal of infamy. This flaming
Tribune of the people has proceeded to an extreme, whither none of the host
of scriblers since the revolution, have dared to lead the way. He has asserted
the expediency of a popular insurrection, he has expressly advised his fellow
citizens to take arms and by a gross and wilful fiction, he has exhibited the
conduct of the inhabitants of New-York, as a precedent to authorize this
odious measure.—So daring and detestable an attempt to establish the
government of a mob, has not been made in this capital, since the downfal
of the "Cosonian faction." The volatile, flashing meteors that have appeared
in the political Hemisphere since that period, may have at one time scorched
an enemy, at another, have consumed a party; but this baleful comet seems
destined to involve the community in a general conflagration. Had this son
of sedition been nurtured among his admired Romans, in any virtuous period
of their Republick, a discovery of similar designs upon their liberty, would

have cost him his life. Neither the dignity of the senators, nor the robe of the patrician had availed him, but like the elder Cassius, he had been thrown from the Tarpeian rock, and his name had long since stood recorded in the sordid annals of treason and rebellion. But his principles as a citizen, need no further comment. I take my leave of the man, and for a while consider the writer. In this capacity he indeed appears a *"glaring spectre."* He refers us to Roman and Athenian histories, in order to be convinced of the *new and wonderful position,* that luxury is fatal to a free nation. To the laborious compilers of these histories, the class of writers to which this man belongs, is chiefly indebted. They have furnished an endless variety of precendents, which serve to support an endless variety of opinions. The most obvious maxims in politicks, and the most trivial incidents in domestic life, must be warranted by a decree of the Areopagus, or by the successful experience of a Roman matron. The general application of the Greek and Roman stories to every casual occurrence, is somewhat singular. The same principle that might induce a Senate to enact a sumptuary law, would justify our Observer in overthrowing a card table. The same causes that might prompt a conqueror to direct the course of a river, and deluge an entire province, would animate our hero to pour hot water on a drawing-room. The sentence of Cato overturned the battlements of Carthage; the voice of the Observer already rattles through the china of the Tea assembly. I am not, Sirs, by any means disposed to deny that luxury is pernicious in every government; nor that Rome and Athens felt its effects, but our Observer must give me leave to inform him that the restless intrigues of disappointed ambition, and the seditious speeches of their popular leaders, produced more important calamities in those Republics, than the spoils of Syria in the one, or the riches of Persia in the other. To exhibit the Tea-assembly in a more odious view, the Observer has been pleased to dubb it, with an appelation, which it never yet assumed. He then by a most pitiful conclusion, infers the depravity of the institution from the pretended import of its name. This, I think is hardly fair, I am sure it is not logical.—Words, says a great man, are the signs of his ideas, by whom they are used. The supposition of a natural connection between names and realities, is a copious source of error. Admitting therefore, that "*Sans Souci*" was the proper name of the Tea-assembly, I know not by what licence the Observer extends his construction of these terms beyond their literal meaning; in themselves, they are harmless, but if he can suppose them connected with vicious ideas in the mind of every person belonging to that society, he must then conclude the metropolis to be already arrived to the last stage of vice and dissipation. In this case one would think it behoved him peaceably to yield to the tide, lest he should be at length carried away by the torrent. If the manners of his fellow citizens are too corrupt, they will not hesitate to raise a subscription to support their virtuous Censor in a voluntary exile. It is intimated by this sagacious writer, that a theatre might be rendered subservient to the purposes of morality. Mr. Addison, as I remember, in one of his Spectators, proposed a system of stage morality; he however thought himself unequal to the task of composing it; may we not think ourselves happy in the superior genous of the Observer, who appears almost ready to compleat the plan. —With reluctance, Sirs have I devoted an hour to remark upon this publication; it has no other claim upon my attention, but what it derives from its novelty and enormity. The Observer may now proceed in his splendid career, without further molestation from the writer of this reply. Neither my leisure or inclination allow me to descend to an examination of the libels of a News-Paper. The subscribers to the Tea-assembly will never suffer this Observer to enjoy the malicious pleasure of obstructing their innocent amusement. The same decorum will continue to preside the same resolution against gaming will not fail to influence them; while the Observer in some sequestered corner, broods over the virtues of the ancient Republics, and pines upon the contemplation of pleasures which he is not qualified to enjoy. I bid him an eternal adieu, with the question of the Poet. *Cur in theatrum, Cato severe, venisti?*   *Sans Souci*

TO THE OBSERVER

You have been pleased, Sir, to set yourself up as Censor of the age, and in that capacity, have attacked with more zeal than prudence, an amusement lately instituted, in order to pass away a few of the gloomy evenings of winter. I wish that the tenor of your late publication had shewn that you was possessed of age and experience sufficient to command that respect which is due to the office you have assumed: But I am to imagine that both are wanting; for it is almost impossible that a man who has liv'd long in the world can be so ignorant as you seem to be of the government of the human heart. What is the method by which you propose to rule it?—Great criticiser of our morals! Is it not violence—the first resort of ignorance and arbitrary will. Are you the guardians of our city, and propose to one part of the inhabitants to embroil themselves with the other—to endeavour to break the amiable bands of harmony and friendship, and to blow up the dire flames of discord and fanaticism, perhaps to embrue their hands in each other's blood; for know that force by force will be repelled; but God forbid that there should be any more such over rigid people as the Observer. I owe no man a farthing more than I can pay this minute—have I not then a right to spend some part of the fruits of my industry to procure amusements most agreeable to myself, whilst I do not act contrary to the laws of my country, or so as to injure my neighbour. To what end do we toil, if not to promote our ease, and to procure an exemption from labour; for my part I think it is better to die at once than for years, and without relaxing, to be a slave to what is called our interest. Let misers enjoy the supreme rational pleasure of counting over their hoards of money, whilst their meagre, haggard looks denote extreme poverty. Ask the naturally poor, the laborious tradesman and mechanick, whose living depends upon the circulation of cash, of what advantage the existence of such virtuous men is in the world; for such I imagine the Observer calls virtuous men who are most fortunate in getting money, and most careful to keep it; but surely those, whose follies, if you please to call them so, contribute to the maintenance of the majority of mankind, have as much right to stand candidates for the palm of virtue. Men are not born like blank sheets of paper, ready to receive any impression, but virtue and vice, lie latent in their nature until time brings them into action, and from chance receive their form: if you allow this, you are not to learn the vicious never want opportunities to indulge their passions. At the Tea Assembly propriety of conduct is sufficiently provided for by the presence of ladies of the first character: As for its being an encouragement to gaming, I cannot consider it as such; this is a vice so generally disapproved of that it is not to be supposed that a man who is addicted to it, wishes to have a number of spectators of his own ruin; he can do it more conveniently at clubs and private parties, and I know not how the Observer will prevent this, but by reviving the Corfu Bell.

For the example you bring of the conduct of the inhabitants of New-York, you have grossly misrepresented it, or I have been exceedingly misinformed: Instead of attributing it to conscience, which you would insinuate was the cause of the riot, it was quite another matter, and no ways connected, being entirely political. The subscribers to the Sans Souci were chiefly composed of that set of people formerly stiled tories, and had remained in the country under sanction of the law; the people at large not being able so soon to forget their animosity occasioned by the distresses of war, and urged on by a few who were excluded from subscribing, committed an action which is a disgrace to any civilized State.

I am sorry your eagerness for the welfare of our countrymen has led you into such an error, and was happy to receive such lessons as came from your pen, while you kept yourself within the bounds of advice; but you have encouraged the spirit of faction once more to rage among us, and by endeavouring, by other means than is allowed to the philosophy you taught, to correct what you call a vice, would make them guilty of the greatest enormities! How admirably well does this agree with your intention of making us more perfect and happy. You refer us to Rome and Athens for examples by which we ought to conduct ourselves: Every age has its great men, but rapine, assassinations, and the basest treachery have sullied the glory of their noblest characters, in the times of their greatest *simplicity*. Aratus the famous Achaean General, who for 33 years had been the strongest opposer of tyranny that lived in that age of freedom, was so only because he acquired more honour than he could by other means, for the moment he saw the probability of a rival, he sold his country, and all Greece to crush the rising fame of Cleomenes.—This is not the only instance, but history furnishes us with them in abundance, that when their favourite passions were opposed, there was no excess of vice that ever cursed the human race, by which they would not defend them. I wish not to deprive them of the merit of having given birth to men of unspotted reputation, but while we boast of a Washington, and many other truly virtuous men, I cannot think the ancients were more deserving than the present age, nor can I think that you would wish us to exchange our amusements for those of Rome—for even the Romans your favourites had amusements from their first existence, and whilst savage barbarity shall stain the historick page, their gladiators will appear the most shocking to nature.

If you wish to separate commerce from luxury you expect an impossibility; let us break the bands of society, refuse all connection with the arts and sciences which live under the patronage of commerce and retire to the woods; let us learn of the savages *simplicity* of life, to forget humanity, and cut each other's throats without remorse, and even with satisfaction, for the inestimable reward of a garland of parsley, or a wreath of pine; or else, let every one who cries shame upon the manners of the times, begin with correcting his own, let him preserve himself immaculate and free from them, we shall then have a speedy and through reformation.

January 17, 1785   *One of a Number*

FOR THE INDEPENDENT CHRONICLE
Messi'rs. Adams & Nourse,

When a writer, under the garb of patriotism, and with a pretence of supporting virtue, comes forward with violent assertions for the base purpose of misleading, and strings out declamatory periods, with the professed design of rousing public indignation either against an individual or a collection of citizens, his misrepresentations call for exposure, and the man himself ought to meet that resentment which he has laboured to turn against the innocent. I am led to these remarks by a paper called the

OBSERVER, No. 7, in last Saturday's Centinel, and will, if you can find room in your useful press, endeavour to point out some of the author's errors, and expose the malignancy of his inferences, which he doubtless intended should lead to some kind of outrageous acts.

"There never was a period," (exclaims this well-informed Demagogue) "when reason was more bewildered and stupified by dissipation, nor was there ever a day when effeminacy, with her languid train, met a greater welcome in society. New amusements are invented, and new dissipations are introduced," &c.—Now, Mess'rs. Printers, I wish to enquire if any person remembers the season when the reverse of this assertion was so true. An assembly holden once in a fortnight, to beguile the tedious evenings of December, and to cheat rough winter of some of its horrors, is all the public amusement this large city knows of, excepting a very harmless meeting, which, though decent even to dullness, has alarmed this furious guardian of the State's morality. His pedantic reference to Greek and Roman manners, is totally inapplicable to an American Commonwealth. The period in the Roman story which he adduces, was indisputably the age of Hardihood; but what was the main object of their inexorable sternness, but to enable those mighty Plunderers to invade the territories of their neighbours, as well as those of distant nations, and to subjugate all who lay within the reach of their violence. Roman virtue, scrutinized to its motive, and measured by the standard of humanity and reason, will be found seldom to rise above senseless ferocity. But even these godlike men, these mighty Romans, at the most conspicuous aera |era | of their savage virtue, had public spectacles and city amusements, not only instituted by the Senate or Consuls, but defrayed out of the treasury of the Republic; and at the most elevated epoch of her history, when learning, wit, philosophy and national glory was at the height, elegant amusement and public exhibitions at Rome, were still more common. As well might the *Observer* quote the Jaggas of Africa, as call our attention to the Romans. Our situation, views and principles are extremely dissimilar. The objects of the one were conquest, and unlimited domination; Ours Peace, *Liberty* and Safety.

But this writer is not content with striving to mislead by false historic deductions; he presumes to tell the world, that there is an assembly in this town publicly resorted to by both sexes, "*so totally repugnant to* VIRTUE, *as in its very name to banish that idea.*" In what quarter of the town so infamous a meeting convenes, is known only, I believe, to this invenomed scribler. If he means the *Tea Assembly*, which meets every other week, for the purpose of promoting decent manners, polite attentions, and preserving our young men from being ruined at taverns, by leading them into the company of the young, the innocent, and the amiable of the other sex, in whose refined converse they must find an additional tie to bind them to their country, then, whatever he has insinuated is *false, malicious* and *libellous*, and his attempt to excite a tumult with the design of suppressing so laudable an institution, deserves and ought to meet with marked contempt.

There are some Beings in all communities who are cursed with such a callousness of fibre, that no refinements can move them; who consider all improvements as innovations on the principles of their grandfathers, and that all those who wish to be either wiser or happier than their ancestors, are heretical upstarts and degenerate citizens. Last Summer, when a few American oaks were set out on the sides of the Mall, a miserable *Observer* remarked, that the Common had for a hundred years served people very well to walk on, without any expence; that the money then expending was useless and ante-rebublican, and that he could plainly trace in that luxurious walk (only a little well-cemented gravel, reader) the outlines of this country's ruin. Patriots of this stamp, can only be laughed at; but when a malicious partizan calls upon the populace to throw mud, and breaks into your house to *scatter water on your floor,"* because you are dancing upon it, it is full time for the free and the peaceable to be prepared to oppose some to such daring outrage.

Crito

Jan. 20, 1785

THE OBSERVER, NO. VIII
Friday, January 21, 1785

> A soul immortal, spending all her Fires,
> Wasting her strength in *strenuous Idleness*,
> Thrown into *Tumult*, raptur'd or alarm'd,
> At ought this scene can threaten, or *indulge*,
> Resembles *Ocean* into tempest wrought,
> To waft a Feather, or to drown a Fly.
>   Young.

The several pieces, directed to the Observer in the last Centinel, oblige the writer of that paper, to reply: That a true idea of the Institution may be laid before the publick, and that it may appear the author has not published, "as truths, the most egregious falsehoods" he will state only undeniable facts, and from the serious and well disposed part of the community, who regard its good order and morals, he has not a doubt he shall receive applause.

From the printed rules of the Tea Assembly he observes, Gentlemen of nineteen, and ladies of fifteen years of age, are admitted;—that the rooms at Concert-Hall, are opened at 6 o'clock, and CARD TABLES provided for EIGHTY GENTLEMEN and LADIES;—*Musick, Dancing, Tea, Coffee, Chocolate, Cards, Wine, Negus, Punch* and *Lemonade*, make up the entertainment; therefore eat, drink and be merry. Certainly it is not proper for such young people, to be from under their parents or guardians care; especially at such late hours, unless they are proof against every temptation. This Assembly is pregnant with fatal consequences, by heads of families leading the way to vice, and setting a publick example by their appearance at the gaming table; from them we have a right to expect better things. If private card parties are esteemed prejudicial, which they are by many persons, are not publick examples of gaming of serious consequence to the people among whom they are permitted? A tavern keeper is not suffered by law to permit gaming in his house; shall then a publick institution be approbated when it derogates from the law of the land? Is not this a precedent at which we have cause to shudder. Those who play frequently get an itch for it, and although they may begin small, will play more largely as they are more attached to it. The gamester by being fortunate this night, is desirous to risk again:—Or by being unfortunate the last night, again plays in hopes of regaining it;—thus he is led on step by step until he has imbibed such a desire for gaming, as never to be easy but when at play. Have ye not cause to blush ye fathers who are thus forfeiting your claim to the parental name, by countenancing an institution that may issue in the rule of your children? Suffer me for a few moments to lead you to the door of the Hall:—There see arranged a number of card tables, seated at which are many of those who are to succeed our present rulers. When these young gentlemen shall have stepped into office, from their education, and present conduct, we may expect laws against gaming, will be repealed, and such as will favour their pleasures, be substituted in their room—Melancholy prospect this. Your daughters fall equally under the censure of the serious, by thus promoting publick gaming, which is fatal in its tendency to society. Can a thoughtful man see this without remorse? Can he reflect on the examples thus publickly set, and not determine to restrain and caution those immediately under his inspection?

The writers of Wednesday have taken up the matter intirely wrong with respect to the Observer's wishing to encourage a mob: He detests the idea, as much as those whose only weapons are satire, and abuse: He only wished to raise in the minds of the serious part of the community an idea that, the Tea Assembly will be pernicious in its consequences, seeing it promotes *publick gaming*, and is destructive of the good order of families, by turning day into night, and night into day. The Observer did not wish to suggest that the characters which attended the Tea Assembly are at this early period of its institution, arrived at that carelessness, and inattention, which the nature of it is likely to introduce.

ONE OF A NUMBER, says, "I owe no man a farthing more than I can pay this minute." However independent this writer may be, he will certainly allow that every youth of nineteen is not equally so: But admit every individual is in the same happy independent state with himself, he then says "have I not a right to spend some part of the fruits of my industry to procure amusements most agreeable to myself, whilst I do not act contrary to the laws of my country, or so as to injure my neighbour?" That he has I allow, if this be the case; but I can scarcely think this writer ignorant of the law of this Commonwealth against *publick gaming* or believe that he will contradict that at the Tea Assembly it is carried on.

With regard to the permission of a theatre among us, the Observer is happy to find, by *Sans Souci*, that his idea of the stage is exactly the same with the great Addison's.

The writer of the first piece, in Wednesday's Centinel, says, "The affair respecting New-York, is a gross and willful fiction,"—that is in plain English, *you lie, Sir*. In this the "Gentleman appears entirely unshackled by the restraints of *ceremony*, and *feelingly alive* to those *polite attentions*, which can alone preserve ease from sinking into negligence, and smiling mirth from deviating into *noisy illiberal humour*." This is a striking proof that the Tea Assembly is a school of refinement and politeness.

The second writer observes, that the conduct of the inhabitants of New York has been grossly misrepresented, or he has been exceedingly misinformed, and just before throws out that thou'd the publick take it in hand here, they will be repelled force by force! This foolish youth—this hero of nineteen, by this threat proves the necessity of his being under parental government. And as to the last writer he is like those incorrect unintelligible story tellers; who having got scent of a matter, runs himself out of breath to tell it abroad, without knowing where to begin, how to go on, or what he would be after. For the Observer's part he supposes him to be a mad man, and would advise his friends to send him to Bedlam, least he should do some injury. In short if the numerous writers in favour of the Tea Assembly have nothing better to advance in its behalf than what has already been offered to the publick, it would have been more to their honour to have let it alone. The Observer cannot, however, help applying to them the following expression of Calvin, "I KNOW BY THEIR ROARING I HAVE HIT THEM RIGHT."

Jan. 27, 1785

Messieurs Adams and Nourse,

The piece in the Centinel, signed an *Observer*, has raised the resentment of many individuals, and they have, with a zeal of rancour and resentment, attacked the observations made by this writer. With a most vehement enthusiasm: Not pretending to justify the Observer in all his sentiments, I shall not commence an advocate in his behalf, but shall deliver my thoughts with a diffidence becoming a person who is *opposed* to an institution, altho' considered as very *innocent*, and even laudable, by a very respectable number of my townsmen. As the Tea-Assembly is now become a subject which has interested the attention of many writers, I shall consider my sentiments as offered to a body of gentlemen who are not so fixed on their amusements, as to admit only what may be advanced in *vindication* of their institution, without giving any attention to what may be said in *opposition*; I have too great an opinion of their candour to suppose the contrary, and shall therefore presume my observations will be read with that same *impartiality* with which they are wrote.

My ideas respecting the Tea-Assembly, although they are not carried to the great length with the Observer, as "banishing every idea of virtue, and throwing aside every restraint," yet I cannot but view it as a measure which, if pursued, *will in time* produce the most alarming consequences. I am sensible that the idea of *alarming consequences* are received as the meer whim of a stern republican's brain, and are sentiments which are considered as *cant* and *inconclusive*; but however they may be thus viewed at first blush, yet they are sentiments which *will stand the test* of the most determined opposers.

I am not one of those who judge on every subject by certain *prejudiced* rules; I have so much candor that I can see new measures introduced, and many old things done away; I can observe many sentiments which have prevailed from the days of our fathers, entirely blasted and rooted out; yet however liberal I may be in general, I cannot but consider *maturely* before I explode their opinions, and with a respect which is due to their many virtues, I consign them with *reluctance* to the *grave of oblivion*.

On these principles I shall consider the late institution of our Tea-Assembly: If it is a measure which can only be objected to on the contracted sentiment that *our fathers did not practice it*, I should declare most fervently in its favour; but if on mature consideration we find it is a measure which at this *particular crisis* is considered by a very respectable MAJORITY of the community, as a very *dangerous* and *destructive situation*, we ought, from every principle of *modesty* and *propriety*, to halt between *two opinions*, til we have carefully attended to what may be said on the subject.

"*Circumstances alter cases*," is a sentiment which is universally known; what may appear innocent, and even laudable, in one person, may be viewed in a very different light in another; what one nation or set of men might practice with impunity, would be with the greatest propriety judged as most pernicious and destructive in another; not therefore to enlarge on this sentiment, I would draw this conclusion, that an *institution* which may be *laudable* (at least not unexceptionable) in the long established Courts of *Europe*, may, by being early *introduced* among the *infant States of America*, be attended with the most fatal consequences.

We, my countrymen, have a character to *establish*, which must become respectable in the world by our well regulated government, national manners, and our attention to those *republican principles* which gave us our INDEPENDENT STATION: The stability of our credit, depend on our practicing these *first principles*, as they are the *chief corner stones* on which rest the *honor, reputation* and *security* of these States; the line of conduct to us, therefore, is *plain* and *certain*; we have too long been engaged in a severe conflict, not to know *how much depend* on our strict observance of these principles, which first gave rise to our opposition.

I shall consider the arguments which have been offered in favour of the Tea-Assembly; and shall observe on those by a person under the signature of "*One of a Number*;" He says, "every one has a right to spend some part of the *fruits* of his industry, to procure amusements agreeable to himself, while he does not act contrary to the laws of his country, or injure his neighbour." This is an argument in theory no one will pretend to deny; but is very flimsy when applied in support of any institution which is thought *dangerous to society*; for if *only those* attended which were spending the "fruits of their industry," this might be some palliation of the measure; but while the institution will admit ALL which make a *respectable appearance* in life, the danger lies that the greater part which attend the amusement, will not spend solely the "*fruits*," but even the *seeds* of their industry: The fault therefore is, in not making a just distinction between *the abilities* of the individuals which compose a publick society of this kind, and the *natural tendency* of the generality to partake of these entertainments from *fashionable motives*, when perhaps their *circumstances* will not justify their continuing them. This is also more fatal in a *republican government*, when all the individuals of the State are so nearly on an equality, for while we are so apparently on a level as to circumstances, each one is for keeping up that *publick appearance*, and will, without considering *consequences*, pursue the amusement, tho' inevitably to the *ruin of their fortunes*, and *misery of their families*: The institution, therefore, cannot be justified on the principle, "that a man can spend his money as he pleases;" for though this independent gentleman may claim this right, within his *private sphere*, yet a *public amusement* may prove fatal to a community, and may with propriety be *supprest as such*.

Another argument is, "That a person who is addicted to gaming, will do it more readily at *Clubs* and *private parties*, than at a *publick assembly*" This can by no means be considered as conclusive. "Examples are more forceable than precepts." Can any one pretend to say seriously, that a *publick institution*, where is practiced card playing, is not *more likely* to introduce YOUTH and others to the practice of *gaming*, than meerly the common herding of a few *despicable characters* over a bottle at a *Tavern* or *Coffee-House*: Human nature is not so depraved; all *introductions* to vice must be first gilded with the glittering outside of *fashion*, and when it has become *established* on this principle, we pursue it with a peculiar relish, and are apt to deceive ourselves by supposing that we are practicing only the *polite amusements* of life, and do not feel their *baneful tendency*, till the *consequences* of our imprudence too loudly call on us to refrain from them.

I suppose this town never has been so free from the vice of gaming as at this day; particularly among the youth at public houses: none but the lowest characters now meet for this purpose, so that but very little mischief is to be dreaded from this quarter: But when *card playing* is instituted as a *public amusement*; when the parade of the card rooms are heightened by the *politeness* and *gentility* of the assembly, and when all around wear the pleasing countenance of *pleasure*; these are allurements *too powerful* to be viewed with indifference, and the gentlemen of the society pay but a *poor compliment* to themselves, if they think that all this *etiquete* and *stile* are not more *inticing*, than an evening spent in a *back chamber* of a tavern, among a group of wretches as despicable in their *characters*, as their PRACTICE is destructive.

Another observation made by this writer signed "One of a Number," is rather curious; he supposes "Commerce will inevitably introduce luxury," and seem to think we must support *luxury* as a kind of AID DE CAMP to commerce; otherways, he says, "we must refuse all connections with the *arts* and *sciences*, and live in savage simplicity; cut one anothers throats, forget humanity." &c. &c. What a long train of misery are here pictured? and all this dreadful calamity will arise unless we nourish luxury as the grand cement of "the bands of society." I could hardly suppose this writer was in earnest; he has broached quite a new doctrine, viz. *commerce intro-*

duces luxury; and still stranger, LUXURY SUPPORTS THE ARTS AND SCIENCES:" bravo! Rome, Athens, and all ye cities of renown, whence came your fall?

So far from mentioning commerce as any reason why we should support luxury, I should not desire to have a more forcible argument to oppose it; particularly the present situation of our commerce; we are too sensible of the embarrassments of our trade; the great difficulty we find in discharging our arrears in Europe; how perplex'd we are to fulfil our engagements even among ourselves; the general complaint of our want of cash; the low profits of merchandise; the slowness of sales; and on the other hand the largeness of our debts; the demands of our creditors; the interest daily increasing the already too ponderous sum; All these considerations are more powerful arguments for us to DESIST, rather than for to pursue the measure, by preaching up a poor cant observation, that commerce will inevitably introduce luxury.

A writer under the signature of CRITO, I should suppose was not a member of the society, as he speaks of the institution in terms not the most exalted; he says it is "a very harmless meeting, *decent even to dullness;*" If he means "the Tea Assembly, which meets every other week for the purpose of promoting decent manners, polite attentions, and preserving our young men from being ruined at taverns, by leading them into the company of the young, the innocent and amiable of the other sex;" surely if he means *this Assembly,* he must be "curs'd with a callousness of fibre," that amid so "laudable an assembly and refin'd converse," he should even admit the idea of "DULNESS." Certainly, Mr. Crito, you mistake, if you suppose, an institution calculated to "cheat rough winter of its horrors, and beguile the tedious evenings of December," can with propriety be called "dull," and insipid:—You will therefore, Sir, please to "reverse your assertion."

The writer signed *Sans Souci,* seems armed with the whole force of HISTORY; he appears like a *self-confident* champion, shrouded within the security of his *own valour,* and declares he shall "not reply to any observations made on his remarks;" it is best therefore to leave this HERO of literature to enjoy the full GLORY of his own sentiments.

Before I conclude, I cannot but observe on the many severe reflections cast on a CERTAIN GENTLEMAN among us, who is supposed to be the writer of the Observer' as a friend to the Independence of this country; as a REPUBLICAN who ever means to act on such principles; I cannot but feel myself injured by such *illiberal treatment.* A gentleman who throughout the war has been *foremost in opposition;* who from the *beginning of our disputes* with Britain, has ever been UNIFORM in his sentiments; whose *life* was early the object of a British ministry: Now, (because he strenuously endeavours to support those *first sentiments* of our opposition) to be so *ungratefully* treated by some of his own TOWNSMEN, must ever be a mark of such ingratitude *as no plea can justify*. Conscious of the rectitude of his heart, he can apply the words of the Poet:—

> *"To virtue only, and her friends agrieved,*
> *The world beside may murmur or commend:*
> *Know all the distant din this world can keep,*
> *Rolls o'er my grotto and but sooths my sleep."*

I must acknowledge, I am somewhat surpriz'd that we have not had many more forcible arguments in *vindication* of the Tea Assembly, as so many gentlemen of a *certain profession* are members; but however, I suppose they are so used to be engaged in a GOOD CAUSE, they feel themselves a little embarrassed to undertake one not so *"perfectly clear."*

Candidus

10. Education

It is obvious from the flood of writings on education during the Revolutionary era that Americans assumed that their experiment in republicanism demanded something very different from the colonial experience in the training of young minds. Indeed, the boldness and innovativeness of the various educational proposals made in the years following the Revolution can only be appreciated in the context of colonial educational practice. Prior to the Revolution, outside New England, there had been no public provision for elementary education. While charity schools and itinerant tutors accounted for some of the formal training of the period, the responsibility for education still rested with parents. Beyond the elementary level the situation was worse. The few secondary schools that existed concentrated on the classics, leading to college and a career in one of the learned professions. Colonial education was haphazard and elitist, and except in New England, was scarcely thought of as a social obligation. Intellectuals thus rightly saw the Revolution as marking a turning point in the development of American educational theory.

Among the Revolutionary intellectuals concerned with education Noah Webster (1758-1843) is undoubtedly one of the most famous. Webster was an indefatigable worker; he edited one magazine and two newspapers, compiled a series of dictionaries, and wrote scores of books and essays, including his well-known reader, grammar, and speller. More than anyone else in the post-Revolutionary period, he stressed that cultural independence must accompany political independence, and to this end he advocated a standardized national language distinct from the English of England. While many of his orthographic reforms were eccentric and unenthusiastically received—for example, the omission of all superfluous silent letters (give as *giv*, built as *bilt*) and the substitution of letters with a definite sound for those that were vague and indeterminate (*greef* for grief, *laf* for laugh)—his educational proposals were typical of many being set forth at the same time. All were grounded on the commitment to a national and universal system of publicly supported schools designed for a republican culture.

But education then as now could never be simply a matter of formal schooling. In the summer of 1771, Robert Skipwith, the brother-in-law of the future Mrs. Jefferson, asked the twenty-eight-year-old Thomas Jefferson for help in choosing some books, which, Skipwith said, would be "suited to the capacity of a common reader who understands but little of the classicks and who has not leisure for any intricate or tedious study. Let them be improving as well as amusing. . . . Let them amount to about five and twenty pounds sterling, or, if you think proper, to thirty pounds." Jefferson's reply went well beyond Skipwith's request and revealed the taste of a superbly well-read eighteenth-century gentleman.

On the Education of Youth in America

NOAH WEBSTER

The Education of youth is, in all governments, an object of the first consequence. The impressions received in early life, usually form the characters of the individuals; a union of which forms the general character of a nation.

The mode of Education and the arts taught to youth, have, in every nation, been adapted to its particular stage of society or local circumstances.

In the martial ages of Greece, the principal study of its Legislators was, to acquaint the young men with the use of arms, to inspire them with an undaunted courage, and to form in the hearts of both sexes, an invincible attachment to their country. Such was the effect of their regulations for these purposes, that the very women of Sparta and Athens would reproach their own sons, for surviving their companions who fell in the field of battle.

Among the warlike Scythians, every male was not only taught to use arms for attack and defence; but was obliged to sleep in the field, to carry heavy burthens, and to climb rocks and precipices, in order to habituate himself to hardship, fatigue and danger.

In Persia, during the flourishing reign of the great Cyrus, the Education of youth, according to Xenophon, formed a principal branch of the regulations

Noah Webster, *A Collection of Essays and Fugitive Writings on Moral, Historical, Political and Literary Subjects* (Boston, 1790), pp. 1–5, 11–18, 22–32, 35–36.

of the empire. The young men were divided into classes, each of which has some particular duties to perform, for which they were qualified by previous instructions and exercise.

While nations are in a barbarous state, they have few wants, and consequently few arts. Their principal objects are, defence and subsistence; the Education of a savage therefore extends little farther, than to enable him to use, with dexterity, a bow and a tomahawk.

But in the progress of manners and of arts, war ceases to be the employment of whole nations; it becomes the business of a few, who are paid for defending their country. Artificial wants multiply the number of occupations; and these require a great diversity in the mode of Education. Every youth must be instructed in the business by which he is to procure subsistence. Even the civilities of behavior, in polished society, become a science; a bow and a curtesy are taught with as much care and precision, as the elements of Mathematics. Education proceeds therefore, by gradual advances, from simplicity to corruption. Its first object, among rude nations, is safety; its next, utility; it afterwards extends to convenience; and among the opulent part of civilized nations, it is directed principally to show and amusement.

In despotic states, Education, like religion, is made subservient to government. In some of the vast empires of Asia, children are always instructed in the occupation of their parents; thus the same arts are always continued in the same families. Such an institution cramps genius, and limits the progress of national improvement; at the same time it is an almost immoveable barrier against the introduction of vice, luxury, faction and changes in government. This is one of the principal causes, which have operated in combining numerous millions of the human race under one form of government, and preserving national tranquillity for incredible periods of time. The empire of China, whose government was founded on the patriarchical discipline, has not suffered a revolution in laws, manners or language, for many thousand years.

In the complicated systems of government which are established among the civilized nations of Europe, Education has less influence in forming a national character; but there is no state, in which it has not an inseparable connection with morals, and a consequential influence upon the peace and happiness of society.

Education is a subject which has been exhausted by the ablest writers, both among the ancients and moderns. I am not vain enough to suppose I can suggest any new ideas upon so trite a theme as Education in general; but perhaps the manner of conducting the youth in America may be capable of some improvement. Our constitutions of civil government are not yet firmly established; our national character is not yet formed; and it is an object of vast magnitude that systems of Education should be adopted and pursued, which may not only diffuse a knowledge of the sciences, but may implant, in the minds of the American youth, the principles of virtue and of liberty; and inspire them with just and liberal ideas of government, and with an inviolable attachment to their own country. It now becomes every American to examin the modes of Education in Europe, to see how far they are applicable in this country, and whether it is not possible to make some valuable alterations, adapted to our local and political circumstances. Let us examin the subject in two views. First, as it respects arts and sciences. Secondly, as it is connected with morals and government. In each of these articles, let us see what errors may be found, and what improvements suggested, in our present practice.

The first error that I would mention, is, a too general attention to the dead languages, with a neglect of our own.

This practice proceeds probably from the common use of the Greek and Roman tongues, before the English was brought to perfection. There was a long period of time, when these languages were almost the only repositories of science in Europe. Men, who had a taste for learning, were under a necessity of recurring to the sources, the Greek and Roman authors. These will ever be held in the highest estimation both for stile and sentiment; but the most valuable of them have English translations, which, if they do not contain all the elegance, communicate all the ideas of the originals. The English language, perhaps, at this moment, is the repository of as much learning, as one half the languages of Europe. In copiousness it exceeds all modern tongues; and though inferior to the Greek and French in softness and harmony, yet it exceeds the French in variety; it almost equals the Greek and Roman in energy, and falls very little short of any language in the regularity of its construction.

In deliberating upon any plan of instruction, we should be attentive to its future influence and probable advantages. What advantage does a merchant, a mechanic, a farmer, derive from an acquaintance with the Greek and Roman tongues? It is true, the etymology of words cannot be well understood, without a knowledge of the original languages of which ours is composed. But a very accurate knowledge of the meaning of words and of the true construction of sentences, may be obtained by the help of Dictionaries and good English writers; and this is all that is necessary in the common occupations of life. But suppose there is some advantage to be derived from an acquaintance with the dead languages, will this compensate for the loss of five or perhaps seven years of valuable time? Life is short, and every hour should be employed to good purposes. If there are no studies of more consequence to boys, than those of Latin and Greek, let these languages employ their time; for idleness is the bane of youth. But when we have an elegant and copious language of our own, with innumerable writers upon ethics, geography, history, commerce and government; subjects immediately interesting to every man; how can a parent be justified in keeping his son several years over rules of Syntax, which he forgets when he shuts his book; or which, if remembered, can be of little or no use in any branch of business? This absurdity is the subject of common complaint; men see and feel the impropriety of the usual practice; and yet no arguments that have hitherto been used, have been sufficient to change the system; or to place an English school on a footing with a Latin one, in point of reputation.

It is not my wish to discountenance totally the study of the dead languages. On the other hand I should urge a more close attention to them, among young men who are designed for the learned professions. The poets, the orators, the philosophers and the historians of Greece and Rome, furnish the most excellent models of Stile, and the richest treasures of Science. The slight attention given to a few of these authors, in our usual course of Education, is rather calculated to make pedants than scholars; and the time employed in gaining superficial knowledge is really wasted.

> "A little learning is a dangerous thing,
> Drink deep, or taste not the Pierian spring."

But my meaning is, that the dead languages are not necessary for men of business, merchants, mechanics, planters, &c. nor of utility sufficient to indemnify them for the expense of time and money which is requisite to acquire a tolerable acquaintance with the Greek and Roman authors. Merchants often have occasion for a knowledge of some foreign living language, as, the French, the Italian, the Spanish, or the German; but men, whose business is wholly domestic, have little or no use for any language but their own; much less, for languages known only in books. . . .

With respect to literary institutions of the first rank, it appears to me that their local situations are an object of importance. It is a subject of controversy, whether a large city or a country village is the most eligible situation for a college or university. But the arguments in favor of the latter, appear to me decisive. Large cities are always scenes of dissipation and amusement, which have a tendency to corrupt the hearts of youth and divert their minds from their literary pursuits. Reason teaches this doctrine, and experience has uniformly confirmed the truth of it.

Strict discipline is essential to the prosperity of a public seminary of science; and this is established with more facility, and supported with more uniformity, in a small village, where there are no great objects of curiosity to interrupt the studies of youth or to call their attention from the orders of the society.

That the morals of young men, as well as their application to science, depend much on retirement, will be generally acknowledged; but it will be said also, that the company in large towns will improve their manners. The question then is, which shall be sacrificed; the advantage of an *uncorrupted heart* and an *improved head*; or of polished manners. But this question supposes that the virtues of the heart and the polish of the gentleman are incompatible with each other; which is by no means true. The gentleman and the scholar are often united in the same person. But both are not formed by the same means. The improvement of the head requires close application to books; the refinement of manners rather attends some degree of dissipation, or at least a relaxation of the mind. To preserve the purity of the heart, it is sometimes necessary, and always useful, to place a youth beyond the reach of bad examples; whereas a general knowledge of the world, of all kinds of company, is requisite to teach a universal propriety of behavior.

But youth is the time to form both the head and the heart. The understanding is indeed ever enlarging; but the seeds of knowledge should be planted in the mind, while it is young and susceptible; and if the mind is not kept untainted in *youth*, there is little probability that the moral character of the *man* will be unblemished. A genteel address, on the other hand, *may* be acquired at any time in life, and *must* be acquired, if ever, by mingling with good company. But were the cultivation of the understanding and of the heart, inconsistent with genteel manners, still no rational person could hesitate which to prefer. The goodness of a heart is of infinitely more consequence to society, than an elegance of manners; nor will any superficial accomplishments repair the want of principle in the mind. It is always better to be *vulgarly right*, than *politely wrong*. . . .

Perhaps it may also be numbered among the errors in our systems of Education, that, in all our universities and colleges, the students are all restricted to the same course of study, and by being classed, limited to the same progress. Classing is necessary, but whether students should not be removeable from the lower to the higher classes, as a reward for their superior industry and improvements, is submitted to those who know the effect of emulation upon the human mind.

But young gentlemen are not all designed for the same line of business, and why should they pursue the same studies? Why should a merchant trouble himself with the rules of Greek and Roman syntax, or a planter puzzle his head with conic sections? Life is too short to acquire, and the mind of man too feeble to contain, the whole circle of sciences. The greatest genius on earth, not even a Bacon, can be a perfect master of *every* branch; but any moderate genius may, by suitable application, be perfect in any *one* branch. By attempting therefore to teach young gentlemen every thing, we make the most of them mere smatterers in science. In order to qualify persons to figure in any profession, it is necessary that they should attend closely to those branches of learning which lead to it.

There are some arts and sciences which are necessary for every man. Every man should be able to speak and write his native tongue with correctness; and have some knowledge of mathematics. The rules of arithmetic are indispensably requisite. But besides the learning which is of common utility, lads should be directed to pursue those branches which are connected more immediately with the business for which they are destined.

It would be very useful for the farming part of the community, to furnish country schools with some easy system of practical husbandry. By repeatedly reading some book of this kind, the mind would be stored with ideas, which might not indeed be understood in youth, but which would be called into practice in some subsequent period of life. This would lead the mind to the subject of agriculture, and pave the way for improvements.

Young gentlemen, designed for the mercantile line, after having learned to write and speak English correctly, might attend to French, Italian, or such other living language, as they will probably want in the course of business. These languages should be learned early in youth, while the organs are yet pliable; otherwise the pronunciation will probably be imperfect. These studies might be succeeded by some attention to chronology, and a regular application to geography, mathematics, history, the general regulations of commercial nations, principles of advance in trade, of insurance, and to the general principles of government.

It appears to me that such a course of Education, which might be completed by the age of fifteen or sixteen, would have a tendency to make better merchants than the usual practice which confines boys to Lucian, Ovid and Tully, till they are fourteen, and then turns them into a store, without an idea of their business, or one article of Education necessary for them, except perhaps a knowledge of writing and figures.

Such a system of English Education is also much preferable to a university Education, even with the usual honors; for it might be finished so early as to leave young persons time to serve a regular apprenticeship, without which no person should enter upon business. But by the time a university Education is completed, young men commonly commence *gentlemen*; their age and their pride will not suffer them to go thro the drudgery of a compting house, and they enter upon business without the requisite accomplishments. Indeed it appears to me that what is now called a *liberal Education*, disqualifies a man for business. Habits are formed in youth and by practice; and as business is, in some measure, mechanical, every person should be exercised in his employment, in an early period of life, that his habits may be formed by the time his apprenticeship expires. An Education in a university interferes with the forming of these habits; and perhaps forms opposite habits; the mind may contract a fondness for ease, for pleasure or for books, which no efforts can overcome. An academic Education, which should furnish the youth with some ideas of men and things, and leave time for an apprenticeship, before the age of twenty one years, would in my opinion, be the most eligible for young men who are designed for activ employments.

The method pursued in our colleges is better calculated to fit youth for the learned professions than for business. But perhaps the period of study, required as the condition of receiving the usual degrees, is too short. Four years, with the most assiduous application, are a short time to furnish the mind with the necessary knowledge of the languages and of the several sciences. It might perhaps have been a period sufficiently long for an infant settlement, as America was, at the time when most of our colleges were founded. But as the country becomes more populous, wealthy and respectable, it may be worthy of consideration, whether the period of academic life should not be extended to six or seven years. . . .

The rod is often necessary in school; especially after the children have been accustomed to disobedience and a licentious behavior at home. All government originates in families, and if neglected there, it will hardly exist in society; but the want of it must be supplied by the rod in school, the penal laws of the state, and the terrors of divine wrath from the pulpit. The government both of families and schools should be absolute. There should, in families, be no appeal from one parent to another, with the prospect of pardon for offences. The one should always vindicate, at least apparently, the conduct of the other. In schools the master should be absolute in command; for it is utterly impossible for any man to support order and discipline among children, who are indulged with an appeal to their parents. A proper subordination in families would generally supersede the necessity of severity in schools; and a strict discipline in both is the best foundation of good order in political society. . . .

Respect for an instructor will often supply the place of a rod of correction. The pupil's attachment will lead him to close attention to his studies; he fears not the *rod* so much as the *displeasure* of his teacher; he waits for a smile, or dreads a frown; he receives his instructions and copies his manners. This generous principle, the fear of offending, will prompt youth to exertions; and instead of severity on the one hand, and of slavish fear, with reluctant obedience on the other, mutual esteem, respect and confidence strew flowers in the road to knowledge.

With respect to morals and civil society, the other view in which I proposed to treat this subject, the effects of Education are so certain and extensiv that it behooves every parent and guardian to be particularly attentiv to the characters of the men, whose province it is to form the minds of youth.

From a strange inversion of the order of nature, the cause of which it is not necessary to unfold, the most important business in civil society, is, in many parts of America, committed to the most worthless characters. The Education of youth, an employment of more consequence than making laws and preaching the gospel, because it lays the foundation on which both law and gospel rest for success; this Education is sunk to a level with the most menial services. In most instances we find the higher seminaries of learning intrusted to men of good characters, and possessed of the moral virtues and social affections. But many of our inferior schools, which, so far as the heart is concerned, are as important as colleges, are kept by men of no breeding, and many of them, by men infamous for the most detestable vices. . . .

The only practicable method to reform mankind, is to begin with children; to banish, if possible, from their company, every low bred, drunken, immoral character. Virtue and vice will not grow together in a great degree, but they will grow where they are planted, and when one has taken root, it is not easily supplanted by the other. The great art of correcting mankind therefore, consists in prepossessing the mind with good principles.

For this reason society requires that the Education of youth should be watched with the most scrupulous attention. Education, in a great measure, forms the moral characters of men, and morals are the basis of government. Education should therefore be the first care of a Legislature; not merely the institution of schools, but the furnishing of them with the best men for teachers. A good system of Education should be the first article in the code of political regulations; for it is much easier to introduce and establish an effectual system for preserving morals, than to correct, by penal statutes, the ill effects of a bad system. I am so fully persuaded of this, that I shall almost adore that great man, who shall change our practice and opinions, and make it respectable for the first and best men to superintend the Education of youth.

Another defect in our schools, which, since the revolution, is become inexcuseable, is the want of proper books. The collections which are now used consist of essays that respect foreign and ancient nations. The minds of youth are perpetually led to the history of Greece and Rome or to Great Britain; boys are constantly repeating the declamations of Demosthenes and Cicero, or debates upon some political question in the British Parliment. These are excellent specimens of good sense, polished stile and perfect oratory; but they are not interesting to children. They cannot be very useful, except to young gentlemen who want them as models of reasoning and eloquence, in the pulpit or at the bar.

But every child in America should be acquainted with his own country. He should read books that furnish him with ideas that will be useful to him in life and practice. As soon as he opens his lips, he should lisp the praise of liberty, and of those illustrious heroes and statesmen, who have wrought a revolution in her favor.

A selection of essays, respecting the settlement and geography of America; the history of the late revolution and of the most remarkable characters and events that distinguished it, and a compendium of the principles of the federal and provincial governments, should be the principal school book in the United States. These are interesting objects to every man; they call home the minds of youth and fix them upon the interests of their own country, and they assist in forming attachments to it, as well as in enlarging the understanding.

"It is observed by the great Montesquieu, that the laws of education ought to be relative to the principles of the government."

In despotic governments, the people should have little or no education, except what tends to inspire them with a servile fear. Information is fatal to despotism.

In monarchies, education should be partial, and adapted to the rank of each class of citizens. But "in a republican government," says the same writer, "the whole power of education is required." Here every class of people should *know* and *love* the laws. This knowledge should be diffused by means of schools and newspapers; and an attachment to the laws may be formed by early impressions upon the mind.

Two regulations are essential to the continuance of republican governments: 1. Such a distribution of lands and such principles of descent and alienation, as shall give every citizen a power of acquiring what his industry merits. 2. Such a system of education as gives every citizen an opportunity of acquiring knowledge and fitting himself for places of trust. These are fundamental articles; the *sine qua non* of the existence of the American republics.

Hence the absurdity of our copying the manners and adopting the institutions of Monarchies.

In several States, we find laws passed, establishing provisions for colleges and academies, where people of property may educate their sons; but no provision is made for instructing the poorer rank of people, even in reading and writing. Yet in these same States, every citizen who is worth a few shillings annually, is entitled to vote for legislators. This appears to me a most glaring solecism in government. The constitutions are *republican*, and the laws of education are *monarchical*. The *former* extend civil rights to every honest industrious man; the *latter* deprive a large proportion of the citizens of a most valuable privilege.

In our American republics, where governments is in the hands of the people knowlege should be universally diffused by means of public schools. Of such consequence is it to society, that the people who make laws, should be well informed, that I conceive no Legislature can be justified in neglecting proper establishments for this purpose.

When I speak of a diffusion of knowlege, I do not mean merely a knowlege of spelling books, and the New Testament. An acquaintance with ethics, and with the general principles of law, commerce, money and government, is necessary for the yeomanry of a republican state. This acquaintance they might obtain by means of books calculated for schools, and read by the children, during the winter months, and by the circulation of public papers.

"In Rome it was the common exercise of boys at school, to learn the laws of the twelve tables by heart, as they did their poets and classic authors." What an excellent practice this in a free government!

It is said, indeed by many, that our common people are already too well informed. Strange paradox! The truth is, they have too much knowledge and spirit to resign their share in government, and are not sufficiently informed to govern themselves in all cases of difficulty.

There are some acts of the American legislatures which astonish men of information; and blunders in legislation are frequently ascribed to bad intentions. But if we examin the men who compose these legislatures, we shall find that wrong measures generally proceed from ignorance either in the men themselves, or in their constituents. They often mistake their own interest, because they do not foresee the remote consequence of a measure.

It may be true that all men cannot be legislators; but the more generally knowlege is diffused among the substantial yeomanry, the more perfect will be the laws of a republican state.

Every small district should be furnished with a school, at least four months in a year; when boys are not otherwise employed. This school should be kept by the most reputable and well informed man in the district. Here children should be taught the usual branches of learning; submission to superiors and to laws; the moral or social duties; the history and transactions of their own country; the principles of liberty and government. Here the rough manners of the wilderness should be softened, and the principles of virtue and good behavior inculcated. The *virtues* of men are of more consequence to society than their *abilities*; and for this reason, the *heart* should be cultivated with more assiduity than the *head*.

Such a general system of education is neither impracticable nor difficult; and excepting the formation of a federal government that shall be efficient and permanent, it demands the first attention of American patriots. Until such a system shall be adopted and pursued, until the Statesman and Divine shall unite their efforts in *forming* the human mind, rather than in loping its excrescences, after it has been neglected; until Legislators discover that the only way to make good citizens and subjects, is to nourish them from infancy; and until parents shall be convinced that the *worst* of men are not the proper teachers to make the *best*; mankind cannot know to what a degree of perfection society and government may be carried. America affords the fairest opportunities for making the experiment and opens the most encouraging prospect of success.

In a system of education, that should embrace every part of the community, the female sex claim no inconsiderable share of our attention.

The women in America (to their honor it is mentioned) are not generally above the care of educating their own children. Their own education should therefore enable them to implant in the tender mind, such sentiments of virtue, propriety and dignity, as are suited to the freedom of our governments. Children should be treated as children, but as children that are, in a future time, to be men and women. By treating them as if they were always to remain children, we very often see their childishness adhere to them, even in middle life. The silly language called *baby talk*, in which most persons are initiated in infancy, often breaks out in discourse, at the age of forty, and makes a man appear very ridiculous. In the same manner, vulgar, obscene and illiberal ideas, imbibed in a nursery or a kitchen, often give a tincture to the conduct through life. In order to prevent every evil bias, the ladies, whose province it is to direct the inclinations of children on their first appearance, and to choose their nurses, should be possessed, not only of amiable manners, but of just sentiments and enlarged understandings.

But the influence of women in forming the dispositions of youth, is not the sole reason why their education should be particularly guarded; their influence in controling the manners of a nation, is another powerful reason. Women, once abandoned, may be instrumental in corrupting society; but such is the delicacy of the sex, and such the restraints which custom imposes upon them, that they are generally the last to be corrupted. There are innumerable instances of men, who have been restrained from a vicious life, and even of very abandoned men, who have been reclaimed, by their attachment to ladies of virtue. A fondness for the company and conversation of ladies of character, may be considered as a young man's best security against the attractives of a dissipated life. A man who is attached to *good* company, seldom frequents that which is *bad*. For this reason, society requires that females should be well educated, and extend their influence as far as possible over the other sex.

But a distinction is to be made between a *good* education, and a *showy* one; for an education, merely superficial, is a proof of corruption of taste, and has a mischievous influence on manners. The education of females, like that of males, should be adapted to the principles of the government, and correspond with the stage of society. Education in Paris differs from that in Petersburg, and the education of females in London or Paris should not be a model for the Americans to copy.

In all nations a *good* education, is that which renders the ladies correct in their manners, respectable in their families, and agreeable in society. That education is always *wrong*, which raises a woman above the duties of her station.

In America, female education should have for its object what is *useful*. Young ladies should be taught to speak and write their own language with purity and elegance; an article in which they are often deficient. The French language is not necessary for ladies. In some cases it is convenient, but, in general, it may be considered as an article of luxury. As an accomplishment, it may be studied by those whose attention is not employed about more important concerns.

Some knowledge of arithmetic is necessary for every lady. Geography should never be neglected. Belles Letters learning seems to correspond with the dispositions of most females. A taste for Poetry and fine writing should be cultivated; for we expect the most delicate sentiments from the pens of that sex, which is possessed of the finest feelings.

A course of reading can hardly be prescribed for all ladies. But it should be remarked, that this sex cannot be too well acquainted with the writers upon human life and manners. The Spectator should fill the first place in every lady's library. Other volumes of periodical papers, tho inferior to the Spectator, should be read; and some of the best histories.

With respect to novels, so much admired by the young, and so generally condemned by the old, what shall I say? Perhaps it may be said with truth, that some of them are useful, many of them pernicious, and most of them trifling. A hundred volumes of modern novels may be read, without acquiring a new idea. Some of them contain entertaining stories, and where the descriptions are drawn from nature, and from characters and events in themselves innocent, the perusal of them may be harmless.

Were novels written with a view to exhibit only one side of human nature, to paint the social virtues, the world would condemn them as defective: But I should think them more perfect. Young people, especially females, should not see the vicious part of mankind. At best novels may be considered as the toys of youth; the rattle boxes of sixteen. The mechanic gets his pence for his toys, and the novel writer, for his books; and it would be happy for society, if the latter were in all cases as innocent play things as the former.

In the large towns in America, music, drawing and dancing, constitute a part of female education. They, however, hold a subordinate rank; for my fair friends will pardon me, when I declare, that no man ever marries a woman for her performance on a harpsichord, or her figure in a minuet. However ambitious a woman may be to command admiration *abroad,* her real merit is known only at *home.* Admiration is useless, when it is not supported by domestic worth. But real honor and permanent esteem, are always secured by those who preside over their own families with dignity.°

°Nothing can be more fatal to domestic happiness in America, than a taste for copying the luxurious manners and amusements of England and France. Dancing, drawing and music, are principal articles of education in those kingdoms; therefore every girl in America must pass two or three years at a boarding school, tho her father cannot give her a farthing when she marries. This ambition to educate females above their fortunes pervades every part of America. Hence the disproportion between the well bred females and the males in our large towns. A mechanic or shopkeeper in town, or a farmer in the country, whose sons get their living by their father's employments, will send their daughters to a boarding school, where their ideas are elevated, and their views carried above a connexion with men in those occupations. Such an education, without fortune or beauty, may possibly please a girl of fifteen, but must prove her greatest misfortune. This fatal mistake is illustrated in every large town in America. In the country, the number of males and females, is nearly equal; but in towns, the number of genteelly bred women is greater than of men; and in some towns, the proportion is, as three to one.

The heads of young people of both sexes are often turned by reading descriptions of splendid living, of coaches, of plays, and other amusements. Such descriptions excite a desire to enjoy the same pleasures. A fortune becomes the principal object of pursuit; fortunes are scarce in America, and not easily acquired; disappointment succeeds, and the youth who begins life with expecting to enjoy a coach, closes the prospect with a small living, procured by labor and economy.

Thus a wrong education, and a taste for pleasures which our fortune will not enable us to enjoy, often plunge the Americans into distress, or at least prevent early marriages. Too fond of show, of dress and expense, the sexes wish to please each other; they mistake the means, and both are disappointed.

Before I quit this subject, I beg leave to make some remarks on a practice which appears to be attended with important consequences; I mean that of sending boys to Europe for an education, or sending to Europe for teachers. This was right before the revolution; at least so far as national attachments were concerned; but the propriety of it ceased with our political relation to Great Britain.

In the first place, our honor as an independent nation is concerned in the establishment of literary institutions, adequate to all our own purposes; without sending our youth abroad, or depending on other nations for books and instructors. It is very little to the reputation of America to have it said abroad, that after the heroic achievements of the late war, these independent people are obliged to send to Europe for men and books to teach their children A B C.

But in another point of view, a foreign education is directly opposite to our political interests, and ought to be discountenanced, if not prohibited.

Every person of common observation will grant, that most men prefer the manners and the government of that country where they are educated. Let ten American youths be sent, each to a different European kingdom, and live there from the age of twelve to twenty, and each will give the preference to the country where he has resided.

The period from twelve to twenty is the most important in life. The impressions made before that period are commonly effaced; those that are made during that period *always* remain for many years, and *generally* thro life.

Ninety nine persons of a hundred who pass that period in England or France, will prefer the people, their manners, their laws, and their government, to those of their nativ country. Such attachments are injurious, both to the happiness of the men, and to the political interests of their own country. As to private happiness, it is universally known how much pain a man suffers by a change of habits in living. The customs of Europe are and ought to be different from ours; but when a man has been bred in one country, his attachments to its manners make them, in a great measure, necessary to his happiness. On changing his residence, he must therefore break his former habits, which is always a painful sacrifice; or the discordance between the manners of his own country, and his habits, must give him incessant uneasiness; or he must introduce, into a circle of his friends, the manners in which he was educated. These consequences may follow, and the last, which is inevitable, is a public injury. The refinement of manners in every country should keep pace exactly with the increase of its wealth; and perhaps the greatest evil America now feels is, an improvement of taste and manners which its wealth cannot support.

A foreign education is the very source of this evil; it gives young gentlemen of fortune a relish for manners and amusements which are not suited to this country; which however, when introduced by this class of people, will always become fashionable. . . .

It is time for the Americans to change their usual route, and travel thro a country which they never think of, or think beneeth their notice: I mean the United States.

While these States were a part of the British Empire, our interest, our feelings, were those of Englishmen; our dependence led us to respect and imitate their manners and to look up to them for our opinions. We little thought of any national interest in America; and while our commerce and governments were in the hands of our parent country, and we had no common interest, we little thought of improving our acquaintance with each other, or of removing prejudices, and reconciling the discordant feelings of the inhabitants of different Provinces. But independence and union render it necessary that the citizens of different States should know each others characters and circumstances; that all jealousies should be removed; that mutual respect and confidence should succeed, and a harmony of views and interests be cultivated by a friendly intercourse. . . .

Americans, unshackle your minds, and act like independent beings. You have been children long enough, subject to the control, and subservient to the interest of a haughty parent. You have now an interest of your own to augment and defend: You have an empire to raise and support by your exertions, and a national character to establish and extend by your wisdom and virtues. To effect these great objects, it is necessary to frame a liberal plan of policy, and built it on a broad system of education. Before this system can be formed and embraced, the Americans must *believe*, and *act* from the belief, that it is dishonorable to waste life in mimicking the follies of other nations and basking in the sunshine of foreign glory.

A Gentleman's Library
THOMAS JEFFERSON

I sat down with a design of executing your request to form a catalogue of books amounting to about 30. lib. sterl. but could by no means satisfy myself with any partial choice I could make. Thinking therefore it might be as agreeable to you, I have framed such a general collection as I think you would wish, and might in time find convenient, to procure. Out of this you will chuse for yourself to the amount you mentioned for the present year, and may hereafter as shall be convenient proceed in completing the whole. A view of the second column in this catalogue would I suppose extort a smile from the face of gravity. Peace to it's wisdom! Let me not awaken it. A little attention however to the nature of the human mind evinces that the entertainments of fiction are useful as well as pleasant. That they are pleasant when well written, every person feels who reads. But wherein is it's utility, asks the reverend sage, big with the notion that nothing can be useful but the learned lumber of Greek and Roman reading with which his head is stored? I answer, every thing is useful which contributes to fix us in the principles and practice of virtue. When any signal act of charity or of gratitude, for instance, is presented either to our sight or imagination, we are deeply impressed with it's beauty and feel a strong desire in ourselves of doing charitable and grateful acts also. On the contrary when we see or read of any atrocious deed, we are disgusted with it's deformity and conceive an abhorrence of vice. Now every emotion of this kind is an exercise of our virtuous dispositions; and dispositions of the mind, like limbs of the body, acquire strength by exercise. But exercise produces habit; and in the instance of which we speak, the exercise being of the moral feelings, produces a habit of thinking and acting virtuously. We never reflect whether the story we read be truth or fiction. If the painting be lively, and a tolerable picture of nature, we are thrown into a reverie, from which if we awaken it is the fault of the writer. I appeal to every reader of feeling and sentiment whether the fictious murther of Duncan by Macbeth in Shakespeare does not excite in him as great horror of villainy, as the real one of Henry IV by Ravaillac as related by Davila? And whether the fidelity of Nelson, and generosity of Blandford in

Thomas Jefferson to Robert Skipwith, 3 August, 1771, in Julian P. Boyd, ed., *The Papers of Thomas Jefferson* (Princeton, 1950–), vol. I, pp. 76–80.

Marmontel do not dilate his breast, and elevate his sentiments as much as any similar incident which real history can furnish? Does he not in fact feel himself a better man while reading them, and privately covenant to copy the fair example? We neither know nor care whether Lawrence Sterne really went to France, whether he was there accosted by the poor Franciscan, at first rebuked him unkindly, and then gave him a peace offering; or whether the whole be not a fiction. In either case we are equally sorrowful at the rebuke, and secretly resolve *we* will never do so: we are pleased with the subsequent atonement, and view with emulation a soul candidly acknowleging it's fault, and making a just reparation. Considering history as a moral exercise, her lessons would be too unfrequent if confined to real life. Of those recorded by historians few incidents have been attended with such circumstances as to excite in any high degree this sympathetic emotion of virtue. We are therefore wisely framed to be as warmly interested for a fictitious as for a real personage. The spacious field of imagination is thus laid open to our use, and lessons may be formed to illustrate and carry home to the mind every moral rule of life. Thus a lively and lasting sense of filial duty is more effectually impressed on the mind of a son or daughter by reading King Lear, than by all the dry volumes of ethics and divinity that ever were written. This is my idea of well-written Romance, of Tragedy, Comedy, and Epic Poetry.—If you are fond of speculation, the books under the head of Criticism, will afford you much pleasure. Of Politicks and Trade I have given you a few only of the best books, as you would probably chuse to be not unacquainted with those commercial principles which bring wealth into our country, and the constitutional security we have for the enjoiment of that wealth. In Law I mention a few systematical books, as a knowlege of the minutiae of that science is not necessary for a private gentleman. In Religion, History, Natural philosophy I have followed the same plan in general.—But whence the necessity of this collection? Come to the new Rowanty, from which you may reach your hand to a library formed on a more extensive plan. Separated from each other but a few paces, the possessions of each would be open to the other. A spring, centrically situated, might be the scene of every evening's joy. There we should talk over the lessons of the day, or lose them in Musick, Chess, or the merriments of our family companions. The heart thus lightened, our pillows would be soft, and health and long life would attend the happy scene. Come then and bring our dear Tibby with you; the first in your affections, and second in mine. Offer Prayers for me too at that shrine to which, tho' absent, I pay continual devotion. In every scheme of happiness she is placed in the fore-ground of the picture, as the principal figure. Take that away, and it is no picture for me.

Bear my affections to Wintipock, cloathed in the warmest expressions of sincerity; and to yourself be every human felicity, Adieu.

ENCLOSURE

FINE ARTS[1]

Observations on gardening. Payne. 5/
Webb's essay on painting. 12mo 3/
Pope's Iliad. 18/
———— Odyssey. 15/
Dryden's Virgil. 12mo. 12/
Milton's works. 2 v. 8vo. Donaldson. Edinburgh 1762. 10/
Hoole's Tasso. 12mo. 5/
Ossian with Blair's criticisms. 2 v. 8vo. 10/
Telemachus by Dodsley. 6/
Capell's Shakespear. 12mo. 30/
Dryden's plays. 6 v. 12mo. 18/
Addison's plays. 12mo. 3/
Otway's plays. 3 v. 12mo. 9/
Rowe's works. 2 v. 12mo. 6/
Thompson's works. 4 v. 12mo. 12/
Young's works. 4 v. 12mo. 12/
Home's plays. 12mo. 3/
Mallet's works. 3 v. 12mo. 9/
Mason's poetical works. 5/
Terence. Eng. 3/
Moliere. Eng. 15/
Farquhar's plays. 2 v. 12mo. 6/
Vanbrugh's plays. 2 v. 12mo. 6/[2]
Steele's plays. 3/
Congreve's works. 3 v. 12mo. 9/
Garric's dramatic works. 2 v. 8vo. 10/
Foote's dramatic works. 2 v. 8vo. 10/
Rousseau's Eloisa. Eng. 4 v. 12mo. 12/
———— Emilius and Sophia. Eng. 4 v. 12mo. 12/
Marmontel's moral tales. Eng. 2 v. 12mo. 9/
Gil Blas. by Smollett 6/
Don Quixot. by Smollett 4 v. 12mo. 12/[3]
David Simple. 2 v. 12mo. 6/

Roderic Random. 2 v. 12mo. 6/
Peregrine Pickle. 4 v. 12mo. 12/
Launcelot Graves. 6/
Adventures of a guinea. 2 v. 12mo. 6/
} *these are written by Smollett.*

Pamela. 4 v. 12mo. 12/
Clarissa. 8 v. 12mo. 24/
Grandison. 7 v. 12mo. 21/
Fool of quality. 3 v. 12mo. 9/
} *these are by Richardson.*

Feilding's works. 12 v. 12mo. £1.16
Constantia. 2 v. 12mo. 6/
Solyman and Almena 12 mo. 3/
} *by Langhorne.*

Belle assemblee. 4 v. 12mo. 12/
Vicar of Wakefeild. 2 v. 12mo. 6/. by Dr. Goldsmith
Sidney Bidulph. 5 v. 12mo. 15/
Lady Julia Mandeville. 2 v. 12mo. 6/
Almoran and Hamet. 2 v. 12mo. 6/
Tristam Shandy. 9 v. 12mo. £1.7
Sentimental journey. 2 v. 12mo. 6/
Fragments of antient poetry. Edinburgh. 2/
Percy's Runic poems. 3/
Percy's reliques of antient English poetry. 3 v. 12mo. 9/
Percy's Han Kiou Chouan. 4 v. 12mo. 12/
Percy's Miscellaneous Chinese peices.

2 v. 12mo. 6/
Chaucer. 10/
Spencer. 6 v. 12mo. 15/
Waller's poems. 12mo. 3/
Dodsley's collection of poems. 6 v. 12
mo. 18/
Pearch's collection of poems. 4 v. 12
mo. 12/
Gray's works. 5/
Ogilvie's poems. 5/
Prior's poems. 2 v. 12mo. Foulis. 6/
Gay's works. 12mo. Foulis. 3/
Shenstone's works. 2 v. 12mo. 6/
Dryden's works. 4 v. 12mo. Foulis.
12/
Pope's works. by Warburton. 12mo.
£1.4
Churchill's poems. 4 v. 12mo. 12/
Hudibrass. 3/
Swift's works. 21 v. small 8vo. £3.3
Swift's literary correspondence. 3 v.
9/
Spectator. 9 v. 12mo. £1.7
Tatler. 5 v. 12mo. 15/
Guardian. 2 v. 12mo. 6/
Freeholder. 12mo. 3/
Ld. Lyttleton's Persian letters. 12mo.
3/

CRITICISM ON THE
FINE ARTS

Ld. Kaim's elements of criticism. 2 v.
8vo. 10/
Burke on the sublime and beautiful. 8
vo. 5/
Hogarth's analysis of beauty. 4to.
£1.1
Reid on the human mind. 8vo. 5/
Smith's theory of moral sentiments.
8vo. 5/
Johnson's dictionary. 2 v. fol. £3
Capell's prolusions. 12mo. 3/

POLITICKS, TRADE.

Montesquieu's spirit of laws. 2 v. 12
mo. 6/

Locke on government. 8vo. 5/
Sidney on government. 4to. 15/
Marmontel's Belisarius. 12mo. Eng. 3/
Ld. Bolingbroke's political works. 5 v.
8vo. £1.5
Montesquieu's rise & fall of the Roman
governmt. 12mo. 3/
Steuart's Political oeconomy. 2 v. 4to.
£1.10
Petty's Political arithmetic. 8vo. 5/

RELIGION.

Locke's conduct of the mind in search
of truth. 12mo. 3/
Xenophen's memoirs of Socrates. by
Feilding. 8vo. 5/
Epictetus. by Mrs. Carter. 2 v. 12mo.
6/
Antoninus by Collins. 3/
Seneca. by L'Estrange. 8vo. 5/[4]
Cicero's Offices. by Guthrie. 8vo. 5/
Cicero's Tusculan questions. Eng. 3/
Ld. Bolingbroke's Philosophical works.
5 v. 8vo. £1.5
Hume's essays. 4 v. 12mo. 12/
Ld. Kaim's Natural religion. 8vo. 6/
Philosophical survey of Nature. 3/
Oeconomy of human life. 2/
Sterne's sermons. 7 v. 12mo. £1.1
Sherlock on death. 8vo. 5/
Sherlock on a future state. 5/

LAW

Ld. Kaim's Principles of equity. fol.
£1.1
Blackstone's Commentaries. 4 v. 4to.
£4.4
Cuningham's Law dictionary. 2 v. fol.
£3

HISTORY. ANTIENT.

Bible. 6/
Rollin's Antient history. Eng. 13 v. 12
mo. £1.19
Stanyan's Graecian history. 2 v. 8vo.
10/
Livy. (the late translation). 12/

Sallust by Gordon. 12mo. 12/
Tacitus by Gordon. 12mo. 15/
Caesar by Bladen. 8vo. 5/
Josephus. Eng. 1.0[2]
Vertot's Revolutions of Rome. Eng. 9/
Plutarch's lives. by Langhorne. 6 v. 8vo. £1.10
Bayle's Dictionary. 5 v. fol. £7.10.
Jeffrey's Historical & Chronological chart. 15/

HISTORY. MODERN.

Robertson's History of Charles the Vth. 3 v. 4to. £3.3
Bossuet's history of France. 4 v. 12mo. 12/
Davila. by Farneworth. 2 v. 4to. £1.10.
Hume's history of England. 8 v. 8vo. £2.8.
Clarendon's history of the rebellion. 6 v. 8vo. £1.10.
Robertson's history of Scotland. 2 v. 8vo. 12/
Keith's history of Virginia. 4to. 12/
Stith's history of Virginia. 6/

NATURAL PHILOSOPHY.
NATURAL HISTORY &C.

Nature displayed. Eng. 7 v. 12mo.
Franklin on Electricity. 4to. 10/
Macqueer's elements of Chemistry. 2 v. 8vo. 10/[4]
Home's principles of agriculture. 8vo. 4/
Tull's horse-hoeing husbandry. 8vo. 5/
Duhamel's husbandry. 4to. 15/
Millar's Gardener's dict. fol. £2.10.
Buffon's natural history. Eng. £2.10.
A compendium of Physic & Surgery. Nourse. 12mo. 1765. 3/
Addison's travels. 12mo. 3/
Anson's voiage. 8vo. 6/
Thompson's travels. 2 v. 12mo. 6/
Lady M. W. Montague's letters. 3 v. 12mo. 9/

MISCELLANEOUS

Ld. Lyttleton's dialogues of the dead. 8vo. 5/
Fenelon's dialogues of the dead. Eng. 12mo. 3/
Voltaire's works. Eng. £4.
Locke on Education. 12mo. 3/
Owen's Dict. of arts & sciences. 4 v. 8vo. £2.

These books if bound quite plain will cost the prices affixed in this catalogue. If bound elegantly, gilt, lettered, and marbled on the leaves, they will cost 20. p. cent more. If bound by Bumgarden in fine Marbled bindings, they will cost 50. p. cent more.

Apply to Thomas Waller, bookseller, Fleet-street London.
This whole catalogue as rated here comes to £107.10.

11. The Federalist Augustan Age

The Federalist quarrel with the Jeffersonian Republicans in post-Revolutionary America was not strictly a political battle between contending parties. It was actually a cultural conflict of immense significance for the future of American literature and art. The Federalists, or many of them, ideally saw the post-Revolutionary period as a new Augustan age in which the gains of the Revolution would be justified and stabilized in a republic noted as much for its literary achievement as for its political grandeur. Like the age of Pope and Johnson, the Federalist era of the 1790's seemed to be a monument of classical elegance beset by the brawling and boorish tendencies of Revolutionary mobs. The Jeffersonian Republicans, the Federalists feared, were trying to usher in not simply a new political order, but an entirely new way of life, and to create a coarse and visionary society, like Jonathan Swift's land of Laputa, run by men with their heads in the clouds.

The 1799 oration by David Daggett (1764-1851) is a particularly sharp attack on the Jeffersonian Republicans and is one of the first of many Federalist pieces to use Swift's Laputan imagery to make its point. Daggett was a young New Haven lawyer who became prominent as a member of the Connecticut government, as United States Senator in 1813, as Mayor of New Haven in 1828, and as Chief Justice of the Supreme Court of Errors in 1832.

Sun-Beams May Be Extracted from Cucumbers, But the Process is Tedious

DAVID DAGGETT

History informs us that at Lagado, in Laputa, there was a grand academy established, in which there was a display of much curious learning.

One artist, of a very philosophic taste, was racking his invention to make a pin-cushion out of a piece of marble.

Another had formed an ingenious project to prevent the growth of wool upon two young lambs, by a composition of gums, minerals and vegetables, applied inwardly, and thus he hoped in a reasonable time to propagate the breed of naked sheep throughout the Kingdom.

A third had contrived a plan to entirely abolish words; and this was urged as a great advantage in point of health as well as brevity. For it is plain that every word we speak is an injury to our lungs, by corrosion, and consequently contributes to the shortening of our lives. An expedient was therefore offered, that since words were only names for things, it would be more convenient for all men to carry about them such things as were necessary to express the particular business on which they were to discourse; and the historian adds "that he had often beheld two of these sages almost sinking under the weight of their packs, who when they met in the streets would lay down their loads, open their sacks, and hold conversation for an hour together; then put up their implements, help each other to resume their burdens, and take their leave.

A fourth appeared with sooty hands and face, his hair and beard long, ragged and singed in several places. His clothes, shirt and skin were all of the same colour. He had been eight years upon a project for extracting sun-beams out of cucumbers, which were to be put into vials, hermetically sealed, and let out to warm the air in raw inclement summers. He said he did not doubt but that in *eight years more* he should be able to supply the Governor's gardens with sunshine at a reasonable rate.

These Theorists were very patient, industrious and laborious in their pursuits—had a high reputation for their singular proficiency, and were re-

David Daggett, *Sun-Beams May be Extracted from Cucumbers, But the Process is Tedious: An Oration Pronounced on the Fourth of July*, 1799 . . . (New Haven, 1799), pp. 5–18, 24–28.

garded as prodigies in science. The common laborers and mechanics were esteemed a different race of beings, and were despised for their stupid and old-fashioned manner of acquiring property and character. If the enquiry had been made whether any of these projects had succeeded, it would have been readily answered that they had not; but that they were reasonable—their principles just—and of course, that they must ultimately produce the objects in view. Hitherto no piece of marble had been made into a pincushion, and few, very few sun-beams had been extracted from cucumbers; but what then? Are not all great and noble and valuable things accomplished with immense exertion, and with an expense of much time? If a farther enquiry had been made what would be the great excellence of marble pincushions, or the superior advantage of a breed of naked sheep, the answer would have been, it is unphilosophical to ask such questions.

In more modern times we have witnessed projects not unlike those of the learned of Laputa, above mentioned. A machine called an *Automaton*, was not long since constructed. This was designed to transport from place to place, by land, any load without the aid of horses, oxen, or any other animal. The master was to sit at helm, and guide it up hill and down, and over every kind of road. This machine was completed, and proved demonstrably capable of performing the duties assigned to it, and the only difficulty which attended it, and which hath hitherto prevented its universal use was, *that it would not go.*—Here, if any ignorant fellow had been so uncivil, he might have doubted why, if wood and iron were designed to go alone and carry a load, the whole herd of oxen, horses and camels were created.

A few years ago the learned insisted that it was grovelling to travel either by *land* or *water*, but that the truly *philosophical* mode was to go by air. Hence, in all parts of the world speculatists were mounted in balloons, with the whole apparatus of living and dying, and were flying through the Heavens, to the utter astonishment and mortification of those poor illiterate wretches who were doomed to tug and sweat on the earth. To be sure this method of travelling was somewhat precarious.—A flaw of wind, regardless of the principles of this machine, might destroy it, or by the giving way of one *philosophical pin, peg or rope*, it might be let into the sea, or dashed against a rock, and thus its precious contents miserably perish. But doubtless reason will in time, provide sufficient checks against all these casualties. Here again some "busy body in other men's matters" might ask, if it was intended that men should fly through the air, why were they not made with feathers and wings, and especially why are there so many who are justly called *Heavy-moulded men?*

Another class of the literati of our age, scorning to travel either *on* the *sea,* or on the *land,* or in the air, have constructed a *submarine* boat or *diving machine,* by which they were constantly *groping* among shark, sturgeon and sea-horses. To say nothing of the hazard which these gentlemen encounter of running on rocks or shoals, or of being left in the lurch, on the bottom of the sea, by a leak, may we not wonder that they were not made with fins and scales, and may they not esteem themselves very fortunate that they have hitherto escaped being cut up to be made into oil?

These are a few among many modern inventions. All the principles of these various machines are capable of defence, and the inventors are all great, and learned, and ingenious men. Yet strange as it may seem, the stupid, foolish plodding people of this and other countries still keep their oxen and their horses—their carriages are still made as they were an hundred years ago, and our coasters will still go to New-York on the surface of the Sound, instead of sinking to the bottom or rising into the clouds—and they still prefer a fair wind and tide to the greatest profusion of steam, produced in the most scientific manner.

This species of enterprise, and this spirit of learning, has entered deeply into the business of agriculture. Discoveries have been made which have rendered sowing and reaping unnecessary. The plow, harrow, spade, hoe, sickle and scythe have undergone a thorough change, on mathematical principles, and the speculative husbandman has yearly expected to see the fields covered with grass, and the hills and vallies with corn and wheat, without the clownish exercise of labor. With Varlow on husbandry in his hands, and a complete collection of philosophical farming utensils, he has forgotten that by the "sweat of his brow he was to eat his bread," and is hourly expecting to "reap where he hath not sown, and gather where he hath not strawed."—Still here and there an old-fashioned fellow, and New-England abounds with them, "will rise early and set up late, and eat the bread of industry; will sow his seed in the morning and in the evening withhold not his hand," and is secretly flattering himself that this is the surest road to peace and plenty.

Hypocrates, Galen and Sydenham have been successively and conjointly attacked by the Physicians of the present refined age, and the medical learning of ancient times, or even of the last century, pronounced quackery and nonsense. A few years since, if a man were attacked with a most violent disease, he was directed to stimulate. Stimulants, powerful stimulants, were all the fashion; and instead of Apothecaries shops and Lancets, the nurse was directed to the brandy-pipe and the gin-case. Thus the Brownonian system had superceded all others, and it was proved demonstrably, that the reason why the children of men were subject to death was, that they did not sufficiently fortify against its attacks, with beef steaks and wine. These principles had slain but a few when they were universally exploded, and men going into the opposite extreme, were literally bled to death, and thus, lest the system should be overcharged, all its props were cautiously, but entirely removed.

At length *reason, unerring reason*, appeared, and patients, writhed with agonies by the most subduing maladies, were solemnly directed to the Points. Yes, to the *Points*, as the great antidote against disease, and the certain restorer of health; and thus it was found, to the everlasting contempt of all the learned of the faculty of ancient and modern days, that the *materia medica* was useless, for that being *plus* electrified, in one part of the body, and *minus* in the other, was the true radix of every disease, and that the sovereign remedy was to restore an equilibrium by an external application of brass and steel.

Yet there are many so bigotted to the customs and practices of their ancestors, that they insist on the foolish habit of temperance, industry and exercise, and express some doubts respecting the entire efficacy of the *tractors*.

A more extensive field for the operation of these principles has been opened, in the new theories of the education of children. It has lately been discovered that the maxim, "Train up a child in the way he should go, and when he is old he will not depart from it," is an erroneous translation, and should read thus—"Let a child walk in his own way, and when he is old he will be perfect." Volumes have been written, and much time and labor expended, to shew that all reproof, restraint and correction, tend directly to extinguish the fire of genius, to cripple the faculties and enslave the understanding. Especially we are told (and the system of education now adopted in the great Gallic nursery of arts, is entirely on this plan) that the prejudices of education, and an inclination to imitate the example of parents and other ancestors, is the great bane of the peace, dignity and glory of young men, and that reason will conduct them, if not fettered with habits, to the perfection of human nature. Obedience to parents is expressly reprobated, and all the tyranny and despotism in the world ascribed to parental authority. This sentiment is explicitly avowed by Mr. Volney, who is the friend and associate of many distinguished men in the United States, and who has, in this opinion, shewed that Paul was a fool or knave when he said, "Children obey your parents in the Lord, for this is right."

If any person, groping in darkness, should object to these sentiments and enquire, how it is possible that children should become thus excellent if left entirely to themselves, when the experience of ages has been that with great and continued exertions, no such facts have existed, it may be replied, *the projector of Laputa had not been able in* EIGHT YEARS *to extract sun-beams from Cucumbers, but he was certain it would be done* IN EIGHT YEARS MORE.

We all recollect when these principles began to impress our Colleges—when it was seriously contended that the study of mathematics and natural philosophy was ruinous to the health, genius and character of a young gentleman—That music and painting, and dancing and fencing, and *speaking French,* were the only accomplishments worth possessing; and that Latin and Greek were fitted only for stupid divines or black-letter-lawyers. An indispensible part of this *philosophical,* and *polite,* and *genteel* and *pretty* education was, to travel into foreign countries, and there reside long enough to forget all the early habits of life—to forget all domestic connexions—to forget the school-house where he was first taught his New England primer—to forget the old-fashioned meeting-house where he was first led to worship God, and especially to forget his native country, and to *remember* only, but remember always and effectually, that he was a polished cosmopolite, or citizen of the world.

The system of morals which has been reared by the care, anxiety and wisdom of ages, has, in its turn, been assailed by these Theorists. The language of modern reformers to those who venerate ancient habits, ancient manners, ancient systems of morals and education, is, "O fools, when will ye be wise?" To first shake, and then destroy the faith of every man on these interesting subjects, has been attempted by many distinguished men, with an industry, labor and perseverance which deserved a better cause, and has been for many years a prime object of pursuit in that nation which has been the great hot-bed of premature and monstrous productions. To particularize on this subject would be impossible, but I cannot forbear to hint at a few of those doctrines now strenuously supported.

That men should love their children precisely according to their worth, and that if a neighbor's child be more deserving, it should be preferred.

That men are to regard the general good in all their conduct, and of course to break promises, contracts and engagements, or perform them, as will conduce to this object.

That to refuse to lend a sum of money, when possible, and when the applicant is in need of it, is an act equally criminal with theft or robbery, to the same amount.

If a difficulty should here be started, that men may judge erroneously as to the desert of a neighbor's child—the demands of the public as to the fulfilment of a promise, or the necessity for the loan in the case mentioned, the answer is ready, *reason*, mighty reason, will be an infallible guide. A plain old-fashioned man will say, this is indeed a beautiful system, but there appears one difficulty attending it, that is, it is made for a race of beings entirely different from men. Again, says he—Why for six thousand years the love of parents to children has been considered, as the only tie by which families have been connected; and families have been considered as the strongest band and most powerful cement of society—destroy then this affection, and what better than miserable vagabonds will be the inhabitants of the earth?— This part of the project really strikes me, he adds, *like the attempt to propagate the breed of naked sheep*. Then again, it is quite doubtful whether parents of ordinary nerves can, at once, divest themselves of natural affection.—Indeed, there is a strong analogy between this part of the scheme, and *making a pin-cushion out of a piece of marble*.—But to the cosmopolite, who belongs nowhere, is connected with nobody, and who has been from his youth progressing to perfection, these sentiments are just, and the exercise of them quite feasible.

But these modern theories have appeared in their native beauty, and shone with the most resplendent lustre, in the science of politics. We are seriously told that men are to be governed only by reason. *Instruct* men and there will be an end of punishment. It is true, since the world began, not a family, a state or a nation has been, on these principles, protected; but this is because reason has not been properly exercised. The period now approaches when reason unfolds itself—one more *hot-bed* will mature it, and then behold the glorious harvest!

But it may be *stupidly* asked what shall be done in the mean time? men are now *somewhat imperfect*—Theft, burglary, robbery and murder are now and then committed, and it will be some years before the perfection of human nature will shield us from these evils. This interregnum will be somewhat calamitous.—And also, is it certain that the commission of crimes has a tendency to refine and perfect the perpetrator? These questions never should be asked at the close of the eighteenth century.—They are manifestly too uncivil.

Again, say modern theories, men are all equal, and of course no *restraints* are imposed by society—no *distinctions* can exist, except to gratify the pride of the *ambitious*, the cruelty of the *despotic*. Hence it is the plain duty of every individual, to hasten the reign of liberty and equality. It is not a novel opinion, that men are by nature possessed of equal rights, and that "God hath made of one blood all nations of men to dwell on the face of the earth," but 'tis somewhat doubtful whether every man should be permitted to do as he pleases.—Such *liberty*, it may be said, is *unsafe* with men who are not perfect.—A cosmopolite, to be sure, will not abuse it, because he loves all mankind in an equal degree: but the expediency of the general principle may be questioned—any opinion of great and learned men in any wise, to the contrary notwithstanding.

If, however, by liberty and equality is intended the power of acting with as much freedom as is consistent with the public safety—and that each man has the same right to the protection of law as another, there is no controversy; but these terms, as now explained, advocated and adopted, mean the power of acting without any other restraint than reason, and the levelling |of| all distinctions by right or wrong, and thus understood, they are of rather too suspicious a character for men of *ordinary talents* to admit.

But these principles extend still farther—their grasp is wider. They aim at the actual destruction of every government on earth.

Kings are the first object of their attack—then a nobility—then commons.

To prepare the way for the accomplishment of these objects, all former systems of thinking and acting must be annihilated, and the reign of reason firmly established.

But it will be enquired, where have these novel theories appeared? I answer—They have dawned upon New-England—they have glowed in the southern states—they have burnt in France. We have seen a few projectors in Boats, Balloons and Automatons—A few philosophical farmers—A few attempts to propagate the breed of naked sheep—and we have at least one Philosopher in the United States, who has taken an accurate mensuration of the Mammoth's bones—made surprising discoveries in the doctrine of vibrating pendulums, and astonished the world with the precise gauge and dimensions of all the aboriginals in America.

But in France, for many years, these speculations in agriculture, the mechanic arts, education, morals and government, have been adopted and pursued. It is there declared and established by law, that ancient habits, customs and manners, modes of thinking, reasoning and acting, ought to be ridiculed, despised and rejected, for that a totally new order of things has taken place. All those rules of action which civilized nations have deemed necessary to their peace and happiness, have been declared *useless* or *arbitrary, unnecessary* or *unjust*. The most distinguished treatises on the laws of nations—treatises which have been considered as containing rules admirably adapted to the situation of different countries, and therefore of high authority, have not only been disregarded, but publicly contemned as musty, worm-eaten productions. Even that accomplished Cosmopolite, Mr. Genet, who came the messenger of *peace* and *science* to this guilty and deluded people, and who treated us precisely according to those assumed characters, opened his budget with an explicit renunciation of the principles of Puffendorf, Vattel, and other writers of that description, and declared that his nation would be governed by none of their obsolete maxims.

Indeed, this learned nation have yielded implicity to the sentiments of Mr. Volney, Mr. Paine, and Mr. Godwin, in all questions of morals and policy; and in all matters of religion there is associated with them that learned and pious divine the Bishop of Autun, who had the Cosmopolitism to boast that he had preached twenty years, under an oath, without believing a word which he uttered.

To aid the establishment of these projects, the credulity of the present age has become truly astonishing. There appears to be a new machinery for the mind, by which its capacity at believing certain things is perfect. It is believed that Socrates, and Plato and Seneca—Bacon, Newton and Locke, and all who lived and died prior to the commencement of the French Revolution, were either fools or slaves. That in no country but France is there *science* or *virtue*. That the body of the people in England are now groaning under the most oppressive bondage and tyranny. That this was precisely the case in Holland, Italy and Switzerland, till France introduced them to their present happy condition. It is believed by all the Cosmopolites in Europe, and by many in America—by all genuine Jacobins, by many Democrats, by the greater part of the readers of the *Aurora,* the *Argus* and the *Bee,* and by an innumerable multitude who don't read at all, that the citizens of these States, and particularly of New-England, are miserable, benighted, enslaved and wretched dupes; and that the President and his adherents are in a firm league to injure and destroy them. That our members of Congress, and the heads of departments, are bribed with British gold, and are exerting all their faculties to forge chains for their posterity. That all in any way connected with the government are constantly plundering the Treasury—amassing wealth—becoming independent—and thus establishing an abominable, cruel, wicked, despotic and devilish aristocracy, which is to continually enlarge its grasp till it shall embrace all the valuable interests of America, and leave the people "destitute, afflicted, tormented." And finally, it is believed by many that John Adams has entered into co-partnership with John Q. Adams, his son, now Minister at Berlin, for the express purpose of importing Monarchy, by wholesale, into this country. And to increase and perpetuate the stock of the house, that the son is to marry one of the daughters of the King of England.

If you enquire respecting the truth of these things, they cite Gallatin, Nicholas and Lyon—They quote from the *Aurora,* the *Argus* and the *Bee;* and who can doubt these sources of information, since the various publications, within a year past, respecting Connecticut, this City, and our College?

But it may be asked, where is your proof that the sentiments and theories which you have been describing, in fact, have an existence? Where is your proof, Sir, that the modern Literati are attempting to extract sun-beams from Cucumbers—to travel without exertion—to reap without sowing—to educate children to perfection—to introduce a new order of things as it respects *morals* and *politics, social* and *civil duties*, and to establish this strange species of credulity? I reply—those who have not yet become Cosmopolites, need no proof. They have seen and heard and read these wild vagaries, and are therefore satisfied of their existence. As to the others, I have only to remark that this same new machinery of the mind, by which *certain* things are believed, necessarily, and by the plain axiom that action and reaction are equal, produces *absolute* incredulity as to certain other thing, and of course *no testimony will have any effect.* Thus genuine Jacobins do not believe a word published in the *Spectator*, the *Connecticut Journal*, the *Connecticut Courant*, or the *Centinel*. They do not believe that France has any intention to destroy the government of this country—They do not believe that our ministers at Paris were treated with any neglect or contempt.—Indeed some doubt whether Mr. Pinkney ever was in France. They do not believe that Italy or Holland or Germany has ever been pillaged by the armies of the Republic, or that the path of those armies has been marked with any scenes of calamity and distress. In short, they do not believe but that the Directory, with their associates, are a benevolent society established in that regenerate country, for the great purpose of propagating religion and good government through the world; and that their armies are their missionaries to effect these glorious objects.

o   o   o

If many of our countrymen approve the measures of France, and applaud them in their mad career of domination, I speak with confidence, the body of our citizens entertain different opinions. Such will cordially join in protecting our government, and in supporting an energetic administration. They will, particularly as a mean to accomplish this object, and the only one I shall now urge, discountenance that unparalleled abuse of all those to whom is entrusted the management of our national interests, which is now so prevalent.

Not a man, tho' his private character were like tried gold, has escaped the most malignant censure.—The President, each head of department, each member of the Legislature, and every other man who supports the administration, is daily charged with the most vile and degrading crimes. They are openly vilified, as parties to a conspiracy against the peace, the dignity, and the happiness of the United States.

And who are these reformers, that exhibit these charges?—Are they the virtuous, meek, unspotted and holy of the earth?

Who are these thus reproached? They are your neighbors, chosen to protect your interests.—What is their object? Wealth?—If so, they are miserably employed. There is not a man among them who can, with the utmost economy, secure as much money as hundreds of merchants, lawyers, physicians, masters of vessels, and farmers, annually make by their various pursuits.

But alas! they wish to enslave us. Is this their character in private life? Have they not, with you, houses and lands, character and liberty to defend? —Have they not wives and children, whose happiness is near their hearts?— And do they, indeed, labour and toil to forge chains and fetters for their children, and children's children, that their names and memories may go down to future generations covered with the bitterest curses?

I have made these observations, my Fellow-Citizens, that we may, on this anniversary of our National existence, a day which I hope may be kept sacred to that solemn employment, contemplate the labours, the exertions and the characters of those venerable men who founded, and have hitherto, protected this nation. I wish them to be seen, and compared with the speculating theorists and mushroom politicians of this age of reason.

It is now less than two hundred years, since the first settlement of white people was effected, in these United States; less than one hundred and eighty, since the first settlement was made in New-England, and less than one hundred and seventy, since the first settlement was made in Connecticut. The place where we are now assembled was then a wild waste. Instead of cultivated fields, *dens and caves*. Instead of a flourishing city, *huts and wigwams*. Instead of polite, benevolent, and learned citizens, *a horde of savages*. Instead of a seat of science, full of young men qualifying to adorn and bless their country, here was only taught the art of tormenting ingeniously, and here were only heard the groans of the dying.

What is here said of New-Haven may, with little variation, be said of all New-England, and of many other parts of the United States.

We have now upwards of four millions of inhabitants, cultivating a fertile country, and engaged in a commerce, with 876,000 tons of shipping, and second only to that of Great Britian.

How has this mighty change been effected?—Was it by magic? By supernatural aid? or was it by ingenious theories in morals, economics and government? My Fellow-Citizens, it was accomplished by the industry, the labour, the perseverance, the sufferings and virtues of those men from whom we glory in being descended.

These venerable men spent no time in extracting sun-beams from cucumbers—in writing letters to Mazzei, or perplexing the world with the jargon of the perfectability of human nature.

They and their illustrious descendants pursued directly, and by those means which common sense dictate, the erection and support of good government and good morals. To effect these great objects they stood like monuments, with their wives, their children, and their lives in their hands.—They fought—they bled—they died.—At this expence of ease, happiness and life, they made establishments for posterity—they protected them against savages—they cemented them with their blood—they delivered them to us as a sacred deposit, and if we suffer them to be destroyed by the tinselled refinements of this age, we shall deserve the reproaches, with which impartial justice will cover such a pusillanimous race. . . .

At this day there exist two parties in these United States. At the head of one are Washington, Adams and Ellsworth.—The object of this party is to protect and defend the government from that destruction with which they believe it threatened, by its enemies. To preserve and transmit to posterity those establishments which they believe important to the happiness of society.

At the head of the other, is the gentleman who drank toasts at Fredericksburgh in May 1798, in direct contempt of our government, who wrote the letter to Mazzei, with Gallatin and Nicholas, and *Lyon*, and to grace the company they shine, with the borrowed lustre of Talleyrand, that dissembler to God and Man. The object of this party is to destroy ancient systems—ancient habits—ancient customs—to introduce a new liberty, new equality, new rights of man, new modes of education, and a new order of things.

Let them meet and make a full, fair, and perfect exposition of their principles—their objects, and the means by which they are to be accomplished—And let there be present at this display, the departed spirits of Davenport, Hooker, Winthrop, Wolcott, Hopkins, Haynes and Heaton, and let there also appear a Lawrence, a Warren, a Mercer, and a Wooster, and to which of these parties would they give their blessing?—For which of these causes, if it were possible to bleed and die again in the cause of America, would the beloved WARREN AGAIN BLEED AND DIE?

12. American Scenes

Illustrations

1. John Vanderlyn, engraved by J. Merigot, *Niagara Falls* (1804).

2. [*Lucy Knox?*], *Tremont Street, Boston* (c. 1800).

190

3. William R. Birch, *Penn's Tree, with the City and Port of Philadelphia* (1800).

4. William R. Birch. *The North, or Senate, Wing of the Capitol* (c. 1800).

5. Pavel Svinin, *Travel by Stagecoach near Trenton, New Jersey* (c. 1811).

6. Pavel Svinin, *Deck Life on the Paragon* (c. 1811).

7. Anonymous. *The Old Plantation* (c. 1777-1794).

8. Alexander Lawson, after John Lewis Krimmel, *Election Day at the State House* (n.d.).

9. Anonymous, *Pawtucket Bridge and Falls* (1812).

10. Anonymous, *The Burning of the Richmond Theater* (1812).

PART FOUR

The Useful Arts

13. Rational Amusement

Charles Willson Peale (1741-1827)—artist, politician, scientist, tinker, and showman—was one of those variegated men who were produced by the American Enlightenment and the fertile scientific environment of post-Revolutionary Philadelphia. Peale began life as a saddler and clock repairman, but soon took to painting portraits for money. After a year in London, studying with Benjamin West, he returned to involvement in the Pennsylvania revolution on the side of the radicals against the wealthy elite of Philadelphia, a stand that soon cost him subscriptions for his portraits. At the end of the war he formally renounced politics and devoted all his efforts to painting, to science, and to raising his family of ten children, a veritable menagerie in itself. In the mid-1780's Peale added to his gallery of paintings a collection of mammoth bones and other curious animal remains. When interest in the conglomeration picked up, he included an exhibition of his latest of many novelties, a miniature theater with transparent moving pictures. The resultant Peale Museum became Peale's life's masterpiece, eventually turning into a profitable institution attended by thousands of viewers. Although he had no real scholarly understanding of the natural world, Peale always sought to keep the scientific side of his museum from being corrupted by the temptations of popular entertainment. With his death, however, his natural history collections became simply aggregations of curiosities and freaks, and his lecture room and concert hall a variety theater. The whole business eventually passed into the enterprising hands of P. T. Barnum, becoming part of his dime museum and traveling circus—a romantic ending for an Enlightenment institution.

The Science of Nature

CHARLES WILLSON PEALE

With an ardent desire of rendering myself not unconspicuously useful to my country, I may undertake works, perhaps, of greater magnitude than may be thought perfectly prudent for an individual of my years;—means of support;—and mental powers.

But when so much pleasure is felt in the contemplation of the wonderful works of an All-wise Creator!—Can I leave any difficulty untried to display those beauties which, in every step we take, unfold scenes calculated to teach adoration to that finger which directs a universe? —Grant thou divine Architect strength to those nerves, light to this mind, to explore the true line of connection and dependence of all thy creatures; and give powers of language, to display, to my fellow man, thy goodness to every being!

In my introductory Lecture, delivered last year, I endeavoured to shew how important is the knowledge of Natural Science to every class of citizens.

I addressed the Farmer; the Merchant, and the Mechanic; I shewed that the Swedish government was aided by Linnaeus's knowledge of Natural Science, and that even Poets, and all those professing the fine arts, must from thence derive their models of elegance. And again I repeat, "that the comfort, happiness, and support of all ranks, depend on their knowledge of nature:" otherwise how could they be fed, clothed, and even sheltered from the inclemency of the seasons?

In short, it is a source from which man is taught to know himself; whose lessons teach him to bear with patience, or to alleviate, the various sufferings to which human beings are liable. Can he properly know himself without having some knowledge of the numerous animals, and such substances as aid, comfort, and even support him?—with this knowledge he is enabled to do justice to the feelings of others, he will bend to that sweet sympathy which cherishes the love of harmony; that peace and tranquillity so powerfully sweetening human life! Need it be said that all the other branches of the Science claim his attention? Minds accustomed to

Charles Willson Peale, *Discourse Introductory to a Course of Lectures on the Science of Nature* . . . (Philadelphia, 1800), pp. 3–16, 32–45, 48–50.

1. Charles Willson Peale, *Exhuming the First American Mastodon* (1806-1808).

2. Titian Ramsay Peale, *The Peale Museum* (1822).

investigate the causes of the various Phenomena of Nature, will be more or less acquainted with the elements, and from the known properties of some, they will enjoy speculative ideas of the more abstruse, or unaccountable appearances of others.

The local organized bodies, as well as those that grow without organs, vegetable and mineral productions, will engage the attention of every person, in a greater or less degree, and are of much consequence in a physical, moral, or commercial view through life.

Many enlightened authors have given their sentiments in elegant language on the importance of the study of Nature and all the judicious part of mankind accord in their wishes to encourage so fruitful a science. It is only the most inconsiderate mind which could possibly turn its face against so pleasing, and useful an employment as the study of Nature. —I must here pause. —This is a heavy charge,—I have said there is a want of taste for this my favourite science,—on reflection, I really do not believe, that a being so out of Nature can be found. —I am sure it would be more monstrous than any *lusus naturae* belonging to the Museum, (and I have several which I have never wished to exhibit.) —No, it cannot be,—there is not such a character to be found,—it is only a difference of sentiment in the manner of obtaining this knowledge of Nature:—It is the means of encouragement to this science, and not against it, that one dissenting vote would be found amongst millions of men.—

Therefore, in future, I shall set it down as an established principle, that all men are agreed to join in the admiration, promotion, and cultivation of the knowledge of Nature.

The BEAUTIES of CREATION.

Mark the beauties of Creation,
   Mark the harmony that reigns!
Each, supported in its station,
   Age to age unchang'd remains.

Water, earth, and air surrounding,
   Teem with life in every mode;
Foodful plants and herbs abounding,
   Fossils in their dark abode.

Flitting thro' the yielding heaven,
   Hark! the warblers of the grove!
Deck'd in plumage richly given,
   All their souls attun'd to love.

Food and raiment, use and pleasure,
　　Each, attend the bestial train;
Seas pour forth their finny treasure;
　　Earth its fruits and plenteous grain.

Flutt'ring gay from flower to flower,
　　See the vivid insect stray—
Changeful form! within the hour,
　　Winged, bursting into day.

These, ten thousand times repeated
　　Fill Creation's boundless plan;
Mark the finger that created
　　Each, in proper place, as man.

Let us then, the whole surveying,
　　Guide the moral to our heart—
Let us, Nature's voice obeying,
　　Live in bliss and bliss impart.

May reason at last, among all nations, obtain its empire; that they may feel their relative situations to other beings; and thus knowing their reciprocal dependence, learn to cultivate the arts of peace,—and may war be no more named, but with horror! How absurdly they reason who say, that mankind would multiply too fast, without wars. —Is there not an abundance of employment for all the human species? —Is there not yet an immensity of land even in Europe uncultivated?—do not other quarters of the globe furnish their millions, yet unexplored?—will not disease make ravages sufficient among us mortals?—must we still go on to murder one another, because we do not speak the same language? or can nations find no other way to settle their differences, but by the sword? will any substantial, or permanent profit arise to those nations which promote wars?—have they calculated the expence of armanents, can they fully weigh the profits and losses, and strike the balance? If one hundreth part of the sums lavished on war, were applied to the encouragement of science, would not the condition of millions of inhabitants be ameliorated, and the world then be a Paradise compared to its present situation! and as to individual profit, what kind of being can he be, who could enjoy riches, the price of his murdered fellow creatures? —Were we cannibals we might have some excuse—but alas! we have none.

Example has sometimes been able to effect more, than the strongest laws of depotism. If I give a very strong contrast, the blush may rise on the cheek of some, not yet lost to all sense of feeling.

To this end, let us take a cursory survey of the manners of other animals; —those, which we say, are inferior to our species. —Do they levy war against their kind?—Does the Lyon destroy the Lyon?—does the Hawk prey upon Hawk?—were Sharks ever known to depredate on their own species?— No! so foul an infamy is found alone on man! —Our traders to the Faulkland and other Isles on the coast of Patagonia and Chili, tell us, that Sea-Lyons, Sea-Wolves, and other such animals, are often found so numerous, as to cover the shores; so thickly are they inhabited, that a man with a short bludgeon, may kill hundreds of them before his breakfast!—yet among this immense number of creatures, a perfect harmony prevails!—Suppose we descend, and view the smallest animals,—here, myriads of insects, present themselves to our view. They are far more numerous than any other class of animals, and yet behold among them also, a perfect harmony.

This is a serious comparative view of animated creation, permit me to ask, if it yields much credit, or honour to our boasted reason?—most assuredly not. And if we study the manners of such animals in general, we shall find amongst them, most excellent models of friendship, constancy, parental care, and every other social virtue.

Although we generally find so much harmony among the inferior animals, yet they sometimes, have their battles, but it rarely happens, where their wants are bountifully supplied.

That one species of animals should prey upon another, is perfectly consistent with the order of things, and it is wisely provided, that the number of each kind should correspond, so as to keep up that equilibrium of supply, which constantly prevails.

It would be digressing from the object of this address, were I to enlarge on the folly of wars, or note the proper means to avoid them. But I have thus pointedly spoken my disapprobation, because I do not hate mankind, and am fully impressed, that if they do not act wisely, the fault only arises from a want of education. The mind of man is ever active, it must be employed continually, and the greater number of inlets that can be opened for him to receive instruction, with rational amusements, the more effectually will he be drawn from vicious habits.

Can we find a more pleasing study, than by gaining a thorough acquaintance with the properties of the various substances, whether animate, or inanimate, that constantly are presented to our view?—

I am sure this polite audience will agree with me, that it would be a source of infinite pleasure, could we say, when we put our hand on this or that object (be it what it may,) such are its component parts; such its derivation; and such are its uses. Perhaps it is not possible for an individual to be so learned in the science of nature, as to possess a complete knowledge of all the objects of each branch; yet possessing the general principles of those systems which have been invented of late years, by several ingenious and learned men, (with a view to facilitate the study of natural history,) he may, with a little application, acquire the knowledge necessary to know any object, although he had never seen it before.

Such is the precision of character stamped by the Creator on all his works! —such the beautiful uniformity in an infinite variety of beings, that the more we see, and know of their marked characters, the more ardent will be our thirst for knowledge in this edifying and charming science,—the greater will our astonishment and admiration of boundless Wisdom!—such contemplations raise us above ourselves!—our astonished souls are elevated as it were to a converse with the great moving Power, who governs worlds!—we feel unspeakable pleasure, and soar above this earth in rapturous praise!

The exercise of our reasoning faculties in making ourselves acquainted with all the objects presented to our view, in each moment of our waking hours, opens a boundless field of contemplation!

Possessing such a turn of mind, we acquire an unceasing fund of entertainment, from which no situation whatever in life, could wholly deprive us. This may be called the food of reason, and ought to be inculcated on the minds of our children, as soon as they can lisp a sentence.

We might begin with the most simple questions; pick up a straw, and question and instruct the child as to its growth; its grain and their uses; and as their little minds expand, teach them not only useful arts, but at the same time a little of every branch of natural history.

One caution only should be premised, which is, never to put abstruse questions to them, such as cannot be comprehended by their experience, or reason; therefore familiar visible things; substances at hand, should be the medium through which we ought to convey our instructions. If education is essential for obtaining happiness,—have not our daughters an equal right with our sons to our instruction? and if we consider what kind of education is most useful, we will find generally that which benefits our sons, may equally be serviceable to our daughters; and it is, with real concern, I have noticed the neglect of female education in some of the states. Happily of late years, the citizens of Philadelphia, have turned their attention to the establishment of particular schools, for the instruction of young ladies,—this reflects much honour on the city, and may excite other cities to establish similar institutions.

The lively fancy of the youthful fair, would quickly catch a fondness for a science of such infinite variety.—What a charming topic for conversation would this afford in their social parties! And if we reflect how the various parts of natural science branch out into all the household and economical concerns, can we find any part of female education of greater import? To proceed a little further, we find that, for the most part, the early education of children must naturally fall to the mother, hence how important that she should be well informed in the history of Nature. What a delightful amusement it must be, to teach her sweet prattlers, as their minds expand, the various changes, from the creeping caterpillar to the dormant chrysalis, and afterward the gay flitting butterfly; and also the various metamorphosis other insects undergo;—to know their uses in the support of other animals, —that hence they may be led to abstain from cruelly, or wantonly tormenting them. Thus instilling and extending, as they advance in years, a sweet benevolence of temper toward their brethren.

What charming conversations will a knowledge of this Science afford between the father and his sons, at the age when they become agreeable and useful companions to each other. —How often in their morning or evening walks might the infirmities of age be beguiled, while recounting their observations, and explaining the vivifying scenes of Nature, and often by judicious remarks, the high toned passions of the youthful nerve, might be restrained until it gains maturity. Whereas from the natural restlessness of that age, unless diverted by some useful amusements, they are heedlessly led into scenes of folly,—and too often, vices that embitter all their future days!

I have not yet spoken of this study in a religious point of view. —Were it necessary, I could give chapter and verse, from the Holy Writings, not only according with the subject of this address, but expressly recommending the study of Nature as an essential duty of man. —Our divines, I flatter myself, will aid me on this subject with more forceable language than I possess. —Into whose hands, with sentiments of regard for their office, I respectfully submit this fruitful theme, wishing them honor, comfort in their labours, energy in their discourses, to make men wiser and better.

Very few words are requisite to prove that the Science of Nature, when viewed in its full extent and true meaning, is one of the most important studies of man. —All men agree, that the study of morals is in the highest degree important. We shall therefore only add that the former is the foundation on which morality is built; in as much as the study of man forms a part of it; and the whole creation teems with the most striking examples which the Moralist can desire.

But enough is already said on the importance of the study of nature—and yet, what a variety of instances, are left unnoticed, which prove the beneficial effects such knowledge has on the conduct of men to render them pious and happy!

Yet not to engross more of your time by illustrating a subject so self evident, let us proceed to point out the most easy method for obtaining this knowledge.

This will be by the aid of a MUSEUM. . . .

First let us suppose we have before us a spacious building, with a suite of rooms of several hundred feet in length, even the length of one of the squares of our city, in which are arranged specimens of all the various animals of this vast continent, and of all other countries;—these in high preservation, under glass to secure them from injury. —Let us suppose them classically arranged, so that the mind may not be confused and distracted in viewing and studying such a multitude of objects.

Whether we begin at the first or last link of the chain is of little consequence; whether we first view the simple naked animals destitute of limbs, such as worms, and ascend through all the various classes of different organized matter until we reach the most intelligent creature, man;—

Or whether we commence our view from those standing erect, and then descend through all the gradation to such as creep in the dust,—is of little consequence, provided we proceed step by step, to trace the beauties which we shall find that each possesses, in its relative situation to other beings;— its force, its intelligence, and its activity to supply its wants, and protect its young.

It is by this kind of order, we may with ease and pleasure, acquire knowledge from the great book of nature.—Thus reading one leaf at a time, progress to a comprehensive acquaintance with the subjects of every country yet explored,—enjoying the whole world! —An elegant author says, "he who views only the produce of his own country, may be said to inhabit a single world; while those who see and consider the productions of other climes, bring many worlds as it were in review before them."

In this manner, while we pass through these rooms, we may see the link that separates our species from the brute creation, in the gentle intelligent Oran Outang, little less than human, only by the want of speech; yet the lack of that, alone, is sufficient to place it far from our species, and nearer to the Monkey tribe. —And in the Flying-squirrel, Ostrich, Cassawary and

Batt, connecting links between quadrupeds and birds.—In the amphibious, the division between quadrupeds and fishes, and even the minuter link, in a quadruped I possess with gills. Amongst the animals of the deep, the variety similar to those that inhabit the air and land.

In short, in an extensive collection should be found, the various Inhabitants of every element, not only of the animal, but also specimens of the vegetable tribe,—and all the brilliant and precious stones, down to the common gritt,—all the minerals in their virgin state. —Petrefactions of the human body, of which two instances are known, and through that immense variety which should grace every well stored Museum. Here should be seen no duplicates, and only the varieties of each species, all placed in the most conspicuous point of light, to be seen to advantage, without being handled.

When we have imagined that specimens of every kind were placed before us,—in varieties equal to any Museum yet formed, so numerous are the works of creation, that others will still be found in that bounteous store. Wherefore, space should always be left, in every division for the reception of more.

Then in rooms, as appendages to this suite of rooms, should be placed every curious article of dress; arms and untensils of the Aborigines of this, and of other new discovered countries.

Besides a classical catalogue, descriptive of every article belonging to so extensive a Museum, there ought to be also a Library consisting of the writings of the best authors on natural history, from Aristotle and Theophrastus down to the present time.

Can the imagination conceive any thing more interesting than such a Museum? —Or can there be a more agreeable spectacle to an admirer of the divine Wisdom! Where, within a magnificent pile, every art and every science should be taught, by plans, models, pictures, real subjects and lectures. To this central magazine of knowledge, all the learned and ingenious would flock, as well to gain, as to communicate, information.

May every person that hears me, feel as I feel, an enthusiastic desire to establish a similar institution to what I have barely given the outline of, in the city of Philadelphia; and let it like that of Ptolemus Philadelphus at Alexandria, be the first in America.

I see no great difficulty in laying the foundation of such an establishment in this city. The progress I have made in a few years, in forming a Museum, by my sole exertions, almost without funds, is a proof of what may be done in a series of time with moderate means. And since I have subjects, a sufficient number of every class to make a brilliant display in a large building, why not with my labours make a beginning? —Why not employ a few persons of proper talents to bring forward a work of which you and your children will reap the benefit; and may feast on continually, with as much delight as the Elysian fields afforded to the antient philosophers! —Not imaginary but substantially, by opening a perpetual stream of useful knowledge; a stream flowing from every quarter of the world! where you might sweetly sip, digest, and still desire more!— If we lay a good foundation for an extensive and permanent Museum, every seaman returning home, will add his mite; our travellers, while exploring the western regions, interested in its progress, would collect for its increase; and our merchants and their friends in foreign countries would shew their zeal to encrease our store.

Why should this be delayed till you my hearers and myself are no more. —Let it not be! We have the resources;—or may obtain them by some exertions. We have the ground, and the building may be spacious without great expence, for, internal ornament would be useless: The building would be but a narrow lengthy shell, plain finished within. However, to support it, some funds are absolutely necessary,—perhaps not more than the real value of articles which would be presented to such an Institution.

A few persons well acquainted with the methods of preserving subjects, should be continually employed; one for each department of nature:—For although things that are once well prepared, require no other care than what any attentive person, is able to perform, yet new subjects will be continually increasing from such an inexhaustible store. Gentlemen of talents, should be allowed to deliver lectures in the several branches of natural history; having the articles of nature before them. But, if the persons who prepare the subjects, are capacitated to deliver lectures, they should be preferred, because they would be the most likely to use those articles with delicacy. Besides, if a profit is to be had from the delivery of lectures, it may be thrown into the salary of such artist.

It will readily be conceived that some person should have the superintendance of the Museum; under whose directions, every addition should be made and the care of every thing rest with him. The support of this officer should arise from the monies paid by the visitors to the Museum: thus giving him an interest in the improvements and in keeping them in good order.

The price of admission should be small, and at stated periods, proportioned to some certain staple, or necessary article of our market. The evil of depreciation of money, is, by this procedure avoided.

The advantages of opening a Museum on these terms are manifest. A small sum paid for admission, would keep out the idle rabble, who, otherwise, by having free ingress, might injure the subjects. Those really desirous of information, would freely pay a triffle, and they would visit it more frequently, as in a well organized repository, there would always be found something new, or unnoticed before.

I verily believe, that this Museum, has already diffused much knowledge, and, no doubt, by the improvements meditated, in a few years the inhabitants near it will possess a more accurate knowledge than people who can-' not have the easy opportunities of seeing it.

One very important effect may be produced,—persons having different sentiments in politicks, being drawn together for the purpose of studying the beauties of nature, while conversing on those agreeable subjects, may find a concordance of sentiments, and most probably from a slight acquaintance, would think better of each other, than while totally estranged. An instance of this is in the memory of many of my hearers. The chiefs of several nations of Indians, who had an hereditary enmity to each other, happened to meet unexpectedly in the Museum in 1796; they regarded each other with considerable emotion, which in some degree subsided when, by their interpreters, they were informed, that each party, ignorant of the intention of the other, had come merely to view the Museum. Never having before met, but in the field of battle, where the recollection of former scenes of bloodshed, only roused the spirit of revenge; no room was left for the feelings of the social man. —Now, for the first time, finding themselves in peace, surrounded by a scene calculated to inspire the most perfect harmony, the first suggestion was,—that as men of the same species they were not enemies by nature; but ought forever to bury the hatchet of war.

After leaving the Museum they formed a treaty so far as their powers extended, and wishing the white people to be witnesses to the sincerity of their intentions, at the request of the Secretary of War, I supplied them with a room.—Sixty-four chiefs of eight or ten nations met; they heard a speech sent by General WASHINGTON, recommending peace.—Their orators spoke; and they departed friends.

Quarrels in politicks are something like those in matrimony, almost always about triffles; seldom on things of consequence;—each comparing their notes with candour, their differences, are soon settled.

I wish to be understood. The institution of a Museum can have no more to do with the politicks of a country, than with particular religious opinions.

Its basis has a much broader bottom. Facts, and not theories, are the foundation on which the whole superstructure is built. Not on theoretical, speculative things, but on the objects of our sight and feelings;—with the laws which govern them; on real subjects, with their general, or specific characters, economy, or manners;—the production, preservation, and destruction of all material things deduced from facts.

Hence pursuing the proper course of this science, we cannot offend any human laws, either political or religious. And by a knowledge of nature all will be benefited.

We might travel for years to obtain knowledge in natural science, and although we might thus get considerable acquaintance with some things, yet many would be hid from our view, if we had not previously studied them in an orderly, classical, or scientific Museum: as it is here, that a better acquaintance of things generally may be had, and even in a shorter time, than in any other mode. So that the expence of travelling, to acquire this knowledge, especially into foreign countries, may, in a considerable degree, be dispensed with.

A correct catalogue of the subjects before us, would be very satisfactory; but a more perfect acquaintance with those things would be obtained by well digested lectures, where the specific description is gone into, with such accounts of them, as may be thought sufficiently interesting.

The sight of some things, which had before caused uneasiness, nay, fright, by a proper investigation, we may learn to look on, to handle, and examine with a considerable degree of pleasure. In short, it is the duty of the Lecturer to shew what we should avoid as dangerous, as well as what we may approach with impunity, and also the particular uses to which they may be applied for the benefit of mankind.

These lectures should not only make us acquainted with the useful properties of all its objects, but since very frequent examples of extraordinary virtues occur, it becomes the Lecturer's duty, occasionally to intersperse in them some moral reflections, because, (according to an old adage,) example is generally more powerful than precept.

In fact, he must be a very superficial observer of nature, who does not see, with what infinite goodness the bountiful hand of Providence, has given powers to all his creatures, to know what is good, and what is hurtful for them; and by attentively observing their manners, we may frequently learn of them, useful lessons. Could it be for any other purpose that the Creator has endowed us with reasoning faculties? which enable us to observe the creatures placed in our power, but that we might compare their conduct with our own? and has also given us freedom of will, to apply it, for our edification, comfort and happiness.

Do not the holy scriptures every where tell us, these are our monitors? I will bring it nearer home, and say, if we consult our own feelings, and then exercise that reason so benevolently bestowed upon us, we must form a proper result. And the comforts immediately, or ultimately flowing therefrom, independent of all other considerations, should arm us with resolution sufficiently strong to induce us, never to do wrong. Otherwise, instead of superior beings, we are really inferior to the reptiles that crawl on the ground.

My friends, if we are not the most cheerful, pious, and happiest creatures that inhabit this globe the fault arises wholly from our want of a proper education, and remember, to that end I give my mite by beginning the establishment of a MUSEUM.

Gaze stranger, there!
And let thy soften'd heart intensely feel
How good, how lovely, nature! when from hence;
Departing to the city's crowded streets,
Thy sickening eye at every step revolts
From scenes of vice and wretchedness; reflect
That man creates the evil he endures.

This Museum is known to contain in good preservation, many of our large, as well as small quadrupeds;—many of the amphibious animals;—the American birds generally, with some Europeans; all in classical arrangement; as, is also a numerous and beautiful collection of insects, even to the minute ones, too small to be seen by the naked eye: these are placed in new invented microscopes; forming a classical continuation in numerical order from the larger kinds. Minerals and shells, &c. properly arranged to advance study,—besides many other articles, the proper appendages of a Museum.

Application has been made to me from Sweden, England, Holland, Germany, France and Italy, for supplies of articles of natural history generally: some have offered money and other similar articles in exchange. My answer uniformly has been, I am willing to exchange, but never to sell. —And some reciprocal exchanges had taken place,—but war has prevented me from getting, in some instances suitable returns, wherefore can it be wondered that I so pointedly reprobate that curse of mankind? Which besides its other enumerable baneful effects, also deprives us of the sight of such desireable objects;—and dreading the claws of those sea monsters, privateer robbers, I have preferred filling my store boxes with the duplicates of my Museum, which now contain hundreds of preserved subjects in readiness to exchange for such articles as my Museum is in want of, such as I can command with very little further trouble, when Europe returns to her proper senses!

Several plans of important additions to my Museum I have meditated the execution of, year after year,—One of them is, preserving the variety of fishes; the product of our waters, which should form a more interesting part of this repository, than many may suppose; since in New York market alone, as I am creditably informed, by a gentleman who had taken the trouble to count and name them, are forty-two different kinds for the table. . . .

Since the death of my son, struck more particularly with the uncertainty of human life, I have hastened to prepare a course of lectures, under the impression, that if I gave them their natural and proper turn; that of manifesting by those works the goodness and wisdom of the Creator, in making every being in the best form to endure its happiness, obtaining its support, with its connection and dependence toward the support of other beings; —In short, to display by visible objects the harmony of the universe.—That having once laid this firm and solid foundation, no one who follows me, however flowery his language, masterly his rhetorick may be; henceforward will chuse to deviate from a system so plain; so morally and religiously beneficial, and yet so demonstrable in its merits to every capacity; not because I have chosen it, but because the world has proved that Linnaeus has judiciously adopted it.

Here I think it proper, to take notice that the Philosopher and Naturalist have been viewed, by some people, as irreligious. How this opinion could be conceived I cannot imagine; unless from the conduct of some rash impassioned men, who have assumed those characters, without being possessed of penetration and judgment sufficient to view things on the great scale of universal laws, which support every atom of matter in its proper place; that bind together or support a universe. Those superficial men, catch at some things that appear strange to them, and with a desire of becoming singular, take on themselves the part of censors; they find fault with that order, the depth of which they do not penetrate.

They affect to be learned, which is sufficient to catch the wonder of the vulgar, and thus they obtain the name of Philosopher or Naturalist, without the least title whatever to the character. When in fact, no man is entitled, or deserves the name, whose words and actions do not prove him to be patient under afflictions,—forbearing when injured,—benevolent to all creatures,—promoting harmony among men. And who also admires the works of creation, and through them adores the Creator. If this is not religion, in the name of charity, what is?

My course of lectures is now comprised in forty discourses, which I propose to deliver this season at my Museum. And in order that too great a number of objects may not distract the attention of those who will honour me with their presence, I shall select from other articles of the Museum, those which are the subjects of each Lecture, and dispose them, while described, in the most favorable light to be seen.

As I have endeavored to shew how important it is for the fair sex to possess this knowledge of nature it would be unpardonable to deliver such Lectures as might offend the most delicate Ear. —Therefore I have prepared them expressly for the Ladies as well as Gentlemen.

As I am the first in America who has made the attempt to deliver lectures particularly on the animal department of Natural History, with preserved subjects, it is hoped the public will regard it with an indulgent ear, and give the encouragement necessary to induce a continuation of this Infant School, which hereafter may be filled by Professors of Talents, better qualified to do the subject Justice.

14. The American Medical Revolution

Benjamin Rush (1746-1813) was the personification of the American Enlightenment. Since, as a physician, he believed that "the science of medicine is related to everything," he considered everything within his intellectual domain and had something to say about everything. Apart from clinical medicine, his writings deal with subjects as diverse as political theory and penology, chemistry and forestry, animal husbandry and steam navigation, psychiatry and education. He was undoubtedly the most influential scientist of his generation and contributed more than anyone else to making Philadlphia the leading center of medical training in the first half of the nineteenth century.

As a man of the Enlightenment, Rush believed that all the scattered facts and ideas relating to various subjects could be brought into comprehensive order. All knowledge—in politics, religion, philosophy and medicine—could be reduced to unity and simplicity. Rush's great aim was to purge medicine of its complications and mystery and to make of it a plain and popular science. Like American politics and society, medicine was to be republicanized, and every man was to become his own doctor.

The Comparative State of Medicine

in the Revolutionary Era

BENJAMIN RUSH

In estimating the progress and utility of medicine, important advantages may be derived from taking a view of its ancient, and comparing it with its present state. To do this upon an extensive scale, would be difficult, and foreign to the design of this inquiry. I shall therefore limit it, to the history of the diseases and medical opinions which prevailed, and of the remedies which were in use, in the city of Philadelphia, between the years 1760 and 1766, and of the diseases, medical opinions, and remedies of the year 1805. The result of a comparative view of each of them, will determine whether medicine has declined or improved, in that interval of time, in this part of the world.

To derive all the benefits that are possible from such an inquiry, it will be proper to detail the causes, which, by acting upon the human body, influence the subjects that have been mentioned, in those two remote periods of time.

Those causes divide themselves into climate, diet, dress, and certain peculiar customs; on each of which I shall make a few remarks.

After what has been said, in the history of the Climate of Pennsylvania, in the first volume of these Inquiries, it will only be necessary in this place

Benjamin Rush, "An Inquiry into the Comparative State of Medicine, in Philadelphia, Between the Years 1760 and 1766, and the Year 1805," *Medical Inquiries and Observations*, 2d ed. (Philadelphia, 1805), vol. IV, pp. 364–405.

briefly to mention, that the winters in Philadelphia, between the years 1760 and 1766, were almost uniformly cold. The ground was generally covered with snow, and the Delaware frozen, from the first or second week in December, to the last week in February, or the first week in March. Thaws were rare during the winter months, and seldom of longer duration than three or four days. The springs began in May. The summers were generally warm, and the air seldom refreshed by cool north-west winds. Rains were frequent and heavy, and for the most part accompanied with thunder and lightning. The autumns began in October, and were gradually succeeded by cool and cold weather.

The diet of the inhabitants of Philadelphia, during those years, consisted chiefly of animal food. It was eaten, in some families, three times, and in all, twice a day. A hot supper was a general meal. To two and three meals of animal food in a day, many persons added what was then called "a relish," about an hour before dinner. It consisted of a slice of ham, a piece of salted fish, and now and then a beef-steak, accompanied with large draughts of punch or toddy. Tea was in the interval between dinner and supper.

In many companies, a glass of wine and bitters was taken a few minutes before dinner, in order to increase the appetite.

The drinks, with dinner and supper, were punch and table beer.

Besides feeding thus plentifully in their families, many of the most respectable citizens belonged to clubs, which met in the city in winter, and in its vicinity, under sheds, or the shade of trees, in summer, once and twice a week, and, in one instance, every night. They were drawn together by suppers in winter, and dinners in summer. Their food was simple, and taken chiefly in a solid form. The liquors used with it were punch, London porter, and sound old Madeira wine.

Independently of these clubs, there were occasional meetings of citizens, particularly of young men, at taverns, for convivial purposes. A house in Water-street, known by the name of the Tun tavern, was devoted chiefly to this kind of accidental meetings. They were often followed by midnight sallies into the streets, and such acts of violence and indecency, as frequently consigned the perpetrators of them afterwards into the hands of the civil officers and physicians of the city.

Many citizens, particularly tradesmen, met every evening for the purpose of drinking beer, at houses kept for that purpose. Instances of drunkenness were rare at such places. The company generally parted at ten o'clock, and retired in an orderly manner to their habitations. Morning drams, consisting of cordials of different kinds, were common, both in taverns and private houses, but they were confined chiefly to the lower class of people.

From this general use of distilled and fermented liquors, drunkenness was a common vice in all the different ranks of society.

The dresses of the men, in the years alluded to, were composed of cloth in winter, and of thin woollen or silk stuffs in summer. Wigs composed the covering of the head, after middle life, and cocked hats were universally worn, except by the men who belonged to the society of friends.

The dresses of the women, in the years before mentioned, consisted chiefly of silks and calicoes. Stays were universal, and hoops were generally worn by the ladies in genteel life. Long cloth or camblet cloaks were common, in cold weather, among all classes of women.

The principal custom under this head, which influenced health and life, was that which obliged women, after lying-in, "to sit up for company;" that is, to dress themselves, every afternoon on the second week after their confinement, and to sit for four or five hours, exposed to the impure air of a crowded room, and sometimes to long and loud conversations.

Porches were nearly universal appendages to houses, and it was common for all the branches of a family to expose themselves upon them, to the evening air. Stoves were not in use, at that time, in any places of public worship.

Funerals were attended by a large concourse of citizens, who were thereby often exposed to great heat and cold, and sometimes to standing, while the funeral obsequies were performed, in a wet or damp church-yard.

The human mind, in this period of the history of our city, was in a colonized state, and the passions acted but feebly and partially upon literary and political subjects.

We come now to mention the diseases which prevailed in our city between the years 1760 and 1766.

The cholera morbus was a frequent disease in the summer months.

Sporadic cases of dysentery were at that time common. I have never seen that disease epidemic in Philadelphia.

The intermitting fever prevailed in the month of August, and in the autumn, chiefly in the suburbs and neighbourhood of the city. In the year 1765, it was epidemic in Southwark, and was so general, at the same time, as to affect two thirds of the inhabitants of the southern states. This fact is mentioned by Dr. Bond, in a lecture preserved in the minutes of the managers of the Pennsylvania hospital.

The slow chronic fever, called at that time the nervous fever, was very common, in the autumnal months, in the thickly settled parts of the city.

The bilious fever prevailed, at the same time, in Southwark. The late Dr. Clarkson, who began to practise medicine in that part of the city, in the year 1761, upon hearing some of his medical brethren speak of the appearance of bilious remittents in its middle and northern parts, about the year 1778, said they had long been familiar to him, and that he had met with them every year since his settlement in Philadelphia.

The yellow fever prevailed in the neighbourhood of Spruce-street wharf, and near a filthy stream of water which flowed through what is now called Dock-street, in the year 1762. Some cases of it appeared likewise in Southwark. It was scarcely known in the north and west parts of the city. No desertion of the citizens took place at this time, nor did the fear of contagion drive the friends of the sick from their bed-sides, nor prevent the usual marks of respect being paid to them after death, by following their bodies to the grave. A few sporadic cases of the same grade of fever appeared in the year 1763.

Pneumonies, rheumatisms, inflammatory sore throats, and catarrhs were frequent during the winter and spring months. The last disease was induced, not only by sudden changes in the weather, but often by exposure to the evening air, on porches in summer, and by the damp and cold air of places of public worship in winter.

The influenza was epidemic in the city in the spring of the year 1761.

The malignant sore throat proved fatal to a number of children in the winter of 1763.

The scarlet fever prevailed generally in the year 1764. It resembled the same disease, as described by Dr. Sydenham, in not being accompanied by a sore throat.

Death from convulsions in pregnant women, also from parturition, and the puerperile fever, were common between the years 1760 and 1766. Death was likewise common between the 50th and 60th years of life from gout, apoplexy, palsy, obstructed livers, and dropsies. A club, consisting of about a dozen of the first gentlemen in the city, all paid, for their intemperance, the forfeit of their lives between those ages, and most of them with some one, or more of the diseases that have been mentioned. I sat up with one of that club on the night of his death. Several of the members of it called at his house, the evening before he died, to inquire how he was. One of them, upon being informed of his extreme danger, spoke in high and pathetic terms of his convivial talents and virtues, and said, "he had spent 200 evenings a year with him, for the last twenty years of his life." These evenings were all spent at public houses.

The colica pictonum, or dry gripes, was formerly a common disease in this city. It was sometimes followed by a palsy of the upper and lower extremities. Colics from crapulas were likewise very frequent, and now and then terminated in death.

Many children died of the cholera infantum, cynanche trachealis, and hydrocephalus internus. The last disease was generally ascribed to worms.

Fifteen or twenty deaths occurred, every summer, from drinking cold pump water, when the body was in a highly excitable state, from great heat and labour.

The small-pox, within the period alluded to, was sometimes epidemic, and carried off many citizens. In the year 1759, Dr. Barnet was invited from Elizabeth-town, in New-Jersey, to Philadelphia, to inoculate for the small-pox. The practice, though much opposed, soon became general. About that time, Dr. Redman published a short defence of it, and recommended the practice to his fellow-citizens in the most affectionate language. The success of inoculation was far from being universal. Subsequent improvements in the mode of preparing the body, and treating the eruptive fever, have led us to ascribe this want of success to the deep wound made in the arm, to the excessive quantity of mercury given to prepare the body, and to the use of a warm regimen in the eruptive fever.

The peculiar customs and the diseases which have been enumerated, by inducing general weakness, rendered the pulmonary consumption a frequent disease among both sexes.

Pains and diseases from decayed teeth were very common, between the years 1760 and 1766. At that time, the profession of a dentist was unknown in the city.

The practice of physic and surgery were united, during those years, in the same persons, and physicians were seldom employed as man-midwives, except in preternatural and tedious labours.

The practice of surgery was regulated by Mr. Sharp's treatise upon that branch of medicine.

Let us now take a view of the medical opinions which prevailed at the above period, and of the remedies which were employed to cure the diseases that have been mentioned.

The system of Dr. Boerhaave then governed the practice of every physician in Philadelphia. Of course diseases were ascribed to morbid acrimonies, and other matters in the blood, and the practice of those years was influenced by a belief in them. Medicines were prescribed to thin, and to incrassate the blood, and diet drinks were administered in large quantities, in order to alter its qualities. Great reliance was placed upon the powers of nature, and critical days were expected with solicitude, in order to observe the discharge of the morbid cause of fevers from the system. This matter was looked for chiefly in the urine, and glasses to retain it were a necessary part of the furniture of every sick room. To ensure the discharge of the supposed morbid matter of fevers through the pores, patients were confined to their beds, and fresh, with [*sic*] cool air, often excluded by close doors and curtains. The medicines to promote sweats were generally of a feeble nature. The spiritus mindereri, and the spirit of sweet nitre were in daily use for that purpose. In dangerous cases, saffron and Virginia snakeroot were added to them.

Blood-letting was used plentifully in pleurisies and rheumatisms, but sparingly in all other diseases. Blood was often drawn from the feet, in order to excite a revulsion of disease from the superior parts of the body. It was considered as unsafe, at that time, to bleed during the monthly disease of the female sex.

Purges or vomits began the cure of all febrile diseases, but as the principal dependence was placed upon sweating medicines, those powerful remedies were seldom repeated in the subsequent stages of fevers. To this remark there was a general exception in the yellow fever of 1762. Small doses of glauber's salts were given every day after bleeding, so as to promote a gentle, but constant discharge from the bowels.

The bark was administered freely in intermittents. The prejudices against it at that time were so general among the common people, that it was often necessary to disguise it. An opinion prevailed among them, that it lay in their bones, and that it disposed them to take cold. It was seldom given in the low and gangrenous states of fever, when they were not attended with remissions.

The use of opium was confined chiefly to ease pain, to compose a cough, and to restrain preternatural discharges from the body. Such were the prejudices against it, that it was often necessary to conceal it in other medicines. It was rarely taken without the advice of a physician.

Mercury was in general use in the years that have been mentioned. I have said it was given to prepare the body for the small-pox. It was administered by my first preceptor in medicine, Dr. Redman, in the same disease, when it appeared in the natural way, with malignant or inflammatory symptoms, in order to keep the salivary glands open and flowing, during the turn of the pock. He gave it likewise liberally in the dry gripes. In one case of that disease, I well remember the pleasure he expressed, in consequence of its having affected his patient's mouth.

But to Dr. Thomas Bond the city of Philadelphia is indebted for the introduction of mercury into general use, in the practice of medicine. He called it emphatically "a revolutionary remedy," and prescribed it in all diseases which resisted the common modes of practice. He gave it liberally in the cynanche trachealis. He sometimes cured madness, by giving it in such quantities as to excite a salivation. He attempted to cure pulmonary consumption by it, but without success; for, at that time, the influence of the relative actions of different diseases and remedies, upon the human body, was not known, or, if known, no advantage was derived from it in the practice of medicine.

The dry gripes were cured, at that time, by a new and peculiar mode of practice, by Dr. Thomas Cadwallader. He kept the patient easy by gentle anodynes, and gave lenient purges only in the beginning of the disease; nor did he ever assist the latter by injections till the fourth and fifth days, at which time the bowels discharged their contents in an easy manner. It was said this mode of cure prevented the paralytic symptoms, which sometimes follow that disease. It was afterwards adopted and highly commended by the late Dr. Warren, of London.

Blisters were in general use, but seldom applied before the latter stage of fevers. They were prescribed, for the first time, in hemorrhages, and with great success, by Dr. George Glentworth.

Wine was given sparingly, even in the lowest stage of what were then called putrid and nervous fevers.

The warm and cold baths were but little used in private practice. The former was now and then employed in acute diseases. They were both used in the most liberal manner, together with the vapour and warm air baths, in the Pennsylvania hospital, by Dr. Thomas Bond. An attempt was made to erect warm and cold baths, in the neighbourhood of the city, and to connect them with a house of entertainment, by Dr. Lauchlin M'Clen, in the year 1761. The project was considered as unfriendly to morals, and petitions, from several religious societies, were addressed to the governor of the province, to prevent its execution. The enterprize was abandoned, and the doctor soon afterwards left the city.

Riding on horseback, the fresh air of the seashore, and long journies, were often prescribed to invalids, by all the physicians of that day.

I come now to mention the causes which influence the diseases, also the medical opinions and remedies of the present time. In this part of our discourse, I shall follow the order of the first part of the inquiry.

I have already taken notice of the changes which the climate of Philadelphia has undergone since the year 1766.

A change has of late years taken place in the dress of the inhabitants of Philadelphia. Wigs have generally been laid aside, and the hair worn cut and dressed in different ways. Round hats, with high crowns, have become fashionable. Umbrellas, which were formerly a part of female dress only, are now used in warm and wet weather, by men of all ranks in society; and flannel is worn next to the skin in winter, and muslin in summer, by many persons of both sexes. Tight dresses are uncommon, and stays are unknown among our women. It is to be lamented that the benefits to health which might have been derived from the disuse of that part of female dress, have been prevented by the fashion of wearing such light coverings over the breasts and limbs. The evils from this cause, shall be mentioned hereafter.

A revolution has taken place in the diet of our citizens. Relishes and suppers are generally abolished; bitters, to provoke a preternatural appetite, also meridian bowls of punch, are now scarcely known. Animal food is eaten only at dinner, and excess in the use of it is prevented, by a profusion of excellent summer and winter vegetables.

Malt liquors, or hydrant water, with a moderate quantity of wine, are usually taken with those simple and wholesome meals.

Clubs, for the exclusive purpose of feeding, are dissolved, and succeeded by family parties, collected for the more rational entertainments of conversation, dancing, music, and chess. Taverns and beer-houses are much less frequented than formerly, and drunkenness is rarely seen in genteel life. The tea table, in an evening, has now become the place of resort of both sexes, and the midnight serenade has taken place of the midnight revels of the young gentlemen of former years.

In doing justice to the temperance of the modern citizens of Philadelphia, I am sorry to admit, there is still a good deal of secret drinking among them. Physicians, who detect it by the diseases it produces, often lament the inefficacy of their remedies to remove them. In addition to intemperance from spiritous liquors, a new species of intoxication from opium has found its way into our city. I have known death, in one instance, induced by it.

The following circumstances have had a favourable influence upon the health of the present inhabitants of Philadelphia.

The improvements in the construction of modern houses, so as to render them cooler in summer, and warmer in winter.

The less frequent practice of sitting on porches, exposed to the dew, in summer evenings.

The universal use of stoves in places of public worship.

The abolition of the custom of obliging lying-in women to sit up for company.

The partial use of Schuylkill or hydrant water, for culinary and other purposes.

The enjoyment of pure air, in country seats, in the neighbourhood of the city. They not only preserve from sickness during the summer and autumn, but they render families less liable to diseases during the other seasons of the year.

And, lastly, the frequent use of private, and public warm and cold baths. For the establishment of the latter, the citizens of Philadelphia are indebted to Mr. Joseph Simons.

The following circumstances have an unfavourable influence upon the health of our citizens.

Ice creams taken in excess, or upon an empty stomach.

The continuance of the practice of attending funerals, under all the circumstances that were mentioned in describing the customs which prevailed in Philadelphia, between the years 1760 and 1766.

The combined influence of great heat and intemperance in drinking, acting upon passions unusually excited by public objects, on the 4th of July, every year.

The general and inordinate use of segars.

The want of sufficient force in the water which falls into the common sewers to convey their contents into the Delaware, renders each of their apertures a source of sickly exhalations to the neighbouring streets and squares.

The compact manner in which the gutters are now formed, by preventing the descent of water into the earth, has contributed very much to retain the filth of the city, in those seasons in which they are not washed by rain, nor by the waste water of the pumps and hydrants.

The timbers of many of the wharves of the city have gone to decay. The docks have not been cleaned since the year 1774, and many of them expose large surfaces to the action of the sun at low water. The buildings have increased in Water-street, and with them there has been a great increase of that kind of filth which is generated in all houses; the stores in this street often contain matters which putrify; from all which there is, in warm weather, a constant emission of such a fetid odour, as to render a walk through that street, by a person who does not reside there, extremely disagreeable, and sometimes to produce sickness and vomiting.

In many parts of the vicinity of the city are to be seen pools of stagnating water, from which there are exhaled large quantities of unhealthy vapours, during the summer and autumnal months.

The privies have become so numerous, and are often so full, as to become offensive in most of the compact parts of the city, more especially in damp weather.

The pump water is impregnated with many saline and aërial matters of an offensive nature.

While these causes exert an unfriendly influence upon the bodies of the citizens of Philadelphia, the extreme elevation or depression of their passions, by the different issues of their political contests (now far surpassing, in their magnitude, the contests of former years), together with their many new and fortuitous modes of suddenly acquiring and losing property, predispose them to many diseases of the mind.

The present diseases of Philadelphia come next under our consideration.

Fevers have assumed several new forms since the year 1766. The mild bilious fever has gradually spread over every part of the city. It followed the filth which was left by the British army in the year 1778. In the year 1780, it prevailed, as an epidemic, in Southwark, and in Water and Front-streets, below Market-street. In the years 1791 and 1792, it assumed an inflammatory appearance, and was accompanied, in many cases, with hepatic affections. The connection of our subject requires that I should barely repeat, that it appeared in 1793 as an epidemic, in the form of what is called yellow fever, in which form it has appeared, in sporadic cases, or as an epidemic, every year since. During the reign of this high grade of bilious fever, mild intermittents and remittents, and the chronic or nervous forms of the summer and autumnal fever, have nearly disappeared.

Inflammations and obstructions of the liver have been more frequent than in former years, and even the pneumonies, catarrhs, intercurrent, and other fevers of the winter and spring months, have all partaken more or less of the inflammatory and malignant nature of the yellow fever.

The pulmonary consumption continues to be a common disease among both sexes.

The cynanche trachealis, the scarlatina anginosa, the hydrocephalus internus, and cholera infantum, are likewise common diseases in Philadelphia.

Madness, and several other diseases of the mind, have increased since the year 1766, from causes which have been mentioned.

Several of the different forms of gout are still common among both sexes.

Apoplexy and palsy have considerably diminished in our city, It is true, the bills of mortality still record a number of deaths from the former, every year; but this statement is incorrect, if it mean a disease of the brain only, for sudden deaths from all their causes are returned exclusively under the name of apoplexy. The less frequent occurrence of this disease, also of palsy, is probably occasioned by the less consumption of animal food, and of distilled and fermented liquors, by that class of citizens who are most subject to them, than in former years. Perhaps the round hat, and the general use of umbrellas, may have contributed to lessen those diseases of the brain.

The dropsy is now a rare disease, and seldom seen even in our hospital.

The colica pictonum, or dry gripes, is scarcely known in Philadelphia. I have ascribed this to the use of flannel next to the skin as a part of dress, and to the general disuse of punch as a common drink.

The natural small-pox is nearly extirpated, and the puerperile fever is rarely met with in Philadelphia. The scrophula is much less frequent than in former years. It is confined chiefly to persons in humble life.

I proceed, in the order that was proposed, to take notice of the present medical opinions which prevail among the physicians of Philadelphia. The system of Dr. Boerhaave long ago ceased to regulate the practice of physic. It was succeeded by the system of Dr. Cullen. In the year 1790, Dr. Brown's system of medicine was introduced and taught by Dr. Gibbon. It captivated a few young men for a while, but it soon fell into disrepute. Perhaps the high-toned diseases of our city exposed the fallacy and danger of the remedies inculcated by it, and afforded it a shorter life than it has had in many other countries. In the year 1790, the author of this inquiry promulgated some new principles in medicine, suggested by the peculiar phaenomena of the diseases of the United States. These principles have been so much enlarged and improved by the successive observations and reasonings of many gentlemen in all the states, as to form an American system of medicine. This system rejects the nosological arrangement of diseases, and places all their numerous forms in morbid excitement, induced by irritants acting upon previous debility. It rejects, likewise, all prescriptions for the names of diseases, and, by directing their applications wholly to the forming and fluctuating states of diseases, and the system, derives from a few active medicines all the advantages which have been in vain expected from the numerous articles which compose European treatises upon the materia medica. This system has been adopted by a part of the physicians of Philadelphia, but a respectable number of them are still attached to the system of Dr. Cullen.

A great change has taken place in the remedies which are now in common use in Philadelphia. I shall briefly mention such of them as are new, and then take notice of the new and different modes of exhibiting such as were in use between the years 1760 and 1766.

Vaccination has been generally adopted in our city, in preference to inoculation with variolous matter.

Digitalis, lead, zinc, and arsenic are now common remedies in the hands of most of our practitioners.

Cold air, cold water, and ice are among the new remedies of modern practice in Philadelphia.

Blood-letting is now used in nearly all diseases of violent excitement, not only in the blood-vessels, but in other parts of the body. Its use is not, as in former times, limited to ounces in specific diseases, but regulated by their force, and the importance of the parts affected to health and life; nor is it forbidden, as formerly, in infancy, in extreme old age, in the summer months, nor in the period of menstruation, where symptoms of a violent, or of a suffocated disease, manifested by an active or a feeble pulse, indicate it to be necessary.

Leeches are now in general use in diseases which are removed, by their seat or local nature, beyond the influence of the lancet. For the introduction of this excellent remedy into our city we are indebted to Mr. John Cunitz.

Opium and bark, which were formerly given in disguise, or with a trembling hand, are now, not only prescribed by physicians, but often purchased, and taken without their advice, by many of the citizens of Philadelphia. They even occupy a shelf in the closets of many families.

The use of mercury has been revived, and a salivation has been extended, with great improvements and success, to nearly all violent and obstinate diseases. Nor has the influence of reason over ignorance and prejudice, with respect to that noble medicine, stopped here. Cold water, once supposed to be incompatible with its use, is now applied to the body, in malignant fevers, in order to insure and accelerate its operation upon the salivary glands.

Wine is given in large quantities, when indicated, without the least fear of producing intoxication.

The warm and cold baths, which were formerly confined chiefly to patients in the Pennsylvania hospital, are now common prescriptions in private practice.

Exercise, country air, and the sea shore, are now universally recommended in chronic diseases, and in the debility which precedes and follows them.

Great pains are now taken to regulate the quantity and quality of aliments and drinks, by the peculiar state of the system.

Let us now inquire into the influence of the new opinions in medicine, and the new remedies which have been mentioned, upon human life.

The small-pox, once the most fatal and universal of all diseases, has nearly ceased to occupy a place in our bills of mortality, by the introduction of vaccination in our city. For the prompt adoption of this great discovery, the citizens of Philadelphia owe a large debt of gratitude to Dr. Coxe, and Mr. John Vaughan.

Fevers, from all their causes, and in all their forms, with the exception of the bilious yellow fever, now yield to medicine. Even that most malignant form of febrile diseases is treated with more success in Philadelphia than in other countries. It would probably seldom prove mortal, did a belief in its being derived from an impure atmosphere, and of its exclusive influence upon the body, while it prevailed as an epidemic, obtain universally among the physicians and citizens of Philadelphia.

The pulmonary consumption has been prevented, in many hundred instances, by meeting its premonitory signs, in weakness and feeble morbid excitement in the whole system, by country air, gentle exercise, and gently stimulating remedies. Even when formed, and tending rapidly to its last stage, it has been cured by small and frequent bleedings, digitalis, and a mercurial salivation.

The hydrocephalus internus, the cynanche trachealis, and cholera infantum, once so fatal to the children of our city, now yield to medicine in their early stages. The two former are cured by copious bleeding, aided by remedies formerly employed in them without success. The last is cured by moderate bleeding, calomel, laudanum, and country air.

The gout has been torn from its ancient sanctuary in error and prejudice, and its acute paroxysms now yield with as much certainty to the lancet, as the most simple inflammatory diseases.

The dropsy is cured by renouncing the unfortunate association of specific-remedies with its name, and accommodating them to the degrees of excitement in the blood-vessels.

The tetanus from wounds is now prevented, in most cases, by inflaming the injured parts, and thereby compelling them to defend the whole system, by a local disease. Where this preventing remedy has been neglected, and where tetanus arises from other causes than wounds, it has often been cured by adding to the diffusible stimulus of opium, the durable stimuli of bark and wine.

Death from drinking cold water, in the heated state of the body, is now obviated by previously wetting the hands or feet with the water; and when this precaution is neglected, the disease induced by it is generally cured by large doses of liquid laudanum.

Madness, which formerly doomed its miserable subjects to cells or chains for life, has yielded to bleeding, low diet, mercury, the warm and cold baths, fresh air, gentle exercise, and mild treatment, since its seat has been discovered to be in the blood-vessels of the brain.

The last achievement of our science in Philadelphia, that I shall mention, consist in the discovery and observation of the premonitory signs of violent and mortal diseases, and in subduing them by simple remedies, in their forming state. By this means, death has been despoiled of his prey, in many hundred instances.

In this successful conflict of medicine with disease and death, midwifery and surgery have borne a distinguished part. They derive their claims to the gratitude of the citizens of Philadelphia from the practice of each of them being more confined, than formerly, to a few members of our profession. It is in consequence of the former being exercised only by physicians of regular and extensive educations, that death from pregnancy and parturition is a rare occurrence in Philadelphia.

I should greatly exceed the limits prescribed to this inquiry, should I mention how much pain and misery have been relieved, and how often death has been baffled in his attempts upon human life, by several late improvements in old, and the discovery of new remedies in surgery. I shall briefly name a few of them.

In cases of blindness, from a partial opacity of the cornea, or from a closure of the natural pupil, a new pupil has been made; and where the cornea has been partially opaque, the opening through the iris has been formed, opposite to any part of it, which retained its transparency.

The cure of fractures has been accelerated by blood-letting, and, where the union of a broken bone has not taken place from a defect of bony matter, it has been produced by passing a seton between the fractured ends of the bone, and effecting a union thereby between them. Luxations, which have long resisted both force and art, have been reduced in a few minutes, and without pain, by bleeding at deliquium animi.

Old sores have been speedily healed, by destroying their surfaces, and thereby placing them in the condition of recent accidents.

The fruitless application of the trepan, in concussions of the brain, has been prevented by copious bleeding, and a salivation.

A suppression of urine has been cured, by the addition of a piece of a bougie to a flexible catheter.

Strictures in the urethra have been removed by means of a caustic, also, in a more expeditious way, by dividing them with a lancet.

Hydrocele has been cured by a small puncture, and afterwards exciting inflammation and adhesion by an injection of wine into the tunica vaginalis testis.

The popliteal aneurism and varicose veins have both been removed by operations that were unknown a few years ago.

For the introduction of several of those new surgical remedies, and for the discovery and improvement of others, the citizens of Philadelphia are indebted to Dr. Physick. They are likewise indebted to him and Dr. Griffitts for many of the new and successful modes of practice, in the diseases that have been mentioned. Even the few remedies that have been suggested by the author of these inquiries, owe their adoption and usefulness chiefly to the influence of those two respectable and popular physicians.

Before I dismiss this part of our subject, I have only to add, that since the cure and extraction of the teeth have become a distinct branch of the profession of medicine, several diseases which have arisen from them, when decayed, have been detected and cured.

We have thus taken a comparative view of the medical theories and remedies of former and modern times, and of their different influence upon human life. To exhibit the advantages of the latter over the former, I shall mention the difference in the number of deaths in three successive years, at a time when the population of the city and suburbs was supposed to amount to 30,000 souls, and in three years, after the population exceeded double that number.

Between the 25th of December, 1771, and the 25th of December, 1772, there died 1291 persons.

Between the same days of the same months, in 1772 and 1773, there died 1344 persons.

Within the same period of time, between 1773 and 1774, the deaths amounted to 1021, making in all 3,656. I regret that I have not been able to procure the returns of deaths in years prior to those which have been mentioned. During the three years that have been selected, no unusually mortal diseases prevailed in the city. The measles were epidemic in 1771, but were not more fatal than in common years.

Between the 25th of December, 1799, and the 25th of December, 1800, there died 1525 persons.

Between the same days of the same months, in the years 1801 and 1802, there died 1362 persons.

Within the same period of time, between 1802 and 1803, the deaths amounted to 1796, making in all 4,883.

Upon these returns it will be proper to remark, that several hundreds of the deaths, in 1802 and 1803, were from the yellow fever, and that many of them were of strangers. Of 68 persons, who were interred in the Swedes' church-yard alone, one half were of that description of people. Deducting 500 from both those causes of extra-mortality in the three years, between 1799 and 1803, the increase of deaths above what they were in the years 1771 and 1774 is but 727. Had diseases continued to be as mortal as they were thirty years ago, considering the present state of our population, the number of deaths would have been more than 7,312.

To render the circumstances of the statement of deaths that has been given perfectly equal, it will be necessary to add, that the measles prevailed in the city, in the year 1802, as generally as they did in 1771.

From the history that has been given, of the effects of the late improvements and discoveries in medicine upon human life, in Philadelphia, we are led to appreciate its importance and usefulness. It has been said, by its enemies, to move; but its motions have been asserted to be only in a circle. The facts that have been stated clearly prove, that it has moved, and rapidly too, within the last thirty years, in a straight line.

To encourage and regulate application and enterprize in medicine hereafter, let us inquire to what causes we are indebted for the late discoveries and improvements in our science, and for their happy effects in reducing the number of deaths so far below their former proportion to the inhabitants of Philadelphia.

1. The first cause I shall mention is the great physical changes which have taken place in the manners of our citizens in favour of health and life.

2. A second cause, is the assistance which has been afforded to the practice of physic, by the numerous and important discoveries that have lately been made in anatomy, natural history, and chemistry, all of which have been conveyed, from time to time, to the physicians of the city, by means of the Philadelphia and hospital libraries, and by the lectures upon those branches of science which are annually delivered in the university of Pennsylvania.

3. The application of reasoning to our science has contributed greatly to extend its success in the cure of diseases. Simply to observe and to remember, are the humblest operations of the human mind. Brutes do both. But to *theorize*, that is, to *think*, or, in other language, to compare facts, to reject counterfeits, to dissolve the seeming affinity of such as are not true, to combine those that are related, though found in remote situations from each other, and, finally, to deduce practical and useful inferences from them, are the high prerogatives and interest of man, in all his intellectual pursuits, and in none more, than in the profession of medicine.

4. The accommodation of remedies to the changes which are induced in diseases by the late revolutions in our climate, seasons, and manners, has had a sensible influence in improving the practice of medicine in our city. The same diseases, like the descendants of the same families, lose their resemblance to each other by the lapse of time; and the almanacks of 1803 might as well be consulted to inform us of the monthly phases of the moon of the present year, as the experience of former years, or the books of foreign countries, be relied upon to regulate the practice of physic at the present time, in any of the cities of the United States.

5. From the diffusion of medical knowledge among all classes of our citi-

zens, by means of medical publications, and controversies, many people have been taught so much of the principles and practice of physic, as to be able to prescribe for themselves in the forming state of acute diseases, and thereby to prevent their fatal termination. It is to this self-acquired knowledge among the citizens of Philadelphia, that physicans are in part indebted for not being called out of their beds so frequently as in former years. There are few people who do not venture to administer laudanum in bowel complaints, and there are some persons in the city, who have cured the cynanche trachealis when it has occurred in the night, by vomits and bleeding, without the advice of a physician. The disuse of suppers is another cause why physicians enjoy more rest at night than formerly, for many of their midnight calls, were to relieve diseases brought on by that superfluous meal.

6.   The dispensary instituted in our city, in the year 1786, for the medical relief of the poor, has assisted very much in promoting the empire of medicine over disease and death. Some lives have likewise been saved by the exertions of the humane society, by means of their printed directions to prevent sudden death; also, by the medical services which have lately been extended to outpatients, by order of the managers of the Pennsylvania hospital.

7thly and lastly. A change, favourable to successful practice in Philadelphia, has taken place in the conduct of physicians to their patients. A sick room has ceased to be the theatre of imposture in dress and manners, and prescriptions are no longer delivered with the pomp and authority of edicts. On the contrary, sick people are now instructed in the nature of their diseases, and informed of the names and design of their medicines, by which means faith and reason are made to co-operate in adding efficacy to them. Nor are patients left, as formerly, by their physicians, under the usual appearances of dissolution, without the aid of medicine. By thus disputing every inch of ground with death, many persons have been rescued from the grave, and lived, years afterwards, monuments of the power of the healing art.

From a review of what has been effected within the last nine and thirty years, in lessening the mortality of many diseases, we are led to look forward with confidence and pleasure to the future achievements of our science.

Could we lift the curtain of time which separates the year 1843 from our view, we should see cancers, pulmonary consumptions, apoplexies, palsies, epilepsy, and hydrophobia struck out of the list of mortal diseases, and many others which still retain an occasional power over life, rendered perfectly harmless, *provided* the same number of discoveries and improvements shall be made in medicine in the intermediate years, that have been made since the year 1766.

But in vain will the avenues of death from those diseases be closed, while the more deadly yellow fever is permitted to supply their place, and to spread terror, distress, and poverty through the city, by destroying the lives of her citizens by hundreds or thousands every year. Dear cradle of liberty of conscience in the western world! nurse of industry and arts! and patron of pious and benevolent institutions! may this cease to be thy melancholy destiny! May Heaven dispel the errors and prejudices of thy citizens upon the cause and means of preventing their pestilential calamities! and may thy prosperity and happiness be revived, extended, and perpetuated for ages yet to come! . . .

15. Republican Technology

The coincidence in time between the American Revolution and the beginnings of what came to be called the Industrial Revolution had momentous consequences for the way Americans came to identify technological progress with the promise of their own history. Political and physical science seemed to be providentially linked, and technology became as important as virtue in achieving America's realization of itself as a moral republic. The useful arts were designed not only to promote the physical well-being of Americans, but more important, to enhance their liberty and republicanism as well. Even the invention of the submarine torpedo was regarded by Robert Fulton (1765-1815) as a device for the moral improvement of the American people.

Fulton, like several other American inventors, began his career as an artist, but moved easily from the fine to the mechanic arts out of the belief that technology could contribute more of what the spirit of the age demanded. He went abroad in 1786 to study with Benjamin West and did not return to the United States for two decades. By the 1790's Fulton had patented several inventions and had become particularly interested in schemes for internal transportation, especially canals. He worked on the use of steam power for boat propulsion from the beginning, but it was not until he gained the friendship of Robert Livingston that he was able to develop a successful steamboat. From 1797 through the first decade of the nineteenth-century, Fulton devoted himself to the invention of the submarine and the torpedo. At first he tried to interest the French and British governments, but unable to demonstrate the practicality of his invention to their satisfaction, he turned to the United States. In 1807 he blew up a brig in New York harbor, an experiment mocked by *Salmagundi* as the destruction of the British fleet in effigy. Congress was sufficiently impressed with the demonstration and with Fulton's speeches and writings on the submarine and torpedo to grant him $5000 to carry on further experiments under the direction of the Secretary of the Navy. But some unsuccessful trials and his growing absorption in the steamboat ended his work on liberating the seas.

Fulton's lack of success in promoting his submarine torpedo, however, stemmed not from any American aversion to such ingenious devices but from Fulton's inability to demonstrate its usefulness. By the second decade of the nineteenth century it was clear that utility, identified most often with profitability, had become the principal criterion of scientific achievement. One of the great prophets of the utility of American science in these years, and indeed the originator of the modern use of the term "technology," was Jacob Bigelow (1786-1879). Bigelow was a physician and botanist of considerable influence, and held the presidency of the American Academy of Arts and Sciences from 1847 to 1863. Although he was already professor of *materia medica* in the Harvard Medical School, in 1816 he was appointed to a Harvard professorship in the application of the sciences to the useful arts, newly endowed by Count Rumford, the former American Tory Benjamin Thompson. In 1829 Bigelow published his Harvard lectures as *Elements of Technology*.

Torpedo War and Submarine Explosion

ROBERT FULTON

To JAMES MADISON, Esq. President of the United States, and to the Members of both Houses of Congress.

GENTLEMEN,

In January last, at Kalorama, the residence of my friend Joel Barlow, I had the pleasure of exhibiting to Mr. Jefferson, Mr. Madison, and a party of gentlemen from the senate and house of representatives, some experiments and details on Torpedo defence and attack; the favourable impression which the experiments appeared to make on the minds of the gentlemen then present; and my conviction that this invention, improved and practised to the perfection which it is capable of receiving, will be of the first importance to our country, has induced me to present you in the form of a pamphlet a description of my system, with five engravings, and such demonstrations as will give each of you an opportunity to contemplate its efficacy and utility at your leisure; and enable you to form a correct judgment on the propriety of adopting it as a part of our means of national defence. It being my intention to publish hereafter a detailed account of the origin and progress of this invention, and the embarrassments under which I have laboured to bring it to its present state of certain utility; I will now state only such experiments

Robert Fulton, *Torpedo War and Submarine Explosions* (New York, 1810), reprinted in *The Magazine of History*, Extra No. 35 (1914), pp. 5–6, 20–23, 30–31, 37, 40–42, 51–53.

and facts as are most important to be known, and which, proving the practicability of destroying ships of war by this means, will lead the mind to all the advantages which we may derive from it. I believe it is generally known that I endeavoured for many years to get torpedoes introduced into practice in France, and in England; which, though unsuccessful, gave me the opportunity of making numerous very interesting experiments on a large scale; by which I discovered errors in the combinations of the machinery and method of fixing the torpedoes to a ship; which errors in the machinery

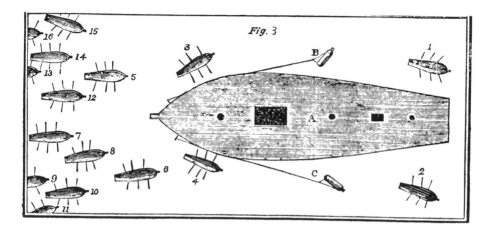

Fig. 3

have been corrected: and I believe I have found means of attaching the torpedoes to a vessel which will seldom fail of success. It is the result of my experience which I now submit to your consideration; and hoping that you will feel an interest in the success of my invention, I beg for your deliberate perusal and reflection on the following few pages. Gentlemen who have traced the progress of the useful arts, know the years of toil and experiment, and difficulties which frequently pass, before the utility and certain operation of new discoveries have been established; hence it could not be expected, that torpedoes should be rendered useful without encountering many difficulties; and I am aware, that in the course of farther essays other difficulties will appear; but from my past experience I feel confident, that any obstacle which may arise can be surmounted by attention and perseverance. . . .

Figure 3 is a bird's eye view of a ship of the line, either at anchor or under sail, and the Torpedo boats rowing on to the attack. I am sensible that there are strong prejudices against the possibility of row-boats attacking a ship or ships of the line, with any reasonable hope of success; I will, therefore, commence my reasoning and demonstrations by the following questions. What is the basis of the aggression and injustice of one nation towards another? Is it not a calculation on their power to enforce their will? What is the basis of all courage and obstinate perseverance in battle? Is it not a calculation on some real or presumed advantage? A frigate of 30 guns is not expected to engage a ship of eighty guns, for every rational calculation is against her, and to strike her colours would be no dishonour. If I now prove that all the calculations are in favour of the Torpedo boats, it shall hereafter be no dishonour for a ship of the line to strike her colours, and tamely submit to superior science and tactics.

I will run my calcualtions against a third rate, an 80 gun ship, she being the medium between first rates of 110 guns and fifth rates of 44 guns. I will suppose her to enter one of our ports or harbours in a hostile manner; her draft of water, when loaded, is twenty-two feet; her full complement of men six hundred. Were we to oppose to the enemy an 80 gun ship, she would cost four hundred thousand dollars; we would also have to give her a full complement of six hundred men. If she engaged the enemy, the chances are equal that she would be beaten; if an obstinate engagement, she might have from one to two hundred men killed and wounded, and be so shattered as to require repairs to the amount of forty or fifty thousand dollars; she might be taken and lost to the nation, and add to the strength of the enemy. It is now to be seen if six hundred men and a capital of four hundred thousand dollars, the value of an eighty gun ship, cannot be used to better advantage in a Torpedo attack or defence.

600	men at 12 to a boat, would man 50 boats,	
50	boats at one hundred dollars each	$5,000
50	Torpedoes complete, one hundred and fifty dollars each, powder included	7,500
50	harpoon guns, thirty dollars each	1,500
200	blunderbusses, twenty dollars each	4,000
100	pair of pistols, fifteen dollars a pair	1,500
600	cutlasses, three dollars each	1,800
	Contingencies	3,000
	Total	$24,300

The pay and provisions for six hundred men, whether in an 80 gun ship or in Torpedo boats, may be estimated, for the present, to amount to the same sum annually.

Here is an establishment of fifty boats with their Torpedoes, and armed complete, for 24,300 dollars; the economy 375,700 dollars. It is evident the ship could not put out fifty boats to contend with our fifty; she could not, in fact, put out twenty; therefore, as to boat fighting, the enemy could have no chance of success, and would have to depend for protection on her guns and small arms. Unless in a case of great emergency, the attack should be in the night, for if an enemy came into one of our harbours to do execution, the chances would be much against her getting out and to any great distance before night. In a night usually dark, rowboats, if painted white, and the men dressed in white, cannot be seen at the distance of three hundred yards; and there are nights so dark, that they cannot be seen if close under the bow. I might here draw into my calculations on chances that an enemy, who understood the tremendous consequences of a successful attack with Torpedoes, would not like to run the risk of the night being dark. But in any night, the fifty boats closing on the vessel in all direction, would spread or divide her fire, and prevent it becoming concentered on any one or more boats. Boats which row five miles an hour, and which all good boats can do for a short time, run at the rate of one hundred and forty yards a minute. At the distance of three hundred yards from the ship, they take the risque of cannon shot, which must, from necessity, be random and without aim, on so small a body as a boat, running with a velocity of one hundred and forty yards a minute. At two hundred yards from the ship, the boats must take the chance of random discharges of grape and cannister shot; and at one hundred yards from the ship, they must run the risque of random musket; each boat will, therefore, be two minutes within the line of the enemy's fire before she harpoons, and two minutes after she has harpooned before she gets out of the line of fire, total, four minutes in danger: the danger, however, is not of a very serious kind, for, as before observed, no aim can be taken in the night at such quick moving bodies as rowboats; yet some men might be killed, and some boats crippled; in such an event, the great number of boats which we should have in motion, could always help the unfortunate. But what would be the situation of the enemy, who had their six hundred men in one vessel? The Torpedo boats closing upon her, twenty-five on the larboard and twenty-five on the starboard bow, some of them would certainly succeed to harpoon her between the stem and main chains, and if so, the explosion of only one Torpedo under her would sink her, killing the greatest part of the people who were between decks, and leave those who might escape to the mercy of our boats to save them.

I now beg of my reader to meditate on this kind of attack, and make up his mind on which are in the greatest danger, the six hundred men in the ship or the six hundred men in the boats? Are not the chances fifty to one against the ship, that she would be blown up before she could kill two hundred men in the boats? Should this appear evident, or be proved by future practice, no commander would be rash enough to expose his ship to such an attack. . . .

Thoughts on the probable effect of this invention

At the time a new discovery is made in physics or mathematical science, the whole of its consequences cannot be foreseen. In the year 1330, Bartholomew Schwartz is said to have invented gun-powder; twenty-five years after, a very imperfect kind of cannon was constructed of welded bars of iron, others of sheet-iron, rolled in the form of a cylinder and hooped with iron rings; in some cases, they were made of leather, strengthened with plates of iron or copper; balls of stone were used; and it was not until the beginning of the fifteenth century, that is, one hundred and seventy years after the invention of powder, that iron balls were introduced into practice. Muskets were not used until the year 1521, or one hundred and ninety-one years after the invention of gun-powder. The Spaniards were the first who armed their foot-soldiers in this manner—they had matchlocks; but firelocks, that is, locks with flints, were not used until the beginning of the eighteenth century, one hundred and eighty years after the invention of muskets, and three hundred and eighty years after the invention of powder. When firelocks were first invented, Marshal Sax had so little confidence in a flint, that he ordered a match to be added to the lock with a flint, lest the flint should miss fire: such is the force of habit and want of faith in new inventions.

Although cannon, fire-arms, and the whole detail of ammunition, now appear extremely simple, yet we here see the very slow advances to their present state of perfection; and they are still improving: hence I conclude, that it is now impossible to foresee to what degree Torpedoes may be improved and rendered useful. When Schwartz invented powder, it may be presumed that his mind did not embrace all its consequences, or perceive that his discovery would supercede the use of catapultas, armour, bows and arrows, and totally change the whole art of war. He certainly could have no conception of such a combination of art as we now see in ships of the line; those movable fortifications, armed with thirty-two pounders, and furnished with wings, to spread oppression over every part of the ocean, and carry destruction to every harbour of the earth. In consequence of the invention of gunpowder, ships of war have been contrived, and increased to their present enormous size and number; then may not science, in her progress, point out a means by which the application of the violent explosive force of gun-powder shall destroy ships of war, and give to the seas the liberty which shall secure perpetual peace between nations that are separated by the ocean? My conviction is, that the means are here developed, and required only to be organized and practised, to produce that liberty so dear to every rational and reflecting man; and there is a grandeur in persevering to success in so immense an enterprise—so well calculated to excite the most vigorous exertions of the highest order of intellect, that I hope to interest the patriotic feelings of every friend to America, to justice, and to humanity, in so good a cause.

I have shewn that a ship of 80 guns and six hundred men, could have little chance of resisting fifty Torpedo boats of twelve men each, equal six hundred men. . . .

In all my reflections on this kind of war, I see no chance for their escape other than by retreat; and the moment English ships of war retreat before Torpedo boats, that moment the power of the British marine is for ever lost, and with it the political influence of the nation. . . .

On the imaginary inhumanity of Torpedo war

In numerous discussions which I have had on this subject and its consequences, it has been stated, that instead of giving liberty to the seas, its tendency would be to encourage piracy and buccaneering, by enabling a few men in a boat to intimidate and plunder merchant vessels, thereby producing greater evil than the existing military marines. This idea, is similar to one which might have arisen on the invention of muskets, which, giving to an individual the power of certain death at the distance of fifty or a hundred yards, robbers might infest the highways, and from an ambush, shoot the traveller and take his property; yet there is not so much robbery now as before the invention of gun-powder; society is more civilized; it is not so much divided into feuds, or clans, to secrete and protect villainy; and all civilized society will, in their own defence, combine against the robber, who has little chance to escape. In like manner, as an individual, instigated by revenge, might with an air-gun shoot his neighbour, or by means of gunpowder blow up his barn or buildings; but society combine against such atrocious acts, and he who would commit them, could have little other prospect before him than the gibbet. In the case of pirates or buccaneers, they could not make a Torpedo without some intelligent workmen, who would be a means of discovery. Were they to take a prize, they must have some port to carry it to, or it could be of no use to them; were they to plunder a ship, they could not carry much in a Torpedo boat, and the boat must have a port to go to, where neighbours or spectators, observing her suspicious character, would lead to investigation; added to which, pirates are seldom constant in their attachment to each other, and each would suspect the other turning informer. It would be difficult for a Torpedo boat to depart from any port of America, and return without being detected. It is certainly much more easy and secure for an individual to go on the highway and rob, yet how seldom is that done. When nations combine against pirates, there is no reason to fear that individuals can make a bad use of this invention.

But men, without reflecting, or from attachment to established and familiar tyranny, exclaim, that it is barbarous to blow up a ship with all her crew. This I admit, and lament that it should be necessary; but all wars are barbarous, and particularly wars of offence. It is barbarous for a ship of war to fire into a peaceable merchant vessel, kill part of her people, take her and the property, and reduce the proprietor with his family from affluence to penury. It was barbarous to bombard Copenhagen, set fire to the city, and destroy innocent women and children. It would be barbarous for ships of war to enter the harbour of New-York, fire on the city, destroy property, and murder many of the peaceable inhabitants; yet we have great reason to expect such a scene of barbarism and distress, unless means are taken to prevent it; therefore, if Torpedoes should prevent such acts of violence, the invention must be humane.

When a fortress is besieged, and a mine driven under the citadel, the powder laid, and the train ready to light, it is the custom for the besiegers to send to the commander of the besieged, to inform him of the preparations, and leave it to his judgment to surrender or risque the explosion; if he will not surrender after such warning, and he, with his men, should be blown up, he is to be charged with the inhumanity, and not the besiegers. Should government adopt Torpedoes as a part of our means of defence, the Europeans will be informed of it, after which, should they send hostile ships into our ports among anchored Torpedoes or Torpedo boats, and such ships should be blown up, the inhumanity must be charged to them, and not to the American government or to this invention. . . .

My feelings are wholly attached to my country, and while I labour for her interest in this enterprise, I am happy that the liberty of the seas, which I believe can be effected, will not only benefit America; it will be an immense advantage to England, to France, and to every other nation. Convinced of this, I have viewed military marines as remains of ancient warlike habits, and an existing political disease, for which there has hitherto been no specific remedy. Satisfied in my own mind, that the Torpedoes now discovered, will be an effectual cure for so great an evil. To introduce them into practice, and prove their utility, I am of opinion, that blowing up English ships of war, or French, or American, were there no other, and the men on shore, would be humane experiments of the first importance to the United States and to mankind. . . .

If science and energy should sweep military marines from the ocean, America will be the garden of the world—an example for Europe to imitate. When we contemplate the immense sums which are expended in European marine establishments, and calculate the infinite good which might have been done with the capital, we have to lament that man, instead of gratifying his ambition in wars and devastation, has not sought a more noble and lasting fame in promoting the arts, and sciences, and civilization.

The annual expence of the navy of Great Britain amounts to upwards of thirteen millions a year; as long as war continues, the expence will not be diminished; but taking the chance of war and peace for the succeeding twenty-five years, and estimate that the marine will cost ten millions a year, the expenditure in twenty-five years will be two hundred and fifty millions of pounds sterling. If driven to have a marine, such might be the expenditure of our successors; if we can avoid it, the capital might be expended in useful work. I will now give a short sketch of the improvements which might be made in America for such a sum:

First, twelve canals, running from the eastern and northern parts of the United States to the south, each fifteen hundred miles long, and fifty miles distant from each other, equal to eighteen thousand miles; thirty canals, running from the sea coast to the interior, each six hundred miles long and fifty miles apart, or eighteen thousand miles—total, thirty-six thousand miles, at three thousand pounds sterling a mile, amounting to one hundred and eight millions. Canals to this extent, would intersect a country fifteen hundred miles long six hundred miles wide, equal nine hundred thousand square miles, or seven hundred and fifty-six millions of acres, not an acre of which would be more than twenty-five miles from canal carriage; and which acres, allowing six to an individual which is equal to the density of English population, or say seven, allowing for rivers, roads, and canals, would be ample space in a country which, by its improvements, must be fertile for one hundred and eight millions of inhabitants.

2d, Two thousand bridges, at thirty thousand
pounds sterling each, equal; 60,000,000
Two thousand and fifty public establishments
for education, at forty thousand
pounds sterling each 82,000,000
The canals; 108,000,000

Total   250,000,000

The two hundred and fifty millions, raised by loan and funded at five per cent, would, if expended on a marine, lay a tax on the people of 12,500,000[£] sterling a year, equal to 55,555,555 dollars a year, with a horde of excise-men and tax gatherers, to torment honest industry. But if expended on canals, the profits to transport would pay the interest, and give inconceivable advantages to the people. Such communications would facilitate every species of industry. Canals bending round the hills, would irrigate the grounds beneath, and convert them into luxuriant pasturage. They would bind a hundred millions of people in one inseparable compact—alike in habits, in language, and in interest; one homogeneous brotherhood, the most invulnerable, powerful, and respectable on earth. Say, legislators, you who direct the destinies of this great nation, shall Americans, like servile creatures of extablished habits, imitate European vices, or copy them because they are familiar? Shall they nourish a useless marine, lay the basis for its increase, and send it down the current of time to futurity with all its complicated evils? Shall such a system consume our resources, deprive the earth of improvements, draw into its vortex ambitious men, divert the best talents of our country from useful works, and interest them in its support—creating non-productive labourers, who must be the consumers of the produce of the productive class, and diminish their enjoyments? Or will you search into the most hidden recesses of science, to find a means for preventing such incalculable evils? And direct the genius and resources of our country to useful improvements, to the sciences, the arts, education, the amendment of the public mind and morals. In such pursuits, lie real honour and the nation's glory; such are the labours of enlightened republicans—those who labour for the public good. Every order of things, which has a tendency to remove oppression and meliorate the condition of man, by directing his ambition to useful industry is, in effect, republican. Every system, which nourishes war and its consequent thousands of idlers and oppressors, is aristocratic in its effects, whatever may be its name. These sentiments exhibit my political creed, the object of all my exertions; and these principles, practised by Americans, will create for them a real grandeur of character, which will secure to them the respect and admiration of the civilized world.

A Nation of Inventors

JACOB BIGELOW

Human ingenuity, in all ages of the world, has been directed to the acquisition of power. The simple bodily strength, with which nature has endowed every one; the inventions which we have sought out to extend and improve our physical ability; the craft and subtlety with which we learn to operate on our fellow-beings have been strikingly employed, at all times, for the promotion of this object. Those men have been great, who have brought others under their dominion; who have swayed them by their eloquence, or influenced them by the ascendency of their character; or who, by enlarging the boundaries of human knowledge, have increased the extent of their own resources, and obtained a control over the creation around them.

Power, when acquired, may have centred and terminated with the individual, or it may have become the common stock of society, and descended from one age to another. In this respect, we find a remarkable difference between the civil and the philosophical history of the world. The power which men and nations exercise in regard to each other, is temporary and transient. The greatest individuals have lived to see the decline of every thing upon which their greatness reposed. Societies and political institutions, which have been distinguished in their ascent, have been not less remarkable in their fall. Those nations and governments which, in former times, have subdued their competitors and controlled, for a time, the destinies of a great portion of the world; are now erased from the list of empires, and, perhaps, recognised only in name.

In the history of philosophy, on the other hand, every thing is permanent and progressive. The triumphs of the human mind over the obstacles that oppose its progress, have never been suspended in any period of the world. The ingenuity of mankind has never ceased to devise successful means of perpetuating its own empire. It has never forgotten how to subjugate the elements to its will, and to reduce all natural agents into ministers of its pleasure and power. What one age has acquired, another has not lost, but each succeeding generation have [*sic*] taken up the conquest where their [*sic*] predecessors had relinquished it; and if they have not been able to ad-

Jacob Bigelow, "Inaugural Address, Delivered in the Chapel at Cambridge, December 11, 1816," *North American Review,* vol. 4 (1816–17), pp. 271–277, 281.

vance into unexplored regions, they have, at least, sacrificed nothing of what was already won. Those sciences and arts, which give mankind an ascendency over the creation about them, have never, for a moment, escaped from their direction and use. The navigation of the sea and the cultivation of the earth, the forging of metals and the fashioning of wood, though their origin is beyond the memory of man, yet have continued without ceasing, even to the present day, to be extended and improved.

In the progress of philosophy, we have also the consoling evidence, that its uniform tendency has been to meliorate the condition and promote the happiness of mankind. Its effect is not merely to aggrandize the individuals who cultivate it, but likewise to benefit those who may be within the sphere of its influence. The branches of natural science, in particular, have this excellence, that they do not terminate in mere speculation, but that most of them have a direct bearing upon the wants of society, and tend to objects of real use. But these are not the only inviting features in their character. As they have hitherto been uniformly progressive, so they will continue to be; and the analogy of their previous growth affords an unlimited prospect for the future. Even at the present period of improvement, there is much to be learned in natural science; and the student, who would be serviceable to his country, may enlist himself in this department of labour, almost with the certainty of being able to contribute something to the general good. He need not despair at the amount of preparatory acquisition which seems necessary to qualify him for usefulness. The paths to eminence are less circuitous in this, than in some of the more abstract departments of knowledge. Many of the important discoveries in physics have been made by men young in life, restricted in leisure, and perhaps uninformed in the elegant branches of literature. The avenues to distinction in natural science, are proportionate to the multiplicity of its objects. Independent of the general subjects of investigation, which are open in all countries alike, there are opportunities exclusively local, peculiar to the place of one's own residence, by the study and improvement of which his labours may become interesting and valuable. This remark may well be brought home to our own country. If any one here despair of successfully cultivating those branches of physical science, which are pursued by learned men in other parts of the globe, with large establishments and expensive endowments, let him see if there are not subjects within the circle of his own walks, which are neither arduous in their character nor expensive in their cultivation, and which lie open to his unassisted industry. A multitude of such subjects he may find in the face and features of our continent: its structure and composition; its capacity for the different branches of agriculture, the improvements of which its present appropriations are susceptible; its geography; its climate and meteorology; its influence on the human body and the human mind; its diseases; its natural productions, minerals, plants, and animals; the resources which it has already derived from these, and those which it has yet to discover; the local exigences and wants, which may be supplied by the application of foreign inventions and known improvements, or by the contrivance and adaptation of new ones; in short, whatever may tend to increase the facilities of subsistence, and the welfare of those among whom we live.

Motives of philanthropy may urge the pursuit of subjects like these, but the calls of patriotism prefer even a stronger claim. The place of our birth and residence is the proper sphere and object of our exertions. It does not become us to complain of its disadvantages, and descant upon the superiority of more favoured spots. We should rather consider how we may overcome its defects, and improve its real advantages. We should also see, whether its irremediable faults are not in some instances, productive to us of good as well as of evil.

The portion of country in which it is our fortune to live, is not one of exuberant soil and spontaneous plenty. The summer of New-England does not elicit a second burden from our trees, nor is even our annual harvest exempt from the contingency of failure. Winter maintains here a long and late influence upon the seasons, and frosts are visiting us in the latest breezes of spring. Our territory is interrupted by extensive masses of rock, and broken by mountains intractable to cultivation. Our thin and penurious soil rests upon beds of granite, upon flint and sand, which drain it of its moisture, while themselves afford no pabulum for its vegetation. Whatever is raised from the bosom of the earth must be extorted by assiduous and painful culture, and a laborious vigilance is necessary to insure the fruits of the year.

Yet has this part of our country become the most populous and enlightened in the continent upon which we live. The very causes which seemed at variance with our prosperity, have proved its most powerful promoters. A vigor and hardihood of character have grown up, out of the evils which they had to combat; and a spirit of enterprise and perseverance, unknown in more luxurious climates, has become the characteristic of our population. The intelligence and the untiring application which were at first the offspring of necessity, have eventually exhibited ample fruits in the features of our land. Cultivated grounds and ornamental dwellings, wealthy cities and flourishing institutions have arisen upon a spot, where nature was never lavish of her gifts. A spirit of frugality and a talent of invention, have more than supplied the disadvantages of our natural situation. Around us is comfort, and plenty, and health. Our faculties are not exhausted by the debilitating heats of a sultry summer, nor our constitutions assaled by the miasmata of pestilential marshes. In our climate youth is active, and manhood is hardy. A spirit of adventure carries us every where in pursuit of the means of living, and there is no part of the world in which the New-England character is not represented. The means of information are cherished in our humblest villages; our cities are but little infested with the crimes of the older continent, and among us to an extent perhaps unexampled, the rein of intelligence and of principle supersedes the coercion of law.

Under so distinguished advantages, let us not complain of our lot in a country which gives us natural talents, and a climate which calls them into action. We should rather consider, that the health and alacrity which we possess, are not the common tenants of a rank and luxuriant clime, that the sultry and tepid breezes which multiply the fruits of the earth and render their qualities more exquisite, do not bring with them a keener relish, a more healthy circulation or a more vigorous frame. Few countries can boast of being what Italy was in the time of her ancient poets, at once the parent of fruits and of men. Luxury and indolence are the well known concomitants of a torrid atmosphere and an exuberant soil. If, in our northern and wintry climate, we are strangers to the rich profusion of a southern soil; we have the consolation that this climate, while it yields us but a scanty harvest for a laborious cultivation, yields us at the same time a blessing, for which there can be no equivalent, the capacity of enjoyment that results from vigour of body and activity of mind.

In science and the arts, notwithstanding the infancy of our institutions, and the embarrassment which most individuals experience from the necessity of attending to the calls of business, we have not been wholly without improvement, and are perhaps not destitute of a name. The researches of most of our ingenious men have had utility for their object. They have been performed in intervals taken from professional duties, and have been impeded by a deficiency of books and means. We have had little of the parade of operation, yet we have sometimes seen the fruits of silent efficiency and perserverance. We have had few learned men, but many useful ones. We have not often seen individuals among us, like the laborious Germans, spending their lives in endless acquisitions, while perhaps themselves add little to the general stock of knowledge; yet we have had men of original talents, who have been fortunate enough to discover some province in which they were qualified to be serviceable to their country and mankind. We have had ingenious mechanicians, skilful projectors, profound mathematicians, and men well versed in the useful learning of their time. The progress of our internal improvements, and the high state of the mechanic arts among us, as well as in our sister states, has entitled us to the character of a nation of inventors. The individuals who have originated and promoted such improvements, have often been men unambitious of fame, whose lives have past in obscurity; yet there have somethimes been those among us, whose labours have attracted the honourable notice of foreigners, and reflected lustre upon the country of their birth. It has ever been our fortune to impose obligations on others, and there are services of our citizens which are now better known than their names. There are some things which, if gathered from the ashes of obscurity, might serve to shed a gleam upon our literary reputation, and to make known at least the light they have kindled for others. It is a fact perhaps not generally realized, that the American Philosophical Society at Philadelphia, the Royal Society of Great Britain, and

Among those whom we shall longest remember, are men whose memory is associated with our own institutions, or with the sciences, which they laboured to promote. While we pass over the distinguished names of the Winthrops and Bowdoins, we should not forget that Franklin, the philosopher of the western world, was a native of New-England, and a son of our own metropolis. It was his fortune to live in times of political importance, and to find in science some paths untrodden by his predecessors. The great national events which he contributed to promote, and the brilliant and imposing nature of his philosophic discoveries, have been sufficient to aggrandize his character and immortalize his fame. Many men have been as learned, and many patriots as ardent, but few have left behind them a character to be summed up in a sublimer epitaph, than his,—who snatched the thunderbolt from heaven and the sceptre from tyrants.

It is with peculiar emotions of gratitude, of patriotism and pride, that we this day recall the memory of a son of Massachusetts, of one who was transplanted from us at an early period, and destined to flourish under other skies than ours; but who has left us the memorial that he was not unmindful of the country of his birth, and that for us he has not lived in vain. Few among us are ignorant that Benjamin Count Rumford received his birth and education in the near vicinity of these walls. . . .

To the country of his birth, Count Rumford has bequeathed his fortune and his fame. The lessons of patriotism which _we_ should learn from his memorable life, are important and convincing. It should teach us to respect ourselves, to value our resources, to cultivate our talents. Let those who would depreciate our native genius, recollect that he was an American. Let those who would make us the dependants and tributaries of the old world, recollect that he has instructed mankind. Let those who would despond as to our future destinies, remember, that his eye, which had wandered over the continent and capitals of Europe, settled at last upon the rising prospects of this western world.—For us, who are destined to labour in the path that he has marked out, and to follow with our eyes, though not with our steps, the brilliancy of his career; it may suffice to acknowledge, that we are not indifferent to the honour that has befallen us; that we are sensible of the magnitude of the example before us; that we believe, that the true end of philosophy is to be useful to mankind, and that we will cheerfully and anxiously enter upon the duties that await us; happy, if by our efforts, we can hope to add even a humble trophy to the monument of philanthropy and science, that commemorates the name of *him*, of whom it may in truth be said, that he lived for the world, and that he died for his country.

16. Newspapers

It was in the decades of the Revolution and the early republic that America became, as the *Port Folio* contemptuously noted in 1800, "a nation of newspaper readers." The remarkable proliferation of newspapers in the post-Revolutionary years was not the consequence of any technological revolution. Although iron presses and rollers were slowly being introduced at the beginning of the nineteenth century, most presses were still made of wood and differed little from Gutenberg's, nearly three centuries earlier. Until the exploitation of steam power, printing remained a laborious process, involving for a page of newspaper a dozen separate manual operations and the printing of only about two hundred pages per hour. In format, the early nineteenth-century papers still resembled the colonial newspaper, consisting of four pages, in size somewhat smaller than a modern tabloid. It was these traditional vehicles that helped to revolutionize American culture. The growth of the press and its influence was both a stimulant and a response to the increasing democratization of American politics and society.

That democratization, together with technological changes, would eventually transform the role of printers. As yet, however, most printers were still their own reporters, editors, and circulation and advertising managers. Probably the greatest printer of the day was Isaiah Thomas (1749-1831), who, with no formal schooling, became the head of a large publishing establishment with branches in towns in New England and in Albany and Baltimore. In 1802 he retired a rich man to devote the rest of his life to writing his *History of Printing in America* and to the founding of the American Antiquarian Society.

Printing in America

ISAIAH THOMAS

The first public journals, printed in British America, made their appearance in 1704. In April of that year, the first Anglo-American newspaper was printed at Boston, in Massachusetts Bay, by the postmaster, whose office was then regulated by the colonial government. At that period, I believe, there were only four or five postmasters in all the colonies. It was not until after the expiration of fifteen years, that another publication of the kind issued from any press in this part of the world.

On the 21st day of December, 1719, the second Anglo-American newspaper was published in Boston; and, on the following day, December 22, the third paper appeared, which was printed in the city of Philadelphia.

In 1725, a newspaper was first printed in New York; and after that time, gazettes were gradually introduced into the other colonies on the continent, and into the West Indies.

There are now, 1810, more newspapers published in the United States, than in the United Kingdom of Great Britain and Ireland.

In 1754, four newspapers only were printed in New England, these were all published in Boston, and, usually, on a small sheet; they were published weekly, and the average number of copies did not exceed six hundred from each press. No paper had then been issued in Connecticut, or New Hampshire. Some years before, one was printed for a short time in Rhode Island, but had been discontinued for want of encouragement. Vermont as a state did not exist, and the country which now composes it was then a wilderness. In 1775, a period of only twenty-one years, more copies of a newspaper were issued weekly from the village press at Worcester, Massachusetts, than were printed in all New England, in 1754; and one paper now published contains as much matter as did all the four published in Boston, in the year last mentioned.

At the beginning of 1775, there were five newspapers published in Boston, one at Salem, and one at Newburyport, making seven in Massachusetts. There was, at that time, one published at Portsmouth; and no other in New

Isaiah Thomas, *The History of Printing in the United States*, 2 vols. (1810), in American Antiquarian Society, *Trans. and Coll.*, vols. V–VI (1874), II, pp. 7–10, 199–204.

Hampshire. One was printed at Newport, and one at Providence, making two in Rhode Island. At New London there was one, at New Haven one, one at Hartford and one in Norwich; in all four in Connecticut; and fourteen in New England. In the province of New York, four papers were then published; three in the city, and one in Albany. In Pennsylvania there were, on the first of January, 1775, six; three in English and one in German, in Philadelphia; one in German, at Germantown; and one in English and German, at Lancaster. Before the end of January, 1775, three newspapers, in English, were added to the number from the presses in Philadelphia, making nine in Pennsylvania. In Maryland, two; one at Annapolis, and one at Baltimore. In Virginia, there were but two, and both of these at Williamsburg. One was printed at Wilmington, and one in Newbern, in North Carolina; three at Charleston, South Carolina; and one at Savannah, in Georgia. Making thirty-seven newspapers in all the British colonies, which are now comprised in the United States. To these may be added one at Halifax, in Nova Scotia; and one in Canada, at Quebec.

In 1800, there were at least one hundred and fifty publications of this kind printed in the United States of America, and since that time, the number has increased to three hundred and sixty. Those published before 1775 were weekly papers. Soon after the close of the Revolutionary war, daily papers were printed at Philadelphia, New York, &c., and there are now, 1810, more than twenty published, daily, in the United States.

It was common for printers of newspapers to subjoin to their titles "*Containing the freshest Advices both Foreign and Domestic;*" but gazettes and journals are now chiefly filled with political essays. News do not appear to be always the first object of editors, and, of course, "containing the freshest advices," &c., is too often out of the question.

For many years after the establishment of newspapers on this continent, very few advertisements appeared in them. This was the case with those that were early printed in Europe. In the first newspapers, advertisements were not separated by lines from the news, &c., and were not even begun with a two line letter; when two line letters were introduced, it was some time before one advertisement was separated from another by a line, or rule as it is termed by printers. After it became usual to separate advertisements, some printers used lines of metal rules; others lines of flowers irregularly placed. I have seen in some New York papers, great primer flowers between advertisements. At length, it became customary to "set off advertisements," and from using types not larger than those with which the news were printed, types of the size of French canon have often been used for names, especially of those who advertised English goods.

In the troublesome times, occasioned by the stamp act in 1765, some of the more opulent and cautious printers, when the act was to take place, put their papers in mourning, and, for a few weeks, omitted to publish them; others not so timid, but doubtful of the consequence of publishing newspapers without stamps, omitted the titles, or altered them, as an evasion; for instance the *Pennsylvania Gazette*, and some other papers, were headed "Remarkable Occurrences, &c.," —other printers, particularly those in Boston, continued their papers without any alteration in title or imprint. . . .

From the foregoing statement it appears that, from the time when the first public journal was published in the country, viz. in April, 1704, to April 1775, comprising a period of seventy-one years, seventy-eight different newspapers were printed in the British American continental colonies; that during this period, thirty-nine, exactly one-half of that number, had been, occasionally, discontinued; and that thirty-nine continued to be issued from the several establishments at the commencement of the revolution. The papers published in the West Indies are not included in this computation.

In the course of thirty-five years, newspaper establishments were, as previously remarked, multiplied in a surprising degree; insomuch, that the number of those printed in the United States in June, 1810, amounted to upwards of three hundred and sixty. . . .

A large proportion of the public papers at that date were established, and supported, by the two great contending political parties, into which the people of these states are usually divided; and whose numbers produce nearly an equipollence; consequently, a great augmentation of vehicles for carrying on the political warfare have been found necessary.

I cannot conclude what I have written on the subject of public journals, better than by extracting the following pertinent observations on newspapers, from the Rev. Dr. [Samuel] Miller's *Retrospect of the Eighteenth Century*.

"It is worthy of remark that newspapers have almost entirely changed their form and character within the period under review. For a long time after they were first adopted as a medium of communication to the public, they were confined, in general, to the mere statement of *facts*. But they have gradually assumed an office more extensive, and risen to a more important station in society. They have become the vehicles of discussion, in which the principles of government, the interests of nations, the spirit and tendency of public measures, and the public and private characters of individuals, are all arraigned, tried, and decided. Instead, therefore, of being considered now, as they once were, of small moment in society, they have become im-

mense moral and political engines, closely connected with the welfare of the
state, and deeply involving both its peace and prosperity.

"Newspapers have also become important in a literary view. There are few
of them, within the last twenty years, which have not added to their political
details some curious and useful information, on the various subjects of literature, science and art. They have thus become the means of conveying, to
every class in society, innumerable scraps of knowledge, which have at once
increased the public intelligence, and extended the taste for perusing periodical publications. The *advertisements*, moreover, which they daily contain,
respecting new books, projects, inventions, discoveries and improvements,
are well calculated to enlarge and enlighten the public mind, and are worthy
of being enumerated among the many methods of awakening and main-
taining the popular attention, with which more modern times, beyond all
preceding example, abound.

"In ancient times, to sow the seeds of civil discord, or to produce a spirit of
union and co-operation through an extensive community, required time,
patience, and a constant series of exertions. The art of printing being unknown, and many of the modern methods of communicating intelligence to
distant places not having come into use, the difficulty of conducting public
affairs must have been great and embarrassing. The general circulation of
Gazettes forms an important era, not only in the moral and literary, but also
in the political world. By means of this powerful instrument, impressions on
the public mind may be mad with a celerity, and to an extent, of which
our remote ancestors had no conception, and which cannot but give rise
to the most important consequences in society. Never was there given
to man a political engine of greater power; and never, assuredly, did
this engine before operate upon so large a scale as in the eighteenth
century.

"Our own country in particular, and especially for the last twelve or fifteen years, has exhibited a spectacle never before displayed among men,
and even yet without a parallel on earth. It is the spectacle, not of the learned
and the wealthy only, but of the great body of the people; even a large portion of that class of the community which is destined to daily labor, having
free and constant access to public prints, receiving regular information of
every occurrence, attending to the course of political affairs, discussing
public measures, and having thus presented to them constant excitements to
the acquisition of knowledge, and continual means of obtaining it. Never, it
may be safely asserted, was the number of political journals so great in proportion to the population of a country as at present in ours. Never were they,
all things considered, so cheap, so universally diffused, and so easy of

access." And never were they actually perused by so large a majority of all classes since the art of printing was discovered.°

"The general effect of this unprecedented multiplication and diffusion of public prints, forms a subject of most interesting and complex calculation. On the one hand, when well conducted, they have a tendency to disseminate useful information; to keep the public mind awake and active; to confirm and extend the love of freedom; to correct the mistakes of the ignorant, and the impositions of the crafty; to tear off the mask from corrupt and designing politicians; and, finally, to promote union of spirit and of action among the most distant members of an extended community. But to pursue a path calculated to produce these effects, the conductors of public prints ought to be men of talents, learning, and virtue. Under the guidance of such characters, every Gazette would be a source of moral and political instruction, and, of course, a public blessing.

"On the other hand, when an instrument so potent is committed to the weak, the ignorant, and the vicious, the most baneful consequences must be anticipated. When men of small talents, of little information, and of less virtue, undertake to be (as the editors of public gazettes, however contemptible their character may, in a degree, be considered) the directors of public opinion, what must be the result? We may expect to see the frivolities of weakness, the errors and malignity of prejudice, the misrepresentations of party zeal, the most corrupt doctrines in politics and morals, the lacerations of private character, and the poluting language of obscenity and impiety, daily issuing from the press, poisoning the principles, and disturbing the response of society; giving to the natural and salutary collisions of parties the most brutal violence and ferocity; and, at length, consuming the best feelings and noblest charities of life, in the flame of civil discord.

"In the former part of the eighteenth century, talents and learning, at least, if not virtue, were thought necessary in the conductors of political journals.† Few ventured to intrude into this arduous office, but those who had some claims to literature. Towards the close of the century, however,

---

°"The extreme cheapness with which newspapers are conveyed by the mail, in the United States, added to the circumstances of their being altogether unincumbered with a stamp duty, or any other public restriction, renders their circulation more convenient and general than in any other country."

†"This has not been, generally, so much the case in America as in Europe. From the earliest period too many of our Gazettes have been in the hands of persons who were destitute both of talents and literature. But in later times, the number of editors who fall under this description has become even greater than formerly."

persons of less character, and of humbler qualifications, began, without scruple, to undertake the high task of enlightening the public mind. This remark applies, in some degree, to Europe; but it applies with particular force to our own country, where every judicious observer must perceive, that too many of our gazettes are in the hands of persons destitute at once of the urbanity of gentlemen, the information of scholars, and the principles of virtue. To this source, rather than to any peculiar depravity of national character, we may ascribe the faults of American newspapers, which have been pronounced by travellers the most profligate and scurrilous public prints in the civilized world.°

"If the foregoing remarks be just, then the friend of rational freedom, and of social happiness, cannot but contemplate with the utmost solicitude, the future influence of political journals on the welfare of society. As they form one of the great safeguards of free government, so they also form one of its most threatening assailants. And unless public opinion (the best remedy that can be applied) should administer an adequate correction of the growing evil, we may anticipate the arrival of that crisis in which we must yield either to an abridgment of the liberty of the press, or to a disruption of every social bond."

OBSERVATION.

There are few instances in which I would presume to differ with the ingenious author of these remarks, in opinion: but, on this occasion, I must be allowed to observe, that I conceive there are among the men who conduct the public journals of America, many, whose literary acquirements are not inferior to those of their predecessors. The great difficulty proceeds from the rage of party spirit, which is kept alive by the frequency of elections, in which the conductors of newspapers engage as partizans; and some of them, it is true, as is also the case in Great Britain, display a greater degree of asperity and opprobriousness than can be justified, which must be a subject of regret to those who are truly interested in the welfare of the country.

°"These considerations, it is conceived, are abundantly sufficient to account for the disagreeable character of American newspapers. In every country the selfish principle prompts men to defame their personal and political enemies; and where the supposed provocations to this are numerous, and no restraints are imposed on the indulgence of the disposition, an inundation of filth and calumny must be expected. In the United States, the frequency of elections leads to a corresponding frequency of struggle between political parties; these struggles naturally engender mischievous passions, and every species of coarse invective; and, unhappily, too many of the conductors of our public prints have neither the discernment, the firmness, nor the virtue to reject from their pages the foul ebullitions of prejudice and malice. Had they more diligence, or greater talents, they might render their gazettes interesting, by filling them with materials of a more instructive and dignified kind; but wanting these qualifications, they must give such materials, accompanied with such a seasoning, as circumstances furnish. Of what kind these are no one is ignorant."

PART FIVE

The Fine Arts

17. Painting and Engraving

By the late colonial period the paucity of materials and patronage in provincial America was driving young aspiring artists like John Singleton Copley and Benjamin West abroad for training and for visual confrontation with the great art they had only read about. West (1728-1820), born into a Pennsylvania Quaker family, lived by the painting of signs and portraits until his savings and some fortunate assistance enabled him to travel to Italy in 1760. West's *Life,* by his friend John Galt, the British writer, is sometimes unreliable, but the scene he describes of the Pennsylvanian's encounter with Rome is based on West's often repeated reminiscences. West went on to England in 1763, planning to stay only a short while, but he found such favor there that he never left. He became extremely popular, eventually gained the patronage of George III, and became president of the Royal Academy of Arts. He trained a succession of American artists, including Charles W. Peale, Gilbert Stuart, Robert Fulton, John Trumbull, Samuel Morse, Thomas Sully, and Washington Allston.

West, sharing the ideals of Sir Joshua Reynolds, sought to create a noble and classical art that would express the heroic qualities of man and reveal virtue through beauty. The lack of American subjects for such a grandiose art was suddenly transformed by the American Revolution, and West himself, although historical painter to the King, toyed with the idea of painting the great scenes of the Revolution. The project, however, passed to his student John Trumbull (1756-1843), who laid out his plans in his 1789 letter declining Jefferson's offer to become his personal secretary. Trumbull went on to become the painter of the American Revolution, depicting some of its great events and painting hundreds of portraits of its participants. Trumbull thought he would make a fortune from the sale of engravings of his paintings, but after an initial encouraging reception subscriptions soon ceased.

Trumbull's disappointments, however, did not discourage others from exploiting American patriotism. Numerous painters and engravers, both refined and primitive, sought through symbolic art to represent the personages and character of the new republic.

The Life of Benjamin West

JOHN GALT

It was not . . . the native inhabitants of Rome who constituted the chief attractions of society there, but the number of accomplished strangers of all
countries and religions, who, in constant succession, came in pilgrimage to
the shrine of antiquity; and who, by the contemplation of the merits and
glories of departed worth, often felt themselves, as it were, miraculously endowed with new qualities. The collision of minds fraught with learning, in
that high state of excitement which the genius of the place produced on the
coldest imaginations, together with those innumerable brilliant and
transitory topics which were never elicited in any other city, made the
Roman conversations a continual exercise of the understanding. The
details of political intrigue, and the follies of individuals, excited but
little interest among the strangers in Rome. It seemed as if by an universal
tacit resolution, national and personal peculiarities and prejudices
were forgotten, and that all strangers simultaneously turned their attention to the transactions and affairs of former ages, and of statesmen and
authors now no more. Their mornings were spent in surveying the
monuments raised to public virtue, and in giving local features in
their minds to the knowledge which they had acquired by the perusal
of those works that have perpetuated the dignity of the Roman character.
Their evenings were often allotted to the comparison of their respective
conjectures, and to ascertain the authenticity and history of the relics
which they had collected of antient art. Sometimes the day was consumed in
the study of those inestimable ornaments of religion, by which the
fraudulent disposition of the priesthood had, in the decay of its power, rendered itself venerable to the most enlightened minds; and the night was
devoted to the consideration of the causes which contribute to the de-
velopement of genius, or of the events which tend to stifle and overwhelm
its powers. Every recreation of the stranger in Rome was an effort of the
memory, of abstraction, and of fancy.—Society, in this elevated state of
enjoyment, surrounded by the greatest works of human creation, and placed
amidst the monuments of the most illustrious of mankind, and that of the

John Galt, *The Life and Studies of Benjamin West, Esq., President of the
Royal Academy of London, Prior to His Arrival in England; Compiled from
Materials Furnished by Himself* (London, 1816), pp. 97–107.

Quakers of Pennsylvania, employed in the mechanical industry of felling timber, and amid the sobriety of rural and commercial economy, were like the extremes of a long series of events, in which, though the former is the necessary consequence of the latter, no resemblance can be traced in their respective characteristics. In America all was young, vigorous and growing,— the spring of a nation, frugal, active, and simple. In Rome all was old, infirm, and decaying,—the autumn of a people who had gathered their glory, and were sinking into sleep under the disgraceful excesses of the vintage. On the most inert mind, passing from the one continent to the other, the contrast was sufficient to excite great emotion; on such a character as that of Mr. West, who was naturally disposed to the contemplation of the sublime and beautiful, both as to their moral and visible effect, it made a deep and indelible impression. It confirmed him in the wisdom of those strict religious principles which denied the utility of art when solely employed as the medium of amusement; and impelled him to attempt what could be done to approximate the uses of the pencil to those of the pen, in order to render Painting, indeed, the sister of Eloquence and Poetry.

But the course of study in the Roman schools was not calculated to enable him to carry this grand purpose into effect; for the principles by which Michael Angelo, and Raphael had attained their excellence, were no longer regarded. The study of Nature was deserted for that of the antique; and pictures were composed according to rules derived from other paintings, without respect to what the subject required, or what the circumstances of the scene probably appeared to be. It was, therefore, not one of the least happy occurrences in his life that he went to Rome when society was not only in the most favourable state for the improvement of his mind, and for convincing him of the deleterious influence of the arts when employed as the embellishments of voluptuousness and luxury; but also when the state of the arts was so mean, that the full effect of studying the antique only, and of grouping characters by academical rules, should appear so striking as to satisfy him that he could never hope for any eminence, if he did not attend more to the phenomena of Nature, than to the productions of the greatest genius. The perusal of the works of other painters, he was sensible, would improve his taste; but he was convinced, that the design which he had formed for establishing his own fame, could not be realised, if, for a single moment, he forgot that their works, however exquisite, were but the imitations and forms of those eternal models to which he had been instinctively directed.

It was on the 10th of July, 1760, that he arrived at Rome. The French Courier conducted him to a hotel, and, having mentioned in the house that he was an American, and a Quaker, come to study the fine arts, the circum-stance seemed so extraordinary, that it reached the ears of Mr. Robinson, afterwards Lord Grantham, who immediately found himself possessed by an irresistible desire to see him; and who, before he had time to dress or refresh himself, paid him a visit, and insisted that he should dine with him. In the course of dinner, that gentleman inquired what letters of introduction the Artist had brought with him; and West having informed him, he observed it was somewhat remarkable that the whole of them should be addressed to his most particular friends, adding, that as he was engaged to meet them at a party in the evening, he expected West would accompany him. This atten-tion and frankness was acknowledged as it deserved to be, and is remembered by the Artist among those fortunate incidents which have rendered the recollection of his past life so pleasant, as scarcely to leave a wish for any part of it to have been spent otherwise than it was. At the hour appointed, Mr. Robinson conducted him to the house of Mr. Crispigné, an English gentleman who had long resided at Rome, where the evening party was held.

Among the distinguished persons whom Mr. West found in company, was the celebrated Cardinal Albani. His eminence, although quite blind, had acquired, by the exquisite delicacy of his touch, and the combining powers of his mind, such a sense of antient beauty, that he excelled all the virtuosi then in Rome, in the correctness of his knowledge of the verity and pecularities of the smallest medals and intaglios. Mr. Robinson conducted the Artist to the inner apartment, where the Cardinal was sitting, and said, "I have the honour to present a young American, who has a letter of intro-duction to your eminence, and who has come to Italy for the purpose of studying the fine arts." The Cardinal fancying that the American must be an Indian, exclaimed, "Is he black or white?" and on being told that he was very fair, "What as fair as I am?" cried the Cardinal still more surprised. This latter expression excited a good deal of mirth at the Cardinal's expence, for his complexion was of the darkest Italian olive, and West's was even more than the usual degree of English fairness. For some time after, if it be not still in use, the expression of "as fair as the Cardinal" acquired proverbial currency in the Roman conversations, applied to persons who had any inordinate conceit of their own beauty.

The Cardinal, after some other short questions, invited West to come near him, and running his hands over his features, still more attracted the attention of the company to the stranger, by the admiration which he expressed at the form of his head. This occasioned inquiries respecting the youth; and the Italians concluding that, as he was an American, he must, of course, have received the education of a savage, became curious to witness the effect which the works of art in the Belvidere and Vatican would produce on him. The whole company, which consisted of the principal Roman nobility, and strangers of distinction then in Rome, were interested in the event; and it was arranged in the course of the evening that on the following morning they should accompany Mr. Robinson and his protegé to the palaces.

At the hour appointed, the company assembled; and a procession, consisting of upwards of thirty of the most magnificent equipages in the capital of Christendom, and filled with some of the most erudite characters in Europe, conducted the young Quaker to view the master-pieces of art. It was agreed that the Apollo should be first submitted to his view, because it was the most perfect work among all the ornaments of Rome, and, consequently, the best calculated to produce that effect which the company were anxious to witness. The statute then stood in a case, enclosed with doors, which could be so opened as to disclose it at once to full view. West was placed in the situation where it was seen to the most advantage, and the spectators arranged themselves on each side. When the keeper threw open the doors, the Artist felt himself surprised with a sudden recollection altogether different from the gratification which he had expected; and without being aware of the force of what he said, exclaimed, "My God, how like it is to a young Mohawk warrior!" The Italians, observing his surprise, and hearing the exclamation, requested Mr. Robinson to translate to them what he said; and they were excessively mortified to find that the god of their idolatry was compared to a savage. Mr. Robinson mentioned to West their chagrin, and asked him to give some more distinct explanation, by informing him what sort of people the Mohawk Indians were. He described to him their education; their dexterity with the bow and arrow; the admirable elasticity of their limbs; and how much their active life expands the chest, while the quick breathing of their speed in the chace, dilates the nostrils with that apparent consciousness of vigour which is so nobly depicted in the Apollo. "I have seen them often," added he, "standing in that very attitude, and pursuing, with an intense eye, the arrow which they had just discharged from the bow." This descriptive explanation did not lose by Mr. Robinson's translation. The Italians were delighted, and allowed that a better criticism had rarely been pronounced on the merits of the statue. The view of the other great works did not awaken the same vivid feelings. Those of Raphael, in the Vatican, did not at first particularly interest him; nor was it until he had often visited them alone, and studied them by himself, that he could appreciate the fulness of their excellence. His first view of the works of Michael Angelo, was still less satisfactory:

indeed, he continued always to think, that, with the single exception of the Moses, that Artist had not succeeded in giving a probable character to any of his subjects, notwithstanding the masterly hand and mind which pervade the weakest of his productions.

Commemorating the Revolution

JOHN TRUMBULL

London, June 11th, 1789.

To Thos. Jefferson, Esq., &c. &c., at Paris.

Dear Sir—

. . .If my affairs were in other respects as I could wish them, I should have given at once a positive answer to your proposition. It would have been an answer of thankfulness and acceptance, for nothing could be proposed to me more flattering to my pride, or more consonant, at least for a time, to my favorite pursuit. The greatest motive I had or have for engaging in, or for continuing my pursuit of painting, has been the wish of commemorating the great events of our country's revolution. I am fully sensible that the profession, as it is generally practiced, is frivolous, little useful to society, and unworthy of a man who has talents for more serious pursuits. But, to preserve and diffuse the memory of the noblest series of actions which have ever presented themselves in the history of man; to give to the present and the future sons of oppression and misfortune, such glorious lessons of their rights, and of the spirit with which they should assert and support them, and even to transmit to their descendants, the personal resemblance of those who have been the great actors in those illustrious scenes, were objects which gave a dignity to the profession, peculiar to my situation. And some superiority also arose from my having borne personally a humble part in the great events which I was to describe. No one lives with me possessing this advantage, and no one can come after me to divide the honour of truth and authenticity,

John Trumbull to Thomas Jefferson, 11 June 1789, in *Autobiography, Reminiscences and Letters of John Trumbull from 1756 to 1841* (New York, 1841), pp. 157–162.

however easily I may hereafter be exceeded in elegance. Vanity was thus on the side of duty, and I flattered myself that by devoting a few years of life to this object, I did not make an absolute waste of time, or squander uselessly, talents from which my country might justly demand more valuable services; and I feel some honest pride in the prospect of accomplishing a work, such as had never been done before, and in which it was not easy that I should have a rival.

With how much assiduity, and with what degree of success, I have pursued the studies necessarily prepatory to this purpose, the world will decide in the judgment it shall pass on the picture (of Gilbraltar) which I now exhibit to them; and I need not fear that this judgment will deceive me, for it will be biased here, to a favorable decision, by no partiality for me, or my country.

But, while I have done whatever depended upon my personal exertions, I have been under the necessity of employing, and relying upon the exertions of another. The two paintings which you saw in Paris three years ago, (Bunker's Hill and Quebec,) I placed in the hands of a print-seller and publisher, to cause to be engraved, and as the prospect of profit to him was considerable, I relied upon his using the utmost energy and dispatch; instead of which, three years have been suffered to elapse, without almost the smallest progress having been made in the work. Instead therefore of having a work already far advanced to submit to the world and to my countrymen, I am but where I was three years since, with the deduction from my ways and means of three years' expenses, with prospects blighted, and the hope of the future damped by the experience of past mismanagement. And the most serious reflection is, that the memory and enthusiasm for actions however great, fade daily from the human mind; that the warm attention which the nations of Europe once paid to us, begins to be diverted to objects more nearly and immediately interesting to themselves; and that France, in particular, from which country I entertained peculiar hopes of patronage, is beginning to be too much occupied by her own approaching revolution, to think so much of us as perhaps she did formerly.

Thus circumstanced, I forsee the utter impossibility of proceeding in my work, without the warm patronage of my countrymen. Three or four years more must pass before I can reap any considerable advantage from what I am doing in this country, and as I am far from being rich, those years must not be employed in prosecuting a plan, which, without the real patronage of my country, will only involve me in new certainties of great and immediate expense, with little probability of even distant recompense. I do not aim at opulence, but I must not knowingly rush into embarrassment and ruin.

I am ashamed to trouble you with such details, but without them, I could not so well have explained my reason for not giving you at once a decided answer. You see, sir, that my future movements depend entirely upon my reception in America, and as that shall be cordial or cold, I am to decide whether to abandon my country or my profession. I think I shall determine without much hesitation; for although I am secure of a kind reception in any quarter of the globe, if I will follow the general example of my profession by flattering the pride or apologizing for the vices of men, yet the ease, perhaps even elegance, which would be the fruit of such conduct, would compensate but poorly for the contempt which I should feel for myself, and for the necessity which it would impose upon me of submitting to a voluntary sentence of perpetual exile. I hope for better things. Monuments have been in repeated instances voted to her heroes; why then should I doubt a readiness in our country to encourage me in producing monuments, not of heroes only, but of those events on which their title to the gratitude of the nation is founded, and which by being multiplied and little expensive, may be diffused over the world, instead of being bounded to one narrow spot?

Immediately therefore upon my arrival in America, I shall offer a subscription for prints to be published from such a series of pictures as I intend, with the condition of returning their money to subscribers, if the sum received shall not prove to be sufficient to justify me in proceeding with the work; and I shall first solicit the public protection of Congress.

I am told that it is a custom in France, for the king to be considered as a subscriber for one hundred copies of all elegant works engraved by his subjects; that these are deposited in the Bibliothéque du Roi, and distributed as presents to foreigners of distinction and taste, as specimens of the state of the fine arts in France. Would this be a mode of diffusing a knowledge of their origin, and at the same time a lesson on the rights of humanity, improper to be adopted by the United States? And if the example of past greatness be a powerful incentive to emulation, would such prints be improper presents to their servants? The expense would be small, and the purpose of monuments and medals as rewards of merit, and confirmations of history, would receive a valuable support, since perhaps it may be the fate of prints, sometimes to outlast either marble or bronze.

If a subscription of this sort should fill in such a manner as to justify me, I shall proceed with all possible diligence, and must of course pass some years in Europe; and as I have acquired that knowledge in this country which was my only object for residing here, and shall have many reasons for preferring Paris hereafter, I shall in that case be happy and proud to accept your flattering proposal. But if, on the contrary, my countrymen should not give me such encouragement as I wish and hope, I must give up the pursuit, and of course I shall have little desire to return for any stay in Europe. In the mean time, viewing the absolute uncertainty of my situation, I must beg you not to pass by any more favorable subject which may offer, before I have the happiness to meet you in America, which I hope will be ere long.

I have the honor to be, very gratefully,

Dear sir, your most faithful servant,

JOHN TRUMBULL.

NEW-YORK, April 2, 1790.

PROPOSALS
BY
JOHN TRUMBULL,
For PUBLISHING by SUBSCRIPTION,

TWO PRINTS,

From ORIGINAL PICTURES painted by himself:

REPRESENTING

The DEATH of Gen. WARREN,
At the Battle of BUNKER's-HILL;

AND

The DEATH of Gen. MONTGOMERY,
In the Attack of QUEBEC.

IN the Battle of Bunker's Hill, the following Portraits are introduced,—

AMERICAN.	BRITISH.
Major General WARREN,	General Sir WILLIAM HOWE,
PUTNAM.	Sir HENRY CLINTON,
	Lieut. Colonel JOHN SMALL,
	Major PITCAIRN, and
	Lieut. PITCAIRN.

In the Attack of Quebec, are seen,—
General MONTGOMERY,
Colonel THOMPSON;
Major MACPHERSON,
Captain CHEESMAN.

CONDITIONS of SUBSCRIPTION.

The Prints will be engraved by two of the most eminent Artists in Europe.—The Size will be 30 Inches by 20.—The Price to Subscribers, Three Guineas for each Print, one half to be paid at the Time of subscribing, the Remainder on the Delivery of the Prints, which will be as soon as the Work (which is already considerably advanced) can possibly be completed.

SUBSCRIPTIONS are received in America, only by Mr. Trumbull.—All subscription Receipts will be signed by him, as well as by Mr. Poggi, of London; under whose Direction the Prints are engraving, and will be published.

(2)

These Prints are the first of a Series, in which it is proposed to represent the most important Events of the American Revolution.

No Period of the History of Man, is more interesting than that in which we have lived.—The Memory of Scenes, in which were laid the Foundations of that free Government, which secures our national and individual Happiness, must remain ever dear to us, and to Posterity;—and if national Pride be in any Case justifiable, Americans have a right to glory in having given to the World an Example, whose Influence is rapidly spreading the Love of Freedom through other Nations, and every where ameliorating the Condition of Men.

To assist in preserving the Memory of the illustrious Events which have marked this Period of our Country's Glory, as well as of the Men who have been the most important Actors in them, is the Object of this Undertaking.—Historians will do justice to an Æra so important; but to be read, the Language in which they write, must be understood;—the Language of Painting is universal, and intelligible in all Nations, and every Age.

As several Years of his Time, and a very considerable Expence, are necessary to accomplish this Undertaking, it would be an imprudent Sacrifice to the mere Hope of Reputation to go more deeply into it, without a Probability of ultimate Success:—That He may judge of the Degree of this Probability, Mr. Trumbull, by the Advice of his Friends, proposes this Subscription, and flatters himself with a Hope of meeting that Patronage from his Countrymen, which will justify his pursuing the Object with Ardor; and without which it is impossible that so expensive a Work should be continued.

The Subjects proposed to be represented, in Addition to the two foregoing, of Bunker's-Hill and Quebec, are—

* The DECLARATION of INDEPENDENCE,
* BATTLE at TRENTON,
* BATTLE of PRINCETOWN,
SURRENDER of General BURGOYNE,
TREATY with FRANCE,
BATTLE of EUTAW SPRINGS,
* SURRENDER of YORK-TOWN,
TREATY of PEACE,
EVACUATION of NEW-YORK,
RESIGNATION of General WASHINGTON,
The ARCH at TRENTON,
INAUGURATION of the PRESIDENT of the UNITED STATES.

Each Picture will contain Portraits of the principal Characters, who were present at the Scene represented.—Those marked with Stars, are considerably advanced;—and the Prints from the Whole will be executed of the same Size, and by the most eminent Engravers.

1. The Advertising of Art, 1790: *Proposals by John Trumbull* (1790).

2. John Trumbull, *Battle of Bunker's Hill* (1775).

3. John Trumbull, *The Declaration of Independence* (1786-1797).

4. Gilbert Stuart, *George Washington* (The Lansdowne Portrait, 1796).

276

5. Edward Savage, *The Washington Family* (1798).

6. Anonymous. *Polly Botsford and Her Children* (c. 1813).

7.   Amos Doolittle, *A New Display of the United States* (1799).

8. Catherine T. Warner, *Mourning Picture: George Washington* (c. 1800).

18. Theater

The theater did not begin to have much effect on American culture until about the middle of the eighteenth century, when traveling troupes from England like the Hallam company, and later the combined Hallam-Douglass group, began touring the colonies. The most immediate communal response, at least outside of the South, was hostile, resulting in mob action and laws against plays in several colonies. Under such adverse circumstances the players were forced to resort to all sorts of subterfuges in order to advertise their plays. Following the Revolution, however, the atmosphere for theater gradually began to improve. Various groups in the leading cities were successful in the 1780's and 1790's in having laws against the stage repealed, and Americans themselves began writing and acting.

Othello, American Style

(Playbill, 1761)

KINGS ARMS TAVERN—NEWPORT—RHODE ISLAND.

On Monday, June 10th, at the Public Room of the above Inn,
will be delivered a series of
MORAL DIALOGUES,
IN FIVE PARTS,

Depicting the evil effects of jealousy, and other bad passions, and proving that happiness can only spring from the pursuit of virtue.

Mr. Douglas—will represent a noble and magnanimous Moor, called Othello, who loves a young lady named Desdemona, and after he has married her, harbors (as in too many cases) the dreadful passion of jealousy.

> Of jealousy, our being's bane,
> Mark the small cause, and the most dreadful pain.

Mr. Allyn—will depict the character of a specious villain, in the regiment of Othello, who is so base as to hate his commander on mere suspicion, and to impose on his best friend. Of such characters, it is to be feared, there are thousands in the world, and the one in question may present to us a salutary warning.

> The man that wrongs his master and his friend,
> What can he come to but a shameful end?

Mr. Hallam—will delineate a young and thoughtful officer, who is traduced by Mr. Allyn, and getting drunk, loses his situation and his general's esteem. All young men, whatsoever, take example from Cassio.

> The ill effects of drinking would you see?
> Be warn'd, and fly from evil company.

Mr. Morris—will represent an old gentleman, the father of Desodemona, who is not cruel or covetous, but is foolish enough to dislike the noble Moor, his son-in-law, because his face is not white, forgetting that we all spring from one root. Such prejudices are very numerous, and very wrong.

William W. Clapp, Jr., *A Record of the Boston Stage* (Boston, 1853), pp. 8–10.

> Fathers beware what sense and love ye lack,
> 'Tis crime, not color, makes the being black.

Mr. Quelch—will depict a fool, who wishes to become a knave, and trusting to one, gets killed by him. Such is the friendship of rogues—take heed.

> When fools would knaves become, how often you'll
> Perceive the knave not wiser than the fool.

Mrs. Morris—will represent a young and virtuous wife, who being wrongfully suspected, gets smothered (in an adjoining room) by her husband.

> Reader, attend; and e'er thou goest hence
> Let fall a tear to helpless innocence.

Mrs. Douglas—will be her faithful attendant, who will hold out a good example to all servants, male and female, and to all people in subjection.

> Obedience and gratitude
> Are things as rare as they are good.

Various other dialogues, too numerous to mention here, will be delivered at night, all adapted to the improvement of the mind and manners. The whole will be repeated on Wednesday and Saturday. Tickets six shilling each, to be had within. Commencement at seven, conclusion at half-past ten, in order that every spectator may go home at a sober hour, and reflect upon what he has seen before he retires to rest.

> God save the king,
> And long may he sway
> East, North, and South,
> And fair America.

The Morality of the Stage

(Philadelphia, 1788)

1

Report of a committee of the assembly of Pennsylvania, to whom had been referred a petition of messrs. Hallam and Henry, praying to have a bill passed to licence a theatre in or near Philadelphia.

THAT they would not have it understood, that in the present report, which will be favourable to the petition, they are in the least influenced by any particular or personal wish for the establishment of a theatre—but a question of such importance, it is their duty to examine with care, as it is the part of integrity to propose their genuine sentiments upon it, even should it be foreseen that they will differ from those entertained by many persons truly estimable for their moral and religious virtues.

The committee have had to withstand the force of a very serious and important objection made to the stage, that it has ever been a great corrupter of the public morals; but this position, as one of a speculative nature, is not capable of complete demonstration—it is even doubted whether it is to be maintained; the better opinion seems to be, that dramatic pieces, in common with other works of taste and sentiment, tend to the general refinement of manners and the polish of society, than which nothing can be more favourable to the growth of the virtues.

In this regard, it may be said, that men, in appearance the farthest removed from the influence of the stage, have obligations to it, which they neither perceive nor own.

But your committee have been led to contemplate the stage as the great mart of genius, and as such, a natural and necessary concomitant of our independence.—We have cast off a foreign yoke in government, but shall still be dependent for those productions of the mind, which do most honour to human nature, until we can afford due protection and encouragement to every species of our own literature.

In these sentiments, your committee offer the following resolution:

Resolved, That a special committee be appointed to bring in a bill to license a theatre in or near the city of Philadelphia for dramatic representations.

American Museum, V (1789), pp. 185–90.

To the general assembly of Pennsylvania.
The memorial and petition of the people called quakers, in
the city of Philadelphia.

Respectfully sheweth.

THAT at the early settlement of Pennsylvania the preservation of the morals of the inhabitants was considered, by the legislature, essential to the well-being and prosperity of the community, and many wise laws were enacted for the suppression of vice and immorality, which appeared to them likely to be greatly promoted by stage entertainments, wherever they were permitted: and accordingly, the assemblies passed divers acts from time to time, to prohibit them, although disallowed by the rulers in Great Britain, who then exercised a controul over the legislature here; their exceptions being founded on maxims of mere human policy, rather than virtuous considerations.—Nevertheless, the virtue of the people, for a considerable time, manifested such an abhorrence of those ensnaring diversions, that the stage actors did not find it their interest to prosecute their corrupting employment. And, since the late revolution, the legislature actuated by laudable motives, enacted a law, entitled, "An act for the prevention of vice and immorality, and unlawful gaming, and to restrain disorderly sports and dissipation," passed in 1786, (for a repeal of which a petition was presented to the late house of assembly by Lewis Hallam and John Henry, in behalf of themselves and other comedians) notwithstanding which, in defiance of its authority, regardless of the penalities, and in contempt of government, those delusive scenes have, in the course of last summer, been exhibited, and, as appears by public advertisements, are of late renewed.

Other persons, also, promoters of licentiousness, at the same time continued amusements among the people of the like pernicious tendency. Whereupon, affected with concern that these exhibitions should be revived at any time, but more especially when a stagnation of commerce, a scarcity of money, and a great appearance of a failure of this country, from the alarming destruction of our wheat by an unusual insect, require a serious attention to an improvement in every moral and religious duty: an address was presented to the executive council on the eighteenth day of the seventh month last, setting forth our full apprehensions, respecting such entertainments, which are not founded on mere speculative opinion; it being not only the sense of divers persons, conspicuous for wisdom and virtue, resulting from their religious observation and experience, but supported by incontrovertible fact. Sir John Hawkins speaking of the pernicious effects of plays, says, "upon setting up or opening a certain theatre, its contiguity to the city soon made it a place of great resort, and what was apprehended from the advertisement of the plays to be exhibited in that quarter of the town, soon followed; the adjacent houses became taverns in name, but in truth they were houses of lewd resort, and the former occupiers of them, useful manufacturers and industrious artificers, were driven to seek elsewhere for a residence." And he further remarks, "that the merchants of London, then a grave, sagacious body of men, found the theatre was a temptation to idleness and to pleasure, that their clerks could not resist; they regretted to see the corruptions of Covent Garden extended, and the seats of industry hold forth allurements to vice and debauchery." And again he observes, "that although of plays it is said, that they teach morality—and of the stage, that it is the mirror of human life—these assertions are mere declamation, and have no foundation in truth or experience; on the contrary, a playhouse, and the regions about it, are the very hot-beds of vice; how else comes it to pass, that no sooner is a playhouse opened in any part of the kingdom, than it becomes surrounded with an hollow (or circle) of brothels? Of this truth the neighbourhood of the place I am now speaking of, has had experience; one parish alone, adjacent thereto, having, to my knowledge, expended the sum of thirteen hundred pounds in prosecutions for the purpose of removing those inhabitants, whom the playhouse had drawn thither."

Such is the account related by this author, of the unhappy and destructive effects of these vain recreations. How consistent such places of dissipation and extravagance are with the profession of christianity, and our present circumstances, requires no great discernment to perceive.

And as the moral, political, and religious interest of the community are, unitedly, the great object of legislative attention; when it becomes evident, by the loud calls of public calamity, that frugality and industry are essential to the well-being of the people; that vice is gaining ground, and religion is in danger of being openly the subject of ridicule—and the serious, important, and self-denying precepts of the gospel set at nought, by the introduction of those seminaries of lewdness and irreligion;—it then becomes the virtuous part of the people of every denomination, to express their feelings with energy, and avow their disapprobation of proceedings so injurious.

Influenced by a sense of duty, and a sincere regard for the youth and others of the present day, we are engaged to request your serious attention to the premises, and that you may reject the application of the said Lewis Hallam and John Henry, however supported by plausible, though fallacious pretensions.

And we earnestly desire the same laudable zeal which influenced your predecessors in their virtuous endeavours to preserve the morals of the people from depravity, may induce you to reject an offer, which proposes to raise a revenue by so corrupt a practice, at the risque of the virtue, happiness, and solid reputation of the people.

And, lastly, that you will such further provision, for the due execution of the law before mentioned, as also to prevent jugglers, mountebanks, rope-dancers, and other immoral and irreligious entertainments, as, under the direction of best wisdom, you may see meet.

Signed on behalf of the said people called quakers, Philadelphia, 11th mo. 6th. 1788, by

Isaac Zane,	Joseph Bringhurst,
Owen Jones,	Nicholas Waln,
J. Pemberon,	Daniel Drinker,
Caleb Carmalt,	Owen Biddle,
John Head,	Benedict Dorsey,
Charles West,	William Clifton,
David Bacon,	Samuel Hopkins,
John Parish,	John Elliott, jun.
Joshua Howell,	Thomas Morris,
Samuel Lewis,	John James,
John Drinker,	Joh. Evans, jun.

[2]

To the honourable the general assembly of Pennsylvania, the subscribers, being a committee of the dramatic association, on behalf of themselves and the many citizens, who have prayed for a repeal of any law, or part of a law, that prohibits dramatic entertainments, beg leave, with the utmost respect, to submit the following representation:

THEY conceive that there are two points to be regarded in every controversy. The first is the weight of the arguments, the second the manner of enforcing them. With respect to the former, the understanding, and not the credulity, of the judge, must be addressed; with respect to the latter, where the adversaries have equal claims in point of reason, decency of manner is a fair foundation for a preference.

The drama is now a subject of earnest discussion; from a topic of private conversation, it has become the object of legislative decision, and contending parties are formed, on the one hand denying, and on the other asserting, the propriety of tolerating the stage.

Let us, therefore, for a moment suppose, that in wisdom, virtue, fortune, and patriotism, these parties are equal—are there any collateral circumstances which can then determine the weight of argument? Here truth dictates a reflexion, on which we appeal to the candour of this honourable house.

Those, who wish the establishment of the drama, desire a thing, which it is in the power of their opponents, deeming it an evil, to avoid, even after it is established; and which, at all events, intrudes upon no right, and interferes with no privilege. But those who wish the prohibition of the drama, seek to deprive their opponents of what they consider as a rational enjoyment, and, by their success, will abridge the natural right of every freeman, to dispose of his time and money, according to his own taste and disposition, when not obnoxious to the real interests of society.

This, we believe, is a statement by no means unfavourable to the enemies of the drama, as to the weight of argument. We will next enquire as to the decency of manner.

The petition in favour of the theatre offers to the legislature an opinion of upwards of two thousand citizens (who think the business of life requires some recreation) that the drama, divested of every other consideration, is a rational amusement: and, at the same time, it is respectfully and temperately intimated, that it is not just to call on the subscribers to sacrifice that opinion, merely in compliment to the prejudices of those of their fellow citizens, who think this, as they do every other amusement, contrary to the laws of conscience and virtue.

But the petition against the theatre, in a spirit less gentle and conciliatory, unequivocally declares that the toleration of a theatre would be impolitic, and injurious to the virtue, happiness, morals, and property of the citizens, and productive of many vices and mischiefs: thence necessarily leading to this inference, that every man of a contrary opinion, (expressed by signing the other petition) is a friend and promoter of the predicted inundation of wickedness and ruin.

This naturally introduces an enquiry into the characters of the persons branded with so gross an obloquy. A spectator, unacquainted with the real state of the business, would be tempted to suppose, that they are men whose understandings are clouded with ignorance, so that they cannot comprehend, and whose hearts are depraved with vice, so that they will not pursue, the plain and fair dictates of reason and morality. He would likewise be induced to suspect, that many among them, were men regardless of the welfare of their country, who had deserted her in the hour of adversity, and who were wilfully employed to undermine the fabric of her liberties, which had been reared by the labour of other hands. Or, perhaps, it might occur to him, that they were enthusiasts, of a melancholy mood, who sought to impose their manners, habits, and sentiments upon mankind, without, in their turn, yielding a single point in theory or practice. But he would err: for, in truth, the petitioners in favour of the drama, are men of science, friends to virtue, and approved guardians of their country. As parents, most of them are anxious for the happiness of posterity; and as men of property, they are generally interested in the order, energy, and stability of government. It is hardly credible, indeed, that an object vilified and depreciated in such positive terms, should, with the countenance of the judges, be promoted by almost every gentleman of the law (a profession perhaps the best qualified to decide upon the propriety of the repeal prayed for) that it should be patronized by almost every whig in the city, and, in short, that it should be approved by every virtuous and sensible man in the state, whose prejudices of education, or professional sanctity, do not exclude the indulgence of public amusements. Even the candour of many of these has led them to declare, that they consider an opposition derogatory to the rights of others, and, in some degree, inconsistent with the independence and purity of their own stations.

We will not undertake the invidious task of examining by what description of citizens, the adverse petition is supported. But, whatever pretensions were originally suggested, respecting the motives which induce them to endeavour to proscribe the sensitivity of their neighbours; it is now certain, by the manner of enforcing their petition, that every scruple of religious delicacy has been superseded by a spirit of party; and an appeal is made from reason and right, to influence and power. There are, among the many strange circumstances of this opposition, three matters of peculiar notoriety. The first is, that which we have already hinted at, an attempt to deprive a freeman of a natural right; the second is, the address by which the real enemies of the drama have, on this occasion, obtained the assistance of some characters with whom they have hitherto lived in a state of political warfare; and the third is, that men, who have suffered under the lash of persecution, should now wage a virulent war against freedom of thought and action—particularly, at the same moment, when they are soliciting the legislature to release them from one fetter, that they should endeavour to prevail on this honourable body, to rivet a fetter upon others.

Here, indeed, is a fair criterion to decide this controversy. An act of assembly has prescribed a certain test, or political obligation, to be taken by every citizen. This, it is said, is incompatible with the opinions of a respectable body. An application is, therefore, made for a repeal of the law, and, we believe, every ingenuous mind entertains a favourable wish upon the subject; for the members of the same community, certainly owe a mutual deference and respect to the sentiments, and even to the conscientious weakness, of each other. But let us suppose that a petition was presented, stating, that allegiance is a debt, which every man incurs, as a necessary consequence of the protection he receives from the government, and picturing a cloud of imaginary evils, which might result from allowing those persons to partake in the administration of public affairs, who were averse from giving a solemn and unequivocal mark of their attachment to the commonwealth—What would be said of a petition of this kind?—Precisely what may be said of the petition against the theatre;—with this difference only, that, in the one instance, the pretence would be for the sake of the political safety, as it is in the other, for the sake of the moral happiness of the people —neither of which would, in fact, be endangered by the repeal of the test law, or the establishment of the drama.

From these premises, we think, the following inferences are fairly deducible:—

1st. That whether the theatre is, or is not a proper institution, rests, on this occasion, merely upon the opinion of the respective subscribers.

2d. That it is thought to be advantageous by men, whose profession best enables them to judge upon the subject; by parents, on whom it is incumbent to suppress every real instrument of corruption; and by citizens, whose experienced patriotism, and extensive interest in the state, entitle them to the consideration of the legislature.

3d. That if a theatre is tolerated, no man sustains an injury, no man is deprived of a means of recreation from the toils and cares of life; nor is any one compelled to act contrary to his principles or his prejudices.

4th. That if a theatre is not tolerated, many respectable citizens will be disappointed in their reasonable hopes, a source of rational amusement will be destroyed, and every freeman must incur a forfeiture of a natural right, which he ought to possess—the right of acting as he pleases, in a matter perfectly indifferent to the well-being of the community.

We do not conceive it to be necessary, at this time, to suggest to your honourable house, the arguments which have been employed in favour of the drama, by the wisest and most virtuous characters, in the most enlightened nations. Nor shall we attempt to deny, that men of a similar description, have controverted the utility of the institution. It is enough for our purpose, that the difference of opinion is so evident, as to render the subject, in that respect, a matter of mere speculation; for in addressing the wisdom of the legislature, while, on the one hand, we cannot admit, that a theatre is the temple of vice, we presume not to insist that it is the school of virtue. As a rational amusement, it is the object of our wishes; and the whole force of our reasoning is directed only to shew, that those who regard it in a contrary light, are not entitled to controul our sentiments, or to compel the adoption of what they profess. If, indeed, a mere difference of opinion, shall be thought a sufficient foundation to curtail our rights, and diminish our enjoyments, the boasted liberality of the present age, will be eclipsed by a comparison with the furious bigotry of the middle centuries; and the same authority which proscribes our amusements, may, with equal justice, dictate the shape and texture of our dress, or the modes and ceremonies of our worship.

This, however, is an evil, which, we are confident, cannot receive the countenance of a legislature, elected to protect and insure the equal rights of the citizens of a free commonwealth. The claim of superior wisdom, virtue, and patriotism, arrogantly enforced—will there be disregarded; and we humbly trust, that the decision of your honourable house will, at last, prove that you think the petitioners in favour of the drama, as capable of judging for their own happiness, as anxious for the prosperity of the state, and as sincere in promoting the welfare of posterity, as those who have testified their opposition in the most positive, though not the most courteous or convincing terms. Signed,

Wal. Stewart,	John Barclay,
Robert Bass,	Jacob Barge,
Jos. Redman,	W. T. Franklin,
T. L. Moore,	James Crawford.
John West,	

19. Architecture

"Architecture," Thomas Jefferson once said, "is my delight, and putting up and pulling down one of my favorite amusements." Even as a young man in his twenties, Jefferson was absorbed in designing and building his home at Monticello. He went at architecture with a mathematical precision; no detail of building—from the chemistry of mortar to the proper technique of laying bricks—was too insignificant for his attention. He cursed the Georgian architecture of colonial Virginia as barbaric and aimed, through books, particularly those of the sixteenth-century Italian architect Palladio and his imitators, to re-create the simplicity and serenity of the architecture of classical antiquity.

With the Revolution and his public role in it, Jefferson was presented with an opportunity that carried him well beyond his early gentleman-amateur interest in architecture. The republic needed new public buildings, and Jefferson wanted a hand in their creation. After 1776 public architecture to Jefferson was no longer simply a matter of creating proportioned forms or practical details that were aesthetically pleasing; it was in truth a matter of the very character of the new republic. Jefferson envisioned the three great buildings he designed—the Capitol in Richmond, Monticello as redesigned during the years of his public life, and the University of Virginia—to be symbols of what the United States now represented in the world. Function, practical convenience, even beauty, had to give way to the overriding concern for public meaning, for the new way of life that the republic stood for.

The decision promoted by Jefferson to remove the seat of Virginia's government from Williamsburg to Richmond gave Jefferson his first chance to realize his vision of a new national aesthetic, a realization that even his departure as minister to France in 1784 could not keep him from. Despite problems of politics and economy in Virginia, the Capitol was completed much as Jefferson designed it, and it became the first monument of the classical renaissance in the United States, a renaissance that fundamentally shaped the character of public building in America.

The Capitol of Virginia

THOMAS JEFFERSON

1. BILL FOR THE REMOVAL OF THE SEAT OF GOVERNMENT OF VIRGINIA, 11 NOVEMBER 1776

WHEREAS great numbers of the Inhabitants of this Commonwealth must frequently, and of necessity resort to the seat of Government, where General assemblys are convened, Superior Courts are held and the Governor and Council usually transact the executive business of Government, and the equal rights of all the said Inhabitants require that such seat of Government should be as nearly central to all, as may be, having regard only to Navigation the benefits of which are necessary for encouraging the growth of a Town. *And Whereas* it has been found by the experience of some of our Sister States a very distressing circumstance, in times of war, that their seats of Government were so situated as to be exposed to the insults, and injuries of the publick enemy, which *(dangers may be avoided)* distresses may be prevented in this Commonwealth and equal Justice done to all *(the)* it's Citizens of this Commonwealth by removing *(the)* it's seat of Government to the town of   in the County of   which is more safe and central than any other Town situated on navigable water.

Be it therefore enacted, by the General Assembly of the Commonwealth of Virginia, that six whole squares of ground, surrounded each of them by four streets, and containing all the ground within such streets situate in the said Town of   and on an open and airy part thereof shall be appropriated to the use and purpose of public buildings.

And be it further enacted that on one of the said squares shall be erected one house for the use of the General assembly to be called the Capitol which said Capitol shall contain two rooms or apartments for the use of the Senate and their Clerk, and two others for the use of the House of Delegates and their Clerk, and others for the purposes of Conferences, Committees, and a Lobby, of such forms and dimensions as shall be adapted to their respective purposes. *And* on one other of the said squares shall be erected another

Julian P. Boyd, ed., *The Papers of Thomas Jefferson* (Princeton, 1950–), I, 598–599; VII, 48–49, 366–368, 534–535, 648; IX, 220–222, 332; X, 133; XI, 332–333; XVI, 26.

Andrew A. Lipscomb and Albert E. Bergh, eds., *The Writings of Thomas Jefferson* (Washington, 1903), XVII, 353–354.

building to be called the General Courthouse which shall contain two rooms
or apartments for the use of the Court of Appeals and its Clerk, two others
fot the use of the High Court of Chancery and its Clerk, two others for the
use of the General Court and its Clerk, two others for the use of the General
Court and its Clerk, two others for the use of the Court of Admiralty and its
Clerk, two others for the use of the Privy Council and its Clerk and others
for the uses of Grand and petty juries of such forms and dimensions as
shall be adapted to their respective purposes, which said houses shall be
built in a handsome manner with walls of Brick, and Porticos, where the
same may be convenient or Ornamental: on one other of the said Squares,
shall be built a house with three apartments for the Ordinary use of the
Clerks of the High Court of Chancery, General Court, and Court of Admiralty; each of them to have one of the said apartments: one other house
with three apartments, to be used as a land office: and one other for a
publick jail with few apartments for the present, but so planned as to admit
of addition in future: two other of the said Squares shall be appropriated to
the use of the Governor of the Commonwealth for the time being, to be built
on hereafter, and one other square shall be appropriated to the use of a
publick Market.

And be it further enacted that five persons shall be appointed by joint
Ballot of both houses of Assembly to be called the Directors of the publick
buildings who, or any three of them, shall be and are hereby empowered
to make choice of such squares of ground situate as before directed as shall
be most proper and convenient for the said publick purposes; to agree on
plans for the said buildings; to employ proper workmen to erect the same;
to procure necessary materials for them; and to draw on the Treasurer of
this Commonwealth from time to time as the same shall be wanting for any
sums of money not exceeding six thousand pounds in the whole; which
draughts he is hereby authorized to answer out of any public money which
shall be in his hands at the time: and in case of the death of any of the said
Directors, or the refusal to act, the Governor is hereby authorized to appoint
others in their stead who shall have the same powers as if they had been
(chosen) appointed by joint Ballot of both houses as before directed.

**2. JAMES BUCHANAN AND WILLIAM HAY, DIRECTORS OF THE PUBLIC BUILDINGS,
TO JEFFERSON, RICHMOND, 20 MARCH 1785**

SIR

The active part which you took before your departure from Virginia, as
a director of the public buildings, leads us to believe, that it will not be now
unacceptable to you, to cooperate with us as far as your engagements will
permit.

We foresee, that in the execution of our commission, the Commonwealth must sustain a heavy expence, and that we can provide no shield so effectual against the censures which await large disbursements of public money, as the propriety of making them. For this purpose we must intreat you to Consult an able Architect on a plan fit for a Capitol, and to assist him with the information of which you are possessed.

You will recollect, Sir, that the first act directed separate houses for the accomodation of the different departments of government. But fearing that the Assembly would not countenance us in giving sufficient magnificence to distinct buildings, we obtained leave to consolidate the whole under one roof, if it should seem adviseable. The inclosed draught will show that we wish to avail ourselves of this licence. But, altho it contains many particulars it is not intended to confine the architect except as to the number and area of the rooms.

We have not laid down the ground, it being fully in your power to describe it, when we inform You that the Hill on which Gunns yellow house stands and which you favoured as the best situation, continues to be preferd by us and that we have allocated 29 half acre lots, including Marsdon's tenement, and Minzies' lots in front of Gunns. The Legislature have [sic] not limited us to any sum; nor can we, as yet at least, resolve to limit ourselves to a precise amount. But we wish to unite oeconomy with elegance and dignity. At present the only funds submitted to our order are nearly about £ 10,000 Virga. Currency.

We have already contract'd with Edward Voss of Culpepper for the laying of 1500 thousand Bricks. He is a workman of the first reputation here, but skilful in plain and rubbed work alone. We suppose he may commence his undertaking by the beginning of August, and have therefore stipulated with him to be in readiness by that time. This circumstance renders us anxious for expedition in fixing the plans, especially to as the foundation of the Capitol will silence the enimies of Richmond in the next October Session.

Should an assistant be thought necessary whose employment will be either independent of Voss or subordinate to him, we will pay him.

We shall send to Europe for any Stone which may be wanted.

The roof will be covered with lead, as we conceive that to be better than Copper or tiles.

In the remarks, which accompany the plan, we have requested a draught for the Governor's house and prison. But we hope that the Capitol will be first drawn and forwarded to us, as there is no hurry for the other buildings.

We trust, Sir, you will excuse the trouble which we now impose on you, and will ascribe it to our belief of your alacrity to serve your Country on this occasion.

3. JEFFERSON TO BUCHANAN AND HAY, PARIS, 13 AUGUST 1785

GENTLEMEN

Your favor of March 20. came to hand the 14th. of June, and the next day I wrote to you acknowleging the receipt, and apprising you that between that date and the 1st. of August it would be impossible to procure and get into your hands the draughts you desired. I did hope indeed to have had them prepared before this, but it will yet be some time before they will be in readiness. I flatter myself however they will give satisfaction when you receive them and that you will think the object will not have lost by the delay. I was a considerable time before I could find an architect whose taste had been formed on a study of the antient models of this art: the style of architecture in this capital being far from chaste. I at length heard of one, to whom I immediately addressed myself, and who perfectly fulfills my wishes. He has studied 20 years in Rome, and has given proofs of his skill and taste by a publication of some antiquities of this country. You intimate that you should be willing to have a workman sent to you to superintend the execution of this work. Were I to send one on this errand from hence, he would consider himself as the Superintendant of the Directors themselves and probably of the Government of the state also. I will give you my ideas on this subject. The columns of the building and the external architraves of the doors and windows should be of stone. Whether these are made here, or there, you will need one good stone-cutter, and one will be enough, because, under his direction, Negroes who never saw a tool, will be able to prepare the work for him to finish. I will therefore send you such a one, in time to begin work in the spring. All the internal cornices and other ornaments not exposed to the weather will be much handsomer, cheaper and more durable in plaister than in wood. I will therefore employ a good workman in this way and have him sent to you. But he will have no employment till the house is covered, of course he need not be sent till next summer. I will take him on wages so long beforehand as that he may draw all the ornaments in detail, under the eye of the architect, which he will have to execute when he comes to you. It will be the cheapest way of getting them drawn and the most certain of putting him in possession of his precise duty. Plaister will not answer for your external cornice, and stone will be too dear. You will probably find yourselves obliged to be contented with wood. For this therefore, and for your windowsashes, doors, forms, wainscoating &c. you will need a capital house-joiner, and a capital one he ought to be, capable of directing all the circumstances in the construction of the walls which the execution of the plans will require. Such a workman cannot be got here. Nothing can be worse done than the house-joinery of Paris. Besides that his speaking the language perfectly would be essential. I think this character must be got from England. There are no workmen in wood in Europe comparable to those of England. I submit to you therefore the following proposition: to wit, I will get a correspondent in England to engage a workman of this kind. I will direct him to come here, which will cost five guineas. We will make proof of his execution. He shall also make himself, under the eye of the architect, all the drawings for the building which he is to execute himself: and if we find him sober and capable, he shall be forwarded to you. I expect that in the article of the drawings and the cheapness of passage from France you will save the expence of his coming here. But as to this workman I shall do nothing unless I receive your commands. With respect to your stone work, it may be got much cheaper here than in England. The stone of Paris is very white and beautiful, but it always remains soft, and suffers from the weather. The cliffs of the Seine from hence to Havre are all of stone. I am not yet informed whether it is all liable to the same objections. At Lyons and all along the Rhone is a stone as beautiful as that of Paris, soft when it comes out of the quarry, but very soon becoming hard in the open air, and very durable. I doubt however whether the commerce between Virginia and Marseilles would afford opportunities of conveiance sufficient. It remains to be enquired what addition to the original cost would be made by the short land carriage from Lyons to the Loire and the water transportation down that to Bordeaux, and also whether a stone of the same quality may not be found on the Loire. In this and all other matters relative to your charge you may command my services freely. . . .

4. JEFFERSON TO JAMES MADISON, PARIS, 20 SEPTEMBER 1785

DEAR SIR

. . . I received this summer a letter from Messrs. Buchanan and Hay as directors of the public buildings desiring I would have drawn for them plans of sundry buildings, and in the first place of a Capitol. They fixed for their receiving this plan a day which was within one month of that on which their letter came to my hand. I engaged an Architect of capital abilities in this business. Much time was requisite, after the external form was agreed on, to make the internal distribution convenient for the three branches of government. This time was much lengthened by my avocations to other objects which I had no right to neglect. The plan however was settled. The gentlemen had sent me one which they had thought of. The one agreed on here is more convenient, more beautiful, gives more room and will not cost more than two thirds of what that would. We took for our model what is called the Maison quarrée of Nismes, one of the most beautiful, if not the most beautiful and precious morsel of architecture left us by antiquity. It was built by Caius and Lucius Caesar and repaired by Louis XIV, and has the suffrage of all the judges of architecture who have seen it, as yielding to no one of the beautiful monuments of Greece, Rome, Palmyra and Balbec which late travellers have communicated to us. It is very simple, but it is noble beyond expression, and would have done honour to our country as presenting to travellers a morsel of taste in our infancy promising much for our maturer age. I have been much mortified with information which I received two days ago from Virginia that the first brick of the Capitol would be laid within a few days. But surely the delay of this piece of a summer would have been repaid by the savings in the plan preparing here, were we to value it's other superiorities as nothing. But how is a taste in this beautiful art to be formed in our countrymen, unless we avail ourselves of every occasion when public buildings are to be erected, of presenting to them models for their study and imitation? Pray try if you can effect the stopping of this work. I have written also to E. R. on the subject. The loss will be only of the laying the bricks already laid, or a part of them. The bricks themselves will do again for the interior walls, and one side wall and one end wall may remain as they will answer equally well for our plan. This loss is not to be weighed against the saving of money which will arise, against the comfort of laying out the public money for something honourable, the satisfaction of seeing an object and proof of national good taste, and the regret and mortification of erecting a monument of our barbarism which will be loaded with execrations as long as it shall endure. The plans are in good forwardness and I hope will be ready within three or four weeks. They could not be stopped now but on paying their whole price which will be considerable. If the Undertakers are afraid to undo what they have done, encourage them to it by a recommendation from the assembly. You see I am an enthusiast on the subject of the arts. But it is an enthusiasm of which I am not ashamed, as it's object is to improve the taste of my countrymen, to increase their reputation, to reconcile to them the respect of the world and procure them it's praise. . . .

5. BUCHANAN AND HAY TO JEFFERSON, RICHMOND, 18 OCTOBER 1785

Sir

Your favour of the 15th. June came duely to hand, and we return you our warmest acknowledgements for undertaking in so obliging a manner to aid the Directors of the public buildings in procuring plans and estimates.

Your ideas upon the subject are perfectly corresponding to those of the Directors, respecting the stile and Ornaments proper for such a work, and we trust the plans will be designed in conformity thereto. We are sorry we did not sollicit your aid in the business at an earlier day, for, from the anxiety of the Public to have the work begun, we have been obliged to carry it on so far, that we may be embarrassed when we are favoured with a more perfect plan for you. As we expect to hear from you, and perhaps receive the plans before this can reach you, we deem it proper to inform you what has been done, that you may judge how far we shall be able to adopt the plan you transmit us. The foundation of the Capitol is laid, of the following demensions, 148 by 118 feet, in which are about 400M bricks; the Center of the building of 75 by 35 to be lighted from above, is designed for the Delegates; the rest is divided in such a manner as to answer every purpose directed by the Assembly; the foundation of the four porticos are not laid, tho' the end and side walls are contrived to receive them. The present plan differs from the One transmitted you, only in the arrangement, and we hope we shall be able to avail ourselves of your assistance without incurring much expence. As we are fully satisfied no expence unnecessarily will be imposed through you, we will chearfully answer your draught for the amount. We have the Honour to be with great respect Sir Your most Obedt. Servants.

6. JEFFERSON TO BUCHANAN AND HAY, PARIS, 26 JANUARY 1786

GENTLEMEN

I had the honour of writing to you on the receipt of your orders to procure draughts for the public buildings, and again on the 13th. of August. In the execution of those orders two methods of proceeding presented themselves to my mind. The one was to leave to some architect to draw an external according to his fancy, in which way experience shews that about once in a thousand times a pleasing form is hit upon; the other was to take some model already devised and approved by the general suffrage of the world. I had no hesitation in deciding that the latter was best, nor after the decision was there any doubt what model to take. There is at Nismes in the South of France a building, called the Maison quarrée, erected in the time of the Caesars, and which is allowed without contradiction to be the most perfect and precious remain of antiquity in existence. It's superiority over any thing at Rome, in Greece, at Balbec or Palmyra is allowed on all hands; and this single object has placed Nismes in the general tour of travellers. Having not yet had leisure to visit it, I could only judge of it from drawings, and from the relation of numbers who had been to see it. I determined therefore to adopt this model, and to have all it's proportions justly observed. As it was impossible for a foreign artist to know what number and sizes of apartments would suit the different corps of our government, nor how they should be connected with one another, I undertook to form that arrangment, and this being done, I committed them to an Architect (Monsieur Clerisseau) who had studied this art 20. years in Rome, who had particularly studied and measured the Maison quarrée of Nismes, and had published a book containing 4 most excellent plans, descriptions, and observations on it. He was too well acquainted with the merit of that building to find himself restrained by my injunctions not to depart from his model. In one instance only he persuaded me to admit of this. That was to make the Portico two columns deep only, instead of three as the original is. His reason was that this latter depth would too much darken the apartments. Economy might be added as a second reason. I consented to it to satisfy him, and the plans are so drawn. I knew that it would still be easy to execute the building with a depth of three columns, and it is what I would certainly recommend. We know that the Maison quarrée has pleased universally for near 2000 years. By leaving out a column, the proportions will be changed and perhaps the effect may be injured more than is expected. What is good is often spoiled by trying to make it better.

The present is the first opportunity which has occurred of sending the plans. You will accordingly receive herewith the ground plan, the elevation of the front, and the elevation of the side. The architect having been much busied, and knowing that this was all which would be necessary in the beginning, has not yet finished the Sections of the building. They must go by some future occas[ion] as well as the models of the front and side which are making in plaister of Paris. These were absolutely necessary for the guide of workmen not very expert in their art. It will add considerably to the expence, and I would not have incurred it but that I was sensible of it's necessity. The price of the model will be 15 guineas. I shall know in a few days the cost of the drawings which probably will be the triple of the model; however this is but my conjecture. I will make it as small as possible, pay it, and render you an account in my next letter. You will find on examination that the body of this building covers an area but two fifths of that which is proposed and begun; of course it will take but about one half the bricks; and of course this circumstance will enlist all the workmen, and people of the art against the plan. Again the building begun is to have 4 porticos; this but one. It is true that this will be deeper than those were probably proposed, but even if it be made three columns deep, it will not take half the number of columns. The beauty of this is ensured by experience and by suffrage of the whole world; the beauty of that is problematical, as is every drawing, however well it looks on paper, till it be actually executed; and tho I suppose there is more room in the plan begun, than in that now sent, yet there is enough in this for all the three branches of government and more than enough is not wanted. This contains 16. rooms, to wit, 4. on the first floor, for the General court, Delegates, Lobby, and Conference; eight on the 2d. floor for the Executive, the Senate, and 6 rooms for committees and [juri]es, and over 4. of these smaller rooms of the 2d floor are 4. Mezzanines or Entresoles, serving as offices for the clerks of the Executive, the Senate, the Delegates and the court in actual session. It will be an objection that the work is begun on the other plan. But the whole of this need not be taken to peices, and of what shall be taken to peices the bricks will do for inner work. Mortar never becomes so hard and adhesive to the bricks in a few months but that it may easily be chipped off. And upon the whole the plan now sent will save a great proportion of the expence. . . .

7. MADISON TO JEFFERSON, ORANGE, VIRGINIA, 18 MARCH 1786

Dear Sir

Your two favours of the 1 and 20 Sepr. under the same cover by Mr. Fitzhugh did not come to hand till the 24th. ult: and of course till it was too late for any Legislative interposition with regard to the Capitol. I have written to the Attorney on the subject. A letter which I have from him dated prior to his receipt of mine takes notice of the plan you had promised and makes no doubt that it will arrive in time for the purpose of the Commissioners. I do not gather from his expressions however that he was aware of the change, which will become necessary in the foundation already laid; a change which will not be submitted to without reluctance for two reasons. 1. The appearance of caprice to which it may expose the Commissioners. 2. Which is the material one, the danger of retarding the work till the next Session of Assembly can impose a vote for its suspension, and possibly for a removal to Williamsburg. This danger is not altogether imaginary. Not a Session has passed since I became a member without one or other or both of these attempts. At the late Session, a suspension was moved by the Williamsburg Interest, which was within a few votes of being agreed to. It is a great object therefore with the Richmond Interest to get the building so far advanced before the fall as to put an end to such experiments. The circumstances which will weigh in the other scale, and which it is to be hoped will preponderate, are the fear of being reproached with sacrificing public considerations to a local policy, and a hope that the substitution of a more oeconomical plan, may better reconcile the Assembly to a prosecution of the undertaking.

8. EDMUND RANDOLPH TO JEFFERSON, RICHMOND, 12 JULY 1786

DEAR SIR

. . . Your favor concerning the capitol came to hand; after the most painful anxiety at the tardy movement of the plan to Virginia. We are at length relieved by its arrival. A council of directors was immediately called, and with some difficulty the plan was carried thro'! But I am exceedingly afraid that we have committed some blunder even now. I directed Mr. Dobie, our superintendant, and an adept in draughtmanship, to furnish me with a narrative of our proceedings in technical language. When completed, it shall be forwarded. At present, however, I will give you some imperfect idea of it.—The plan sent to you was a mere assay; that adopted by us was very different. When your plan was examined, it was conceived, that without adhering to precisely the same front, it would be enough to follow the same proportions. By this doctrine we were rescued from a great embarrassment, for the lowland interest and a strong party of the upland, in the assembly, are labouring to stop the progress of the building. To pull up all that had been done, would have been to strengthen the opposition. We have therefore resolved to pursue your plan in every respect, except the extension of front. By this means we have been obliged to remove only one side wall and a few partition walls. . . .

9. HAY TO JEFFERSON, RICHMOND, 3 MAY 1787

SIR

Your favour of the 26th. December inclosing Bill of Lading for the Model of the Capitol came safe to hand, adressed to Mr. Buchanan and myself, and have to appologize for answering it in my private Capacity. There has not been a Meeting of the Directors of the Public Buildings for some considerable Time past and Mr. Buchanan is now confined by a severe spell of Sickness, so that I could neither have the Advice of the Directors nor the Assistance of Mr. Buchanan in the Business. No Delay in the work has been occasioned by the Models not coming to hand, last Summer, and I fear it will stop where it now is for some Time. The pedestal Basement and the principal story were finished by last October, and nothing has been done since. The fund of the 2 p.ct. Additional Duties upon which was charged £5000 to be applied towards completing the public Buildings, has proved unproductive, for the Treasurer assures me, it will not produce the sum which was charged on it in the first Instance for the support of the Members of Congress. The Directors therefore can make no Contract upon this Fund without sacrificing too much to the extravagance of the Times, and when the Assembly meets again I fear no further Assistance will be given on account of the Distress which is universally complained of thro' the State. The Capitol may then remain in its present state for many Years. The Directors themselves have been neglectful, in many things and in none more, than in the want of Acknowledgements to you, for the great Assistance you have given them in this Business. Permit me therefore, to return my sincere thanks, and I am sure they will be those of the Directors in general, for the Interest you have taken in procuring proper Plans and a model for Ornamenting the Capital of your native country. . . .

10. JEFFERSON TO WILLIAM SHORT, EPPINGTON, 14 DECEMBER 1789

DEAR SIR

. . . Our new Capitol when the corrections are made of which it is susceptible will be an edifice of first rate dignity. Whenever it shall be finished with the proper ornaments belonging to it (which will not be in this age) it will be worthy of being exhibited along side the most celebrated remains of antiquity. It's extreme convenience has acquired it universal approbation. There is one street in Richmond (from the bridge strait on towards Currie's) which would be considered as handsomely built in any city of Europe. The town below Shockoe creek is so deserted, that you cannot get a person to live in a house there rentfree. . . .

11. JEFFERSON, AN ACCOUNT OF THE ORIGINAL PLAN OF THE CAPITOL, 1800

The capitol in the city of Richmond, in Virginia, is the model of the Temples of Erectheus at Athens, of Balbec, and of the Maison quarrée of Nismes. All of which are nearly of the same form and proportions, and are considered as the most perfect examples of cubic architecture, as the Pantheon of Rome is of the spherical. Their dimensions not being sufficient for the purposes of the capitol, they were enlarged, but their proportions rigorously observed. The capitol is of brick, one hundred thirty-four feet long, seventy feet wide, and forty-five feet high, exclusive of the basement. Twenty-eight feet of its length is occupied by a portico of the whole breadth of the house, showing six columns in front, and two intercolonnations in flank. It is of a single order, which is Ionic; its columns four feet two inches diameter, and their entablature running round the whole building. The portico is crowned by a pediment, the height of which is two ninths of its span.

Within the body of the building, which is one hundred and six feet long, are two tiers of rooms twenty-one feet high each. In the lower, at one end, is the room in which the Supreme Court sits, thirty feet by sixty-four feet with a vestibule fourteen feet by twenty-two feet, and an office for their clerk, fourteen feet by thirteen feet. In the other end is the room for the House of Delegates, thirty feet by sixty-four feet, with a lobby fourteen feet by thirty-six feet. In the middle is a room thirty-six feet square, of the whole height of the building, and receiving its light from above. In the centre of this room is a marble statue of General Washington, made at Paris, by Houdon, who came over to Virginia for the express purpose of taking his form. The statue is made accurately of the size of life. A peristile of columns in the same room, six feet from the wall, and twenty-two and a half feet high with their entablature, support a corridor above, serving as a communication for all the upper apartments, the stairs landing in it. In the upper tier is a Senate chamber, thirty feet square, an office for their clerk, five rooms for committees and juries, an office for the clerk of the House of Delegates, a chamber for the Governor and Council, and a room for their clerk. In the basement of the building are the Land Office, Auditor's office, and Treasury.

The drawings of the façade and other elevations, were done by Clarissault, one of the most correct architects of France, and author of the Antiquities of Nismes, among which was the Maison quarrée. The model in stucco was made under his direction, by an artist who had been employed many years in Greece, by the Count de Choiseul, ambassador of France at Constantinople, in making models of the most celebrated remains of ancient architecture in that country.

Travellers' Comments, 1791
DUKE DE LA ROCHEFOUCAULD-LIANCOURT

The Capitol is erected on a point of this hill which commands the town. This edifice, which is extremely vast, is constructed on the plan of the "Maison Quarrée" at Nismes, but on a much more extensive scale. The attics of the Maison Quarrée have undergone an alteration in the Capitol, to suit them for the convenience of the public offices of every denomination, which, thus, perfectly secure against all accidents from fire, lie within reach of the tribunals, the executive council, the governor, the general assembly, who all sit in the Capitol, and draw to it a great afflux of people. This building, which is entirely of brick, is not yet coated with plaster: the columns, the pilasters, are destitute of bases and capitals: but the interior and exterior cornices are finished, and are well executed. The rest will be completed with more or less speed: but, even in its present unfinished state, this building is, beyond comparison, the finest, the most noble, and the greatest, in all America. The internal distribution of its parts is extremely well adapted to the purposes for which it is destined. It was Mr. Jefferson who, during his embassy in France, sent the model of it. Already it is said to have cost a hundred and seventy thousand dollars; and fifteen thousand more are the estimated sum requisite for completing it and remedying some defects which have been observed in the construction.

* * * *

ISAAC WELD

The situation of the upper town is very pleasing; it stands on an elevated spot, and commands a fine prospect of the falls of the river, and of the adjacent country on the opposite side. The best houses stand here, and also the capitol or statehouse. From the opposite side of the river this building appears extremely well, as its defects cannot be observed at that distance, but on a closer inspection it proves to be a clumsy ill shapen pile. The

Duke de la Rochefoucauld-Liancourt, *Travels Through the United States the Years* 1795, 1796, *and* 1797 (London, 1799), pp. 108–109.

Isaac Weld, Jr., *Travels Through the States of North America . . . During the Years* 1795, 1796, *and* 1797 (London, 1799), pp. 108–109.

original plan was sent over from France by Mr. Jefferson, and had great merit; but his ingenious countrymen thought they could improve it, and to do so placed what was intended for the attic story, in the plan, at the bottom, and put the columns on the top of it. In many other respects, likewise, the plan was inverted. This building is finished entirely with red brick; even the columns themselves are formed of brick; but to make them appear like stone, they have been partially whitened with common whitewash. The inside of the building is but very little better than its exterior part. The principal room is for the house of representatives; this is used also for divine service, as there is no such thing as a church in the town. The vestibule is circular, and very dark; it is to be ornamented with a statue of George Washington, executed by an eminent artist in France, which arrived while I was in the town. Ugly and ill contrived as this building is, a stranger must not attempt to find fault with any part of it, for it is looked upon by the inhabitants as a most elegant fabric.

1. Model of the Virginia State Capitol (1785-1790) by Thomas Jefferson and Charles Louis Clerisseau.

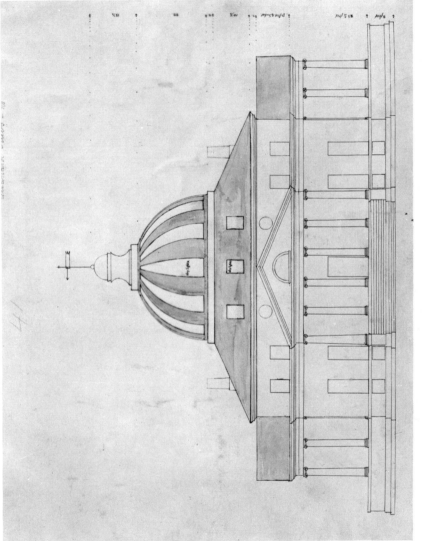

2. Design for President's House (1792) by " A.Z." [Thomas Jefferson].

3. Monticello (orginally built in 1770's.remodeled in 1796-1809) by Thomas Jefferson.

4. The University of Virginia (1819-1826) by Thomas Jefferson.

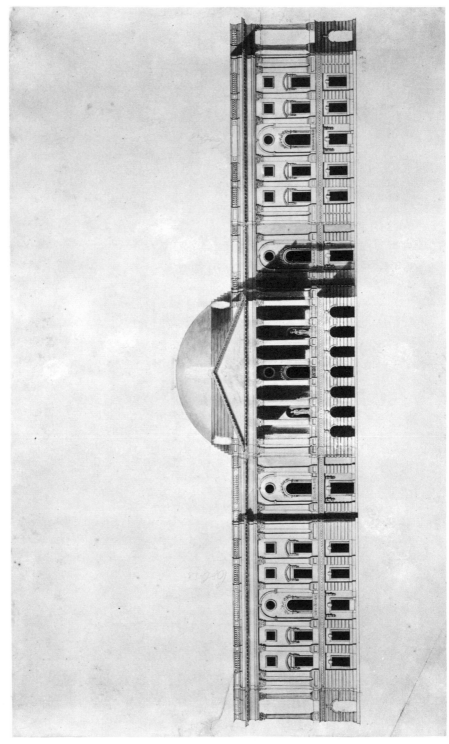

5. Design of the East Elevation of the U.S. Capitol (1794) by William Thornton.

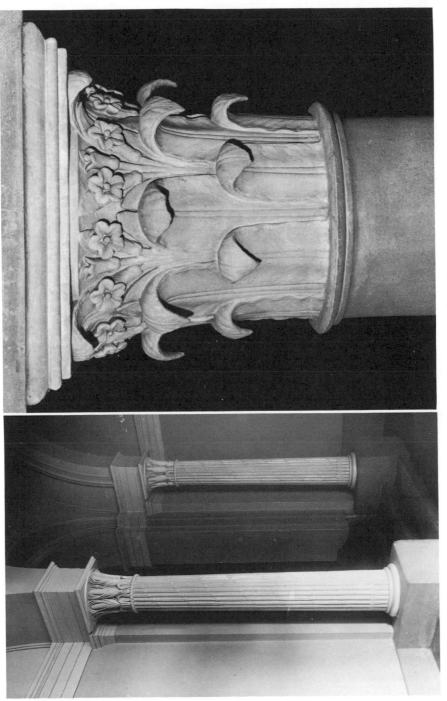

6. "Cornstalk" and "Tobacco Leaf" Capitals (1809 and 1816) by Benjamin Latrobe.

7. Government House, New York (1790) by John McComb. Watercolor by Cotton Milbourne.

Peter Lacour delin.   *A. Doolittle Sculp.*

FEDERAL HALL

The Seat of **CONGRESS**

Printed & Sold by A. Doolittle New Haven 1790

8. Federal Hall (1790) by Pierre Charles L'Enfant. Engraving by Amos Doolittle.

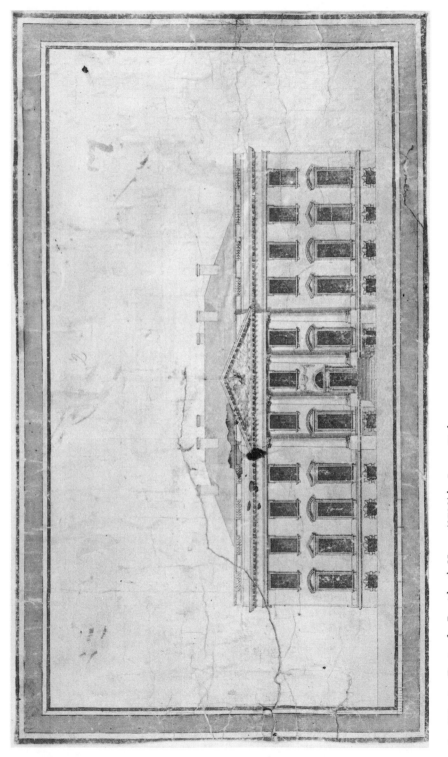

9. Winning Design for President's House (1792) by James Hoban.

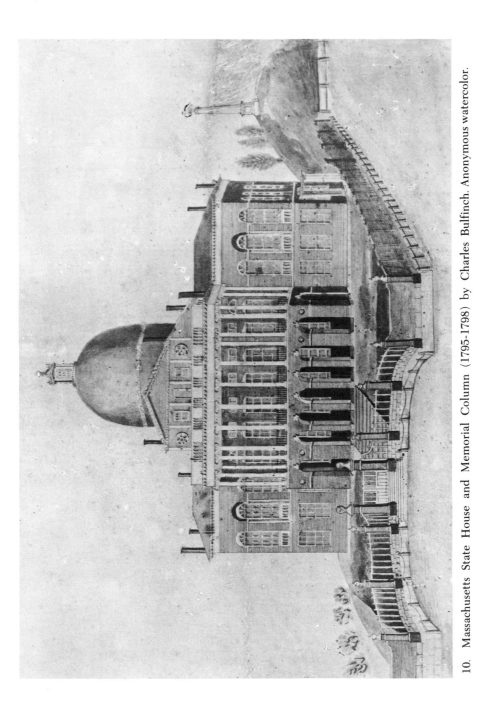

10. Massachusetts State House and Memorial Column (1795-1798) by Charles Bulfinch. Anonymous watercolor.

11. The Bank of Pennsylvania (1799-1801) by Benjamin Latrobe.

20. Republican Art

With the Revolution, Americans were determined to create a truly republican art, an art that necessarily had to be different from that of Europe. No longer could art be simply a plaything of the people of leisure, a dependent creature of an aristocratic few. It now had to belong to the whole people and be nourished by their civic spirit and taste. Yet the disappointments and problems in realizing these aims soon involved artists in institutional arrangements dependent on narrow private patronage that contradicted their goals. Republican genius was peculiarly dependent on the public, but the public had to be educated to appreciate that genius.

It was this pedagogical intent that led to the founding of the first art academies in America, of which the Pennsylvania Academy of the Fine Arts, created in 1805 by well-to-do Philadelphians, was the most successful. In 1810, a large group of Philadelphia painters, sculptors, and engravers—numbering a hundred within six months—organized themselves as the Society of Artists of the United States and sought a union with the lay-dominated Academy. The disparity of interests between the two groups was too great, and they settled for a working relationship, including an annual exhibition of the artists' works in the Academy's newly constructed building. The first exhibition, in 1810, was the occasion of Joseph Hopkinson's oration.

Hopkinson (1770-1842), a successful Philadelphia lawyer and a founder and later president of the Academy, was representative of the many well-to-do Americans in the early nineteenth century who, with mingled hopes and apprehensions, sought through and for art to save the republic. Hopkinson, the son of the Revolutionary poet and satirist, Francis Hopkinson, is perhaps best remembered in American history as the author of "Hail Columbia," written in 1798.

The Pennsylvania Academy of the Fine Arts

JOSEPH HOPKINSON

ONE of the articles of our association, pursuing the plan of other similar societies, directs that a discourse shall be annually delivered, on some subject connected with the views of the institution.

Owing to the difficulties and embarrassments which always oppose the establishment of an institution, especially when it is so entirely new, the Directors have heretofore been obliged to give all their attention to fixing the foundations of the Academy, and arranging those parts which are essentially necessary to its existence. Those ornaments which are to decorate the superstructure and invite the observation of the public, as well as many of the uses finally to proceed from it, were necessarily postponed.

After five years of experiment, not, indeed, without much laborious effort and occasional despondency, the dirctors have infinite satisfaction, mingled with some pride, in being able to say to those gentlemen by whose liberality this house of the arts; this school of our native genius, has been erected and sustained, that the "PENNSYLVANIA ACADEMY OF THE FINE ARTS" may now be considered as completely formed and established; about to unfold the important uses for which it was designed, and beginning already to add some bright beams of lustre to the reputation our city has always enjoyed in the support of liberal and public institutions.

We now begin to find ourselves sufficiently at leisure to look to those parts of the scheme which are calculated to give character to the undertaking and extend its utility. Among the most important of these is the establishment of schools for the improvement of young artists; the devising of inducements to excite a laudable emulation amongst them, by encouraging and stimulating superior merit with honours and rewards. All this, at least in a degree, will speedily be done. Large and commodious additions have been made to our building, which now furnishes ample room for the exhibition of works of art, and convenient apartments for the necessary schools.

The delivery of an annual discourse to the members of the academy is another part of the original plan. The directors have honoured me with

Joseph Hopkinson, *Annual Discourse, Delivered Before the Pennsylvania Academy of the Fine Arts* . . . (Philadelphia, 1819), pp. 5–15, 17–18, 20–36.

the appointment at this time. I am not unconscious that an attempt of this sort is wholly beside my usual pursuits, and that to be qualified to accomplish it properly, requires information which I do not possess, and which my daily and indispensable occupations put it out of my power to acquire. I have, however, been so long in the habit of declining no endeavour to serve this institution, that I accepted, without hesitation or reflection, the task proposed.

It must not be expected that this discourse will resemble those which are delivered to similar institutions in Europe. They are, generally, strictly technical and scientific, being read by a professed artist to artists. Of course, they are lectures of instruction, lessons of art, critical examinations of works of art, and scholastic disquisitions, which none but a professor of the arts can make or entirely comprehend when made. A society has, however, lately arisen here, from which such instructive lessons may be expected, and which I trust will not disappoint the expectation.

It is my humbler design to point out the uses to be derived from this institution; its claims to public patronage; the peculiar propriety of encouraging the arts in our country at this time, and to remove the objections and prejudices which may impede their progress.

Whether it has been the result of accident or may be attributed to the peculiar genius of our people, the fact is certain that the United States, in proportion to their age and population, have produced a very remarkable number of distinguished painters. An American is now, and long has been, at the head of the historical school in England, and president of the royal academy. An American is perhaps unrivalled, certainly not surpassed, in pourtraying the human face beaming with the soul that animates it; and a very respectable catalogue might be added of American painters distinguished in the various departments of the art: but they have been obliged to seek abroad for those means of improvement, which it is the object of this academy to furnish them at home.

That particular climates or portions of the earth have a peculiar fitness for the production of genius has been very strenuously contended for by men eminent in taste and literature. If indeed it be true, as some of these authors assert, that the arts and sciences have not flourished beyond the fifty second degree of northern latitude, nor nearer than twenty five degrees to the line, we are placed in a happy medium between these extremes. Or if climate has an influence in any manner upon the production or growth of genius, the extent and variety to be found in the United States cannot fail to furnish that which is most propitious. The vanity of the European has indeed taught him to believe, and his folly has led him to publish the absurdity, that the liberal arts cannot thrive out of Europe. It is for us to refute, by the unanswerable testimony of experience, the flimsy arguments by which this extravagent hypothesis is maintained.

The sagacity, ardour, and inventive ingenuity of the American character are all calculated to carry us to a high state of perfection in the arts. The enterprise of our merchants, though opposed by the most discouraging difficulties, has extended our commerce to every habitable clime, and spread our flag over every water on which a vessel can float. In implements of agriculture, in the machinery of various mechanic arts, many ingenious and useful inventions and improvements have been made. In agriculture, too, such important knowledge has been acquired, that the face of the country is changed, and plentiful crops cover a soil not long since thought unworthy of culture. Shall we stop here? Shall we not go on to the more elegant and sublime employments of the human faculties, to those arts which polish the manners and refine the morals of a people; which give them character and consequence abroad, while they provide for them at home the most innocent and elevated enjoyments?

When we reflect upon the discovery of this new world; its rapid and prosperous settlement, the independence of that part of it we possess, and the manner and time of its accomplishment, and connect these extraordinary events with the more extraordinary and disastrous fate of a great portion of the old world, we cannot, I think, but discern in them something more than the ordinary course of human affairs; something that indicates a great design of Providence.

Is it but a fanciful theory to say that the discovery and settlement of the western world, was preparatory of those convulsions which are tumbling down the political institutions of Europe, and devastating its fairest countries. The arts fly from the din of arms, and science shrinks from the sight of blood— Industry pines and starves; wealth is plundered to beggary, and poverty trampled under foot. Pride cannot sustain, nor humility avoid the shock. Here the ruined victims find a safe asylum, and honest labour is protected in her gains. Shall we not invite, shall we not joyfully welcome *such* a migration? And can we do so but by establishing institutions for the encouragement of the arts; by cultivating a taste among our citizens for works of genius, and affording to those who excel in them, that liberal patronage, that friendly regard they so truly deserve. Let us for a moment reflect that a vast mass of intellect is acquired in the thousands and tens of thousands who seek refuge in our land; and when we further reflect that these people migrate from countries in which the arts and sciences have long flourished, the value of *such of them* as have been there engaged, in such useful and honourable pursuits, and come here to continue in them, is incalculable. In the present state of our country, every skilful, industrious mechanic; every man of genius and science, is indeed a treasure, a growing treasure which will communicate its virtue, and spread its utility to a boundless extent.

The changes and revolutions of empires, their rise and progress to wealth and power, and their subsequent decline and annihilation are subjects of curious and profound speculation. Whether their destruction should be attributed solely to those causes which immediately produce it, or they have their appointed periods, and it is written by the great Creator of the universe, that all things human shall be transitory; and the works of man, like man himself, have their youth, their maturity, their decay, and their death, cannot be easily decided. Certain it is, that nations more powerful than any that now inhabit our globe; that institutions more vast and splendid than any that now dazzle the imagination, have passed away, leaving not a stone to mark the place of their existence. "Where" cries the pathetic Sterne, "is Troy and Mycene, and Persepolis and Agrigentum? What is become of Nineveh and Babylon, of Cyzicum and Mitylene? The fairest towns that ever the sun rose upon are now no more; the names only are left."

But the destruction of an empire does not imply the annihilation of its people, or of the arts they excelled in. Sometimes they have formed new settlements distant from the scene of their calamities; and sometimes they have incorporated themselves with other nations happily placed beyond the vortex of their ruin. While then we lament the awful afflictions with which Europe is scourged, humanity unites with sound policy in requiring us to receive with liberal favour, the honest industry, the cultivated intellect, the refined taste and improved genius which comes to enrich, and not to disturb us; to find peace and not to destroy it. Such kindness

> "is twice blest,
> It blesses him that gives and him that takes."

If on the arrival of men thus qualified in our country, they find no institutions to foster and exercise their talents; they find the public taste rude, uncultivated, and degraded, the arts unknown or despised, and the accumulation of wealth absorbing every faculty and desire, except the ostentation and folly with which it is afterwards dissipated, how deep will be their disappointment, how deplorable their fate! They have fled from tumult and oppression, to drought and sterility; they have avoided a sudden extermination, to fall into a languishing decay.

This is our peculiar time for transplanting to our western soil, those arts and sciences which have been ripening for ages in Europe. The fruit is offered without the labour of producing it. Let us not reject the precious gift. The observation of a learned French critic, is undoubtedly correct, that the arts flourish when the country in which artists live is in a peaceful and flourishing condition; when the public are not only disposed to encourage them, but enabled to do so, by having no wants but only their pleasures to supply. This is happily our condition. The general prosperity has pervaded almost every mansion; and our citizens are daily seeking new and expensive gratifications. The cook or upholsterer, who brings some new luxury to the opulent votaries of fashion, finds full employment and extravagant reward. Palaces are built from ice creams and sugar plums, and country seats purchased with soups and gravies. The new cut of a curtain ensures a fortune; and the man may keep a carriage who can make one on a new and fantastical model. Let us hasten to elevate our enjoyments; to refine the public taste, and look for pleasure in more noble and dignified objects. Let even the man who consults only his pride in the appropriations of his liberality, reflect upon the satisfaction he may derive from patronizing an academy of arts; a school of American genius, where he will daily see the fruits of his bounty growing and ripening, and diffusing its sweet odour around. Let him compare, fairly and rationally, such pleasures with the mean, the miserable ostentation of a splendid feast, a tumultuous rout; where a few days of anxious, laborious, bustling, uncomfortable preparation, is followed, in its best success, with a shortlived, contemptible triumph, mixed with some mortifying sarcasm, some unexpected discontent. He pampers, at an enormous expense, some hundreds of beings, for the most part wholly indifferent, perhaps disagreeable to him, but as they serve to fill his rooms and swell the pageant; who regard him but as the caterer of their appetites, and remember him and his feast only until another supercedes him. For half the money lavished on such an exhibition, I will not call it an entertainment, this child of fortune might place within these walls some valuable specimen of art, some permanent, honourable, useful monument of his liberality. He might confer a lasting benefit on the arts and artists of his country, and incorporate his fame with theirs. This is a calculation that pride might make, even where higher motives are wanting. But the pride of some men requires more immediate and ostentatious returns for her offerings; and prefers the momentary blaze of vain admiration, to the steady light of real utility.

In the school of Lorenzo Michael Angelo was formed. If all the wealth of Lorenzo had been given to make such a man, it would have been well bestowed. Let me ask the most dull and infatuated vanity, the most selfish and sordid avarice, whether the prospect, the most distant hope, of producing to America some such astonishing genius, whose name, proudly eminent on the rolls of fame, will be connected with theirs for centuries to come, has not an inflaming influence, an irresistible power to open their ponderous coffers to the noble purpose. The wealth of this country is generally deposited with her merchants. They are, in this respect, the nobles of the land. The family of the Medici, the restorers of learning and the arts, the benefactors to whom every civilized man is now grateful; the men whom the historian, the poet, the statuary, and the painter, all delight to honour, were also merchants. But, let it be remembered, if they had done no more to immortalize themselves than import spices from the Indies, and draw wealth from every quarter of the globe, they would have sunk into oblivion with their transitory possessions. Wealth is dissipated by indiscretion; it is lost by misfortune; its gratifications certainly cease with death. But the just and noble employment of it gives it possessor the most rational and exquisite delight while he lives, and a credit with posterity which no honest man can anticipate without pleasure.

The surest mode of securing a lasting fame is to engage the good will and gratitude of some useful and distinguishd class of men. Individual bounties, however benevolent, are transient, and die with their object; but favours bestowed on some permanent institution, are perpetual. If a munificent benefit were to be conferred upon the arts, in any of their branches, in sculpture, painting, or engraving; as long as the arts exist here, its professors will remember and acknowledge the benefaction; and the donor thus enlists in the service of his reputation a lasting and powerful class of men.

I have already observd that quietude is necessary to the culture and growth of the arts. Political independence is not less so. A nation in a state of vassalage cannot excel in them. The mind must be free as air, dreading the inspection of no jealous master: the ardour of genius must not be chilled by conscious dependence, no its flights limited by the weight of chains. A comparative view of our own country before and since the revolution, abundantly proves this position. Before the revolution, a spelling book impressed upon brown paper, with the interesting figure of master Dilworth as a frontispiece, was the extent of American skill in printing and engraving. But when independence and peace were obtained, and when, by the adoption of a regular and free government, that independence and peace were secured, the arts began to show themselves like the verdure of the spring, spare and feeble, but full of health and promise. . . .

The fastidious arrogance with which the reviewers and magazine makers of Great Britain treat the genius and intellect of this country is equalled by nothing but their profound ignoranc of its true situation. Our literature, taste, morals, and progress in the arts, are never failing subjects of the most illiberal sarcasm and abuse. But their blunders in matters of fact are so gross and ridiculous, that the censure founded on them should be met with contempt. They are scarcely acquainted with the geography of our country, and they undertake to decide, with the most disgusting insolence upon our learning, literature, morals, and manners, or rather upon our want of all of them; grounding their charges and opinions upon the tales of some miserable reptiles, who, after having abused the hospitality and patience of this country, levy a tax from their own, by disseminating a vile mass of falsehood and nonsense, under the denomination of "Travels through the United States." In truth nothing is more difficult than to form a just estimate of a foreign country—a wise man, therefore, will say little about it. . . .

I do not, however, mean to be wilfully blind on our deficiencies. They are many and important. We have doubtless much to do; but the means are in our power, if the inclination is not wanting. It is certainly true that the talents of this country have not yet been directed to subjects of erudite literature and profound science. To develop the causes of this deficiency would require more time and explanation than can be given to it on this occasion. Briefly and generally, they may be

1. The want of rich and extensive seminaries of learning, which so young a country cannot possess, to which the scholar may retire, undisturbed by the business or pleasures of the world, and be furnished with the best and most ample means of instruction.

2. The desire which every man has to establish himself as an independent member of society, and become the head of a family; and the facility with which this may be done here by the most moderate exercise of labour and ingenuity.

3. Our natural aversion to seclusion, to deep mental abstraction, to pain and privation (all of which the scholar must endure) while our necessities are not strong enough to drive us, nor our inducements to allure us, to such a course of penance.

4. Our social intercourse is so early and unreserved as very soon to involve a young man of any sensibility in a matrimonial engagement: and at the age when a devoted scholar would be seeking a retired chamber in the university, and collecting his musty volumes, our youth is looking for a convenient dwelling house and purchasing the necessary furniture. In truth a beautiful woman is so much more attractive and easily understood than a

Greek manuscript, that we cannot, very harshly, censure the preference.

5. Another cause may be added, that our young men are, at a very early age, turned into the world to maintain themselves, they must, therefore, adopt some occupation which will yield immediate profit.

None of these causes, however, evince or imply any deficiency of genius or intellect. On the contrary much of both is discovered in the ardour, the reputation, and success, with which law, physic, and commerce, the usual resorts of our young men, are pursued.

The honourable testimonials of merit presented to commodore Truxtun and Mr. Dobel, naturally lead us to a very obvious and important use to be derived from the fine arts, particularly applicable to republican governments. When some eminent citizen, eminent by his virtue, devotes his life, and all his faculties, to the service of his country; when, by an illustrious sacrifice of himself he averts some dreaded calamity, some threatening ruin, what has the gratitude, the justice of a republic to give? How shall she acknowledge and acquit the obligation? Instead of rank and titles incompatible with her principles; instead of grants and pensions which exhaust the public wealth, and excite rather a spirit of avarice or luxury, then patriotism, the vast debt is cheaply paid by the skill of the artist consecrated by the voice of the nation. Such rewards neither encourage nor gratify any sordid disposition, but operate only on the generous, the disinterested, the sublime passions, of the soul. They neither give power nor endanger liberty; yet they satisfy the patriot, and excite the noblest emulation. The greatest minds are impelled to their boldest exploits by the suggestions of honour, and the prospect of some public and permanent testimony of their merit and services. "A peerage or Westminster Abbey" was in the heart and on the lips of the immortal Nelson whenever he was about to plunge into some perilous enterprise. When hereafter our commonwealth shall produce Nelsons blazing with glory; when we shall have statesmen and generals rivaling the heroes of the ancient republics, in the purity of their virtue and importance of their services, performed by incredible exertions, by extreme suffering, by premature death, where is the art or the artist to bear down to future ages the fame of their achievements, or proclaim the gratitude of their country. Shall we disgracefully apply to the very enemy they have defeated, to commemorate the triumph? Must the conqueror thus stoop to the conquered, acknowledging a degrading and mortifying inferiority? Athens was the teacher of Rome in those things which really dignify a nation, after the arms of Rome had subjugated the liberties of Greece; and Athens is now remembered and revered more as the mistress of learning and the arts than for all her victories.

But shall any future patriot hope to have his memory perpetuated, when WASHINGTON lies neglected. Not a stone tells the stranger where the hero is laid. No proud column declares that *his country is grateful*. If but an infant perish, even before its smiles have touched a parent's heart, yet a parent's love marks with some honour the earth that covers it. 'Tis the last tribute which the humblest pay to the most humble.

> "Yet e'en these bones from insult to protect,
> Some frail memorial still erected nigh;
> With uncouth rhymes and shapeless sculpture deck'd;
> Implores the passing tribute of a sigh."

The stranger who, in days to come, shall visit our shore, will exclaim, show me the statue of your WASHINGTON, that I may contemplate the majestic form that encompassed his mighty soul; that I may gaze upon those features once lighted with every virtue; and learn to love virtue as I behold them. Alas! there is no such statue. Lead me then, American, to the tomb your country has provided for her deliverer; to the everlasting monument she has erected to his fame. Alas! his country has not given him a tomb; she has erected no monument to his fame. His grave is in the bosom of *his own soil*, and the cedar, that was watered by his hand, is all that rests upon it. Tell me whence is this inhuman supineness? Is it envy, jealousy, or ingratitude? Or is it that, in the great struggle for power and place, every thing else is forgotten; every noble, generous, and national sentiment desregarded or despised? Whatever be the cause, the curse of ingratitude is upon us until it be removed.

In recommending to our fellow-citizens the cultivation of a general taste in the fine arts, and a liberal attention to every institution calculated to promote it, we should not overlook some of its most interesting uses to society. Every man who is a member of that society and has influence and power in it, either by his rank, his education, or his wealth, has a deep interest, perhaps a serious duty, to attent to on this subject. It is no new doctrine to assert that the fine arts are of great importance to the morals of the community. Their influence, in this respect, may reach where the voice of the preacher is never heard, and the lectures of the moralist, never read. By providing an innocent, an interesting, and dignified source of pleasure, they not only draw the mind from gross and vulgar gratifications; but finally so entirely absorb and purify it; so quicken its sensibility and refine its taste, that pleasures more gross lose their attractions and becoming disgusting. Men, whose inclination and fortune withdraw them from scenes of active and necessary business, still require occupation and amusement. The mind that is stagnant loses its vital principle, and sinks either into a distressing lethargy, or low and corrupting vices. What a resource, what a refuge is opened to such men in the fascinating gardens of Taste.

> "Thou mak'st all nature beauty to his eye,
> Or music to his ear; well pleas'd he scans
> The goodly prospect; and with inward smiles
> Treads the gay verdure of the painted plain;
> Beholds the azure canopy of heaven,
> And living lamps that overarch his head
> With more than regal splendour; bends his ears
> To the full choir of water, air, and earth;
> Nor heeds the pleasing errours of his thoughts,
> So sweet he feels their influence to attract
> The fixed soul; to brighten the dull glooms
> Of care, and make the destin'd road of life,
> Delightful to his feet."

Such are the pleasures of a mind purified by virtue, and cultivated by taste. Can a being capable of such sublime contemplations, and commanding such high sources of pleasure, drop from its dignity into some sink of vice, or be lost in the mazes of sensual dissipation?

When speaking of the morality of the fine arts, I should be unpardonable were I not to fortify myself with the sentiments of the elegant and philosophical critic, Lord Kaims. He remarks that the pleasures of the ear and eye "approach the purely mental, without exhausting the spirits; and exceed the purely sensual, without the danger of satiety."—That they have "a natural aptitude to draw us from immoderate gratifications of sensual appetite," and that the Author of our nature has thus qualified us to rise, by gentle steps, "from the most groveling corporeal pleasures, for which only the mind is fitted in the beginning of life, to those refined and sublime pleasures which are suited to maturity;" and these refined pleasures of sense lead "to the exalted pleasures of morality and religion." We stand therefore, says this eloquent writer "engaged in honour, as well as interest, to second the purposes of Nature, by cultivating the pleasures of the eye and ear, those especially that require extraordinary culture, such as are inspired by poetry, painting, sculpture, music, gardening, and architecture." Shall I say that he adds, "this is chiefly the duty of the opulent, who have leisure to improve their minds and feelings?" He further declares, that "a taste in the fine arts and the moral sense go hand in hand." May I be indulged in a further extract from this distinguished critic and moralist? "Mathematical and metaphysical reasonings," he says, "have no tendency to improve social intercourse; nor are they applicable to the common affairs of life: but a just taste in the fine arts, derived from rational principles, is a fine preparation for acting in the social state with dignity and propriety." It moderates the selfish affections, and "by sweetening and harmonizing the temper, is a strong antidote to the turbulence of passion and the violence of pursuit." It "procures a man so much enjoyment at home, or easily within reach, that in order to be occupied, he is, in youth, under no temptation to precipitate into hunting, gaming, drinking; nor, in middle age to deliver himself over to ambition; nor, in old age, to avarice." "I insist on it," continues he, "with entire satisfaction, that no occupation attaches a man more to his duty than that of cultivating a taste in the fine arts, a just relish of what is beautiful, proper, elegant, and ornamental in writing or painting, in architecture or gardening, is a fine preparation for discerning what is beautiful, just, elegant, or magnanimous in character and behaviour."

> "For the attentive mind,
> By this harmonious action on her powers,
> Becomes herself harmonious: wont so long
> In outward things, to meditate the charm
> Of sacred order, soon she seeks at home
> To find a kindred order: to exert
> Within herself, this elegance of love,
> This fair inspir'd delight; her temper'd powers
> Refine at length, and every passion wears
> A chaster, milder, more attractive mien."

If such pleasures can require any other recommendation than their ex-quisite and dignified delight, their perfect innocence, their entire exemp-tion from all disgust and remorse, do we not find it in their universality and ease of acquirement. To enjoy a fine painting, a correct and elegant building, a beautiful garden, it is not necessary we should own them. It is only necessary we should have chastened and improved that taste of which every man has from nature a portion, to derive from these expensive pos-sessions every pleasure they can bestow. Thus it is that wealth spreads her bounty, even if reluctant, and is compelled, while she gratifies her vanity, to diffuse her enjoyments.

Further; every man has not only the means of gratification, thus cheaply furnished, but also the power of enjoying them. This is given him by nature. Whatever distance there may be between the rude and the refined taste, every one has more or less of it; afforded, indeed, in different portions, but always capable of much improvement. When therefore I have heard gentlemen excuse themselves from contributing their aid to this institution, by alleging they have no taste for such things, I have been astonished. It is not true. Does the gentleman mean to say, he cannot tell a straight line from a crooked one; that he cannot discern whether an imitation be correct or otherwise; that he has no pleasure in beauty, no disgust from deformity? What is this taste they are so eager to disclaim? There is no magic in the word:——

> "What, then, is taste, but these internal powers,
> Active and strong, and feelingly alive
> To each fine impulse; a discerning sense
> Of decent and sublime, with quick disgust
> From things deformed, or disarranged, or gross in species?"

If this be taste, is any one willing to avow himself destitute of it? What does it require? Sight, sensibility, and judgment. That it is possessed in portions almost infinitely different; that it affords pleasure in different degrees to different men, is undoubtedly true; but, every man who sees, feels, and judges, has *taste*, which, by culture, he may enlarge and improve.

Let us imagine some gross disproportion in a building, or deformity in a statue or picture, the most common eye would discover it, and be offended. This deformity may be so diminished, that a more accurate eye, and scrutinizing judgment is necessary to detect it, which is obtained by more experience, and, perhaps, a superiour original sensibility or delicacy of mental organization. When a painter spreads over his canvass some animated scene of nature; or pourtrays the actions or passions of men, what is that taste which decides upon the merit of his work? It is the faculty of discerning whether his imitations are accurate, his combinations just, and whether grace and harmony pervade the whole. No man is without some portion of this discernment.

It is, indeed, so far from being true, that men, in general, are not competent to judge of the productions of the fine arts, that it is by public judgment their merit or demerit is finally established. This is the tribunal before which they stand or fall; and, generally speaking, it is not only impartial, but just and correct. Public opinion has, in more instances than one, triumphed over critics and connoisseurs, and the triumph has been sanctioned by time and experience. Plays and poems finally take their rank in literature by the reception they meet with in the world, and not by the square and compass of the professed critic. Is not this taste, and a high exercise of its prerogatives? And this is all as it should be. The object of the fine arts, in all their branches, is to please; to engage attention, to fascinate. Now, these are emotions of which every man is susceptible. We require no critic or connoisseur to tell us whether we shall be delighted with a play, or subdued by the powers of music. Can any critic prove that we must not be melted with the tenderness of Shakspeare, or prevent him from shaking our souls with terror? Is there a picture which has fascinated every eye; or a piece of music which has touched every heart, and can they be proved, by any course of reasoning, to be bad? It has long since been agreed, that the truest test of eloquence is the impression it makes upon the common audience; even upon the vulgar and unlearned. May not the same test be applied, not, perhaps with equal confidence, or to the same extent, to other efforts of genius?

Professors of an art are frequently prejudiced by attachments to particular schools; to particular masters; by personal friendships; perhaps, sometimes, by envy or dislike: but the public voice speaks over such considerations; and, when combined in one sentiment, is seldom wrong, and always irresistible.

The highest efforts of art are but attempts to imitate Nature; and it is excellent in proportion as it succeeds in the imitation. Is it only to the man of education that Nature unfolds her excellence and offers her enjoyments? Is it only to him she displays her beauties, her perfections, her symmetry?

> "Ask the swain
> Who journeys homewards, from a Summer-day's
> Long làbour, why, forgetful of his toils
> And due repose, he loiters to behold
> The sunshine gleaming, as through amber clouds,
> O'er all the western sky; full soon I ween
> His rude expression and untutor'd airs,
> Beyond the powers of language, will unfold
> The form of Beauty smiling at his heart,
> How lovely! how commanding!"

Nothing can be more obvious and natural than the connexion between what are termed the useful arts and the fine arts; and hence is derived a strong inducement for encouraging the latter. The carpenter, the mason, nay, the mechanic of every description, will improve in the propriety and elegance of his design, and the excellence of his workmanship, by having placed before him models formed with correct proportion, with elegant symmetry, with true taste. By constantly observing what is just and beautiful, a desire of imitating it is excited; a spirit of emulation arises, and superior genius displays itself in the most ordinary works. Instead of immense piles of brick and mortar heaped together, without any unity or propriety of design, or justness of proportion, where expense is substituted for taste, and gaudy ornament for true elegance, we shall have the plain, chaste, but beautiful productions of legitimate architecture.

Nor is it only in constructing our dwellings and public edifices that the aid of the fine arts is necessary. It is equally required in selecting and disposing the internal decorations and furniture; which are sometimes, even in the houses of the most fashionable, most ridiculous and shocking.—Those mechanics, therefore, who are employed in these services, have the most indispensable occasion for cultivating their talents, and improving their taste; especially while their employers are resolved not to do so. It is from the stores of antiquity this improvement is to be drawn. It may surprise some to learn, that most of the ornaments introduced to the persons and houses of the wealthy and the gay, under the irresistible recommendation of being *"new fashions,"* are really some thousand years old; purloined from the relics of former ages. The brilliant trinket that sheds its lustre from the bosom of a modern belle, performed the same kind office for some damsel, equally fair, who, centuries agone, mouldered to imperceptible atoms. How various! how inexhaustible! is the profit and pleasure to be derived from the studies of antiquity.

The collection and exhibition of works of art, in some public institution, furnishes a cheap school, of easy access, to every one disposed to receive the benefit. The labour and expense submitted to by those who have created this school, is, at least, disinterested. They have no advantage in it but that which is common to every member of the community, who has any concern in its welfare; they have no gratification but that of affording the means of improvement to American genius, not always affluent enough to seek it abroad.

The exhibition of fine specimens of art has a further use. It excites curiosity, attracts attention to subjects which might otherwise have been unnoticed, and stimulates the spirit of exertion. The man in whom the spark of genius may be latent, begins to look into his own powers; to inquire whether he might not produce such works; to make the effort; to be crowned with success.

If, on the one hand, we have strong motives for inviting artists, and, with them, the arts, to the American shore, do we not also offer them strong inducements for accepting the invitation? Without recurring to those derived from the afflicted state of Europe, the prospects presented to them here are, surely, flattering. A young and vigorous country, rising, with unexampled rapidity, to the maturity of strength and opulence; increasing in luxury with the multitude of expensive wants or indulgences that walk in her train! The arts, as yet in their infancy, with a people disposed to expense, and desirous of distinction; public buildings erecting, almost daily, in some part of this vast empire, and innumerable private mansions, calling for the aid of the educated artist. In another direction, printing is extending itself with wonderful increase; and, in connexion with it, the necessary arts of designing, drawing, and engraving. Both literature and the arts connected with it have, in England, found their most liberal and effectual patrons in the booksellers. The honourable example is not disregarded here. The same spirit inspires the profession, and the same effects may be expected from it. The history of science and letters amply testifies, that they flourish or decline with the arts.

It would be tedious to enumerate the sources of encouragement which artists of real merit will find in this country; or to state more particularly the facts and reasons which should draw them to us. At this moment, although we have near sixty engravers in this city, as many more would meet employment.

Nor is our country deficient in objects to exercise and elevate the soul of genius. Our public events, in addition to the common stock of ancient fable, furnish subjects for the historic canvass; and private affection or vanity will fully occupy the time and talents of the portrait painter. Do not our vast rivers, vast beyond the conception of the European, rolling over immeasurable space, with the hills and mountains, the bleak wastes and luxuriant meadows through which they force their way, afford the most sublime and beautiful objects for the pencil of Landscape. Look at the rich variety, and dazzling brilliancy of our autumnal foliage. The powers of colouring may be exerted to the utmost in representing it. I speak on certain evidence, when I relate that an English artist, who was requested to paint this American foliage, with an intention of sending the picture to England, refused to put it on his canvass as it really is, lest his painting might be taken for caricature in England, where as this painter supposed, it would never be believed to be an imitation of nature.

I could not hope for pardon were I to conclude this address without some acknowledgement for the patronage this institution has received from the ladies of our city. The first contribution to it was by a lady, equally distinguished for her taste and liberality; for the native powers of her intellect and the improvement they have received from a judicious cultivation. The influence of the female sex, in making any undertaking of this kind fashionable or otherwise, is sovereign and undoubted; and it has been most beneficially exerted in behalf of this academy. Our collection of painting and statuary, from its first exhibition, has been visited by our ladies, with a constancy which acquits them of the motive of mere curiosity, and an ardour which could be found only in minds well improved, touched with the fire of genius, and really capable of enjoying her works. It must be admitted, too, that the objects of the institution were so novel in this country, as well as its exhibitions, that it required no inconsiderable share of good sense and fortitude in a lady to countenance them. But intelligence, taste, and genuine modesty bore down ignorance, prejudice, and affectation, without, in the least, impairing that delicacy which is the most facinating attraction of facinating woman.

In the present state of society, woman is inseparable connected with every thing that civilizes, refines, and sublimates man. The barbarous days are now but dimly seen in the mist of distant ages, when she was considered and treated as the slave of an unfeeling master; born only to perpetuate his savage race, and indulge his grosser appetites. On many subjects of human knowledge her intellect has proved itself equal to the powers of man; and in some of the best properties of our nature she is much his superiour. The gardens of literature are now illumined with many a lamp trimmed by a female hand; and the arts of painting and engraving have softened under the tenderness of the female touch. I hope and trust the walls of our academy will soon be decorated with the productions of female genius; and that no means will be omitted to invite and encourage them.

MR. PRESIDENT,

I have to congratulate you and the members of this academy upon the establishment of the "Society of Artists of the United States;" and their happy union with this institution. This association promises to be eminently useful to the arts, and to have a decided influence in concentrating them in this city. The success, however, of these gentlemen, depends upon the harmony and cooperation of their efforts; upon their having magnanimity enough to keep out every selfish wish, every turbulent passion, every petty jealousy and dissension, suffering nothing to divert them from their great design. In the ensuing spring this society will make their first exhibition of works of art, original and collected from every part of the United States.

This evening, too, for the first time, the Pennsylvania Academy of the Fine Arts, will confer its honours on distinguished professors of the arts. This is a most important and delicate function, and on the just and impartial exercise of it the most interesting consequences depend. Genius must be fostered, encouraged, and sustained by rewards, by honours, by distinction. She is sometimes a wayward child, and must be indulged and cheered. History furnishes us with many anecdotes of the caprices and eccentricties of men of genius, and of the indulgence they have received from the patrons of the arts. If genius has her sublime and ethereal elevations, she has also her discontents, occasional peevishness, her deep and gloomy despondencies, from which she must be drawn by blandishments and kindness. She must be roused and stimulated by public notice and applause. In distributing the honours of the academy, the utmost care must be taken to do it with sound discrimination and honest impartiality, or the charm is gone; the influence lost. It is happily observed by a celebrated French critic, that "The Roman soldiers would have ceased to set a value upon the crown of oaken boughs, for which they exposed themselves to the greatest dangers, had the favour of the general bestowed it, a few times, on those who never deserved it."

I fear, gentlemen, this discourse, though composed of mere hints and sketches put together with unwarranted haste, has exceeded the limits of your patience, and of propriety. My thanks are, therefore, the more due for your indulgent attention.

PART SIX

Order and Disorder

21. Social Mobility

Social mobility lay at the heart of the meaning of the American Revolution. The Americans threw off British authority precisely because they sought to create a society where real merit, and not artificial connections, would determine the shape of the social hierarchy. Republicanism signified equality of opportunity and careers open to talent. Even farmers' sons, if qualified, could become magistrates and governors. But first they must be qualified. The rising self-made men, most of the Revolutionary generation believed, must first acquire the attributes of social superiority—wealth, education, experience, refinement—before they could be considered eligible for political leadership. Any short-circuiting of this orderly movement through clearly discernible ranks would lead to social chaos and would prevent those who were naturally talented from ruling the republic. Yet such irregular rising was precisely what seemed to be happening in the years following the Revolution.

Perhaps no one developed this theme of abused social mobility more fully than did Hugh Henry Brackenridge (1748-1816), in his rambling picaresque novel *Modern Chivalry,* written piecemeal from 1792 to 1815. Brackenridge, as the son of a poor Scottish immigrant farmer, had every reason to believe in the promise of American mobility. He rose through hard work and self-cultivation to graduate from Princeton in 1771, to become a lawyer and man of letters, and, eventually, to become in 1786 an assemblyman from western Pennsylvania. His precipitant electoral defeat the following year by an ex-weaver, William Findley, stunned him, however, and laid the basis for his satirical novel. Brackenridge wrote a number of essays, several plays, and a considerable variety of verse, including, in collaboration with Philip Freneau, the famous Princeton Commencement poem, "The Rising Glory of America." He became a leader of the Republican party in western Pennsylvania and was appointed Justice of the Supreme Court of Pennsylvania in 1799.

Modern Chivalry

HUGH HENRY BRACKENRIDGE

The captain rising early next morning, and setting out on his way, had now arrived at a place where a number of people were convened, for the purpose of electing persons to represent them in the legislature of the state. There was a weaver who was a candidate for this appointment, and seemed to have a good deal of interest among the people. But another, who was a man of education, was his competitor. Relying on some talent of speaking which he thought he possessed, he addressed the multitude.

Fellow-citizens, said he, I pretend not to any great abilities; but am conscious to myself that I have the best good will to serve you. But it is very astonishing to me, that this weaver should conceive himself qualified for the trust. For though my acquirements are not great, yet his are still less. The mechanical business which he pursues, must necessarily take up so much of his time, that he cannot apply himself to political studies. I should therefore think it would be more answerable to your dignity, and conductive to your interest, to be represented by a man at least of some letters, than by an illiterate handicraftsman like this. It will be more honourable for himself, to remain at his loom and knot threads, than to come forward in a legislative capacity: because, in the one case, he is in the sphere suited to his education; in the other, he is like a fish out of water, and must struggle for breath in a new element.

Is it possible he can understand the affairs of government, whose mind has been concentered to the small object of weaving webs; to the price by the yard, the grist of the thread, and such like little matters as concern the manufacturer of cloths? The feet of him who weaves, are more occupied than the head, or at least as much; and the whole must be, at least, but in half, accustomed to exercise his mental powers. For these reasons, all other things set aside, the chance is in my favour with respect to information. However, you will decide, and give your suffrages to him or to me, as you shall judge expedient.

The Captain hearing these observations, and looking at the weaver, could not help advancing, and undertaking to subjoin something in support of

Hugh Henry Brackenridge, *Modern Chivalry: Containing the Adventures of a Captain, and Teague O'Regan, His Servant*, 2 vols. (Philadelphia, 1804), vol. I, pp. 10–24.

what had been just said. Said he, I have no prejudice against a weaver more than another man. Nor do I know any harm in the trade; save that from the sedentary life in a damp place, there is usually a paleness of the countenance: but this is a physical not a moral evil. Such usually occupy subterrancan apartments; not for the purpose, like Demosthenes, of shaving their heads, and writing over eight times the history of Thucydides, and perfecting a stile of oratory; but rather to keep the thread moist; or because this is considered but as an inglorious sort of trade, and is frequently thrust away into cellars, and damp out-houses, which are not occupied for a better use.

But to rise from the cellar to the senate house, would be an unnatural hoist. To come from counting threads, and adjusting them to the splits of a reed, to regulate the finances of a government, would be preposterous; there being no congruity in the case. There is no analogy between knotting threads and framing laws. It would be a reversion of the order of things. Not, that a manufacturer of linen or woolen, or other stuff, is an inferior character, but a different one, from that which ought to be employed in affairs of state. It is unnecessary to enlarge on this subject; for you must all be convinced of the truth and propriety of what I say. But if you will give me leave to take the manufacturer aside a little, I think I can explain to him my ideas on the subject; and very probably prevail with him to withdraw his pretensions. The people seeming to acquiesce, and beckoning to the weaver, they withdrew aside, and the Captain addressed him in the following words;

Mr. Traddle, said he, for that was the name of the manufacturer, I have not the smallest idea of wounding your sensibility; but it would seem to me, it would be more your interest to pursue your occupation, than to launch out into that of which you have no knowledge. When you go to the senate house, the application to you will not be to warp a web; but to make laws for the commonwealth. Now, suppose that the making [of] these laws, requires a knowledge of commerce, or of the interests of agriculture, or those principles upon which the different manufactures depend, what service could you render. It is possible you might think justly enough; but could you speak? You are not in the habit of public speaking. You are not furnished with those common place ideas, with which even very ignorant men can pass for knowing something. There is nothing makes a man so ridiculous as to attempt what is above his sphere. You are no tumbler for instance; yet should you give out that you could vault upon a man's back; or turn head over heels like the wheels of a cart; the stiffness of your joints would encumber you; and you would fall upon your backside to the ground. Such a squash as that would do you damage. The getting up to ride on the state is an unsafe thing to those who are not accustomed to such horsemanship. It is a disagreeable thing for a man to be laughed at, and there is no way of keeping ones self from it by avoiding all affectation.

While they were thus discoursing, a bustle had taken place among the croud [crowd]. Teague hearing so much about elections, and serving the government, took it into his head, that he could be a legislator himself. The thing was not displeasing to the people, who seemed to favour his pretensions; owing, in some degree, to there being several of his countrymen among the croud; but more especially to the fluctuation of the popular mind, and a disposition to what is new and ignoble. For though the weaver was not the most elevated object of choice, yet he was still preferable to this tatter-demalion, who was but a menial servant, and has so much of what is called the brogue on his tongue, as to fall far short of an elegant speaker.

The Captain coming up, and finding what was on the carpet, was greatly chagrined at not having been able to give the multitude a better idea of the importance of a legislative trust; alarmed also, from an apprehension of the loss of his servant. Under these impressions he resumed his address to the multitude. Said he, this is making the matter still worse, gentlemen: this servant of mine is but a bog-trotter, who can scarcely speak the dialect in which your laws ought to be written; but certainly has never read a single treatise on any political subject; for the truth is, he cannot read at all. The young people of the lower class, in Ireland, have seldom the advantage of a good education; especially the descendants of the ancient Irish, who have most of them a great assurance of countenance, but little information, or literature. This young man, whose family name is Oregan, has been my servant for several years; and, except a too great fondness for women, which now and then brings him into scrapes, he has demeaned himself in a manner tolerable enough. But he is totally ignorant of the great principles of legislation; and more especially, the particular interests of the government. A free government is a noble acquisition to a people: and this freedom consists in an equal right to make laws, and to have the benefit of the laws when made. Though doubtless, in such a government, the lowest citizen may become chief magistrate; yet it is sufficient to possess the right; not absolutely necessary to exercise it. Or even if you should think proper, now and then, to shew your privilege, and exert, in a signal manner, the democratic prerogative, yet is it not descending too low to filch away from me a hireling, which I cannot well spare. You are surely carrying the matter too far, in thinking to make a senator of this ostler; to take him away from an employment to which he has been bred, and put him to another, to which he has served no apprenticeship: to set those hands which have been lately employed in currying my horse, to the draughting [of] bills, and preparing business for the house.

The people were tenacious of their choice, and insisted on giving Teague their suffrages; and by the frown upon their brows, seemed to indicate resentment at what had been said; as indirectly charging them with want of judgment; or calling in question their privilege to do what they thought proper. It is a very strange thing, said one of them, who was a speaker for the rest, that after having conquered Burgoyne and Cornwallis, and got a government of our own, we cannot put in it whom we please. This young man may be your servant, or another man's servant; but if we chuse to make him a delegate, what is that to you. He may not be yet skilled in the matter, but there is a good day a-coming. We will empower him; and it is better to trust a plain man like him, than one of your high flyers, that will make laws to suit their own purposes.

I had much rather, said the Captain, you would send the weaver, though I thought that improper, than to invade my household, and thus detract from me the very person that I have about me to brush my boots, and clean my spurs. The prolocutor of the people gave him to understand that his objections were useless, for the people had determined on the choice, and Teague they would have, for a representative.

Finding it answered no end to expostulate with the multitude, he requested to speak a word with Teague by himself. Stepping aside, he said to him, composing his voice, and addressing him in a soft manner: Teague, you are quite wrong in this matter they have put into your head. Do you know what it is to be a member of a deliberative body? What qualifications are necessary? Do you understand any thing of geography? If a question should be put to make a law to dig a canal in some part of the state, can you describe the bearing of the mountains, and the course of the rivers? Or if commerce is to be pushed to some new quarter, by the force of regulations, are you competent to decide in such a case? There will be questions of law, and astronomy on the carpet. How you must gape and stare like a fool, when you come to be asked your opinion on these subjects? Are you acquainted with the abstract principles of finance; with the funding public securities; the way and means of raising the revenue; providing for the discharge of the public debts, and all other things which respect the economy of the government? Even if you had knowledge, have you a facility of speaking. I would suppose you would have too much pride to go to the house just to say, ay, or no. This is not the fault of your nature, but of your education; having been accustomed to dig turf in your early years, rather than instructing yourself in the classics, or common school books.

When a man becomes a member of a public body, he is like a racoon, or other beast that climbs up the fork of a tree; the boys pushing at him with pitchforks, or throwing stones, or shooting at him with an arrow, the dogs barking in the mean time. One will find fault with your not speaking; another with your speaking, if you speak at all. They will put you in the newspapers, and ridicule you as a perfect beast. There is what they call the caricatura; that is, representing you with a dog's head, or a cat's claw. As you have a red head, they will very probably make a fox of you, or a sorrel horse, or a brindled cow. It is the devil in hell to be exposed to the squibs and crackers of the gazette wits and publications. You know no more about these matters than a goose; and yet you would undertake rashly, without advice, to enter on the office; nay, contrary to advice. For I would not for a thousand guineas, though I have not the half it to spare, that the breed of the Oregans should come to this; bringing on them a worse stain than stealing sheep; to which they are addicted. You have nothing but your character, Teague, in a new country to depend upon. Let it never be said, that you quitted an honest livelihood, the taking care of my horse, to follow the new fangled whims of the times, and be a statesman.

Teague was moved chiefly with the last part of the address, and consented to relinquish his pretensions.

The Captain, glad of this, took him back to the people, and announced his disposition to decline the honour which they had intended him.

Teague acknowledged that he had changed his mind, and was willing to remain in a private station.

The people did not seem well pleased with the Captain; but as nothing more could be said about the matter, they turned their attention to the weaver, and gave him their suffrages.

★   ★   ★   ★

The Captain leaving this place, proceeded on his way; and at the distance of a mile or two, met a man with a bridle in his hand; who had lost a horse, and had been at a conjurer's to make enquiry, and recover his property.

It struck the mind of the Captain to go to this conjuring person, and make a demand of him, why it was that the multitude were so disposed to elevate the low to the highest station. He had rode but about a mile, when the habitation of the conjurer, by the direction and description of the man who had lost the horse had given, began to be in view. . . . Coming up to the door, and enquiring if that was not where conjurer Kolt lived, they were answered yes. Accordingly alighting, and entering the domicile, all these things took place which usually happen, or are described in cases of this nature, viz. there was the conjurer's assistant, who gave the Captain to understand that master had withdrawn a little, but would be in shortly.

In the mean time, the assistant endeavoured to draw from him some account of the occasion of his journey; which the other readily communicated; and the conjurer, who was listening through a crack in the partition, overheard. Finding it was not a horse or a cow, or a piece of linen that was lost, but an abstract question of political philosophy which was to be put, he came from his lurking place, and entered, as if not knowing that any person had been waiting for him.

After mutual salutations, the Captain gave him to understand the object which he had in view by calling on him.

Said the conjurer, this lies not at all in my way. If it had been a dozen of spoons, or a stolen watch, that you had to look for, I could very readily, by the assistance of my art, have assisted you in the recovery; but as to this matter of men's imaginations and attachments in political affairs, I have no more understanding than another man.

It is very strange, said the Captain, that you who can tell by what means a thing is stolen, and the place where it is deposited, though at a thousand miles distance, should know so little of what is going on in the breast of man, as not to be able to develope his secret thoughts, and the motives of his actions.

It is not of our business, said the other; but should we undertake it, I do not see that it would be very difficult to explain all that puzzles you at present. There is no need of a conjurer to tell why it is that the common people are more disposed to trust one of their own class, than those who may affect to be superior. Besides, there is a certain pride in man, which leads him to elevate the low, and pull down the high. There is a kind of creating power exerted in making a senator of an unqualified person; which when the author has done, he exults over the work, and like the Creator himself when he made the world, sees that "it is very good." Moreover, there is in every government a patrician class, against whom the spirit of the multitude naturally militates: and hence a perpetual war: the aristocrats endeavouring to detrude the people, and the people contending to obtrude themselves. And it is right it should be so; for by this fermentation, the spirit of democracy is kept alive.

The Captain, thanking him for his information, asked him what was to pay; at the same time pulling out half a crown from a green silk purse which he had in his breeches pocket. The conjurer gave him to understand, that as the solution of these difficulties was not within his province, he took nothing for it. The Captain expressing his sense of his disinterested service, bade him adieu.

★   ★   ★   ★

A Democracy is beyond all question the freest government: because under this, every man is equally protected by the laws, and has equally a voice in making them. But I do not say an equal voice; because some men have stronger lungs than others, and can express more forcibly their opinions of public affairs. Others, though they may not speak very loud, yet have a faculty of saying more in a short time; and even in the case of others, who speak little or none at all, yet what they they do say containing good sense, comes with greater weight; so that all things considered, every citizen has not, in this sense of the word, an equal voice. But the right being equal, what great harm if it is unequally exercised? is it necessary that every man should become a statesman? No more than that every man should become a poet or a painter. The sciences are open to all; but let him only who has taste and genius pursue them. "If any man covets the office of a bishop," says St. Paul, "he covets a good work." But again, he adds this caution, "Ordain not a novice, lest being lifted up with pride, he falls into the condemnation of the devil." It is indeed making a devil of a man to lift him up to a state to which he is not suited. A ditcher is a respectable character, with his over-alls on, and a spade in his hand; but put the same man to those offices which require the head, whereas he has been accustomed to impress with his foot, and there appears a contrast between the individual and the occupation.

There are individuals in society, who prefer honour to wealth; or cultivate political studies as a branch of literary pursuits; and offer themselves to serve public bodies, in order to have an opportunity of discovering their knowledge, and exercising their judgment. It must be matter of chagrin to these, and hurtful to the public, to see those who have no talent this way, and ought to have no taste, preposterously obtrude themselves upon the government. It is the same as if a brick-layer should usurp the office of a taylor and come with his square and perpendicular, to take the measure of a pair of breeches.

It is proper that those who cultivate oratory, should go to the house of orators. But for an Ay and No man to be ambitious of that place, is to sacrifice his credit to his vanity.

I would not mean to insinuate that legislators are to be selected from the more wealthy of the citizens, yet a man's circumstances ought to be such as afford him leisure for study and reflection. There is often wealth without taste or talent. I have no idea, that because a man lives in a great house, and has a cluster of bricks or stones about his backside, that he is therefore fit for a legislator. There is so much pride and arrogance with those who consider themselves the first in a government, that it deserves to be checked by the populace, and the evil most usually commences on this side. Men associate with their own persons, the adventitious circumstances of birth and fortune: So that a fellow blowing with fat and repletion, conceives himself superior to the poor lean man, that lodges in an inferior mansion. But as in all cases, so in this, there is a medium. Genius and virtue are independent of rank and fortune; and it is neither the opulent, nor the indigent, but the man of ability and integrity that ought to be called forth to serve his country: and while, on the one hand the aristocratic part of the government, arrogates a right to represent; on the other hand, the democratic contends the point; and from this conjunction and opposition of forces, there is produced a compound resolution, which carries the object in an intermediate direction. When we see therefore, a Teague Oregan lifted up, the philosopher will reflect, that it is to balance some purse-proud fellow, equally as ignorant, that comes down from the sphere of aristocratic interest.

But every man ought to consider for himself, whether it is his use to be this drawback on either side. For as when good liquor is to be distilled, you throw in some material useless in itself to correct the effervescence of the spirit; so it may be his part to act as a sedative. For though we commend the effect, yet still the material retains but its original value.

But as the nature of things is such, let no man who means well to the commonwealth, and offers to serve it, be hurt in his mind when some one of meaner talents is preferred. The people are a sovereign, and greatly despotic; but, in the main, just.

It might be advisable, in order to elevate the composition, to make quotations from the Greek and Roman history. And I am conscious to myself, that I have read the writers on the government of Italy and Greece, in ancient, as well as modern times. But I have drawn a great deal more from reflection on the nature of things, than from all the writings I have ever read. Nay, the history of the election, which I have just given, will afford a better lesson to the American mind, than all that is to be found in other examples. We see here, a weaver a favoured candidate, and in the next instance, a bog-trotter superseding him. Now it may be said, that this is fiction; but fiction, or no fiction, the nature of the thing will make it a reality. But I return to the adventures of the Captain, whom I have upon my hands; and who, as far as I can yet discover, is a good honest man; and means what is benevolent and useful; though his ideas may not comport with the ordinary manner of thinking, in every particular.

22. The Unsettling of the South

The logic of Revolutionary thought could not be confined to questions of taxation and representation. Many Americans soon grasped the inconsistency of fighting for their freedom from Britain while they were simultaneously enslaving five hundred thousand Negroes. Even before the Declaration of Independence, some of the colonies and the Continental Congress had begun attacking the slave trade. Within two decades following the Revolution, all of the northern states moved in various ways to abolish slavery altogether. Even in the states of the upper South—Delaware, Maryland, and Virginia—antislavery societies began emerging, and criticism of slavery was widespread. Little, however, was done, and southerners lived with a growing fear, fed by the Negro insurrections in Santo Domingo during the 1790's, of the American presumption that men everywhere, white or black, yearned for freedom.

In 1800, in Virginia, the long-dreaded event finally occurred, with momentous consequences for American attitudes toward slavery and the Negro. More than any other single event in post-Revolutionary America, Gabriel's plot confronted white southerners, and Virginians in particular, with the awful implications of their 1776 declarations of liberty and equality, and they reacted by turning against these declarations. The slave uprising of 1800 destroyed the antislavery movement in the South, hardened southern ideas about slavery, and intensified the anomalous position of the black man in what was not supposed to be, but what was clearly becoming, a white man's republic.

Gabriel's Insurrection

1. GOVERNOR MONROE TO THE SPEAKERS OF THE GENERAL ASSEMBLY, RICHMOND, 5 DECEMBER 1800

SIRS,—an important incident has occurred since your last session, which I consider it my duty to submit fully and accurately, in all its details to the wisdom of the General Assembly. On the 30th of August, about two in the afternoon, Mr. Moseby Shephard a respectable citizen of this county called and informed me he had just received advice from two slaves that the negroes in the neighbourhood of Thomas H. Prosser intended to rise that night, kill their masters, and, proceed to Richmond, where they would be joined by the negroes of the city; that they would then take possession of the arms, ammunition, and the town. He added he had long known these two slaves and had no doubt of the truth of the information they gave him, and that he communicated it to me that the proposed insurrection might be defeated if possible. This communication was very interesting, and the source from whence derived, calculated to inspire a belief it was true. The day was far advanced when I received it, so that if any provision was to be made to avert the danger, not a moment was to be lost. I immediately called in the officers commanding the regiment of Militia & troop of Cavalry in town, and made the best disposition for such an emergency the time would allow. A guard of a Captain and thirty men was placed at the Penitentiary where the publick arms were deposited, twenty at the Magazine, and fifteen at the Capitol, and the Horse was ordered to patrol the several routes leading to the city from Mr. Prosser's estate, and to apprize me without de-

Stanislaus M. Hamilton, ed., *The Writings of James Monroe* . . . (New York, 1900), vol. III, pp. 208–209, 234–243, 292–295.

H. W. Flournoy, ed., *Calendar of Virginia State Papers . . . from January 1, 1799, to December* 31, 1807 . . . (Richmond, 1890), vol. IX, pp. 150–152, 164–165.

Dunbar Rowland, ed., *The Mississippi Territorial Archives,* 1798–1803 (Nashville, Tennessee, 1905), vol. I, pp. 311–312.

Paul L. Ford, ed., *The Works of Thomas Jefferson* (New York, 1905), vol. IX, pp. 315–318, 373–375.

lay, if anything like a movement of the negroes was seen, or other circumstance creating a suspicion such was contemplated. The close of the day was marked by one of the most extraordinary falls of rain ever known in our country. Every animal sought shelter from it. Nothing occurred in the night, of the kind suspected, to disturb the tranquility of the city, and in the morning the officer commanding the Horse reported he had seen but one circumstance unusual in the neighbourhood, which was, that all the negroes he passed on the road, in the intervals of the storm, were going from the town, whereas it was their custom to visit it every Saturday night. This circumstance was not otherwise important than as it was said the first rendezvous of the negroes was to be in the country. The same precautions were observed the next night against the threatened insurrection and the same report made the next day by the officers on duty, so that I was on the point of concluding there was no foundation for the alarm, when I was informed by Major Mosby and other gentlemen of character from his neighborhood, they were satisfied a project of insurrection, such as above described, did exist, and that the parties to it meant still to carry it into effect. These gentlemen stated facts and gave details, which left no doubt in my mind of the existence of such a project. From this period the affair assumed a more important aspect. It did not seem probable the slaves in this city and neighbourhood would undertake so bold an enterprise without support from the slaves in other quarters of the State. It was more reasonable to presume an extensive combination had been formed among them for that purpose. Heretofore I had endeavored to give the affair as little importance as the measures necessary for defence would permit. I had hoped it would even pass unnoticed by the community. But as soon as I was satisfied a conspiracy existed it became my duty to estimate the crisis according to its magnitude, and to take regular and systematic measures to avert the danger. In consequence I issued a summons to convene the Council at ten the next day, and in the interim advised the gentlemen who gave me the information, to apprehend and commit to prison without delay all the slaves in the county whose guilt they had good cause to suspect. I also gave a like intimation to the Mayor of the city, which advice was duly attended to. When the Council convened (on the 2d of September) I laid before it the evidence I had received of the meditated insurrection of the slaves, and asked its advice as to the measures necessary to be taken in such an emergency. The Council concurred in opinion that such a project existed and ought to be guarded against with peculiar care. But as the extent of the danger was not yet known, it was thought sufficient at the time to confine our measures of defence to those objects which it was understood were to be first assailed, the Penitentiary, the Capitol, and the Magazine in this city; and the Arsenal at the Point of Fork. It was natural to conclude the attention of the insurgents would be directed in the outset to these objects; and this presentiment was confirmed by every one who knew and communicated to us any thing of their designs. Accordingly guards were established at those places in this city, and an additional force of fifty men ordered to the Point of Fork. At the same time letters were written to the Commandants of every regiment in the Commonwealth, admonishing them of the existing danger, and requesting that vigilant attention be paid to the police of the country, by ordering out suitable and active patrols in every county. In the evening of the same day about twenty of the conspirators were brought to town from Mr. Prosser's and the neighbouring estates, and as the jail could not contain them, they were lodged in the Penitentiary. The chiefs were not to be found. Some of the arms which they had prepared for the occasion, formed of scythe blades, well calculated for execution were likewise brought with them. By the information now received as by former communications, it appeared that the inhabitants of that neighbourhood were in a particular degree, exposed to danger: the conspiracy commenced with their slaves, and they were to be its first victims. It was therefore deemed proper, with a view to their safety, by advice of Council, to order from the thirty third Regiment a guard of a Captain and sixty men to take post near Watson's tavern in the centre of that neighbourhood. By like advice the troop of the city was at the same time subjected to such duty as should be required of it. Every day now threw new light on this affair, and increased the idea of its importance. On the 6th by advice of Council, an order was issued for the removal of the powder from the Magazine to the Penitentiary; the distribution of the arms which were stamped and prepared for the several counties according to a law of the last session, was suspended; the whole militia of the city was armed, its guard increased from sixty to a hundred men, and a power vested in the Chief Magistrate to call out such proportions of the militia of Henrico, Chesterfield and the city of Richmond, as in his judgement the emergency might require. The trials had now commenced whereby the nature and extent of the conspiracy became better understood. It was satisfactorily proven that a general insurrection of the slaves was contemplated by those who took the lead in the affair. A species of organization had taken place among them. At a meeting held for the purpose, they had appointed a commander, to whom they gave the title of General, and had also appointed some other officers. They contemplated a force of cavalry as well as infantry and had formed a plan of attack on the city which was to commence by setting fire to the lower end of the town where the houses consisted chiefly of wood, in expectation of drawing the people to that quarter, while they assailed the Penitentiary, Magazine and Capitol, intending after achieving these, and getting possession of the arms, to meet the people unarmed on their return. The accounts of the number of those who were to commence the movement varied. Some made it considerable, others less so. It was distinctly seen that it embraced most of the slaves in this city and neighbourhood, and that the combination extended to several of the adjacent counties, Hanover, Caroline, Louisa, Chesterfield, and to the neighbourhood of the Point of Fork; and there was as good cause to believe that the knowledge of such a project pervaded other parts, if not the whole of the State. At this time there was no reason to believe if such a project was ever conceived, that it was abandoned. Those who gave the earliest information and were best informed on the subject, thought otherwise. It was understood that the leaders in the conspiracy, who had absconded, were concealed in the neighbourhood. And as several of the parties to it were confined in the Jail condemned to suffer death, and many others in the Penitentiary, likely to experience the same fate, it was probable sympathy for their associates might drive them to despair, and prompt them to make a bolder effort for their relief. The opposite effect was expected from the measures pursued by the Government, but yet the result was uncertain. Other considerations presented themselves to view, in weighing the part it was then incumbent on me to take. The number of slaves in this city and its neighbourhood, comprising those at work on the publick buildings, the canal, and the coal pits, was considerable. These might be assembled in a few hours, and could only be opposed by a respectable force, which force if the city was surprised, could not be collected in a short time. The probability was if their effort succeeded, we should see the town in flames, its inhabitants butchered, and a scene of horror extending through the country. This spectable it is true, would be momentary only, for as soon as a body of militia could be formed the insurrection would be suppressed. The superiority in point of numbers, in the knowledge and use of arms, and indeed every other species of knowledge which the whites have over the blacks in this Commonwealth is so decisive, that the latter could only sustain themselves for a moment in a rebellion against the former. Still it was a crisis to be avoided so far as prudent precautions could accomplish it. There was one other consideration which engaged the mind in the commencement of this affair from which it was not easy to withdraw it. It seemed strange that the slaves should embark in this novel and unexampled enterprise of their own accord. Their treatment has been more favorable since the revolution, and as the importation was prohibited among the first acts of our independence, their number has not increased in proportion with that of the whites. It was natural to suspect they were prompted to it by others who were invisible, but whose agency might be powerful. And if this was the case it became proportionally more difficult to estimate the extent of the combination, and the consequent real importance of the crisis. On consideration of all these circumstances it was deemed necessary to call out such a force as might be fully adequate to the emergency; such an one as would be likely to overawe and keep down the spirit of insurrection, or sufficient to suppress it in case it broke out. On that principle I called into service on the 9th the 19th and 23d regiments, and a detachment of fifty men, additional, from the 33d; which detachment with the whole of the 19th regiment and one hundred men of the 23d, were ordered to take post in this city. The residue of the 23d were stationed in the town of Manchester. While there was a hope the report of this conspiracy was unfounded, or a possibility of controlling it in silence, that object was pursued with zeal. But as its existence had become known to the publick, it only remained to make the incident as harmless in other respects as circumstances would permit. Having with a view to the publick safety, called out a respectable force, I was resolved to derive from it all the aid it could yield in reference to the objects contemplated. It was paraded daily on the Capitol square, and trained as well that it might be prepared for action if occasion required, as that our strength might be known to the conspirators. The effect which this measure produced was easily and soon perceived. It was evident that the collection and display of this force inspired the citizens with confidence, and depressed the spirits of the slaves. The former saw in it a security from the danger which menaced them; the latter a defeat of their nefarious projects. On the 12th of September, five, and on the fifteenth following, five others were executed. On those occasions the whole force in service in the city (infantry and horse) attended the execution. On the 27th Gabriel, one of the chiefs of the conspiracy, for whom a reward had been offered, and who had been apprehended at Norfolk, was delivered up and committed to Jail. As these executions were carried into effect without any movement of the slaves, and their chief apprehended, it was fair to presume the danger of the crisis had passed. It became from that period the object of the Executive to diminish the force with a view to lessen the expense; which object was pursued with undeviating attention. On the 13th it was reduced to 650 men, including those at the Point of Fork. On the 16th to 225; occasional reductions were afterwards made, as circumstances permitted, till finally on the 18th of October, it was reduced to a Serjeant and twelve men at the Penitentiary, and a Corporal and six at the Jail, at which point it now stands. You will receive herewith a copy of the documents which illustrate the transaction, with a report from the Auditor of the expenses attending it: to which is added a letter from the Treasurer, communicating an opinion of the Attorney General respecting payment for some of the slaves who were executed. I cannot too much commend the conduct of the Militia on this occasion. They were obedient to order, exact in their discipline, and prompt in their execution of every duty that was enjoined on them. Their improvement was rapid and far exceeded anything I had ever witnessed. Nor can it be doubted, had a crisis occurred, they would have proved as firm and decisive in action, as they were patient and perservering in the discharge of every other duty. Their example teaches a useful lesson to our country. It tends to confirm the favorable idea before entertained of their competence to every purpose of publick safety. It belongs to the Legislature to weigh with profound attention, this unpleasant incident in our history. What has happened may occur again at any time, with more fatal consequences, unless suitable measures be taken to prevent it. Unhappily while this class of people exists among us we can never count with certainty on its tranquil submission. The fortunate issue of the late attempt should not lull us into repose. It ought rather to stimulate us to the adoption of a system, which if it does not prevent the like in future, may secure the country from any calamitous consequences.

2. CONFESSIONS OF BEN, ALIAS BEN WOOLFOLK, 17 SEPTEMBER 1800

The first time I ever heard of this conspiricy was from Mrs. Ann Smith's George; the second person that gave me information was Samuel alias Samuel Bird, the property of Mrs. Jane Clarke. They asked me last spring to come over to their houses on a Friday night. It was late before I could get there; the company had met and dispersed. I inquired where they were gone, and was informed to see their wives. I went after them and found George; he carried me and William (the property of William Young) to Sam Bird's, and after we got there he (Sam) enquired of George if he had any pen and ink; he said no—he had left it at home. He brought out his list of men, and he had Elisha Price's Jim, James Price's Moses, Sally Price's Bob, Denny Wood's Emanuel. After this George invited me to come and see him the next night, but I did not go. The following Monday night William went over and returned with a ticket for me; likewise one for Gilbert. The Thursday night following, both George and Sam Bird came to see me. Bowler's Jack was with us. We conversed untill late in the night upon the subject of the meditated war. George said he would try to be ready by the 24th of August, and the following Sunday he went to Hungry meeting-house to enlist men. When I saw him again he informed me he had enlisted 37 men there. The Sunday

after he went to Manchester, where he said he had recruited 50-odd men. I
never saw him again untill the sermon at my house, which was about three
weeks before the rising was to take place. On the day of the sermon, George
called on Sam Bird to inform how many men he had; he said he had not his
list with him, but he supposed about 500. George wished the business to be
deferred some time longer. Mr. Prosser's Gabriel wished to bring on the
business as soon as possible. Gilbert said the summer was almost over, and he
wished them to enter upon the business before the weather got too cold.
Gabriel proposed that the subject should be referred to his brother Martin to
decide upon. Martin said there was this expression in the Bible, delays breed
danger; at this time, he said, the country was at peace, the soldiers were discharged, and the arms all put away; there was no patroling in the country,
and that before he would any longer bear what he had borne, he would turn
out and fight with his stick. Gilbert said he was ready with his pistol, but it
was in need of repair; he gave it to Gabriel, who was [to] put it in order for
him. I then spoke to the company and informed them I wished to have something to say. I told them that I had heard in the days of old, when the Israel-
ites were in service to King Pharoah, they were taken from him by the power
of God, and were carried away by Moses. God had blessed him with an angel
to go with him, but that I could see nothing of that kind in these days. Martin
said in reply: I read in my Bible where God says if we will worship Him we
should have peace in all our land; five of you shall conquer an hundred, and
a hundred a thousand of our enemies. After this they went on consultation
upon the time they should execute the plan. Martin spoke and appointed for
them to meet in three weeks, which was to be of a Saturday night. Gabriel
said he had 500 bullets made. Smith's George said he was done the corn and
would then go on to make as many cross-bows as he could. Bowler's Jack said
he had got 50 spiers or bayonets fixed at the end of sticks. The plan was to be
as follows: We were all to meet at the briery spot on the Brook; 100 men were
to stand at the Brook bridge; Gabriel was to take 100 more and go to Greg-
ory's tavern and take the arms which were there; 50 more were to be sent to
Rocketts to set that on fire, in order to alarm the upper part of the town and
induce the people to go down there; while they were employed in extinguish-
ing the fire Gabriel and the other officers and soldiers were to take the Capitol and all the arms they could find and be ready to slaughter the people on
their return from Rocketts. Sam Bird was to have a pass as a free man and was
to go to the nation of Indians called Catawbas to persuade them to join the
negroes to fight the white people. As far as I understood all the whites were
to be massacred, except the Quakers, the Methodists, and the Frenchmen,
and they were to be spared on account as they conceived of their being

friendly to liberty, and also they had understood that the French were at war with this country for the money that was due them, and that an army was landed at South Key, which they hoped would assist them. They intended also to spare all the poor white women who had no slaves.

The above communications are put down precisely as delivered to us by Ben, alias Ben Woolfolk. Given under our hands this 17th day of September, 1800.

GERVAS STORRS,
JOSEPH SELDEN.

Ben, alias Ben Woolfolk, sentenced to death for conspiracy and insurrection Sept. 16th, pardoned Sept. 18th.

3. TRIAL OF GABRIEL, OCTOBER 1800

At a Court of Oyer and Terminer held for the county of Henrico on Monday, the sixth day of October, 1800, for the trial of Gabriel, a negro man slave, the property of Thomas Henry Prosser, of the said county, charged with conspiracy and insurrection, the said Gabriel was convicted and condemned to execution on Tuesday, the seventh day of October, 1800.

Prosor's Ben—Gabriel was appointed Captain at first consultation respecting the Insurrection, and afterwards when he had enlisted a number of men was appointed General. That they were to kill Mr. Prosser, Mr. Mosby, and all the neighbors, and then proceed to Richmond, where they would kill everybody, take the treasury, and divide the money amongst the soldiers; after which he would fortify Richmond and proceed to discipline his men, as he apprehended force would be raised elsewhere to repel him. That if the white people agreed to their freedom they would then hoist a white flag, and he would dine and drink with the merchants of the city on the day when it should be agreed to.

Gabriel enlisted a number of negroes. The prisoner went with the witness to Mr. Young's to see Ben Woolfolk, who was going to Caroline to enlist men there. He gave three shillings for himself and three other negroes, to be expended in recruiting men.

The prisoner made the handles of the swords, which were made by Solomon. The prisoner shewed the witness a quantity of bullets, nearly a peck, which he and Martin had run, and some lead then on hand, and he said he had ten pounds of powder which he had purchased. Gabriel said he had nearly 10,000 men; he had 1,000 in Richmond, about 600 in Caroline, and nearly 500 at the Coal pits, besides others at different places, and that he expected the poor white people would also join him, and that two Frenchmen had actually joined, whom he said Jack Ditcher knew, but whose names he would not mention to the witness. That the prisoner had enlisted nearly all the negroes in town as he said, and amongst them had 400 Horsemen. That in consequence of the bad weather on Saturday night, an agreement was made to meet at the Tobacco House of Mr. Prosser the ensuing night. Gabriel said all the negroes from Petersburg were to join him after he had commenced the Insurrection.

Mr. Price's John—He saw the prisoner at a meeting, who gave a general invitation to the negro men to attend at the Spring to drink grog. That when there he mentioned the Insurrection, and proposed that all present should join them in the same, and meet in 3 weeks for the purpose of carrying the same into effect, and enjoined several of the negroes then present to use the best of their endeavors in enlisting men, and to meet according to the time appointed.

Ben. Woolfolk—The prisoner was present at the meeting at Mr. Young's, who came to get persons to join him to carry on the war against the white people. That after meeting they adjourned to the Spring and held a consultation, when it was concluded that in 3 weeks the business should commence. Gabriel said he had 12 dozen swords made, and had worn out 2 pair of bullet moulds in running bullets, and pulling a third pair out of his pocket, observed that was nearly worn out. That Bob Cooley and Mr. Tinsley's Jim was to let them into the Capitol to get the arms out. That the lower part of the Town towards Rocketts was to be fired, which would draw forth the citizens (that part of the town being of little value); this would give an opportunity to the negroes to seize on the arms and ammunition, and then they would commence the attack upon them. After the assembling of the negroes near Prosser's, and previous to their coming to Richmond, a company was to be sent to Gregorie's Tavern to take possession of some arms there deposited. The prisoner said, at the time of meeting the witness at Mr. Young's, that he had the evening before received six Guns—one of which he had delivered to Col. Wilkinson's Sam. That he was present when Gabriel was appointed General and Geo. Smith second in command. That none were to be spared of the whites except Quakers, Methodists, and French people. The prisoner and Gilbert concluded to purchase a piece of silk for a flag, on which they would have written "death or Liberty," and they would kill all except as before excepted, unless they agreed to the freedom of the Blacks, in which case they would at least cut off one of their arms. That the prisoner told the witness that Bob Cooley had told him if he would call on him about a week before the time of the Insurrection he would untie the key of the room in which the arms and ammunition were kept at the

Capitol and give it to him, or if he did not come, then on the night of the Insurrection being commenced, he would hand him arms out as fast as he could arm his men, and that he had on a Sunday previous to this, been shown by Cooley every room in the Capitol.

4. GOVERNOR WINTHROP SARGENT TO SLAVEHOLDERS IN MISSISSIPPI TERRITORY, 16 NOVEMBER 1800

His Excellency the Governour was pleased to write the following Letter, and in pursuance of his direction, near one hundred Printed Copies of it, were addressed to Respectable Characters, and slave holders, within the Mississippi Territory.

Mississippi Territory
Grove Plantation Novr. 16th 1800

Sir,

I believe it a Duty to Communicate to the Officers of the Territory, and Slave-holders within the *same*, that an *intended* Insurrection amongst the Negroes of Virginia, (in which fifty thousand were to have rose in Arms) is said to have been lately discovered, and that six of the *Principal Blacks* are already Executed at *Richmond*—but my Correspondent observes, that this alarming Business *probably* had its origin in *foreign* influence, and was intended to extend throughout the United States—to reiterate the horrid scenes of Rapine and Murders, which have been Practised in the French Islands—though the Chief and Villanous agents had not been detected at the time of his writing.

It is almost unnecessary sir, after the preface of this interesting Communication to Recommend, to your prudence and understanding the utmost Vigilance to your *own* and the slaves of your neighbours—or to suggest the impolicy of unnecessarily alarming *them*, by informations upon a *subject* which mild and wise Treatment may happily long keep from their Views and wishes.

Violent assaults upon the overseers of Mr. Lintots and Mr. Moores slaves, and the severely wounding one or both, I believe may be *judiciously* urged as the motive for extraordinary Circumspection in the present Moment, and to Completely enforce the Law against slaves retaining any Kind of Weapons.

Upon this occasion it seems more than usually incumbent upon me to demand from the officers Civil and Military—and all good Citizens, according to their Respective Duties, to use their best endeavours to produce perfect submission to the statutes for the Regulation of slaves within the Mississippi Territory.

They will please to Remember that upon Saturday Evenings and sundays when the Negroes of different Plantations assemble, devising means for excess in strong drink and frequently mixing with *such* as have of late been introduced amongst us (some of whom, it is more than probable have been actors in the Bloody scenes that have already devastated whole Countries,) we should take extraordinary care to provide against impending Mischief: —Their Quakers and places of Rendezvous should at such times be particularly attended to by the proper persons—and in the approaching holydays, and whenever *indeed* it may be deemed necessary, the Military Officers will be pleased to use the Ample Provision of Patrols and Guards which the General Orders have Authorized to their discretion.

Characters arriving within the Territory, whose pursuits are doubtful should be immediately reported to the Governour—or some of the Officers in Commission for enquiry and investigation.

A strict observance of such Rule might be the happy preventative means of much and *fatal* Evils.

5. FREDERICKSBURG VIRGINIA HERALD, 23 SEPTEMBER 1800

This dreadful conspiracy originates with some vile French Jacobins, aided and abetted by some of our own profligate and abandoned democrats. Liberty and equality have brought the evil upon us. A doctrine which, however intelligible, and admissible, in a land of freemen, is not only unintelligible and inadmissible, but dangerous and extremely wicked in this country, where every white man is a master and every black man is a slave. This doctrine, in this country, and in every country like this (as the horrors of St. Domingo have already proved) cannot fail of producing either a general insurrection, or a general emancipation. It has been most impudently propogated for several years at our tables while our servants were standing behind our chairs. It has been preached from the pulpits, Methodists and Baptists alike without reserve. Democrats have talked it, what else then could we expect except what has happened? There can be no compromise between liberty and slavery. The man who thinks so is a fool. . . . There is no middle course we must either abolish slavery or continue it. . . . If we continue it, it must be restricted, all the vigorous laws must be reenacted which experience has proved necessary to keep it within bounds. . . . If we will keep a ferocious monster within our country, we must keep him in chains, no one would turn a lion or a tiger out in the streets.—Slavery is a monster,—most horrible of all monsters,—tyranny, excepted. Democracy, therefore, in Virginia is like virtue in Hell. The Ethiopian can never be washed white.

The slaveholder can never be a Democrat. He who affects to be a Democrat and at the same time is a slaveholder is a devil incarnate. He tells a damnable diabolical lie in the face of day, which his own conscious revolts at, the moment he utters it, and which he knows every man of truth, of common sense, of common honesty must turn from with horror.

6. GOVERNOR MONROE TO PRESIDENT JEFFERSON, RICHMOND, 15 JUNE 1801

Sir,—I enclose you a resolution of the General Assembly of this Commonwealth, of the last Session, by which it is made my duty to correspond with you on the subject of obtaining by purchase lands without the limits of this State, to which persons obnoxious to the laws or dangerous to the peace of society may be removed. This resolution was produced by the conspiracy of the slaves which took place in this city and neighbourhood last year, and is applicable to that description of persons only. The idea of such an acquisition was suggested by motives of humanity, it being intended by means thereof to provide an alternate mode of punishment for those described by the resolution, who under the existing law might be doomed to suffer death. It was deemed more humane, and it is hoped would be found in practice not less expedient, to transport such offenders beyond the limits of the State.

It seems to be the more obvious intention of the Legislature, as inferred from the resolution, to make the proposed acquisition of land, in the vacant western territory of the United States, but it does not appear to me to preclude one without the limits of the Union. If a friendly power would designate a tract of country within its jurisdiction, either on this Continent or a neighbouring Island, to which we might send such persons, it is not improbable the Legislature might prefer. In any event an alternative could not otherwise than be desirable, since after maturely weighing the conditions and advantages of each position the Legislature might still prefer that which appeared to it most eligible.

It is proper to remark that the latter part of the resolution which proposes the removal of such persons as are dangerous to the peace of society, may be understood as comprizing many to whom the preceding member does not apply. Whether the Legislature intended to give it a more extensive import, or rather whether it contemplated removing from the Country any but Culprits who were condemned to suffer death, I will not undertake to decide. But if the more enlarged construction of the resolution is deemed the true one, it furnishes in my opinion, a strong additional motive, why the Legislature, in disposing of this great concern should command an alternative of places. As soon as the mind emerges, in contemplating the subject, beyond the contracted scale of providing a mode of punishment for offenders, vast and interesting objects present themselves to view. It is impossible not to revolve in it, the condition of those people, the embarrassment they have already occasioned us, and are still likely to subject us to. We perceive an existing evil which commenced under our Colonial System, with which we are not properly chargeable, or if at all not in the present degree, and we acknowledge the extreme difficulty of remedying it. At this point the mind rests with suspense, and surveys with anxiety obstacles which become more serious as we approach them. It is in vain for the Legislature to deliberate on the subject, in the extent of which it is capable, with a view to adopt the system of policy which appears to it most wise and just, if it has not the means of executing it. To lead to a sound decision and make the result a happy one, it is necessary that the field of practicable expedients be opened to its election, on the widest possible scale.

Under this view of the subject I shall be happy to be advised by you whether a tract of land in the Western territory of the United States can be procured for this purpose, in what quarter, and on what terms? And also whether any friendly power will permit us to remove such persons within its limits, with like precision as to the place and conditions? It is possible a friendly power may be disposed to promote a population of the kind referred to, and willing to facilitate the measure by co-operating with us in the accomplishment of it. It may be convenient for you to sound such persons especially those more immediately in your neighbourhood, on the subject, in all the views which may appear to you to be suitable.

You will perceive that I invite your attention to a subject of great delicacy and importance, one which in a peculiar degree involves the future peace, tranquility and happiness of the good people of this Commonwealth. I do it, however, in a confidence, you will take that interest in it, which we are taught to expect from your conduct through life, which gives you so many high claims to our regard.

7. PRESIDENT JEFFERSON TO GOVERNOR MONROE, WASHINGTON, 24 NOVEMBER 1801

Dear Sir,—I had not been unmindful of your letter of June 15, covering a resolution of the House of Representatives of Virginia, and referred to in yours of the 17th inst. The importance of the subject, and the belief that it gave us time for consideration till the next meeting of the Legislature, have induced me to defer the answer to this date. You will perceive that some circumstances connected with the subject, & necessarily presenting themselves to view, would be improper but for yours' & the legislative ear. Their publication might have an ill effect in more than one quarter. In confidence of attention to this, I shall indulge greater freedom in writing.

Common malefactors, I presume, make no part of the object of that resolution. Neither their numbers, nor the nature of their offences, seem to require any provisions beyond those practised heretofore, & found adequate to the repression of ordinary crimes. Conspiracy, insurgency, treason, rebellion, among that description of persons who brought on us the alarm, and on themselves the tragedy, of 1800, were doubtless within the view of every one; but many perhaps contemplated, and one expression of the resolution might comprehend, a much larger scope. Respect to both opinions makes it my duty to understand the resolution in all the extent of which it is susceptible.

The idea seems to be to provide for these people by a purchase of lands; and it is asked whether such a purchase can be made of the U S in their western territory? A very great extent of country, north of the Ohio, has been laid off into townships and is now at market, according to the provisions of the acts of Congress, with which you are acquainted. There is nothing which would restrain the State of Virginia either in the purchase or the application of these lands; but a purchase, by the acre, might perhaps be a more expensive provision than the H of Representatives contemplated. Questions would also arise whether the establishment of such a colony within our limits, and to become a part of our union, would be desirable to the State of Virginia itself, or to the other States—especially those who would be in its vicinity?

Could we procure lands beyond the limits of the U S to form a receptacle for these people? On our northern boundary, the country not occupied by British subjects, is the property of Indian nations, whose title would be to be extinguished, with the consent of Great Britain; & the new settlers would be British subjects. It is hardly to be believed that either Great Britain or the Indian proprietors have so disinterested a regard for us, as to be willing to relieve us, by receiving such a colony themselves; and as much to be doubted whether that race of men could long exist in so rigorous a climate. On our western & southern frontiers, Spain holds an immense country, the occupancy of which, however, is in the Indian natives, except a few insolated spots possessed by Spanish subjects. It is very questionable, indeed, whether the Indians would sell? whether Spain would be willing to receive these people? and nearly certain that she would not alienate the sovereignty. The same question to ourselves would recur here also, as did in the first case: should we be willing to have such a colony in contact with us? However our present interests may restrain us within our own limits, it is impossible not to look forward to distant times, when our rapid multiplication will expand itself beyond those limits, & cover the whole northern, if not the southern continent, with a people speaking the same language, governed in similar forms, & by similar laws; nor can we contemplate with satisfaction either blot or mixture on that surface. Spain, France, and Portugal hold possessions on the southern continent, as to which I am not well enough informed to say how far they might meet our views. But either there or in the northern continent, should the constituted authorities of Virginia fix their attention, of preference, I will have the dispositions of those powers sounded in the first instance.

The West Indies offer a more probable & practicable retreat for them. Inhabited already by a people of their own race & color; climates congenial with their natural constitution; insulated from the other descriptions of men; nature seems to have formed these islands to become the receptacle of the blacks transplanted into this hemisphere. Whether we could obtain from the European sovereigns of those islands leave to send thither the persons under consideration, I cannot say; but I think it more probable than the former propositions, because of their being already inhabited more or less by the same race. The most promising portion of them is the island of St. Domingo, where the blacks are established into a sovereignty *de facto*, & have organized themselves under regular laws and government. I should conjecture that their present ruler might be willing, on many considerations, to receive even that description which would be exiled for acts deemed criminal by us, but meritorious, perhaps, by him. The possibility that these exiles might stimulate & conduct vindictive or predatory descents on our coasts & facilitate concert with their brethren remaining here, looks to a state of things between that island & us not probable on a contemplation of our relative strength, and of the disproportion daily growing; and it is overweighed by the humanity of the measures proposed, & the advantages of disembarrassing ourselves of such dangerous characters. Africa would offer a last & undoubted resort, if all others more desirable should fail us. Whenever the Legislature of Virginia shall have brought it's mind to a point, so that I may know exactly what to propose to foreign authorities, I will execute their wishes with fidelity & zeal.

8. GOVERNOR MONROE TO PRESIDENT JEFFERSON, RICHMOND, 13 FEBRUARY 1802

Sir,—I enclose you some resolutions of the General Assembly of this Commonwealth, passed at its last session explanatory of a resolution of the preceding session authorizing a correspondence with you relative to the purchase of lands without the limits of the State, to which persons obnoxious to the laws or dangerous to the peace of society might be removed. You will recollect that as the precise import of the first resolution was not clearly understood, it was though proper to submit our communication on it to the General Assembly, that its object and policy might be more accurately defined. The resolutions which I have now the pleasure to communicate to you have removed all doubt on that subject, by confining the attention in procuring the asylum sought to the accommodation of negroes only, and by specifying for what causes, under what circumstances, and (in the case of felons) to what countries it is wished to send them. You will be pleased to observe that there are two descriptions of negroes embraced by these resolutions, the first comprizes those who being slaves may commit certain enumerated crimes. For *such* an asylum is preferred on the continent of Africa or the Spanish or Portuguese settlements in South America. The second respects free negroes and mulattoes, including those who may hereafter be emancipated and sent, or choose to remove to such place as may be acquired. For *these* a preference is not expressed in favor of any particular region or country, nor is the right of sovereignty over such place desired. In removing these people without our limits, no restraint is imposed to preclude the attainment of an asylum anywhere, whereby the object of the State might be defeated, or to prevent that attention to their interests in case an alternative of places is presented, by inhibiting a preference for *that* which may be deemed best adapted to their constitution, genius, and character.

I have therefore to request that you will be so good as to endeavor to promote the views of the State in these important respects; being satisfied that they are founded in a policy equally wise and humane, with respect to ourselves, and the people who are the object of it.

9. PRESIDENT JEFFERSON TO GOVERNOR MONROE, WASHINGTON, 2 JUNE 1802

Dear Sir,—I observe that the resolution of the legislature of Virginia of Jan. 23 in desiring us to look out for some proper place to which insurgent negroes may be sent, expresses a preference of the continent of Africa, or some of the Spanish or Portuguese settlements in S. America: in which preference, and especially as to the former, I entirely concur. On looking towards Africa for our objects the British establishment at Sierra Leone at once presents itself. You know that that establishment was undertaken by a private company and was first suggested by the suffering state of the blacks, who were carried over to England during the revolutionary war, and who were perishing [*illegible*] and misery in the streets of London. A number of benevolent persons subscribed for the establishment of a company who might carry these people to the coast of Africa, and there employ them usefully for themselves, and indemnify the company by commercial operations: Sierre Leone was fixed on as the place, the blacks then in England were carried thither, and a vessel or vessels sent to Nova Scotia which carried to the same place the blacks who had gone to that country. The settlement is consequently composed of negroes formerly inhabitants of the southern states of our union. Having asked a conversation om this subject with Mr. Thornton the British chargé des affaires here, he informs me the establishment is prosperous, and he thinks there will be no objection on the part of the company to receive blacks from us, not of the character of common felons, but guilty of insurgency only, provided they are sent as free persons, the principles of their institution admitting no slavery among them. I propose, therefore, if it meets your approbation, to write to Mr. King our minister in London to propose this matter to the Sierre Leone company who are resident in London and if leave can be obtained to send black insurgents there, to inquire further whether the regulations of the place would permit us to carry or take there any mercantile objects which by affording some commercial profit, might defray the expenses of the transportation. As soon as I can be favored with your sentiments on this proposition and your approbation of it I will write to Mr. King that we may have the matter finally arranged. Should any mercantile operation be permitted to be combined with the transportation of these persons, so as to lessen or to pay the expense, it might then become eligible to make that the asylum for the other description also, to wit, the freed slaves and persons of color. If not permitted, so distant a colonization of them would perhaps be thought too expensive. But while we are ascertaining this point, we may be making inquiry what other suitable places may be found in the West Indies, or the southern continent of America, so as to have some other resource provided if the one most desirable should be unattainable. In looking out for another place we should prefer placing them with whatever power is least likely to become an enemy, and to use the knowledge of these exiles in predatory expeditions against us. Portugal and Holland would be of this character. But I wish to have your sentiments on both branches of the subject before I commit it by an actual step.

10. GOVERNOR MONROE TO PRESIDENT JEFFERSON, RICHMOND, 11 JUNE 1802

Sir,—I find by your letter of the 3d that you think Sierra Leone, on the coast of Africa, a suitable place for the establishment of our insurgent slaves, that it may also become so for those who are or may hereafter be emancipated, and that you are disposed to obtain the assent of the company to such a measure through our minister in London, while your attention will be directed in the interim to such other quarters as may enable us to submit a more enlarged field to the option of our Assembly. By the information of Mr. Thornton, the British chargé des affaires, which you have been so kind as to communicate, it appears that slavery is prohibited in that settlement, hence it follows that we cannot expect permission to send any who are not free to it. In directing our attention to Africa for an Asylum for insurgents it is strongly implied that the Legislature intended they should be free when landed there, as it is not known that there exists any market on that coast for the purchase of slaves from other countries. Still I am persuaded that such was not the intention of the Legislature, as it would put culprits in a better condition than the deserving part of those people. This opinion is further supported by a law still in force which authorizes the Executive to sell, subject to transportation, all slaves who are guilty of that crime. I submit this idea to your consideration not with a view to prevent your application to the company for its assent to the settlement within its limits, but as a motive in case you concur with me in the above construction of the resolution, why you should more particularly seek an establishment for them in the Portuguese, Dutch or Spanish settlements in America. In obtaining permission to send our negroes to that settlement we may avail ourselves of it on the principles of the company as far as it suits our interest and policy.

If the Legislature intends that insurgents shall enjoy their liberty on landing there, the accommodation would be general; but if they are excluded and the door is opened on favorable conditions to such only as are or may hereafter become free, it will nevertheless be important as it will give the Legislature an opportunity to deliberate on and perhaps provide a remedy for an evil which has already become a serious one. I cannot otherwise than highly approve the idea of endeavoring to lighten the charge of transportation to the publick, wheresoever they may be sent. A permission to send certain articles of merchandize, which would be sure to command a profit, if that could be relied on, would contribute much to that end. Perhaps other means not incompatible with the charter of the company might be devised. Do their regulations permit temporary servitude? If they do, might not those who are sent (hereafter to be emancipated) be bound to service for a few years, as the means of raising a fund to defray the charge of transportation? The ancestors of the present negroes were brought from Africa and sold here as slaves, they and their descendants for ever. If we send back any of the race subject to a temporary servitude with liberty to their descendants will not the policy be mild and benevolent?

May not the same idea be held in view in reference to any other place in which an establishment is sought for them? I do not know that such an arrangement would be practicable in any country, but it would certainly be a very fortunate attainment if we could make these people instrumental to their own emancipation, by a process gradual and certain, on principles consistent with humanity, without expense or inconvenience to ourselves.

23. Traveling in America

Even before the turmoil of the Revolution had settled, America was besieged by curious European travelers anxious to find out what kind of people these new republicans were. In the decades following the Revolution the number of published travel accounts multiplied beyond belief, as all kinds and classes of Europeans—English, French, and German—poked and probed into the manners and characteristics of the new society, seeking answers to the promise or the ominousness of the future. Nothing angered Americans more than the hasty, overweening, and contemptuous judgments about America found in many of these travelers' journals. America, the travelers had discovered, was not Europe, and this conclusion seemed to compel them to point up every eccentricity, every absence of civilized life in the United States.

One of the most amusing retorts to these "travelmongers" can be found among the essays of *Salmagundi,* the collaborative literary venture of Washington Irving, James Kirke Paulding, and William Irving, Washington's older brother, written in New York throughout the year 1807. *Salmagundi* was a delightful burlesque in which nothing seemed beyond satire and humor. Even its format was a parody of the traditional eighteenth-century didactic English periodical. The essays were an immediate success and were subsequently republished in many editions. At one point eight hundred copies were sold in a day—a record for that time. While ranging over various aspects of American culture, *Salmagundi* paid considerable attention to traveling and expressed good-natured resentment of the fault-finding arrogance of European accounts of America. Yet, for all of its vexation with the travelers' portrayals, *Salmagundi* itself could not help mocking the barrenness and disorder of American life. In the end *Salmagundi* represents the cultural frustration and the provincial dilemma felt by enlightened and polished but proud and devoted Americans.

The *Salmagundi* essays were a joint production with Washington Irving and Paulding, both in their twenties, doing the major share of the writing. The "Jeremy Cockloft" pieces, reprinted here, were probably Washington Irving's work. Although often labeled a Federalist for his satirical attacks on Jeffersonian rationalism, Irving spent as much time making fun of the social pretensions of the Federalist aristocracy.

Salmagundi

WASHINGTON IRVING

MEMORANDUMS FOR A TOUR TO BE ENTITLED "THE STRANGER IN NEW JERSEY: OR, COCKNEY TRAVELING."

BY JEREMY COCKLOFT, THE YOUNGER

CHAPTER I.

THE man in the moon—preparations for departure—hints to traveller about packing their trunks—straps, buckles, and bed-cords—case of pistols, *à la cockney*—five trunks, three bandboxes, a cocked hat, and a medicine-chest, *à la Française*—parting advice of my two sisters—*quere*, why old maids are so particular in their cautions against naughty women—description of Powles-Hook ferry-boats—might be converted into gunboats, and defend our ports equally well with Albany sloops—BROM, the black ferryman—Charon—river Styx—ghosts;—Major Hunt—good story—ferriage nine-pence,—city of Harsimus—built on the spot where the folk once danced on their stumps, while the devil fiddled—*quere*, why do the Harsimites talk Dutch?—story of the Tower of Babel, and confusion of tongues—get into the stage—driver a wag—famous fellow for running stage races—killed three passengers and crippled nine in the course of his practice —philosophical reasons why stage-drivers love grog—causeway—ditch on each side for folk to tumble into—famous place for *skilly-pots*; Philadelphians call 'em tarapins—roast them under the ashes as we do potatoes—query, may not this be the reason that the Philadelphians are all turtle-heads?—Hackensack bridge—good painting of a blue horse jumping over a mountain—wonder who it was painted by;—mem. to ask the *Baron de Gusto* about it on my return;—Rattle-snake Hill, so called from abounding with butterflies;—salt marsh, *surmounted* here and there by a solitary hay-stack— more tarapins—wonder why the Philadelphians don't establish a fishery here, and get a patent for it—bridge over the Passaic—rate of toll—description of toll-boards—tollman had but one eye—story how it *is possible* he *may* have lost the other—pence-table, etc.

William Irving, James Kirke Paulding, and Washington Irving, *Salmagundi; or the Whim-Whams and Opinions of Launcelot Langstaff, Esq., and Others* [1807] (New York, 1865), pp. 74–82, 201–209, 237–245.

CHAPTER II.

Newark—noted for its fine breed of fat musquitoes—sting through the thickest boots—story about *Gallynippers*—Archy Gifford and his man Caliban—jolly fat fellows—a knowing traveller always judges of everything by the inn-keepers and waiters—set down Newark people all fat as butter—learned dissertation on Archy Gifford's green coat, with philosophical reasons why the Newarkites wear red worsted nightcaps, and turn their noses to the south when the wind blows—Newark academy full of windows—sunshine excellent to make little boys grow—Elizabethtown—fine girls—vile mosquitoes—plenty of oysters—quere, have oysters any feeling?—good story about the fox catching them by his tail—ergo, foxes might be of great use in the pearl fishery—landlord member of the legislature—treats everybody who has a vote—mem. all the inn-keepers members of the legislature in New Jersey; Bridge-town, vulgarly called *Spank-town*, from a story of quondam parson and his wife—real name, according to Linkum Fidelius, Bridge-town, from *bridge*, a contrivance to get dry shod over a river or brook; and *town*, an appelation given in America to the accidental assemblage of a church, a tavern, and a blacksmith's shop—Linkum as right as my left leg;—Rahway River—good place for gunboats —wonder why Mr. Jefferson don't send a *river fleet* here, to protect the hay-vessels?—Woodbridge—landlady mending her husband's breeches—sublime apostrophe to conjugal affection and the fair sex;—Woodbridge famous for its crab-fishery—sentimental correspondence between a crab and a lobster—digression to Abelarde and Eloisa;—mem. when the moon is in *Pisces*, she plays the devil with the crabs.

CHAPTER III.

Brunswick—oldest town in the state—division line between two counties in the middle of the street;—posed a lawyer with the case of a man standing with one foot in each county—wanted to know in which he was *domicil*— lawyer couldn't tell for the soul of him;—mem. all the New Jersey lawyers *nums*;—Miss Hay's boarding-school—young ladies not allowed to eat mustard—and why?—fat story of a mustard-pot, with a good saying of Ding-Dong's;—Vernon's tavern—fine place to sleep, if the noise would let you— another Caliban!—Vernon *slew*-eyed—people of Brunswick, of course, all squint;—Drake's tavern—fine old blade—wears square buckles in his shoes —tells bloody long stories about last war—people, of course, all do the same; —Hook'em Snivy, the famous fortune-teller, born here—contemporary with Mother Shoulders—particulars of his history—died one day—lines to his memory, *which found their way into my pocketbook;*—melancholy reflections on the death of great men—beautiful epitaph on myself.

CHAPTER IV.

Princeton—college—professors wear boots!—students famous for their love of a jest—set the college on fire, and burnt out the professors; an excellent joke, but not worth repeating—mem. American students very much addicted to burning down colleges—reminds me of a good story, nothing at all to the purpose—two societies in the college—good notion —encourages emulation, and makes little boys fight;—students famous for their eating and erudition—saw two at the tavern, who had just got their allowance of spending money—laid it all out in a supper—got fuddled, and d—d the professors for nincoms. N.B. Southern gentleman—Churchyard —apostrophe to grim death—saw a cow feeding on a grave—metempsychosis—who knows but the cow may have been eating up the soul of one of my ancestors—made me melancholy and pensive for fifteen minutes;—man planting cabbages—wondered how he could plant them so straight—method of mole-catching—and all that—query, whether it would not be a good notion to ring their noses as we do pigs'—mem. to propose it to the American Agricultural Society—get a premium perhaps—commencement—students give a ball and supper—company from New York, Philadelphia, and Albany —great contest which spoke the best English—Albanians vociferous in their demand for sturgeon—Philadelphians gave the preference to raccoon and splacnunes—gave them a long dissertation on the phlegmatic nature of a goose's gizzard—students can't dance—always set off with the wrong foot foremost—Duport's opinion on that subject—Sir Christopher Hatton the first man who ever turned out his toes in dancing—favorite with Queen Bess on that account—Sir Walter Raleigh—good story about his smoking— his descent into New Spain—El Dorado—Candide—Dr. Pangloss—Miss Cunegunde—earthquake at Lisbon—Baron of Thundertentronck—Jesuits —Monks—Cardinal Woolsey—Pope Joan—Tom Jefferson—Tom Paine, and Tom the ——whew! N.B. Students got drunk as usual.

CHAPTER V.

Left Princeton—country finely diversified with sheep and hay-stacks—saw a man riding alone in a wagon! why the deuce didn't the blockhead ride in a chair? fellow must be a fool—particular account of the construction of wagons, carts, wheelbarrows, and quail-traps—saw a large flock of crows—concluded there must be a dead horse in the neighborhood—mem. country remarkable for crows—won't let the horses die in peace—anecdote of a jury of crows—stopped to give the horses water—good-looking man came up and asked me if I had seen his wife? heavens! thought I, how strange it is that this virtuous man should ask *me* about his wife—story of Cain and Abel—stagedriver took a *swig*—mem. set down all the people as drunkards—old house had moss on the top—swallows built in the roof—better place than old men's beards—story about that—derivation of words *kippy, kippy, kippy,* and *shoo-pig*—negro driver could not write his own name—languishing state of literature in this country; philosophical inquiry of 'Sbidlikens, why the Americans are so much inferior to the nobility of Cheapside and Shore-ditch, and why they do not eat plum-pudding on Sundays—superfine reflections about anything.

CHAPTER VI.

Trenton—built above the head of navigation to encourage commerce—capital of the State—only wants a castle, a bay, and a mountain, a sea, and a volcano, to bear strong resemblance to the bay of Naples—supreme court sitting—fat chief justice—used to get asleep on the bench after dinner—gave judgment, I suppose, like Pilate's wife, from his dreams—reminded me of Justice Bridlegoose deciding by a throw of a die, and of the oracle of the holy bottle—attempted to kiss the chambermaid—boxed my ears till they rung like our theatre-bell—girl had lost one tooth—mem. all the American ladies prudes, and have bad teeth; Anacreon Moore's opinion on the matter. State-house—fine place to see the sturgeons jump up—quere, whether sturgeons jump up by an impulse of the tail, or whether they bounce up from the bottom by the elasticity of their noses. Linkum Fidelius of the latter opinion—I too—sturgeon's nose capital for tennis-balls—learnt that at school—went to a ball—negro wench principal musician! N.B. People of America have no fiddlers but females!—origin of the phrase, "fiddle of your heart"—reasons why men fiddle better than women; expedient of the Amazons who were expert at the bow; waiter at the city tavern—good story of his—nothing to the purpose—never mind—fill up my book like Carr—make it sell. Saw a democrat get into a stage followed by his dog. N.B. This town remarkable for dogs and democrats—superfine sentiment—good story from Joe Miller—ode to a piggin of butter—pensive meditations on a mouse-hole—make a book as clear as a whistle!

THE STRANGER IN PENNSYLVANIA.

BY JEREMY COCKLOFT, THE YOUNGER.

CHAPTER I.

Cross the Delaware—knew I was in Pennsylvania, because all the people were fat and looked like the statue of William Penn—Bristol—very remarkable for having nothing in it worth the attention of the traveller—saw Burlington on the opposite side of the river—fine place for pigeon-houses—and why?—Pennsylvania famous for barns—cattle in general better lodged than the farmers—barns appear to be built, as the old Roman peasant planted his trees, "for posterity and the immortal gods." Saw several fine bridges of two or three arches, built over dry places—wondered what could be the use of them—reminded me of the famous bridge at Madrid made of pine logs fastened together by ropes of walnut bark—strange that the people who have such a taste for bridges should not have taken advantage of this river to indulge in their favorite kind of architecture!—expressed my surprise to a fellow passenger, who observed to me with great gravity, "that nothing was more natural than that people who build bridges over dry places should neglect them where they are really necessary"—could not, for the head of me, see to the bottom of the man's reasoning—about half an hour after it struck me that he had been quizzing me a little—didn't care much about that—revenge myself by mentioning him in my book. Village of Washington—very pleasant, and remarkable for being built on each side of the road—houses all cast in the same mould—have a very Quakerish appearance, being built of stone, plastered and white-washed, and green doors, ornamented with brass knockers, kept very bright—saw several genteel young ladies scouring them —which was no doubt the reason of their brightness. Breakfasted at the Fox Chase—recommend this house to all gentlemen travelling for information, as the landlady makes the best buckwheat cakes in the whole world; and because it bears the same name with a play, written by a young gentleman of Philadelphia, which, notwithstanding its very considerable merit, was received at that city with indifference and neglect, because it had no puns in it. Frankfort *in the mud*—very picturesque town, situated on the edge of a pleasant swamp—or meadow, as they call it—houses all built of turf, cut in imitation of stone—poor substitute—took in a couple of Princeton students, who were going on to the southward, to tell their papas (or rather their mammas), what fine manly little boys they were, and how nobly they resisted the authority of the trustees—both pupils of Godwin and Tom

Paine—talked about the rights of man, the social compact, and the perfectibility of boys—hope their parents will whip them when they get home, and send them back to college without any spending money. Turnpike gates —direction to keep to the right, as the law directs—very good advice, in my opinion; but one of the students swore he had no idea of submitting to this kind of oppression, and insisted on the driver's taking the left passage, in order to show the world we were not to be imposed upon by such arbitrary rules—driver, who, I believe, had been a student at Princeton himself, shook his head like a professor, and said it would not do. Entered Philadelphia through the suburbs—four little markets in a herd—one turned into a school for young ladies—mem. young ladies early in the market here—pun—good.

CHAPTER II.

Very ill—confined to my bed with a violent fit of the *pun* mania—strangers always experience an attack of the kind on their first arrival, and undergo a *seasoning* as Europeans do in the West Indies. In my way from the stage-office to Renshaw's I was accosted by a good-looking young gentleman from New Jersey, who had caught the infection—he took me by the button and informed me of a contest that had lately taken place between a tailor and shoemaker about I forget what;—Snip was pronounced a fellow of great *capability*, a man of gentlemanly *habits*, who would doubtless *suit* everybody. The shoemaker *bristled* up at this, and *waxed* exceeding wroth—swore the tailor was but a *half-souled* fellow, and that it was to *shew* he was never *cut-out* for a gentleman. The *choler* of the tailor was up in an instant, he swore by his thimble that he would never *pocket* such an insult, but would *baste* any man who dared to repeat it.—Honest Crispin was now worked up to his proper *pitch*, and was determined to yield the tailor no *quarters;*—he vowed he would lose his *all* but what he would gain his *ends*. He resolutely held on to the *last*, and on his threatening to *backstrap* his adversary, the tailor was obliged to *sheer* off, declaring, at the same time, that he would have him *bound over*. The young gentleman, having finished his detail, gave a most obstreperous laugh, and hurried off to tell his story to somebody else—*Licentia punica*, as Horace observes—it did my business—I went home, took to my bed, and was two days confined with this singular complaint.

Having, however, looked about me with the Argus eyes of a traveller, I have picked up enough in the course of my walk from the stage-office to the hotel, to give a full and impartial account of this remarkable city. According to the good old rule, I shall begin with the etymology of its name, which according to Linkum Fidelius, Tom. LV. is clearly derived, either from the name of its first founder, viz. PHILO DRIPPING-PAN, or the singular taste of the Aborigines, who flourished there on his arrival. Linkum, who is as shrewd a fellow as any theorist or F.S.A. for peeping with a dark lantern into the lumber garret of antiquity, and lugging out all the trash which was left there for oblivion by our wiser ancestors, supports his opinion by a prodigious number of ingenious and inapplicable arguments; but particularly rests his position on the known fact, that Philo Dripping-pan was remarkable for his predilection to eating, and his love of what the learned Dutch call *doup*. Our erudite author likewise observes that the citizens are to this day noted for their love of "a sop in the pan," and their portly appearance, "except, indeed," continues he, "the young ladies, who are perfectly genteel in their dimensions—this, however, he ill-naturedly enough attributes to their eating pickles, and drinking vinegar.

The Philadelphians boast much of the situation and plan of their city, and well may they, since it is undoubtedly, as fair and square, and regular, and right angled, as any mechanical genius could possibly have made it. I am clearly of opinion that this hum drum regularity has a vast effect on the character of its inhabitants and even on their looks, "for you will observe," writes Linkum, "that they are an honest, worthy, square, good-looking, well-meaning, regular, uniform, straight-forward, clockwork, clear-headed, one-like-another, salubrious, upright, kind of people, who always go to work, methodically, never put the cart before the horse, talk like a book, walk mathematically, never turn but in right angles, think syllogistically, and pun theoretically, according to the genuine rules of Cicero and Dean Swift; —whereas the people of New York—God help them—tossed about over hills and dales, through lanes and alleys, and crooked streets—continually mounting and descending, turning and twisting—whisking off at tangents, and left-angle-triangles, just like their own queer, odd, topsy-turvy rantipole city, are the most irregular, crazy headed, quicksilver, eccentric, whim-whamsical set of mortals that ever were jumbled together in this uneven, villainous revolving globe, and are the very antipodeans to the Philadelphians."

The streets of Philadelphia are wide and straight, which is wisely ordered, for the inhabitants having generally crooked noses, and most commonly travelling hard after them, the good folks would soon *go to the wall*, in the crooked streets of our city. This fact of the crooked noses has not been hitherto remarked by any of our American travellers, but must strike every stranger of the least observation. There is, however, one place which I would recommend to all my fellow-citizens, who may come after me, as a promenade—I mean Dock street—the only street in Philadelphia that bears any resemblance to New York—how tender, how exquisite, are the feelings awakened in the breast of a traveller, when his eye encounters some object which reminds him of his far distant country! The pensive New Yorker, having drank his glass of porter, and smoked his cigar after dinner (by the way I would recommend Sheaff, as selling the best Philadelphia), may here direct his solitary steps and indulge in that mellow tenderness in which the sentimental Kotzebue erst delighted to wallow—he may recall the romantic scenery and graceful windings of Maiden Lane, and Pearl street, trace the tumultuous gutter in its harmonious meanderings, and almost fancy he beholds the moss-covered roof of the Bear Market, or the majestic steeple of St. Paul's towering to the clouds.—Perhaps, too, he may have left behind him some gentle fair one, who, all the live-long evening, sits pensively at the window, leaning on her elbows, and counting the lingering, lame and broken-winded moments that so tediously lengthen the hours which separate her from the object of her contemplations!—delightful Lethe of the soul—sunshine of existence—wife and children poking up the cheerful evening fire—paper windows, mud walls, love in a cottage—sweet sensibility—and all that.

Everybody has heard of the famous Bank of Pennsylvania, which, since the destruction of the tomb of Mausolus, and the Colossus of Rhodes, may fairly be estimated as one of the wonders of the world. My landlord thinks it unquestionably the finest building upon earth. The honest man has never seen the theatre in New York, or the new brick church at the head of Rector street, which, when finished, will beyond all doubt be infinitely superior to the Pennsylvania barns I noted before.

Philadelphia is a place of great trade and commerce—not but that it would have been much more so, that is had it been built on the site of New York: but as New York has engrossed its present situation, I think Philadelphia must be content to stand where it does at present—at any rate it is not Philadelphia's fault, nor is it any concern of mine, so I shall not make myself uneasy about the affair. Besides, to use Trim's argument, were that city to stand where New York does, it might perhaps have the misfortune to be called New York and not Philadelphia, which would be quite another matter, and this portion of my travels had undoubtedly been smothered before it was born—which would have been a thousand pities indeed.

Of the manufactures of Philadelphia, I can say but little, except that the people are famous for an excellent kind of confectionery, made from the drainings of sugar. The process is simple as any in Mrs. Glass's excellent and useful work (which I hereby recommend to the fair hands of all young

ladies, who are not occupied in reading Moore's poems)—you buy a pot—
put your molasses in your pot—(if you can beg, borrow, or steal your
molasses it will come much cheaper than if you buy it)—boil your molasses
to a proper consistency; but if you boil it too much, it will be none the better
for it—then pour it off and let it cool, or draw it out into little pieces about
nine inches long, and put it by for use. This manufacture is called by the
Bostonians *lasses candy*, by the New Yorkers, *cock-a-nee-nee*—but by the
polite Philadelphians, by a name utterly impossible to pronounce.

The Philadelphia ladies are some of them beautiful, some of them tolerably
good looking, and some of them, to say the truth, are not at all handsome.
They are, however, very agreeable in general, except those who are reckoned
witty, who, if I might be allowed to speak my mind, are very disagreeable,
particularly to young gentlemen, who are travelling for information. Being
fond of tea-parties, they are a little given to criticism—but are in general
remarkably discreet, and very industrious as I have been assured by some of
my friends. Take them all in all, however, they are much inferior to the
ladies of New York, as plainly appears, from several young gentlemen having
fallen in love with some of our belles, after resisting all the female attractions
of Philadelphia. From this inferiority, I except one, who is the most amiable,
the most accomplished, the most bewitching, and the most of everything that
constitutes the divinity of women—mem.—*golden apple!*

The amusements of the Philadelphians are dancing, punning, tea-parties,
and theatrical exhibitions. In the first, they are far inferior to the young
people of New York, owing to the misfortune of their mostly preferring to
idle away time in the cultivation of the head instead of the heels. It is a
melancholy fact that an infinite number of young ladies in Philadelphia,
whose minds are elegantly accomplished in literature, have sacrificed to the
attainment of such trifling acquisitions, the pigeon-wing, the waltz, the
Cossack dance, and other matters of equal importance. On the other hand
they excel the New Yorkers in punning, and in the management of tea-
parties. In New York you never hear, except from some young gentleman
just returned from a visit to Philadelphia, a single attempt at punning, and at
a tea-party, the ladies in general are disposed close together, like a setting of
jewels, or pearls round a locket, in all the majesty of good behavior—and if
a gentleman wishes to have a conversation with one of them, about the
backwardness of the spring, the improvements in the theatre, or the merits
of his horse, he is obliged to march up in the face of such volleys of eye-
shot! such a formidable artillery of glances! If he.escapes annihilation, he
should cry out a miracle! and never encounter such dangers again. I
remember to have once heard a very valiant British officer, who had served

with a great credit for some years in the train-bands, declare with a veteran oath, that sooner than encounter such deadly peril, he would fight his way clear through a London mob, though he were pelted with brick-bats all the time. Some ladies who were present at this declaration of the gallant officer, were inclined to consider it a great compliment, until one, more knowing than the rest, declared, with a little piece of a sneer, "that they were very much obliged to him for likening the company to a London mob, and their glances to brick-bats." The officer looked blue, turned on his heel, made a fine retreat, and went home with a determination to quiz the American ladies as soon as he got to London.

THE STRANGER AT HOME; OR, A TOUR IN BROADWAY.

BY JEREMY COCKLOFT, THE YOUNGER.

PREFACE.

Your learned traveller begins his travels at the commencement of his journey; others begin theirs at the end; and a third class begin any how and anywhere, which I think is the true way. A late facetious writer begins what he calls a "Picture of New York," with a particular description of Glen's Falls, from whence, with admirable dexterity, he makes a digression to the celebrated Mill Rock on Long Island! Now, this is what I like; and I intend, in my present tour, to digress as often and as long as I please. If, therefore, I choose to make a hop, skip, and jump to China, or New Holland, or Terra Incognita, or Communipaw, I can produce a host of examples to justify me, even in books that have been praised by the English reviewers, whose *fiat* being all that is necessary to give books a currency in this country, I am determined, as soon as I finish my edition of travels in seventy-five volumes, to transmit it forthwith to them for judgement. If these trans-Atlantic censors praise it, I have no fear of its success in this country, where their approbation gives, like the Tower stamp, a fictitious value, and makes tinsel and wampum pass current for classic gold.

CHAPTER I.

Battery—flag-staff kept by Louis Keaffee—Keaffee maintains two spy-glasses by subscriptions—merchants pay two shillings a year to look through them at the signal poles on Staten Island—a very pleasant prospect;

but not so pleasant as that from the hill of Howth—quere, ever been there? Young seniors go down to the flag-staff to buy peanuts and beer, after the fatigue of their morning studies, and sometimes to play at ball, or some other innocent amusement—digression to the Olympic, and Isthmian games, with a description of the Isthmus of Corinth, and that of Darien: to conclude with a dissertation on the Indian custom of offering a whiff of tobacco smoke to their great spirit Areskou.—Return to the Battery—delightful place to indulge in the luxury of sentiment. How various are the mutations of this world! but a few days, a few hours—at least not above two hundred years ago, and this spot was inhabited by a race of aborigines, who dwelt in bark huts, lived upon oysters and Indian corn, danced buffalo dances, and were lords "of the fowl and the brute"; but the spirit of time, and the spirit of brandy have swept them from their ancient inheritance: and as the white wave of the ocean, by its ever toiling assiduity, gains on the brown land, so the white man, by slow and sure degrees, has gained on the brown savage, and dispossessed him of the land of his forefathers.—Conjectures on the first peopling of America—different opinions on that subject, to the amount of near one hundred—opinion of Augustine Torniel—that they are the descendants of Shem and Japheth, who came by the way of Japan to America.—Juffridius Petre says they came from Frizeland.—mem. cold journey—Mons. Charron says they are descended from the Gauls—bitter enough—A. Milius from the Celtae—Kircher from the Egyptians—L'Compte from the Phenicians—Lescarbort from the Canaanites, alias the Anthropophagi—Brerewood from Tartars—Grotius from the Norwegians—and Linkum Fidelius has written two folio volumes to prove that America was first of all peopled either by the antipodeans or the Cornish miners, who, he maintains, might easily have made a subterranean passage to this country, particularly the antipodeans, who, he asserts, can get along under ground as fast as moles— quere, which of these is in the right, or are they all wrong? For my part, I don't see why America had not as good a right to be peopled at first, as any little contemptible country in Europe, or Asia; anad I am determined to write a book at my first leisure, to prove that Noah was born here—and that so far is America from being indebted to any other country for inhabitants, that they were every one of them peopled by colonies from her!—mem. Battery a very pleasant place to walk on a Sunday evening—not quite gentel though— everybody walks there, and a pleasure, however genuine, is spoiled by general participation—the fashionable ladies of New York turn up their noses if you ask them to walk on the Battery on Sunday—quere, have they scruples of conscience, or scruples of delicacy? Neither—they have only scruples of gentility, which are quite different things.

CHAPTER II.

Custom-house—origin of duties on merchandise—this place much frequented by merchants—and why?—different classes of merchants —importers—a kind of nobility—wholesale merchants—have the privilege of going to the city assembly!—Retail traders cannot go to the assembly. —Some curious speculations on the vast distinction betwixt selling tape by the piece or by the yard.—Wholesale merchants look down upon the retailers, who in return look down upon the green-grocers, who look down upon the market-women, who don't care a straw about any of them.—Origin of the distinctions of rank—Dr. Johnson once horribly puzzled to settle the point of precedence between a louse and a flea—good hint enough to humble purse-proud arrogance.—Custom-house partly used as a lodging-house for the pictures belonging to the Academy of Arts—couldn't afford the statues house-room, most of them in the cellar of the City Hall—poor place for the gods and godesses—after Olympus.—Pensive reflections on the ups and downs of life—Apollo, and the rest of the set, used to cut a great figure in days of yore.—Mem. every dog has his day—sorry for Venus though, poor wench, to be cooped up in a cellar with not a single grace to wait on her!—Eulogy on the gentlemen of the Academy of Arts, for the great spirit with which they began the undertaking, and the perseverance with which they pursued it—it is a pity, however, they began at the wrong end— maxim—If you want a bird and a cage, always buy the cage first—hem!—a word to the wise!

CHAPTER III.

Bowling Green—fine place for pasturing cows—a perquisite of the late corporation—formerly ornamented with a statue of George the Third— people pulled it down in the war to make bullets—great pity; it might, have been given to the academy—it would have become a cellar as well as any other.—Broadway—great difference in the gentility of streets—a man who resides in Pearl street, or Chatham Row, derives no kind of dignity from his domicil; but place him in a certain part of Broadway, anywhere between the Battery and Wall street, and he straightway becomes entitled to figure in the beau monde, and strut as a person of prodigious consequence! —Quere, whether there is a degree of purity in the air of that quarter which changes the gross particles of vulgarity into gems of refinement and polish? A question to be asked, but not to be answered—New brick church!—What a pity it is the corporation of Trinity church are so poor!—if they could not afford to build a better place of worship, why did they not go about with a subscription?—even I would have given them a few shillings rather than our city should have been disgraced by such a pitiful specimen of economy— Wall street—City Hall, famous place for catch-poles, deputy sheriffs, and young lawyers; which last attend the courts, not because they have business there, but because they have no business anywhere else. My blood always curdles when I see a catch-pole, they being a species of vermin who feed and fatten on the common wretchedness of mankind, who trade in misery, and in becoming the executioners of the law, by their oppression and villainy, almost counterbalance all the benefits which are derived from its salutary regulations—Story of Quevedo about a catch-pole possessed by a devil, who, on being interrogated, declared that he did not come there voluntarily, but by compulsion; and that a decent devil would never of his own free will enter into the body of a catch-pole; instead, therefore, of doing him the injustice to say that here was a catch-pole bedevilled, they should say, it was a devil be-catch-poled; that being in reality the truth—Wonder what has become of the old crier of the court, who used to make more noise in preserving silence than the audience did in breaking it—if a man happened to drop his cane, the old hero would sing out "silence!" in a voice that emulated the "wide mouthed thunder"—On inquiring, found he had retired from business to enjoy *otium cum dignitate*, as many a great man has done before. Strange that wise men, as they are thought, should toil through a whole existence merely to enjoy a few moments of leisure at last! why don't they begin to be easy at first, and not purchase a moment's pleasure with an age of pain?—mem. posed of the jockeys—eh!

CHAPTER IV.

BARBER'S pole; three different orders of *shavers* in New York—those who shave *pigs*; N.B.—freshmen and sophomores,—those who cut beards, and those who *shave notes of hand*; the last are the most respectable, because, in the course of a year, they make more money, and that *honestly*, than the whole corps of other *shavers* can do in half a century; besides, it would puzzle a common barber to ruin any man, except by cutting his throat; whereas your higher order of *shavers*, your true bloodsuckers of the community, seated snugly behind the curtain, in watch for prey, live on the vitals of the unfortunate, and grow rich on the ruin of thousands. Yet this last class of *barbers* are held in high respect in the world; they never offend against the decencies of life, go often to church, look down on honest poverty walking on foot, and call themselves gentlemen; yea, men of honor!—Lottery offices—another set of capital shavers!—licensed gambling houses! good things enough, as they enable a few *honest industrious gentlemen* to humbug the people—according to law; besides, if the people will be such fools, whose fault is it but their own if they get *bit*?—Messrs. Paff—beg pardon for putting them in such bad company, because they are a couple of fine fellows—mem. to recommend Michael's antique snuff-box to all amateurs *in the art.*—Eagle singing Yankee-doodle—N.B.—Buffon, Pennant and the rest of the naturalists, all *naturals* not to know the eagle was a singing bird; Linkum Fidelius knew better, and gives a long description of a bald eagle that serenaded him once in Canada;—digression; particular account of the Canadian Indians;—story about Areskou learning to make fishing nets of a spider—don't believe it, though, because, according to Linkum, and many other learned authorities, Areskou is the same as *Mars,* being derived from his Greek name of *Ares;* and if so, he knew well enough what *a net* was without consulting a spider;—story of Arachne being changed into a spider as a reward for having hanged herself;—derivation of the word spinster from spider;—Colophon, now Altobosco, the birthplace of Arachne, remarkable for a famous breed of spiders to this day;—mem. nothing like a little scholarship—make the *ignoramus,* viz. the majority of my readers, stare like wild pigeons;—return to New York a short cut— meet a dashing belle, in a little thick white veil—tried to get a peep at her face—saw she squinted a little—thought so at first;—never saw a face covered with a veil that was worth looking at;—saw some ladies holding a conversation across the street about going to church next Sunday—talked so loud they frightened a cartman's horse, who ran away, and over set a basket of gingerbread with a little boy under it; mem. I don't much see the use of speaking-trumpets now-a-days.

CHAPTER V.

BOUGHT a pair of gloves; dry-goods stores the genuine schools of politeness —true Parisian manners there—got a pair of gloves and a pistareen's worth of bows for a dollar—dog cheap!—Courtlandt street corner—famous place to see the belles go by—quere, ever been shopping with a lady?—some account of it—ladies go into all the shops in the city to buy a pair of gloves —good way of spending time, if they have nothing else to do.—Oswego Market—looks very much like a triumphal arch—some account of the manner of erecting them in ancient times; digression to the *arch*-duke Charles, and some account of the ancient Germans. N.B.—quote Tacitus on this subject.—Particular description of market-baskets, butchers' blocks, and wheelbarrows;—mem. queer things run upon one wheel!—Saw a cartman driving full tilt through Broadway—run over a child—good enough for it—what business had it to be in the way?—Hint concerning the laws against pigs, goats, dogs, and cartmen—grand apostrophe to the sublime science of jurisprudence;—comparison between legislators and tinkers; quere, whether it requires greater ability to mend a law than to mend a kettle?—injury [inquiry] into the utility of making laws that are broken a hundred times in a day with impunity;—my Lord Coke's opinion on the subject; my Lord a very great man—so was Lord Bacon: a good story about a criminal named Hogg claiming relationship with him.—Hogg's porterhouse;—a great haunt of Will Wizard; Will put down there one night by a sea-captain, in an argument concerning the era of the Chinese empire Whangpo;—Hogg's a capital place for hearing the same stories, the same jokes, and the same songs every night in the year—mem. except Sunday nights; fine school for young politicians too—some of the longest and thickest heads in the city come there to settle the nation.—Scheme of *Ichabod Fungus* to restore the balance of Europe;—digression;—some account of the balance of Europe; comparison between it and a pair of scales, with the Emperor Alexander in one and the Emperor Napoleon in the other: fine fellows—both of a weight, can't tell which will kick the beam:—mem. don't care much either—nothing to me:—*Ichabod* very unhappy about it—thinks Napoleon has an eye on this country—capital place to pasture his horses, and provide for the rest of his family.—Dey street—ancient Dutch name of it, signifying murderers' valley, formerly the site of a great peach orchard; my grandmother's history of the famous *Peach war*—arose from an Indian stealing peaches out of this orchard; good cause as need be for a war; just as good as the balance of power. Anecdote of war between two Italian states about a bucket; introduce some capital new truisms about the folly of mankind, the ambition of kings, potentates, and princes; particularly Alexander, Caesar, Charles the XIIth, Napoleon, little King Pepin, and the great Charlemagne.—Conclude with an exhortation to the present race of sovereigns to keep the king's peace, and abstain from all those deadly quarrels which produce battle, murder, and sudden death:—mem.—ran my nose against a lamp-post—conclude in great dudgeon.

24. A National Character

Inchiquin's Letters was published anonymously in 1810 and consisted of a series of eight letters supposed to be written by an Irish Jesuit, banished from Great Britain and traveling in the United States, to his friends abroad. The book was one of the first avowed defenses of the American national character against foreign, particularly British, criticism, and as such it came from a very unlikely source. Charles Jared Ingersoll (1782-1862), the author, was the grandson of a Tory, the son of a Federalist, and a member of the Anglophile world of Joseph Dennie. Yet, before he was thirty, Ingersoll was already deep in the process of repudiating his class and his heritage in favor of the Republican, and later the Jacksonian Democratic, party. This rejection of the refined society of Philadelphia, painful and difficult as it was for a cultivated man like Ingersoll, represented for him and for others like him the eighteenth-century's coming to terms with the emerging popular and commercial spirit, indeed the very vulgarity, of nineteenth-century American life. Democracy to Ingersoll was losing the problematical quality it had for his father and other Federalists and was fast becoming an article of American faith—a faith that Americans would soon seek to vindicate forcibly in a second war with Britain.

Inchiquin's Letters

CHARLES JARED INGERSOLL

The lien of this "mighty continental nation" is commercial liberty: not mere political liberty, but positive freedom; geographical absolution from all but the slightest restraints; the inherent and inalienable birthright of this adolescent people, upon the enjoyment of which they entered by a lineal title, the moment they felt strength enough to cast off the trammels of infancy: a heritage as natural as the air they breathe, which, whether it sweeten the toil of New England, where the same farmer who sows and reaps his own field, is also the mariner, who attends his produce on distant ventures, or inflate the pride of the south, where the poor black sows the ground and the rich white reaps the harvest, is still and every where the same "brave spirit," pervading the whole republic, and binding it together by an influence, not the less powerful, because its current is propelled by an animating contrariety. The American people, dispersed over an immense territory, abounding in all the means of commercial greatness, to whom an opportunity was presented at an early period of adapting their government to their circumstances, followed the manifest order of nature, when they adopted a free, republican, commercial federation.

The course and catastrophe of the French revolution have cast a gloom over republicanism, which perhaps it may never shake off; and which, at least for the present, renders it in Europe repulsive and discreditable. But the American republic is the natural fruit of the American soil: the spirit of its freedom is impassioned, perhaps factious, but not furious or bloody. It is in vain to attempt, and absurd to desire, the introduction of the republican polity as a general melioration of the lot of nations. Many causes, that are beyond the reach of man, must concur to its establishment; and there have been few countries predisposed, as they should be, for its reception. The English loathed the adulteration they endured during the aera of their commonwealth, when hypocritical lowliness, ferocious fanaticism, and overstained economy, were substituted for the generous and munificent patrio-

[Charles Jared Ingersoll], *Inchiquin, the Jesuit's Letters . . . Containing a Favorable View of the Manners, Literature, and State of Society of the United States, and a Refutation of Many of the Aspersions Cast Upon this Country, by Former Residents and Tourists* (New York, 1810), pp. 110–151, 164–165.

tism which ennobled and perpetuated the ancient republics. Yet short as was its duration, and perverted as were its principles, such is the natural vigour of a free commonwealth, that the English received from theirs an impulse, which while it darkened their character, greatly increased their power, and gave it the direction it has ever since followed. The French had none of the ideas or propensities suited to freedom: and whatever may have been the effects of their revolution in deracinating abuses, and regenerating their national energies, it was not to be supposed that a republican government would endure in France. The French had not the raw material. But the American federation is the natural offspring of commerce and liberty, whose correlative interests will bind it together in principle, even after its formal dissolution. What are the merits of those institutions which have been framed by the people of this country it is not necessary here to inquire, or whether the government be calculated for strength and durability. The states, as now organized, may be consolidated or dismembered, may fall asunder by the weight and weakness of the union, or may separate in a convulsion. But it is the perfection of polity, when it rests on natural bases; and a disunion of the American states, whatever might be its political consequences, could not destroy or materially change their mutual commercial dependence, and would not probably diminish the almost universal attachment of the people to republican institutions. The empire, in point of extent, is unwieldy. The east and the south are already jealous of each other, and the west regards them both with suspicion. But a community of language, of laws, of political attachments, and a reciprocity of interests are strong bonds of union. So many theories have been projected on the excellence of a federal republic, and so much disgrace has of late been cast upon republicanism by both its advocates and enemies, that the American experiment must be regarded with no small anxiety: for certain it is that an enlightened and predominant republic, such as those of Greece, Carthage and Rome, is the most rational and glorious object the mind can contemplate.

The prevailing character of these national elements is the natural result from their geographical and political combination. It is natural that a people descended so lately from pilgrims and sectaries should be enthusiasts—that a commercial people should be enterprising and ingenious—that a republican people, whose press is free, and whose government is a government of laws and opinion, should be intelligent and licentious—that an adolescent and prosperous people should be aspiring, warlike and vainglorious. This is not the character the Americans bear in Europe. The question there is whether they have any national character at all; and the common impression is that they have not.

There is a great proneness to misrepresent national character, which is a consideration extremely obscured by gross prejudices. That verisimilitude of habits, manners and propensities, indicative of the inhabitants of ancient countries, is not an infallible index to the national character: there are vulgar features, striking, but deceptive. Heroes, poets and historians will adapt national greatness to a poor and enslaved people. Peace, plenty and a certain degree of obscurity render a people happy; and if they are happy, they will commonly be virtuous. But virtue and happiness are not so imposing as greatness, in the national, or in the individual estimate. The same principle that induces a preference of the great to the good, bears admiration from the wise and peaceable commonwealth to the belligerent empire. We prize military renown beyond civil or pacific distinction, following the blaze of glory rather than the sober light of wisdom. We eulogize for its national character, a warlike empire, composed of the most despicable materials, with no common spirit but implicit obedience to chiefs, through whose merits alone it is eminent; and deny the same homage to a country composed of a virtuous and intelligent population, governed by one common sentiment of policy, but whose policy happens to be peace. No excellence in the arts, no morals, no refinement, no intelligence, no literary fame, will give national importance, without an ability for war, and a high martial rank among sovereign states. The Chinese, in many respects a wise and original people, consisting of three hundred millions of souls under one head, are despised by the pettiest nation in Europe. The Swiss and the Dutch, the only powers of modern Europe that never wage foreign wars, acquired the only national reputation they ever enjoyed, not by any peculiarity of manners, or wise institutions, but by their capacity for resistance to hostile encroachment. Reflecting men in Europe regard the American revolution as a period when the American character shone forth with considerable distinction. Yet the same nation, in part the same men, after thirty years of peace and prosperity, are supposed to have lost the energy of patriotism they then displayed. An expansion of population, of resources, of territory, of power, of information, of freedom, of every thing that tends to magnify man, is supposed to have degenerated the Americans. Is this the course of nature? All things are said to tend from their origin to a certain degree of perfection, and thence to decline and dissolution. But can the time be so soon arrived for the tide of American declension? According to the common course of events, the genius of the American people should be enhanced, not deteriorated, by the peace and prosperity they have enjoyed since the period of their birth as a nation. By sketches of the present state of their religion, legislation, literature, arts and society, with an aspect never turned from their national characteristics, and embracing no further details that are necessary for their exposition, I propose to endeavour to refute the false opinions inferred from their tranquillity, and at the same time to exhibit their national character.

In this age of infidelity and indifference, to call any people a religious people, is a license, which nothing but a comparative view of the state of religion in this and in other christian countries, can uphold. It is, however, true, that the number of persons devoted to pious exercises, from reflection, independent of education and habit, is greater in the United States, than in any other part of the world, in proportion to the population; and religious morality is more general and purer here than elsewhere. The political ordinance of religious toleration is one of those improvements in the science of politics, for which mankind will acknowledge their obligations to America: and the divorce of church and state is an inestimable pledge for the purity and stability of republican government. Religious toleration, says the Prince of Benevento, is one of the most powerful guaranties of social tranquillity; for where liberty of conscience is respected, every other right cannot fail to be so. As christianity and civilization have hitherto been inseparable companions, it is probable that where the practice of the former is most acceptable, the influence of the latter will be the most pervading. One of the first acts of Penn and Baltimore in their respective provinces, was the absolute separation of ecclesiastical from secular concerns: a catholic and a quaker, the extremes of the christian creed, thus signalizing their administrations by a liberality equally wise and magnanimous, the beneficial effects of which will be felt to the latest generation. In New England, where presbyterianism is the predominant faith, fanaticism expired slowly, and proscription blazed up more than once, after it was believed and ought to have been extinguished. But at this time persecution is impracticable. Laws, and opinions stronger than laws, prevent it. The churches of Rome, of England, of Luther, of Wesley and of Fox, in all their various subdivisions and modifications, subsist in peace and harmony, worshipping without molestation, according to their different tenets. Universal toleration has produced numberless particular sects, each maintained by enthusiastic proselytes. Thus the Americans are a nation of freethinkers; and having moreover not only no established church, but being perfectly unrestrained in their belief, those persuasions are most followed, which involve the utmost refinements of enthusiasm, and rejection of ceremonial. After shaking off entirely the shackles of superstition, it is not easy to avoid the phrensy of fanaticism; for one begins where the other ends. But it is the advantage of the latter, that whereas superstition binds the soul in sloth and fear, fanaticism sets it free from their mortification; and though for a time it may float in an unsettled medium, it will settle at last on the right base.

The civil institutions of this country conduce equally with religious toleration to habits of intelligence and independence. Natural equality perhaps does not exist. Birth, affluence and talents create distinctions, notwithstanding political regulations to the contrary. The pride of family, the vanity of wealth, and other adventitious advantages, are not without their sensation in society, even in this young republic. But patrician and plebeian orders are unknown, and that third or middle class, upon which so many theories have been founded, is a section that has no existence here. Luxury has not yet corrupted the rich, nor is there any of that want, which classifies the poor. There is no populace. All are people. What in other countries is called the populace, a compost heap, whence germinate mobs, beggars, and tyrants, is not to be found in the towns; and there is no peasantry in the country. Were it not for the slaves of the south, there would be but one rank. By the facility of subsistence and high price of labour, by the universal education and universal suffrage, almost every man is a yeoman or a citizen, sensible of his individual importance. Not more than 350,000 of the seven millions composing the population of the American states, reside in large towns. The remainder live on farms or in villages. Most of them are proprietors of the soil; and many of them the wealthiest and most influential natives.° This great repartition of estate has necessarily a great and beneficial influence on the morals and sentiments of the people, which the laws are in general contrived to aid and confirm. The abolition of the rights of primogeniture, and of entails, and the statutes for regulating the transmission of property, are calculated to prevent the accumulation of the fortune of a family in the hands of any one of the children; and by distributing it equally among them all, serve to exalt those sentiments of individual independence, which are

°Not that I by any means subscribe to the sentiment of Mr. Jefferson, that husbandmen are God's chosen people. Far from it. They are more prone to intoxication, litigation, gambling and turbulence, than the inhabitants of cities. The popular insurrections that have threatened the peace of this government since the establishment of the present constitution, have broken out in the interior, remote from any large towns. The late attempt by Burr, was to have been perpetrated not by means of town mobs, but frontier settlers, or what are known here by the denomination of backwoodsmen. In countries where the peasants are so ignorant and poor as to be wholly under the influence of superiors, their laborious simplicity may be more useful to the state and more conducive to their own happiness, than the occupations of the lower classes in great towns; especially in catholic countries, where the lawfulness of innocent recreations prevents a recurrence to vitious amusements. But, in the United States, the people are neither ignorant, poor, nor catholic; and the virtues of contentment, industry and sobriety, are at least as common (if not more so) in cities as in the country.

the roots of patriotism. They are most attached to the soil, who own a part of it; from which attachment spring love of country, glory, and that fine union of public with private feelings, which constitutes the strength and ornament of republics. In monarchies, these sentiments are confined to the great. The mass of the people to be sure instinctively love the spot of their nativity, but are seldom animated with that noble, personal, and selfish and obstinate zeal, which citizens feel for what they call their own. Hard labour and low wages stupify and vitiate the lower classes of most countries. But in the United States wages are very high, and hard labour is altogether optional. Three day's work out of seven yields a support. The lassitude and dissipation, which might be expected from so much leisure, are provided against by natural circumstances. On one side the sea, and on the other rich waste lands, present inexhaustible fields of adventure and opulence. The inducement to labour, the recompense, is so great, that the Americans, with the utmost facilities of subsistence, are a most industrious people. As in higher life, learning and assiduity are certain passports to performent and celebrity, so in the occupations of trade, agriculture, and the sea, persevering industry, almost without a risk of disappointment, leads to comfort and consequence. The proportion of persons of large fortune is small; that of paupers next to nothing. Every one is a man of business; every thing in the progress of emulation and improvement. Universality of successful employment diffuses alacrity and happiness throughout the community. No taxes, no military, no ranks, remove every sensation of restraint. Each individual feels himself rising in his fortunes; and the nation, rising with the concentration of all this elasticity, rejoices in its growing greatness. It is the perfection of civilized society, as far as respects the happiness of its members, when its ends are accomplished with the least pressure from government; and if the principle of internal corruption, and the dangers of foreign aggression, did not render necessary a sacrifice of some of this felicity, to preserve and perpetuate the rest, the Americans might continue to float in undisturbed buoyancy. The happiness, the virtue, and the most desirable character of a people at such a time, and under such circumstances, are most perfect, and should be most distinguished. But a dash of licentiousness already disturbs this happy equilibrium, and it must be overthrown by foreign or domestic violence, unless it be retrenched and protected.

From ignorance and bigotry, the common features of common people, the Americans have less to fear than from the opposite evils of faction and fanaticism. Propensities to the bottle, to conventicles, and to popular assemblies, are founded in enthusiasm, and fomented by freedom. A free and prosperous people will be infected with the lust for novelty; a passion more easily diverted than subdued. It would be practicable for the American government to give such encouragement to public festivals and recreations, as might tend to allay popular restlessness, and to give the popular feeling an innocent and even a patriotic direction. But at present, with all their fondness for public meetings, which is indulged in a numberless variety of associations, religious, political, convivial and social, greatly exceeding that of any other country, the Americans have few national festivals, and they are falling into disuse.

Perhaps this is not the scene for science, literature and the fine arts. Business and tranquillity are not their elements. The poets, painters, architects, or philosophers of America are as yet neither very numerous nor eminent. But the Americans are by no means, as is often asserted in Europe, so absorbed in ignoble pursuits, as to be insensible to the arts that polish and refine society. The natural genius of man is very similar in all climates, and literary excellence has had charms for all civilized men in their turn. Why then should a free, rich and rising nation be lost to the noblest attractions, the groundwork for whose attachment to literature is broadly laid in a far more general dissemination of common learning, than any other people enjoy? There are few Americans, who cannot read and write, and who have not a competent knowledge of figures. Education is more a public concern here than in any other country. In the little state of Connecticut alone, there are not less than 1200 public schools, which contain about 40,000 scholars at a time. The course of education, however, is in general short and superficial: adapted rather to the occasions than the perfection of the student. There is less of that minute division of employment, which obtains in older nations, and which has great tendency toward the extent and certainty of acquirements. But the number of schools is unequalled elsewhere: and in the several colleges there are probably about 2,000 scholars at a time.

For plain rudimental learning, and general, practical good sense, the Americans surpass all other people. The lower classes in England, and even in Scotland, are in this most important respect much their inferiors.

But the national character, in this point, is rather that of an almost universal medicrity, than any particular intensity of acquirement. The literature of the country, to advance our view a grade higher, is rather solid than shining. But the vast number of newspapers, and periodical publications, the immense importations from Europe of books of every description, and their continual sale at very high prices, the printing presses, the public libraries, the philosophical and literary institutions, and, above all, the general education and intelligence of the community, most effectually refute the charges of indifference to literature and science. Germany and England are the only countries where more books are annually published; and in neither of these, though their original writers are more numerous, is the number of readers so great as in the United States. Nor in either of those or any other country whatever, is a genius for writing or speaking a more useful or commanding endowment than in this. The talents displayed in the American state papers, both for composition and legislation are seldom contested. Independent of several public literary works, of sterling and of brilliant merits, almost every state has its historian and other writers: and statistical, professional, commerical, scientific and especially political treaties, are the offspring of every day, and multiply at a prodigious rate. It is not every year, in any country, that produces the *moeonii carminis alite*, which blooms, like the aloe, hardly once an age.

In all the useful mechanic arts, in common and indispensable manufactures, as well as in not a few of the more curious and costly fabrications, in agriculture both practically and scientifcically, in the construction of houses and ships, they rank with the most advanced nations of Europe, and very far surpass some, who upon no better pretension than a higher national ancestry, presume to consider the Americans as totally unacquainted with refinements, which in fact they understand and enjoy much better than themselves. Their architecture is always neat and commodious, often elegant, and in some instances, grand and imposing. In their labour-saving machinery, in their implements of husbandry, and domestic utensils, they are a century more improved than the inhabitants of France and Spain.

When we leave the province of utility, and approach the regions of elegance, or the depths of erudition, it is true they are in a state of minority, when compared with the most improved nations. Some arts and studies require leisure and patronage, perhaps luxury, to foster them into maturity. Though of these the American soil is not entirely unproductive, yet such shoots as have appeared, are rare and spontaneous. There are few individuals with the means and inclination to be patrons: and the government has hitherto afforded little protection or countenance to such improvements.

Most foreigners impute this barbarian niggardliness on the part of the government to the spirit of a republican people, and the policy of their rulers; and I fear there are not wanting native Americans who consider the fine arts and republicanism incompatible. But how rude and false is such a sentiment! How offensive to the history and genius of republics!

Certain it is, however, that there is almost a total absence from this country of those magnificent memorials and incentives of distinction, which the fine arts, particularly those of statuary and painting, create and sanctify. There is scarcely a statue, structure or public monument to commemorate the achievements of their war for independence. The ground where the principal battles were fought, remains unconsecrated—the ashes of the patriots who died for liberty, uninurned—and every disposition toward a suitable emblazonment of those events and characters, which should be perpetually present to the nation, in every captivating form, has been repressed as inimical to the thrifty policy of republicanism. Thousands of pens indeed, and tens of thousands of tongues, vie with each other in their panegyric. And more than one native pencil too has been dedicated to their immortalizing. But these are private effusions. The nation has not the honour of their creation; and remains to this day with scarcely one of those great and splendid edifices, obelisks and monuments, which should be scattered over the land with munificent profusion, to attach and inspire its inhabitants, and embody, identify, and preserve their national feelings and character. Patriotism must have shrines, or its ardour will relent. Permanent public memorials serve not only to invigorate the character of a country, and incite the best emotions of its citizens, but to embellish, civilize and make it happy. . . .

In those efforts which are the production of genius rather than erudition, particularly in the accomplishment of public speaking, the Americans have attained to greater excellence than other modern nations, their superiors in age and refinement. In the prevalence of oratory, as a common talent, in the number of good public speakers, in the fire and captivation of their public harangues, parliamentary, popular, forensic and of the pulpit, the English are the only modern people comparable with the Americans, and the English are far from being their equals. Popular representation and freedom of speech, several sovereignties, each one represented in a debating assembly, always rivals and sometimes directly opposed to each other, cultivate and call forth the most striking powers of oratory; whose conceptions are facilitated by the grandeur of surrounding scenery, and sublimity of the images of nature. Not only oratory, but all the arts and sciences are said to flourish in a fresh soil: and Greece will ever remain an illustrious instance, that a cluster of commercial republics is eminently adapted to their propagation and perfection.

But there are circumstances both natural and moral, promotive or prejudicial to the interests of letters and the fine arts, that have operated on different nations and ages, which baffle research, and are indicated only in effects, not to be traced to any certain cause. Thus Sallust observes of the Greeks, that owing to their great genius for writing, their acts are more celebrated than they deserved to be: wheras the Romans did not write enough for their own renown. . . . It is common in Europe to regard the American states with contempt, because, among other defects, of their supposed in-

aptitude for literary refinements: and the nonproduction of famous performances, is adopted as a proof of the poverty of their taste for literature, which
is ascribed to commerical and republican habits and laws. I have endeavoured to show the falsehood of these premises. But admitting their correctness, does the inference follow? The Romans, who, as I have just shown,
wrote very little, who were not a commerical people, and who, above all
others, were addicted to theatrical spectacles, never had a tragic poet; and
their few comic writers are inferior to those of Greece. Spain has been said to
have produced but one excellent book, and that ridicules most others. Yet
how mistaken our conclusions would be, if we inferred from the nonexistence
of tragic poets at Rome, that the Romans had no taste for tragedy, or from
reading Don Quixotte, that the Spaniards were an ignorant or a lively nation.

There is no subject on which a liberal judgment should proceed so cautiously to condemnation, as that of the literary character of a cotemporaneous
nation. The most distinguished scholars have been the most prejudiced,
when they came to weigh the comparative merits of their own and other nations in this respect. Voltaire, notwithstanding all his learning and impartiality in the abstract, and Johnson, take their stations at the head of the
prejudices of their respective countries. It is not, therefore, to be wondered
at, that the English deny the charms of French poetry, or that the French
cannot relish Shakespeare or blank verse.

When a young people, not yet half a century advanced, have already exhibited a genius for oratory and legislation, and their general intelligence is
so unrivalled as that of the Americans, we should be slow to conclude, from
the paucity of their original writers, that they want an aptitude for composition, or a taste for literature and the arts. Since the invention of printing,
and the improvements in commerce, the antiquated principles of gradual
amelioration are no longer applicable to any people, especially not to the
Americans. Rudiments are obsolete. As the discovery and first settlement of
America were the results of, and simultaneous with, the reappearance of
the arts and sciences during the 15th and 16th centuries, and as the inhabitants of this country have ever since, by the means of commerce and free
presses, been intimately connected with all the most polished nations of the
older world, their imitation of successive improvements has been close and
constant, sometimes enlivened with distinguished discoveries and useful
inventions of their own. While the shackles of a mother country laid upon
their genius, it was necessarily somewhat restricted and mortified. The
revolution called it forth to action, with all the ardour incident to such occasions. During the short period that has elapsed since their independence,
freedom, prosperity and ambition have stimulated its powers; and setting

aside two, or perhaps three, of the most enlightened empires of Europe, the literature, arts and sciences of the people of the United States of America, are equal, and their general information and intelligence superior, to those of any other nation.

A people so lately sprung from Europe, so closely connected with it, and so much younger in the annals of civilization, naturally adopts European customs. At the same time there being few rich, and no poor, there is less disparity, little luxury, and morals predominate over manners in this country. As civilized society rests on reciprocal concessions, its structure is most harmonious when they are best regulated; for, perhaps, the most we can say of human nature is, that it is capable of being rendered amiable by a reciprocity of good offices. The arts of hospitality and politeness, the alternation of business and pleasure, social assemblies, innocent recreations and good breeding, while they give zest to existence, undoubtedly tend to refine and cement socity, and to render mankind more virtuous as well as more elegant. Up to the period of enervation, refinements mend the affections as well as the manners: but it is the misfortune of society, that civilization, after a certain point, begins to lose its seemliness; morals give way to manners, and character has no weight against rank, appearance or behaviour.

Though there are few men of very large fortunes in the United States, a great proportion are in easy circumstances, and hospitality and politeness are common virtues. Commerical people are said to be inhospitable. The English and the Dutch are the least hospitable people of modern Europe. But, in the United States, abundance overcomes the calculating spirit of trade, and the east and the south vie with each other in unbounded hospitality. Even this, by some of those Europeans who are prepossessed against this country, may be accounted a remnant of simplicity at least, if not of barbarity. Savages are always hospitable. The Romans found it necessary to prohibit the lavish dispensation of this duty among the Germans. But in the exercise of such a virtue, we admire the vanquished more than their conquerors in its extinction.

The amusements of the Americans are gayer and less ferocious than those of the English. They are more addicted to dancing, for instance, and less to boxing, bull-baiting, and cock-fighting. Not that there is more ferocity in the English than in the American character. But the Americans have had opportunities, of which they have availed themselves, to lay aside certain savage attachments, which unbroken custom still maintains in England. Theatrical exhibitions, the sports of the field, and the pleasures of the table, are found by the Americans not incompatible with serious and lucrative occupations, and are followed with a general and increasing relish. Gaming and vitious dissipation are not unpractised, but more commonly by inferior than the better sort of people.

The prevailing vice is inebriety; induced by the relaxing heats of the climate in the southern and middle states, by the absence of all restriction, and the high price of wages. From this odious imputation New England is exempt. But in every other part of the Union, the labourers, and too many of the farmers, are given up to a pernicious indulgence in spirituous liquors.

Marriages in the United States are contracted early, and generally from disinterested motives. With very few exceptions they are sacred. Adultery is rare, and seduction seldom practised. The intercourse of the sexes is more familiar, without vice, than in any other part of the world; to which circumstance may, in great measure, be attributed the happy footing of society. This intercourse, in some countries, is confined, by cold and haughty customs, almost to the circles of consanguinity; in others, from opposite causes, it is unrestrained, voluptuous, and depraved. In the United States, it is free, chaste and honourable. Women are said to afford a type of the state of civilization. In savage life they are slaves. At the middle era of refinement, they are companions. With its excess they become mistresses and slaves again. North America is now at that happy mean, when well educated and virtuous women enjoy the confidence of their husbands, the reverence of their children, and the respect of society, which is chiefly indebted to them for its tone and embellishments. The unobtrusive and insensible influence of the sex is in meridian operation at this time; and as the company of virtuous women is the best school for manners, the Americans, without as high a polish as some Europeans acquire, are distinguished for a sociability and urbanity, that all nations, even the most refined, have not attained.

Commerce, which equalizes fortunes, levels ranks; and parade and stateliness can be kept up only where there is great disproportion of possessions. Expensive establishments, splendid equipages, and magnificient entertainments, are sometimes copied after European models. But they are neither common nor popular. It is difficult and invidious to be magnificent in a republican country, where there is no populace, and so many members of society have wherewithal to be generous and hospitable. A plentiful mediocrity, a hearty hospitality, a steadier and less ostentatious style of living, are more congenial with the habits and fortunes of the Americans.°

°The United States of America seem to have incurred the obloquy of Europe, in proportion as their happiness and power have increased; and now that they are the happiest and least depraved people in the world, others are industriously taught to despise them as the most vitious and miserable. Most countries have suffered in their estimate from the ignorance and antipathies

Having thus sketched the situation of this country, religious, political and social, let me hasten to such results as have not appeared in the course of the retrospect, and to some brief reflections on that commerical spirit, whose infusion is supposed to debilitate and debase the whole. It must always be borne in mind, that estimates of national character are to be formed from that class of the community, whatever it may be in different nations, which is the largest, and constitutes the most important portion of the population; especially when the Americans are the subject; inasmuch as they have, in fact, but one class of society. But in any nation a few individuals, of either the higher or lowest class, are not to be adopted as national types, nor the impressions they communicate, received as the national character. Our opinions of the French or English would be greatly erroneous, if our inquires were circumscribed to Paris or London.

of others, and the misrepresentations of prejudiced travellers and voyage writers. But on this in particular the overflowing phial of falsehood and opprobrium has been emptied. That the genius and character of the people should be misconceived and underrated, is, perhaps, less to be wondered at, than the pictures, alternately fulsome and disgusting, which have been drawn of the state of society, morals and manners; because these can hardly be mistaken by an actual observer; and none other, it might be supposed, would attempt them. When Buffon and D'Aubenton exhibit nature as niggardly, and her offspring as dwarfish and thwarted in America, compared with their species in Europe, such egregious errors are easily assigned to no uncommon cause — a deficiency of practical knowledge. And when the Abbé Raynal, erring from the same cause, on the opposite extreme, taking it for granted that a young and agricultural community must be industrious and virtuous, unpractised in the luxurious refinements of cities and higher civilization, fills a page or two with flattering delineations of their primeval and *bucolic* characteristics; grouping the swains of Florida, Virginia, and Canada altogether in the same paragraph, dressed out in the florid colours of his own imagination, in defiance of all truth, and without the least appearance of even geographical propriety, while we smile, we cannot be surprised at his blunders. But when writers, with the advantages of actual observation, portray the society of these states in the disgusting shades of vulgar, unrelieved depravity, those, whom similar opportunities have made acquainted with the glaring falsehood of these pretended likenesses, are at a loss to account for the motives of their creation; and can ascribe them to nothing but the operation of national prejudice on minds charged with an unusual portion of that popular and universal jealousy. Europe, unwilling to admit that a region so lately peopled from its superabundant population, should be any thing more than a feeble scion from the parent stock, unworthy to be considered as an equal, much less a rival, destined one day to surpass and overshadow the parent stock itself, has disregarded the evidence of nature and history with respect to this country, and received all her impressions from the most perverted and unfounded intelligence. Would such monstrous absurdities be tolerated else as the visions of Brissot and the cumbersome tattle of Liancourt; the ridiculous stories of Weld; the singsong wanderings of Anacreon Moore; and the numberless equally preposterous accounts and opinions that are perpetually issuing forth, in various shapes, from different quarters of Europe, pouring their ignorance and arrogance on America? It is not surpris-

A republican federation, a free press, general education, abundant subsistence, high price of labour, a warm climate, habits of intemperance, a variety of religious creeds, and the universal sensation of improvement and increase, naturally concur to the constitution of a well informed, ardent, enthusiastic, enterprising and licentious people. Where every man is a citizen, every citizen a freeholder, able and allowed to think, speak, and act for himself, the empire of opinion must be omnipotent: and it is impossible that a free and thinking people can be without a character. Enterprise, public spirit, intelligence, faction and love of country are natural to such a people. No series of ages is requisite to form or consolidate their character. At the earliest date the legend is most decided; and though it may be aggravated, is seldom improved by years or refinements.

ing that the lower orders of Europe generally believe the Americans to be copper-coloured, when the communications of statesmen, and the disquisitions of literati, are the first to proclaim and sanction all the narrow prejudices that prevail there on this subject. . . .

But the arrant misrepresentations of this country, which philosophers and historians, travellers and talebearers seem to have conspired to impress on the ignorance and prejudices of others, would not have had the permanent and extensive effect they have had, both here and in Europe, had they not been adopted, patronised and disseminated by those native Americans, of whom, the number, though daily diminishing, is still too great; who, awed by perpetual comparisons with the superior refinement, power, intelligence, and happiness of Europe, have been rebuked into concessions of their own inferiority. That involuntary feeling of respect, with which the American colonists were accustomed to regard Europe, particularly their mother country, it will require a generation or two to wear out. By European individuals it is asserted on all occasions; by many American individuals it is almost as often, sometimes unconsciously, acknowledged, on one side enforced, on the other conceded, to such a degree, as to mark, not indeed the character of the country, for the country in general neither feels nor avows it, but the characters of many respectable and influential individuals, with a tameness and subserviency they themselves are not aware of; which pervade every department, particularly those of social life and the higher classes; and carry abroad among the many who adopt these individuals as types of the nation, those opinions which are so prevalent of its want of an original national genius and character. It is this colonial spirit which causes incessant struggles between an instinctive love of country and an habitual veneration for what is European; in which struggle the latter feeling too often predominates; and with many native Americans of education and affluence, who are by no means deficient in personal independence, the first emotion toward what is American is contempt, the first emotion toward whatever proceeds from that nation of Europe, to which they happen to be most attached, is reverence and admiration. If a custom, production, or institution be American, it costs them an effort to approve; but if foreign, they submit to it with implicit faith. They depreciate not only the politics, literature, science and language, but the morals, manners, and state of society, according to the reduced scale of foreign detraction. But this is not the spirit of the people, but of those small sections, who claim to be their betters. A servile postponement of their own natural and manly habits to the most preposterous European usages, a thirst

Wherever we find foreign commerce, there also we find polished manners. It is commerce that harmonizes the intercourse and dissipates the prejudices of nations; softens their native peculiarities, and approximates their national characters to one common standard. Commerce, and trade, and manufactures, grew under the same shade in which learning flourished.

Such opinions, from such authority, are unanswerable. It is to North America only that their justice is denied. In Europe at least it is a prevailing notion to associate the commercial habits of the United States, with sordid fraud, a distaste for noble pursuits, and a dread of war: and the Americans have incurred the odium and contempt, which will be the lot of any nation that is considered by others to be tame, mercenary and base-spirited. But the policy of the government has been mistaken for the genius of the people. Alert, impetuous, alive to news and public discussions, the vibrations of popular sympathies are in no country so rapid and pervading. As individuals, and as a community, they have exhibited and continue to exhibit every day, the most decided proofs of courage and impetuosity.

The appeal to duels for the decision of private disputes is more frequent in the United States than in any other country whatever: and these private combats are conducted with a scientific ferociousness, and terminate in general with a fatality unknown elsewhere. The severest statutes have in vain pointed their artillery against this chivalric custom, which seems to be inveterate among impassioned and opiniated freeman. It is certain that men

after the company and alliance of foreigners in preference to their own countrymen, an affected reluctance to live and die where they were born, are some of the symptoms of this miserable disease, infinitely more miserable and less pardonable than its opposite *la maladie du pays*. A state of society in the meridian of refinement and virtue, midway between simplicity and corruption; gay and polite, without being profligate; shedding the selectest influence of domestic comfort and public tranquility; to the eye of depravity may present but a homely and insipid scene; but to such as love manly employment and rational recreation, is an enviable state, whose unequalled blessings they do not deserve to partake, who are not grateful for being born in the country where they flourish. Sentiments of repugnance in the natives of such a country are only tolerable, while they remain passive and latent. Whenever they break out into declared opposition, they become obnoxious to detestation and punishment. Such as cannot subdue them, are to be pitied; such as encourage them, abhorred. They are guilty of the most fatal species of treason — not that which boldly devotes a country to stratagem, blood and destruction — but that more insidious and more certain hostility, which flows in unseen perennial channels, traducing, betraying and assassinating. Of such as these there can be, I trust, but few in this happy country.—Wretches, who have no God, household, or supreme — the creeping things of the earth, who feed on the offals of foreigners — who lick the foot that tramples on them — who are despised by all others, even those they worship, and must despise themselves.

have become less free, less courageous, less disposed for great enterprises, than they were in the days of Rome and of suicide, when, as Montesquieu expresses it, they appear to have been born with a greater aptitude for heroism, and by exerting this inconceivable power over themselves, could bid defiance to all other human power. The modern duel is an offspring of this heathen sacrifice, in which similar causes lead to nearly the same effect. The prevalence of the *Catonis nobile lethum* of the Romans may not be an evidence of their good sense or their fortitude; nor the frequency of fatal duels in this country of the superior bravery of its inhabitants. But they prove at least the sensibility of both to that romantic and inexplicable point of honour, which, however indefensible its votaries may be in the eyes of both God and rational man, has ever been a shrine sacred to the brave and high minded.

As a community, the Americans have always shown themselves no less forward, than as individuals, to face their enemies and aggressors. In most countries it is the government that provokes, declares and maintains wars. But the United States have exhibited continual struggles between the government and the people, in which the latter have been clamorous for hostilities, at one time with one foreign power, at another time with another, while all the influence and forbearance of their rulers has been exercised to restrain this martial intoxication. The revolution was lighted up by a national instinct for independence, called early into action by the allurements of liberty and republicanism; when certainly no incapacity for war was evinced. How illustrious indeed should the conduct and termination of that contest render the Americans, when contrasted with the pusillanimous facility with which the most compact and warlike nations of Europe have lately fallen under the arms of their invaders! The American colonies would not have ventured a war singlehanded with the first maritime power of the world, about a trifling tax on tea, had not that military impulse, which inflamed alike the sturdy east, and the impatient south, prompted them to unite for assertion of their independence. It was not oppression that goaded them upon emancipation. But their instinct for liberty: as the author of their epic, with his peculiar propriety of expression, describes their feelings at the time,

"Fame fir'd their courage, freedom edg'd their swords."

A long interval of profound tranquillity and multiplied commerce may have tarnished the fame, perhaps relaxed somewhat the tone of this people. But it was the government, not the nation, who compromised with endurance for emolument; and the same spirit which was once displayed, is still ready to show itself when summoned into action. The same valour, good faith, clemency and patriotism still animate the bosoms of America, as the first burst of their hostilities, whenever it takes place, will convince their calumniators.

Legitimate commerce, instead of demoralizing or debasing a community, refines its sentiments, multiplies its intelligence, and sharpens its ingenuity. Where are the evidences to the contrary in this country?—The Americans, far from being a sordid or venal, are not even a thrifty people. Subsistence is so easy, and competency so common, that those nice calculations of domestic economy which are a branch almost of education in Europe, are scarcely attended to in America; and that long, disgusting catalogue of pretty offences, through which the lower classes of other nations are driven by indigence and wretchedness, has hardly an existence here, though death is almost proscribed from the penal code. Native Americans are very seldom to be met with in menial or the laborious occupations, which are filled by blacks and foreigners, mostly *Europeans*, who are also the common perpetrators of the smaller crimes alluded to. Though the government is supported by the customs, and the punishments for their contravention are merely pecuniary, yet such delinquencies are infinitely less frequent than in Europe or even Asia. The salaries of the public officers are very inconsiderable: yet malversation is a crime of rare occurrence; and that essential venality, which pervades almost every department of government in other countries, is altogether unpractised in this.

In their foreign traffic the Americans have been exposed to all the contumelious indignities which superior power and rapacity could inflict. But have the accusations charged upon them been substantiated? When a young and unarmed people have no other reliance for their advancement than their industry and acuteness, and nevertheless, owing to these and their territorial advantages, succeed against the jealous restrictions and overwhelming maritime strength of older states, it is as natural for the latter to stigmatize them with dishonesty and encroachment, as it was for Rome, when Carthage was half subdued, to proclaim the instability of Punic faith. But the charge contradicts itself: for how could the Americans pursue a successful and augmenting commerce, if their frauds were as numerous as they are declared to be, after the whole world are put on their guard, and in arms, to suppress them? The American merchant can have no other convoy than his neutrality and fairness: and if he have common sense, must perceive that honesty is his only policy. The unfairness with which the trade of these states is charged, is ascribable, not to the American, but to the many desperate foreigners, who assume a neutralized citizenship for the designs of dishonest speculation, and in too many instances abuse the privilege by simulation and iniquity.

While universal occupation, agricultural, mercantile and professional, imbues society with its spirit of punctuality and exactitude, poverty does not vitiate the lower, nor profligacy distinguish the higher classes. The laws of honour, as we have seen, have been adopted in their fullest rigour; and infractions of good faith or propriety are liable to the loss of character, of fortune, and of life itself: nor is there any community, among whom the temptations to debasement are less powerful, or where the laws and morals combine to oppose a more effectual restraint on those crimes that cause it. . . .

An affectation of contempt for America, is one of the only prejudices in which all the nations of Europe seem to concur. The soil, climate, productions, and creatures of this enviable country have been stigmatized as altogether inferior to those of Europe. And the gravest philosophers of the old world have led the way in these ignorant, absurd prejudices, against the new. The soil has been represented as parsimonious and abortive; the climate as froward and pernicious; the creatures as stunted, stupid, and debased below their species; the manners, principles, and government, as suited to this universal depravity. These absurdities appeared engraved with the stamp of knowledge and authority; their circulation was general and accredited; and it is amazing how current they continue to this day, notwithstanding the proofs that have successively adduced themselves of their falsification and baseness. But it is time such opinions were called in, and a new seignorage issued, less alloyed with prejudice; that Europe may be undeceived respecting a people, in many respects the first, and in none the lowest on the scale of nations.

Selected Bibliography

Berman, Eleanor D. *Thomas Jefferson Among the Arts: An Essay in Early American Esthetics.* New York, 1947.

Boorstin, Daniel J. *The Lost World of Thomas Jefferson.* Boston, 1948.

Charvat, William. *The Origin of American Critical Thought, 1810-1835.* Philadelphia, 1936.

Chinard, Gilbert. "Eighteenth-Century Theories on America as a Human Habitat," in American Philosophical Society, *Proceedings*, XCI (1947), 27-57.

Clark, Harry Hayden. "The Influence of Science on American Ideas, from 1775 to 1809," in Wisconsin Academy of Science, Arts and Letters, *Transactions*, 35 (1943), 305-349.

Davis, Richard Beale. *Intellectual Life in Jefferson's Virginia, 1790-1830.* Chapel Hill, N.C., 1964.

D'Elia, Donald J. "Dr. Benjamin Rush and the American Medical Revolution," in American Philosophical Society, *Proceedings*, CX (1966), 227-234.

Dickson, Harold E. *Arts of the Young Republic: The Age of William Dunlap.* Chapel Hill, N.C., 1968.

Elsbree, Oliver Wendell. *The Rise of the Missionary Spirit in America, 1790-1815.* Williamsport, Pa., 1928.

Foster, Charles I. *An Errand of Mercy: The Evangelical United Front, 1790-1837.* Chapel Hill, N.C., 1960.

Gowans, Alan. *Images of American Living.* New York, 1964.

Greene, John C. "Science and the Public in the Age of Jefferson," *Isis*, 49 (1958), 13-25.

Harris, Neil. *The Artist in American Society: The Formative Years, 1790-1860.* New York, 1966.

Heimert, Alan. *Religion and the American Mind: From the Great Awakening to the Revolution.* Cambridge, 1966.

Hindle, Brooke. *Technology in Early America: Needs and Opportunities for Study.* Chapel Hill, N.C., 1966.

————. *The Pursuit of Science in Revolutionary America, 1735-1789.* Chapel Hill, N.C., 1956.

Howard, Leon. *The Connecticut Wits.* Chicago, 1943.

————. "The Late Eighteenth Century: An Age of Contradictions," in Harry Hayden Clark, ed., *Transition in American Literary History.* Durham, N.C., 1954.

Howe, John R. "Republican Thought and the Political Violence of the 1790's," *American Quarterly,* XIX (1967), 147-165.

Huth, Hans. *Nature and the American: Three Centuries of Changing Attitudes.* Berkeley. 1957.

Jordan, Winthrop D. *White Over Black, American Attitudes Toward the Negro, 1550-1812.* Chapel Hill, N.C., 1968.

Kerber, Linda K. *Federalists in Dissent: Imagery and Ideology in Jeffersonian America.* Ithaca, N.Y., 1970.

Kimball, Fiske. *Thomas Jefferson, Architect.* Boston, 1916.

Kirker, Harold and James. *Bulfinch's Boston, 1787-1817.* New York, 1964.

Kraus, Michael. *The Atlantic Civilization: Eighteenth-Century Origins.* Ithaca, N.Y., 1949.

Krout, John Allen, and Fox, Dixon Ryan. *The Completion of Independence, 1790-1830.* New York, 1944.

Nash, Roderick. *Wilderness and the American Mind.* New Haven, Conn., 1967.

Miller, Perry. *The Life of the Mind in America from the Revolution to the Civil War.* New York, 1965.

Nye, Russel B. *The Cultural Life of the New Nation, 1776-1830.* New York, 1960.

Pearce, Roy Harvey. *Savagism and Civilization: The Study of the Indian and the American Mind.* Baltimore, 1967.

Simpson, Lewis P. "Federalism and the Crisis of Literary Order," *American Literature,* XXXII (1960), 253-266.

Spencer, Benjamin T. *The Quest for Nationality: An American Literary Campaign.* Syracuse, 1957.

Sweet, William Warren. *Religion in the Development of American Culture, 1765-1840.* New York, 1952.

Tuveson, Ernest Lee. *Redeemer Nation: The Idea of America's Millennial Role.* Chicago, 1968.

Whitehill, Walter and Wendell D., and Garrett, Jane N. *The Arts in Early American History: Needs and Opportunities for Study.* Chapel Hill, N.C., 1965.

Wood, Gordon S. *The Creation of the American Republic, 1776-1787.* Chapel Hill, N.C., 1969.